Fodor's

BIG ISLAND OF HAWAII

W9-ABI-505

Welcome to the Big Island

Hawaii's largest island has more than 250 miles of coast from Kona to Hilo and beyond, lined with incredible beaches, elegant resorts, coffee farms, rain forests, and waterfalls. History and culture resonate everywhere, from Kealakekua Bay to the rugged Valley of Kings near Waipio. Above it all, snowcapped Maunakea contrasts with fiery Mauna Loa, the centerpiece of Hawaii Volcanoes National Park. As you plan your upcoming travels to the Big Island, please confirm that places are still open and let us know when we need to make updates by emailing us at editors@fodors.com.

TOP REASONS TO GO

★ **Hawaii Volcanoes National Park:** The world's most active volcano is an amazing sight.

★ **Fun towns:** Humming Kailua-Kona, cowboy country Waimea, rainbow-streaked Hilo.

★ **Stargazing:** Maunakea's peak is the best place on Earth to stare out into space.

★ **Beaches:** The Big Island offers sand in many shades—black, white, and even green.

★ **Wildlife:** You can watch sea turtles on the beach and humpback whales in the waves.

★ **Kona coffee:** Farm tours, smooth sips, and a coffee cultural festival are all memorable.

Contents

Fodor's Features

MAPS

Chapter 1

EXPERIENCE BIG ISLAND

17 ULTIMATE EXPERIENCES

The Big Island of Hawaii offers terrific experiences that should be on every traveler's list. Here are Fodor's top picks for a memorable trip.

on Maunakea

zing at Maunakea's summit are both outstanding. The visitor center at as most rental cars are allowed to go) is open daily. Guided summit tours

2 Tour a Kona Coffee Plantation

Local coffee farmers love to share their passion with the public, and most offer free tours. Kona coffee estate farms stretch from Holualoa to South Kona. *(Chs. 3–4)*

3 Be a Cowboy for a Day

Saddle up and get ready to ride the ranges, cliffs, and trails of the Big Island on horseback. It's one of the best ways to take in the island's beautiful scenery. *(Ch. 9)*

4 Hike to the Green Sand Beach

It's worth the effort to drive to the end of South Point Road in Kau and hike about 3 miles to stunning, olivine Papakolea Beach. Take lots of water. *(Ch. 8)*

5 Enjoy a Sunday Stroll in Kailua-Kona

On the third Sunday afternoon of every month, Kailua-Kona town closes off to car traffic so people can take a local stroll with vendors, ending with a free Hawaiian music concert. *(Ch. 3)*

6 Swim at Night with Manta Rays

These gracious, gentle giants feed on plankton in a spot called "Manta Village." An experienced outfitter can get you there. *(Ch. 9)*

7 Go Bowling on a Volcano

Kilauea Military Camp (KMC), within Hawaii Volcanoes National Park, was established in 1916 for military families, but the public is also welcome to bowl, eat, shop, and pump affordable gas. *(Ch. 8)*

8 Walk on a Solid Lava Lake

Both the Halemaumau Crater and Kilauea Iki hikes take you across the floor of volcanic craters, where you'll walk on a solidified lake of formerly red-hot lava flows. *(Ch. 8)*

9 Hover over Cliffs and Waterfalls

Lift off in a helicopter and get a bird's-eye view of the island's incredible landscapes. Valleys, beaches, and volcanoes look even more amazing from several thousand feet up. *(Ch. 9)*

10 Visit Kaloko-Honokohau

At this free, underrated national historical park, boardwalks take visitors past ancient fishponds in addition to beautiful beaches where swimming is allowed. *(Ch. 3)*

11 Go Whale-Watching

From November through May, take a boat trip to watch migrating humpbacks from Alaska. They mate, give birth, and nurture their young in waters off the Hawaiian Islands. *(Ch. 9)*

12 Tour a Royal Palace

Visit the gorgeous Hulihee Palace, which is on the National Register of Historic Places and is one of only three royal palace residences in the United States. *(Ch. 3)*

13 Explore Lava Tubes

Thurston Lava Tube in Hawaii Volcanoes National Park is convenient; Kula Kai Caverns and Kilauea Caverns of Fire are fascinating but require expert guides. *(Ch. 8, 9)*

14 Marvel at the Waipio Valley

This lush, waterfall-laden valley—surrounded by sheer, fluted 2,000-foot cliffs—was once a favorite retreat for Hawaiian royalty. *(Ch. 6)*

15 Sleep on the Volcano's Rim

The historic Volcano House hotel overlooks the Kilauea caldera and is the oldest hotel in Hawaii, offering unforgettable views of the crater. *(Ch. 8)*

16 Check out Sleeping Turtles at a Black Sand Beach

At Punaluu Black Sand Beach, groups of threatened Hawaiian green sea turtles (*honu*) and endangered hawksbill turtles often sun themselves on the hot sand. *(Ch. 8)*

17 Visit a Five-Star Beach

The Big Island's (and the state's) most beautiful white-sand beaches dot the Kohala Coast, including breathtaking Hapuna Beach, Anaehoomalu Bay, and Kaunaoa Beach. *(Ch. 5)*

WHAT'S WHERE

1 Kailua-Kona. This quaint seaside town is packed with restaurants, shops, and a busy waterfront bustling with tourists along the main street, Alii Drive.

2 South Kona. The Kona Coast extends south of Kailua-Kona, including gorgeous Kealakekua Bay. It's the place to take farm tours and taste samples of world-famous Kona coffee.

3 The Kohala Coast and Waimea. The sparkling coast is home to all those long white-sand beaches and the expensive resorts that go with them. Ranches sprawl across the cool upland meadows of Waimea, known as *paniolo* (cowboy) country.

4 The Hamakua Coast. Waterfalls, dramatic cliffs, ocean vistas, ancient hidden valleys, rain forests, and the stunning Waipio Valley are just a few of the treats here. Journey up 13,796-foot Maunakea for what's considered the world's best stargazing, with 11 active telescopes perched on top.

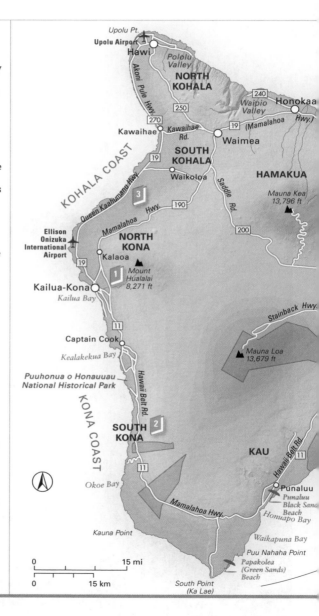

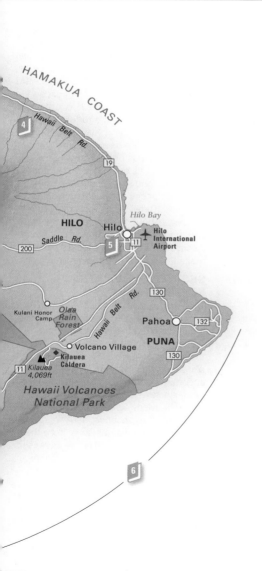

5 Hilo. Known as the City of Rainbows for all its rain, Hilo is often skipped by tourists in favor of the sunny Kohala Coast. But for what many consider the "real" Hawaii, as well as nearby rain forests, waterfalls, and the island's best farmers' market, Hilo can't be beat.

6 Hawaii Volcanoes National Park, Puna, and Kau. The spectacular Halemaumau Crater within Kilauea caldera is not to be missed, especially during eruptions. Take breathtaking hikes across steaming craters, traversing moonscape terrains mingled with lush rain forests. The adjacent hamlet of Volcano Village provides a great base for exploring the park. The remote Puna district is home to the quirky hippie town of Pahoa as well as some of the island's most recent lava flows. Round the southernmost part of the island to Kau for two of the Big Island's most unusual beaches: Papakolea (Green Sand Beach) and Punaluu Black Sand Beach. Ka Lae (South Point) is the southernmost point of land in the United States.

Big Island Today

Stunning topography, breathtaking beaches, memorable sunsets, and the endless potential for adventure mean the Big Island will always remain extremely popular with visitors. But the tiny state of Hawaii (2023 population 1.43 million, with the Big Island population hovering at 205,000) sometimes struggles to balance the demands of the visitor industry with the needs of residents. The high cost of living and doing business, overdevelopment, overtourism, lack of affordable housing, scant health care, and much more combine to make the Big Island a challenging place to live. But despite the difficulties, you will almost always hear nearly all residents use the phrase "Lucky we live in Hawaii" several times a day, and especially at sunset.

BACK-TO-BASICS AGRICULTURE

Emulating how the Hawaiian ancestors lived and returning to their ways of growing and sharing a variety of foods have become statewide initiatives. Hawaiian farmers are dedicated to producing diversity in agriculture, from coffee, avocados, and dragon fruit to flowers, goat cheese, and even wine. The seeds of this movement thrive through various farmers' markets and partnerships between restaurants and local farmers. Localized efforts such as the Hawaii Farm Bureau Federation are collectively leading the organic and sustainable agricultural renaissance. From home-cooked meals and casual plate lunches to fine dining, cooks, farmers, and chefs are blazing a trail of sustainability, helping to enrich the culinary tapestry of Hawaii.

TOURISM AND THE ECONOMY

Tourism is by far the state's largest and most important industry. In 2019, the arrival of 10.4 million visitors to the state surpassed a long-expected milestone. According to the Hawaii Tourism Authority, there were, on average, more than 250,000 visitors in the Islands on any given day, spending about $17.8 billion in 2019 alone. The COVID pandemic stopped Hawaii tourism in its tracks temporarily, a mixed blessing. Residents could enjoy uncrowded beaches and roads, but the state suffered economically from the effects of layoffs, lockdowns, and closures. Although 2023 visitor numbers are expected to match or exceed those posted in 2019, the economy may take several more years to fully recover. Even as Big Island visitor numbers increase in boom times, spending has tended to fall, as people favor lower-cost vacation rentals over hotels, cooking over eating out, and spending less money overall on pricey activities such as golf. With the 10 million visitor threshold met, concerns about overtourism in the state began to creep back into the statewide discussion, along with calls for balance to make the industry more sustainable.

SHORT-TERM VACATION RENTAL REGULATION

The explosive popularity of short-term vacation rentals (STVRs) in Hawaii—and indeed, around the world—has had a major impact on the way visitors travel. Not only are STRVs generally less expensive than hotels, but they can also accommodate larger groups or families who can save money by cooking and eating in. Many visitors, craving a more "authentic" experience, seek to stay in uncrowded, rural areas away from the hotel or resort scene. But the increased number of STVRs has brought significant community backlash. Legislation approved in 2019 allowed existing rentals not in already sanctioned resort zones to apply for a one-time permit to continue operations. All others in nonconforming zones, except for hosted stays, were banned. The county is currently working on new, strict regulations that, if passed, will probably eliminate most hosted (owner on-site) rentals as well.

THIRTY METER TELESCOPE

The Thirty Meter Telescope (TMT) is the latest telescope project to be proposed for the summit of Maunakea, the best place in the world for astronomy. With a planned mirror size of a jaw-dropping 30 meters (98 feet) in diameter, the $1.4 billion TMT will be one of the strongest telescopes on the planet. The TMT has been controversial, as some residents worry about the potential impact of further development on Maunakea and to Native Hawaiian cultural and spiritual practices. Following years of contested case hearings, in 2018, the Hawaii Supreme Court ruled in favor of the TMT, giving the green light to start. Before construction began in July 2019, protesters once again gathered at the base of the mountain, but the pandemic shut down any operations for a time. As of this writing, the TMT is still negotiating with stakeholders.

INVASIVE SPECIES

The Big Island has a long history of imported invasive species devastating to native flora and fauna, as well as to crops such as coffee and macadamia nuts. Although Hawaii has adopted strict regulations on imported species, some inevitably slip through the cracks. As you drive around the island at night, for example, you will encounter the infamous mating call of the coqui, a frog whose single, two-tone shriek can exceed 90 decibels. Originally from Puerto Rico, this teeny frog likely hitched a ride to Hawaii on nursery plants. With no natural predators, they were able to multiply throughout the island's lush forests, and now they are found most everywhere. The frogs are only the latest in a long line of animals that were imported or that hitchhiked in and became difficult to control as they

spread throughout the rugged, inaccessible mountains and rain forests of the Big Island. Goats, wild boars, mongooses, feral cats, mosquitoes, and others have wreaked havoc on local ecosystems and food chains, and have wiped out hundreds of species of endemic Hawaiian birds and other animals.

THE LATEST VOLCANIC ERUPTIONS

In May 2018, startling changes began at Kilauea Volcano. The cessation of the Puu Oo Vent, which had been continuously erupting since 1983, preceded a line of fissure eruptions in a remote neighborhood of Lower Puna, destroying dozens of homes. Meanwhile, in Hawaii Volcanoes National Park, the lava lake at Halemaumau drained quickly, creating enormous ash plumes above the summit caldera and causing steam explosions and earthquakes as it collapsed. The dramatic events claimed several beloved beaches in Lower Puna, including the Kapoho tide pools and the Ahalanui warm ponds. Those same forces also created an enormous black sand beach at Pohoiki, which continues to expand as more black sand builds up on the shore. Hawaii Volcano Observatory (HVO) scientists have since declared this phase of the eruption over, but in late 2020, a new summit eruption began in the caldera, lasted for a few months, paused, and then restarted in September 2021. Throughout 2022 and 2023, summit eruptions were on and off, always producing spectacular viewing. The current eruption is fully contained in the caldera and can be safely viewed from inside the park from several vantage points.

The sleeping giant, Mauna Loa volcano, erupted somewhat suddenly in November 2022, sending lava flows into unpopulated areas for about two weeks.

Best Big Island Beaches

KEKAHA KAI STATE PARK

A treasure of a place lies at the end of a bumpy, unimproved road (2WD with clearance can make it) where beachgoers will find their journey rewarded with the soft sands of Mahaiula Beach. Turtles love to sun on this shore, but please maintain a respectful distance. A moderately difficult hike along an *aa* (rocky lava) path takes you to Kua Bay, on the other side of the park. Local surfers and body boarders love the challenge of the rough waves in winter.

PAPAKOLEA (GREEN SAND BEACH)

This isolated beach at the southern tip of the island came into being thanks to a volcano. Olivine crystals, a semiprecious mineral born of volcanic eruptions, give the sand the famous green hue. It's a 2½-mile hike (one way) from remote South Point Road in Kau, but where else are you going to experience a beach with green sand? Bring water, wear sturdy shoes, and swim only in the calmest of conditions.

PUNALUU BLACK SAND BEACH PARK

Along the desolate southeastern coast in Kau, this pretty little beach park impresses with its shimmering black sands, coconut groves, and the stars of the show basking on shore: *honu* (turtles), both the Hawaiian green sea turtle and sometimes the highly endangered hawksbill.

ANAEHOOMALU BAY

Although less well known than its Kohala Coast cousins, this lovely stretch of beach, with its mature coconut palms and ancient fishponds, is just a stone's throw from two large resorts. It's a spectacular spot for swimming, snorkeling, and stand-up paddleboarding.

HAPUNA BEACH STATE RECREATION AREA

This sugar-white stretch of tropical glory evokes everyone's ideal fantasy of Hawaii and is consistently rated among the world's best beaches. Aquamarine water and wide, sandy shores guarantee idyllic conditions for swimming, snorkeling, wading, and sunbathing.

KAMAKAHONU BEACH (KING KAM BEACH)

In the heart of Kailua-Kona, this gentle spot of sand and surf makes the perfect place for kids and babies. Sometimes known by locals as Kona's "baby beach," Kamakahonu means "eye of the turtle" and was named for a large rock formation now buried by the pier. It fronts the Courtyard King Kamehameha's Kona Beach Hotel.

HONOLII BEACH PARK

This scenic beach park is pure gold to eastside surfers. A couple miles north of Hilo, the cove is surrounded by lush tropical foliage. Because of its constant year-round swells (more vigorous in winter), Honolii regularly hosts local surf contests. It's not particularly favorable for swimming, however, due to murky waters fed by the nearby river mouth, as well as some strong rip currents and other dangerous conditions.

RICHARDSON OCEAN PARK

The black-sand beach park south of town is probably the best beach in the Hilo area. Not only are there protected sections of lava outcrops that make it a good spot for kids and snorkeling, but the vistas from here are also superb. You can see Maunakea in the background and coconut palms create a backdrop for the beach area, giving it a postcard quality.

POHOIKI BLACK SAND BEACH

As the devastating 2018 Puna eruption made its way down to the beloved eastside coastline, it destroyed nearly all in its path, then set its sights on Pohoiki Bay. But the river of molten earth suddenly stopped, fingers of lava reaching only as far as the parking lot at adjacent Isaac Hale Beach Park. Over the years, a large black-sand beach has continued to form and expand where the bay and boat ramp used to be. Beautiful as it is, swimming is not advised, as it's usually too rough.

KAUNAOA (MAUNA KEA BEACH)

If you were given the job of painting a picture of the most scenic spot on the Big Island, your canvas might include this breathtaking crescent of white sand, lapped by extraordinarily clear waters and fronted by the Mauna Kea Beach Hotel, Autograph Collection.

Best Natural Wonders on the Big Island

KEALAKEKUA BAY STATE HISTORICAL PARK
One of the undisputed jewels of the entire state, Kealakekua Bay, a marine-life conservation district, encompasses several miles of shimmering, crystal-clear aquamarine waters, bordered by a long, sloping *pali* (cliff) that ranges in color from emerald green to soft brown.

THURSTON LAVA TUBE
Estimated to be about 500 years old, this giant, easily accessible cavern presents a wonderful example of what happens when molten lava flows through a channel and then hardens around it, leaving a hollowed-out space. It's lush, porous, and damp inside, and the first portion is even lit.

WAILUKU RIVER STATE PARK
A short distance from downtown Hilo, the 80-foot Rainbow Falls is part of the fearsome Wailuku River. The name means "River of Destruction" in Hawaiian. This river is classified as a Class V rapid and is very dangerous. It's for viewing only, never swimming.

AKAKA FALLS STATE PARK
Free-falling 442 feet into a deep gorge, Akaka Falls presents some of the most dramatic and easily accessible (to view) waterfalls on Hawaii Island. A short, ½-mile paved hike through the lush rain forest offers unique vantage points of two different sections of the falls.

HALEMAUMAU CRATER
This famous summit caldera in Hawaii Volcanoes National Park is home to an active lava lake that rises and falls over generations and sometimes disappears. Quiet after the cessation of the Lower East Rift Zone eruption in 2018, the crater awoke with an eruption of its own in December 2020, followed by numerous starts and stops in 2022 and 2023. In fact, so much lava has filled the lake since its 2018 collapse that the lake is now visible from the lookouts for the first time in many years.

MAUNAKEA
Reigning almost 14,000 feet above sea level, Maunakea invokes a plethora of superlatives. It's the best place in the world for astronomy and the tallest peak in the Hawaiian Islands. The mountain also boasts the state's only alpine lake, Lake Waiau. Only about 10 feet deep, the lake is replenished by permafrost from the last ice age, during which monstrous glaciers raked over the summit, leaving deep marks from passing rocks and stones.

MAUNA LOA
Rising 13,679 feet, Mauna Loa ("Long Mountain") is the planet's largest active volcano in terms of mass and volume, its flows comprising more than 50% of the Big Island's slopes. It's so huge and heavy that it has created a sea floor depression in excess of 5 miles, just through its sheer mass. For the first time in almost 40 years, in November 2022, she erupted for about two weeks, sending lava flows in an uninhabited northeastern direction.

POLOLU VALLEY
At the end of the Akoni Pule Highway in North Kohala, a steep ½-mile hike leads to a fantastic gray-sand beach, dotted with large boulders and driftwood and surrounded by ironwood trees and sheer green cliffs. The beach has a contemplative quality, a good thing because as at all east-side beaches, the water can be rough and dangerous, while the scenery is beautiful to observe.

2018 PUNA LAVA FLOWS
In May 2018, fissures of lava erupted near Pahoa Town in the middle of a quiet subdivision called Leilani Estates. By August, it was over. It is quite shocking to drive through what appears to be a dense, lush rain forest and suddenly come across a black, desolate landscape, replete with burned-out tree trunks and brush and with solid walls of lava blocking the road like a commanding fortress built by Pele herself, the Hawaiian volcano goddess.

WAIPIO VALLEY
The Valley of the Kings, on the Hamakua Coast, is full of sky-high waterfalls, lush green cliffs, and a mystical quality that can't quite be described or rivaled. The view from the lookout at the top is breathtaking.

What to Eat and Drink in Hawaii

HAWAIIAN PLATE LUNCH

The Hawaiian plate lunch comprises the delicious, traditional foods of Hawaii, all on one heaping plate. You can find these combo meals anywhere, from roadside lunch wagons to five-star restaurants. Get yours with the melt-in-your-mouth shredded kalua pig, pork, or chicken *laulau* (cooked in ti leaves) with *lomi lomi* salmon (diced salmon with tomatoes and onions) on the side and the coconut-milk *haupia* for dessert. Most Hawaiian plates come with the requisite two scoops of white rice. Don't forget to try *poi*, or pounded and cooked taro.

SHAVE ICE

Shave ice is simple in its composition—fluffy ice drizzled in Technicolor syrups. Shave ice traces its roots to Hawaii's plantation past. Japanese laborers would use the machetes from their field work to finely shave ice from large frozen blocks and then pour fruit juice over it.

POKE

In Hawaiian, *poke* is a verb that means to slice and cut into pieces. It perfectly describes the technique Hawaiians have used for centuries to prepare poke the dish. The cubed raw fish, most commonly *ahi* (yellowfin tuna), is traditionally tossed with Hawaiian sea salt, *limu kohu* (red seaweed), or *inamona* (crushed kukui nuts). Today, countless varieties of this must-try dish are served in all kinds of restaurants across the Islands. Poke shacks offer no-frills, made-to-order poke.

MUSUBI

Musubi are Hawaii's answer to the perfect snack. Portable, handheld, and salty, *musubi* are a great go-to any time of day. The local comfort food is a slice of fried Spam encased in packed white rice and snugly wrapped with nori, or dried seaweed. Available everywhere, *musubi* are usually just a few dollars.

MAI TAI

When people think of a Hawaiian cocktail, the colorful mai tai often comes to mind. It's the unofficial drink to imbibe at a luau and refreshingly tropical. This potent concoction has a rum base and is traditionally made with orange curaçao, orgeat, fresh-squeezed lime juice, and simple syrup.

SAIMIN

This only-in-Hawaii noodle dish is the culinary innovation of Hawaii plantation workers in the late 1800s who created a new comfort food with ingredients and traditions from their home countries.

MANAPUA

When *kamaaina*, or Hawaii residents, are invited to a potluck, business meeting, or even an impromptu party, inevitably there will be a box filled with *manapua*. Inside these airy white buns are pockets of sweet *char siu* pork. Head to cities and towns around the Islands, and you'll find restaurants with manapua on their menus, as well as manapua takeout places serving a variety of fillings. There's sweet potato, curry chicken, *lap cheong* (or Chinese sausage)—and even sweet flavors, such as custard and *ube*, a purple yam popular in Filipino desserts.

LOCO MOCO

The traditional version of one of Hawaii's classic comfort-food dishes consists of white rice topped with a hamburger patty and fried eggs and generously blanketed in rich, brown gravy. Cafe 100 in Hilo on the Big Island is renowned as the home of the *loco moco*, but you'll find this popular staple everywhere. It can be eaten any time of day.

KONA COFFEE

In Kona, on the Big Island, coffee reigns supreme. There are roughly 600 coffee farms dotting the west side of the island, each producing flavorful (and quite expensive) coffee grown in the rich, volcanic soil. Kona coffee is typically hand-harvested from August through December.

MALASADA

Malasadas are a beloved treat in Hawaii. The Portuguese pastries are about the size of a baseball and are airy, deep-fried, and dusted with sugar. They are best enjoyed hot and filled with custard; fillings are a Hawaiian variation on the original.

Flora and Fauna in Hawaii

KUKUI

The kukui, or candlenut, is Hawaii's state tree, and Hawaiians have had many uses for it. Oil was extracted from its nuts and burned as a light source and also rubbed on fishing nets to preserve them. The juice from the husk's fruit was used as a dye. The small kukui blossoms and nuts also have medicinal purposes.

PLUMERIA

Also known as frangipani, this fragrant flower is named after Charles Plumier, the noted French botanist who discovered it in Central America in the late 1600s. Plumeria come in shades of white, yellow, pink, red, and orange. The hearty, plentiful blossoms are frequently used in lei.

GARDENIA

The gardenia is a favorite for lei makers because of its sweet smell. The plant is native to tropical regions throughout China and Africa, but there are also endemic gardenias in Hawaii. The nanu gardenia is found only in the Islands and has petite white blossoms.

HONU

The *honu*, or Hawaiian green sea turtle, is a magical sight. The graceful reptile is an endangered and protected species in Hawaii. It's easier to encounter *honu* during a snorkeling or scuba-diving excursion, but they occasionally can be spotted basking on beaches.

HUMPBACK WHALES

Each year, North Pacific humpback whales make the long journey to Hawaii from Alaska. With its warm, protected waters, Hawaii provides the ideal place for the marine mammals to mate and to birth and to nurse their young. They arrive between November and May, and their presence is an anticipated event. You can see them up close during whale-watching boat tours.

MONK SEAL

Known as the *ilio holo i ka uaua*, meaning "dog that runs in rough water," monk seals are endemic to Hawaii and critically endangered. The majority of these mammals, which can grow to more than 7 feet long, live in the remote, uninhabited Northwestern Hawaiian Islands.

TROPICAL FISH

Approximately 25% of the fish species in the Islands are endemic. Snorkeling in Hawaii is a unique, fun opportunity to see colorful fish found nowhere else on Earth. Interestingly, Hawaii's state fish, the *humuhumunukunukuapuaa*, or reef trigger, is not endemic to the state.

NENE GOOSE

Pronounced *nay-nay*, the endemic nene goose (Hawaii's state bird) is one of the world's rarest. A descendant of the Canada goose, it has been bred back from the edge of extinction and reintroduced into the wild. Use caution driving in national and state parks, which they frequent.

HIBISCUS

In 1923, the Territory of Hawaii passed a law designating hibiscus as Hawaii's official flower. While there are more than 30 introduced species of the large, colorful flowers throughout the Islands, there are five endemic types. The endemic hibiscus has yellow blossoms and is known in Hawaiian as *mao hau hele*, which means the "traveling green tree."

PIKAKE

These small, delicate blossoms are known for their hypnotic, sweet scent. The jasmine flower was introduced from India and was a favorite of Princess Kaiulani. *Pikake*, which is the Hawaiian word for the blossom as well as for a peacock—another favorite of the princess—is the subject of many *mele*, or Hawaiian songs.

What to Buy in Hawaii

MACADAMIA NUT CANDY
Macadamia nuts are native to Australia, but the gumball-sized nut remains an important crop in Hawaii. It was first introduced in the late 1880s as a windbreak for sugarcane crops. Today, mac nuts are a popular local snack and are especially good baked in cookies or other desserts.

LEI
As a visitor to Hawaii, you may well receive a lei, either a shell, kukui nut, or fragrant flower variety, as a welcome to the Islands. *Kamaaina* (Hawaii residents) mark special occasions by gifting lei.

LAUHALA
The hala tree is most known for its long, thin leaves and the masterful crafts that are created from them. Lauhala weavers make baskets, hats, mats, jewelry, and more, using intricate traditional patterns and techniques.

JEWELRY
Island-inspired jewelry comes in many styles. Tahitian pearl pendants and earrings are a local favorite, as are delicate, inexpensive shell pieces. The most coveted are Hawaiian heirloom bracelets in gold or silver with one's name enameled in Old English script.

ALOHA WEAR
Aloha wear in Hawaii has come a long way from the polyester fabrics with too-bright, kitschy patterns (although those still exist). Local designers have been creating dressy, modern aloha attire with softer prints that evoke Island botanicals, heritage, and traditional patterns. Hawaii residents don aloha wear for everything from work to weddings.

HAWAIIAN COFFEE

Reminisce about your Hawaii getaway each time you brew a cup of aromatic, full-bodied coffee, whether it's from Kona or Kauai. All the main islands grow distinctive coffee. Stores and cafés sell bags of varying sizes, and in some places you can buy directly from a farmer.

HAWAIIAN SEA SALT

A long tradition of harvesting salt beds by hand continues today on all the Islands. The salt comes in various colors, including inky black and brick red—the result of the salt reacting and mixing with activated charcoal and *alaea* (volcanic clay). It is renowned by chefs around the state.

HAWAIIAN HONEY

With its temperate climate and bountiful foliage, Hawaii is ideal for honeybees. Its unique ecosystem yields honeys with robust flavors and textures, including elixirs extracted from the blossoms of the macadamia nut tree, the lehua flower, and the invasive Christmas berry shrub.

UKULELE

In Hawaiian, *ukulele* means "the jumping flea." The small instrument made its way to the Islands in the 1880s via Portuguese immigrants who brought with them the four-string, guitarlike *machete de braga*. It is famous as a solo instrument today, with virtuoso artists like Jake Shimabukuro and Taimane Gardner popularizing the ukulele's versatile sound.

KOA WOOD

If you're looking for an heirloom keepsake from the Islands, consider a koa wood product. Grown only in Hawaii, the valuable koa is some of the world's rarest and hardest wood. Hawaiians traditionally made surfboards and canoes from these trees, which today grow only in upland forests.

Kids and Families

With dozens of adventures, discoveries, and fun-filled beach days, Hawaii is a blast with kids. Even better, the things to do here don't appeal only to small fry. The entire family, parents included, will enjoy surfing, discovering a waterfall in the rain forest, and snorkeling with reef fish. If you're at a resort, count on organized activities for kids that will give parents time for a dinner date or a few romantic beach strolls.

CHOOSING A PLACE TO STAY

Resorts: Most big resorts make kids' programs a priority, and it shows. When you are booking your room, ask about "kids eat free" deals and the number of kids' pools at the resort. Also check out the size of the groups in the children's programs, and find out whether the cost of the programs includes lunch, equipment, and activities.

The Hilton Waikoloa Village is every kid's fantasy vacation come true, with multiple pool slides, a lagoon for snorkeling, and even a choice between riding a monorail or taking a boat to your room. Not to be outdone, the Four Seasons Resort Hualalai has a great program that will keep your little ones happy and occupied all day.

Condos: Condo and vacation rentals are a fantastic value for families vacationing in Hawaii. You can cook your own food, which is cheaper than eating out and sometimes easier (especially if you have a finicky eater in your group). You'll also get twice the space of a hotel room for about a quarter of the price. If you decide to go the condo route, be sure to ask about the size of the complex's pool (and whether kids of all ages are allowed) and whether barbecues are available. One of the best reasons to stay in your own place is to hold a sunset family barbecue by the pool or overlooking the ocean.

Updated regulations apply for vacation rentals now, so make sure the one you book is permitted and legal.

Condos in Kailua-Kona (on or near Alii Drive) are some of the best values on the Big Island. You have a choice of older or newer properties with a varying number of amenities (and, as a result, varying prices). Affordable food in a number of cuisines is available at restaurants in Kona, including Kailua-Kona, if you are looking for a family night out or, even better, a date night.

OCEAN ACTIVITIES

On the beach: Most people like being in the water, but toddlers and school-age kids tend to be especially enamored of it. The swimming pool at your condo or hotel is always an option, but don't be afraid to hit the beach with a little one in tow. There are lots of family-friendly beaches on the Big Island with protected bays and pleasant white sand. As always, use your judgment, and heed all posted signs and lifeguard warnings.

Calm beaches to try include Kamakahonu Beach and Kahaluu Beach Park in Kailua-Kona; Spencer Beach Park in Puako; and Onekahakaha Beach Park in Hilo.

On the waves: Surf lessons are a great idea for older kids. Beginner lessons are always on safe and easy waves. Most surf schools also offer instruction in stand-up paddleboarding.

For school-age and older kids, book a two-hour surfing lesson with Hawaii Lifeguard Surf Instructors and either join the kids out on the break or say aloha to a little parents-only time.

The underwater world: If your kids are ready to try snorkeling, Hawaii is a great place to introduce them to the underwater world. Even without the mask and snorkel, they'll be able to see colorful fish darting this way and that below the surface of the water, and they may also spot turtles at many of the island's bays.

The easily accessible Kahaluu Beach, in Kailua-Kona, is a great introductory snorkel spot because of its many facilities. Protected by a natural breakwater, these shallow reefs attract large numbers of sea creatures, including the Hawaiian green sea turtle. These turtles feed on seaweed near shore and sometimes can be spotted basking on the rocks.

Near the southern tip of the island, Punaluu Black Sand Beach provides opportunities to view sea turtles up close. Though the water can be rough, hawksbill turtles nest here, and there are nearly always one or two napping on the beach. Please heed signs and don't get too close. These animals are endangered and protected. At nighttime, you can head to the Outrigger Kona Resort and Spa at Keauhou Bay or Huggo's on the Rocks in Kailua-Kona to view manta rays; each place shines a bright spotlight on the water to attract them. Anyone, but especially kids, could sit and watch manta rays glide through the ocean in graceful circles for hours. No snorkel required!

Another great option is to book a snorkel cruise or opt to stay dry inside the Atlantis Submarine that operates out of Kailua-Kona. Kids love crawling down into a real-life submarine and viewing the ocean world through its portholes.

LAND ACTIVITIES

In addition to beach experiences, the Big Island has easy waterfall hikes, botanical gardens, a zoo, and hands-on museums that will keep your kids entertained and out of the sun for a day.

Hawaii Volcanoes National Park is a must for any family vacation. Even phone-addicted teenagers will acknowledge the coolness of lava tubes, steaming volcanic craters, and a fiery nighttime lava show (when they happen).

On the Hilo side, the Panaewa Rainforest Zoo and Gardens is small but free and lots of fun for the little ones, with a small petting zoo on Saturday. Your kids might even get to hold a Hawaiian hawk. Just a few miles north, on the Hamakua Coast, the the Hawaii Tropical Bioreserve & Garden makes a beautiful, fun stop for kids, filled with huge lily pads and noisy frogs.

School-age and older kids will get a kick out of Kohala UTV Adventure or horseback rides above the waterfalls of Waipio Valley via Waipio on Horseback.

AFTER DARK

At night, younger kids get a kick out of attending a luau, and many incorporate young audience members, adding to the fun. Teens and adults alike are sure to enjoy the music and overall theatrical quality of all of the island's luau shows, which are produced by serious practitioners of all of the Polynesian native dance styles.

Stargazing from Maunakea is another treat. The visitor center has star talk programs and telescopes set up (check online; these are subject to change). If you'd rather leave the planning to someone else, book a tour with Hawaii Forest and Trail. Their knowledgeable guides are great at sharing that knowledge in a narrative form that kids—and adults, for that matter—enjoy. And everyone enjoys the hot chocolate and cookies served during the star talk held at 11,000 feet where stars are actually clearer to the eye than on top.

The History of Hawaii

THE POLYNESIANS

Years before the eras of the Vikings and Christopher Columbus, Polynesian seafarers embarked on journeys across the boundless ocean in wooden, double-hulled canoes. These were no chance voyages—these adventurers possessed an intricate understanding of celestial navigation and sailing. Originating from western Polynesia, they navigated between Samoa, Fiji, Tahiti, the Marquesas, and the Society Isles. By AD 300, they had established settlements in far-flung places like Hawaii and Easter Island.

Around AD 1200, the pinnacle of Polynesian voyaging was reached. Following this, the distant Hawaiian Islands evolved independently, fostering distinct cultural practices and ways of life. The community on these islands beautifully blended religion, mythology, science, and artistry. Each settlement, overseen by an *alii*, a chief, existed within an *ahupuaa*, a pie-shaped division of land that extended from the mountains, through the valleys to the shores. Everyone played a crucial role such as crafting canoes, fishing, or farming.

THE HAWAIIAN KINGDOM

In 1778, when Captain James Cook arrived in Kealakekua Bay on the Big Island, the Hawaiians welcomed him warmly with a sense of great importance. The trade that followed, including the acquisition of guns from foreign ships, provided Kamehameha the Great, the chief of the Big Island, with a strategic advantage over other chiefs. This led to the unification of Hawaii into a single kingdom in 1810, putting an end to the frequent interisland battles that had long defined Hawaiian life.

However, the new kingdom faced many challenges. Native religion was abandoned, and traditions, including *kapu* (laws and regulations) were eventually discarded. In addition, the European explorers brought devastating diseases that decimated the Native Hawaiian population within a few decades.

The fabric of pre-contact Hawaii began to unravel with new laws affecting land ownership and religious practices. As Western influences permeated Hawaiian culture, social unrest took root, marking a major shift in the island's way of life, including the loss of the Hawaiian language.

MODERN HAWAII

In 1893, Queen Liliuokalani, the last Hawaiian monarch, was overthrown by American and European leaders, backed by an armed militia. This upheaval created the Republic of Hawaii, paving the way for 60 years as a U.S. territory. The scars of lost sovereignty and the terms of annexation have lingered, haunting the Hawaiian people since the monarchy's abrupt end.

In 1941, the attack on Oahu's Pearl Harbor thrust the U.S. into World War II. This surprise bombing destroyed or damaged many military ships and airplanes, and killed over 2,000 people. Visitors are encouraged to visit the memorial, which includes the battleships USS *Arizona* and USS *Missouri,* to pay tribute to the fallen.

Hawaii's complex history continued to evolve and in 1959, Hawaii officially became the 50th U.S. state. Despite ongoing challenges, a cultural revival known as the Hawaiian Renaissance began in the 1960s among the Native Hawaiian community, including resurrecting the hula, reviving voyaging canoes, and reinvigorating Hawaiian art, music, and language. Today, tourists can learn about the culture and even volunteer through the *Malama Aina* project, (meaning "to care for the land").

Continued on page 42

HAWAIIAN CULTURAL TRADITIONS HULA, LEI, AND LUAU

HULA: MORE THAN A FOLK DANCE

Hula has been called "the heartbeat of the Hawaiian people" and also "the world's best-known, most misunderstood dance." Both are true. Hula isn't just dance. It is storytelling.

Chanter Edith McKinzie calls it "an extension of a piece of poetry." In its adornments, implements, and customs, hula integrates every important Hawaiian cultural practice: poetry, history, genealogy, craft, plant cultivation, martial arts, religion and protocol. So when 19th-century Christian missionaries sought to eradicate a practice they considered depraved, they threatened more than just a folk dance.

With public performance outlawed and private hula practice discouraged, hula went underground for a generation. The fragile verbal link by which culture was transmitted from teacher to student hung by a thread. Even increasing literacy did not help because hula's practitioners were a secretive and protected circle.

As if that weren't bad enough, vaudeville, Broadway, and Hollywood got hold of the hula, giving it the glitz treatment in an unbroken line from "Oh, How She Could Wicky Wacky Woo" to "Rock-A-Hula Baby." Hula became shorthand for paradise: fragrant flowers, lazy hours. Ironically, this development assured that hundreds of Hawaiians could make a living performing and teaching hula. Many danced 'auana (modern form) in performance; but taught kahiko (traditional) quietly, at home or in hula schools.

Today, decades after the cultural revival known as the Hawaiian Renaissance, language immersion programs have assured a new generation of proficient chanters, songwriters, and translators. Visitors can see more—and more authentic—traditional hula now than at any other time in the last 200 years.

Like the culture of which it is the beating heart, hula has survived.

Lei poo. Head lei. In *kahiko,* greenery only. In auana, flowers.

Face emotes appropriate expression. Dancer should not be a smiling automaton.

Shoulders remain relaxed and still, never hunched, even with arms raised. No bouncing.

Eyes always follow leading hand.

Lei. Hula is rarely performed without a shoulder lei.

Traditional hula skirt is loose fabric, smocked and gathered at the waist.

Arms and hands remain loose, relaxed, below shoulder level— except as required by interpretive movements.

Hip is canted over weight-bearing foot.

Knees are always slightly bent, accentuating hip sway.

Kupee. Ankle bracelet of flowers, shells, or foliage.

In *kahiko*, feet are flat. In *'auana*, they may be more arched, but not tiptoes or bouncing.

BASIC MOTIONS

Speak or sing

Moon or sun

Grass shack or house

Mountains or heights

Love or caress

At backyard parties, hula is performed in bare feet and street clothes, but in performance, adornments play a key role, as do rhythm-keeping implements such as the *pahu* drum and the *ipu* (gourd).

In hula *kahiko* (traditional style), the usual dress is multiple layers of stiff fabric (often with a pellom lining, which most closely resembles *kapa*, the paperlike bark cloth of the Hawaiians). These wrap tightly around the bosom but flare below the waist to form a skirt. In pre-contact times, dancers wore only kapa skirts. Men traditionally wear loincloths.

Monarchy-period hula is performed in voluminous muumuu or high-necked muslin blouses and gathered skirts. Men wear white or gingham shirts and black pants.

In hula *'auana* (modern), dress for women can range from grass skirts and strapless tops to contemporary tea-length dresses. Men generally wear aloha shirts, but sometimes grass skirts over pants or even everyday gear.

SURPRISING HULA FACTS

■ Grass skirts are not traditional; workers from Kiribati (the Gilbert Islands) brought this custom to Hawaii.

■ In olden-day Hawaii, *mele* (songs) for hula were composed for every occasion—name songs for babies, dirges for funerals, welcome songs for visitors, celebrations of favorite pursuits.

■ Hula *mai* is a traditional hula form in praise of a noble's genitals; the power of the *alii* (royalty) to procreate gave *mana* (spiritual power) to the entire culture.

■ Hula students in old Hawaii adhered to high standards: scrupulous cleanliness, no sex, daily cleansing rituals, certain food prohibitions, and no contact with the dead. They were fined if they broke the rules.

WHERE TO WATCH

If you're interested in "the real thing," there are annual hula festivals on each island. Check the individual island visitors' bureaus websites at ⊕ *www.gohawaii.com*.

If you can't make it to a festival, there are plenty of other hula shows—at most resorts, many lounges, and even at certain shopping centers. Ask your hotel concierge for performance information.

ALL ABOUT LEI

Lei brighten every occasion in Hawaii, from birthdays to bar mitzvahs to baptisms. Creative artisans weave nature's bounty—flowers, ferns, vines, and seeds—into gorgeous creations that convey an array of heartfelt messages: "Welcome," "Congratulations," "Good luck," "Farewell," "Thank you," "I love you." When it's difficult to find the right words, a lei expresses exactly the right sentiment.

WHERE TO BUY THE BEST LEI

Most airports in Hawaii have lei stands where you can buy a fragrant garland upon arrival. Every florist shop in the Islands sells lei; you can also treat yourself to a lei while shopping for provisions at any supermarket or box store. And you'll always find lei sellers at crafts fairs and outdoor festivals.

LEI ETIQUETTE

■ To wear a closed lei, drape it over your shoulders, half in front and half in back. Open lei are worn around the neck, with the ends draped over the front in equal lengths.

■ Pikake, ginger, and other sweet, delicate blossoms are "feminine" lei. Men opt for cigar, crown flower, and ti leaf lei, which are sturdier and don't emit as much fragrance.

■ Lei are always presented with a kiss, a custom that supposedly dates back to World War II when a hula dancer fancied an officer at a U.S.O. show. Taking a dare from members of her troupe, she took off her lei, placed it around his neck, and kissed him on the cheek.

■ You shouldn't wear a lei before you give it to someone else. Hawaiians believe the lei absorbs your mana (spirit); if you give your lei away, you'll be giving away part of your essence.

ORCHID

Growing wild on every continent except Antarctica, orchids—which range in color from yellow to green to purple—comprise the largest family of plants in the world. There are more than 20,000 species of orchids, but only three are native to Hawaii—and they are very rare. The pretty lavender vanda you see hanging by the dozens at local lei stands has probably been imported from Thailand.

MAILE

Maile, an endemic twining vine with a heady aroma, is sacred to Laka, goddess of the hula. In ancient times, dancers wore maile and decorated hula altars with it to honor Laka. Today, "open" maile lei usually are given to men. Instead of ribbon, interwoven lengths of maile are used at dedications of new businesses. The maile is untied, never snipped, for doing so would symbolically "cut" the company's success.

ILIMA

Designated by Hawaii's Territorial Legislature in 1923 as the official flower of the island of Oahu, the golden ilima is so delicate it lasts for just a day. Five to seven hundred blossoms are needed to make one garland. Queen Emma, wife of King Kamehameha IV, preferred ilima over all other lei, which may have led to the incorrect belief that they were reserved only for royalty.

PLUMERIA

This ubiquitous flower is named after Charles Plumier, the noted French botanist who discovered it in Central America in the late 1600s. Plumeria ranks among the most popular lei in Hawaii because it's fragrant, hardy, plentiful, inexpensive, and requires very little care. Although yellow is the most common color, you'll also find plumeria lei in shades of pink, red, orange, and "rainbow" blends.

PIKAKE

Favored for its fragile beauty and sweet scent, pikake was introduced from India. In lieu of pearls, many brides in Hawaii adorn themselves with long, multiple strands of white pikake. Princess Kaiulani enjoyed showing guests her beloved pikake and peacocks at Ainahau, her Waikiki home. Interestingly, pikake is the Hawaiian word for both the bird and the blossom.

KUKUI

The kukui (candlenut) is Hawaii's state tree. Early Hawaiians strung kukui nuts (which are quite oily) together and burned them for light; mixed burned nuts with oil to make an indelible dye; and mashed roasted nuts to consume as a laxative. Kukui nut lei may not have been made until after Western contact, when the Hawaiians saw black beads from Europe and wanted to imitate them.

LUAU: A TASTE OF HAWAII

The best place to sample Hawaiian food is at a backyard luau. Aunts and uncles are cooking, the pig is from a cousin's farm, and the fish is from a brother's boat.

But even locals have to angle for invitations to those rare occasions. So your choice is most likely between a commercial luau and a Hawaiian restaurant.

Some commercial luau are less authentic; they offer little of the traditional diet and are more about umbrella drinks, spectacle, and fun.

For greater culinary authenticity, folksy experiences, and rock-bottom prices, visit a Hawaiian restaurant (most are in anonymous storefronts in residential neighborhoods). Expect rough edges and some effort negotiating the menu.

In either case, much of what is known today as Hawaiian food would be as foreign to a 16th-century Hawaiian as risotto or chow mien. The pre-contact diet was simple and healthy—mainly raw and steamed seafood and vegetables. Early Hawaiians used earth ovens and heated stones to cook seafood, taro, sweet potatoes, and breadfruit and seasoned their food with sea salt and ground kukui nuts. Seaweed, fern shoots, sweet potato vines, coconut, banana, sugarcane, and select greens and roots rounded out the diet.

Successive waves of immigrants added their favorites to the ti leaf–lined table. So it is that foods as disparate as salt salmon and chicken long rice are now Hawaiian—even though there is no salmon in Hawaiian waters and long rice (cellophane noodles) is Chinese.

AT THE LUAU: KALUA PORK

The heart of any luau is the *imu*, the earth oven in which a whole pig is roasted. The preparation of an imu is an arduous affair for most families, who tackle it only once a year or so, for a baby's first birthday or at Thanksgiving, when many Islanders prefer to imu their turkeys. Commercial luau operations have it down to a science, however.

THE ART OF THE STONE

The key to a proper imu is the *pohaku*, the stones. Imu cook by means of long, slow, moist heat released by special stones that can withstand a hot fire without exploding. Many Hawaiian families treasure their imu stones, keeping them in a pile in the backyard and passing them on through generations.

PIT COOKING

The imu makers first dig a pit about the size of a refrigerator, then lay down *kiawe* (mesquite) wood and stones, and build a white-hot fire that is allowed to burn itself out. The ashes are raked away, and the hot stones covered with banana and ti leaves. Well-wrapped in ti or banana leaves and a net of chicken wire, the pig is lowered onto the leaf-covered stones. *Laulau* (leaf-wrapped bundles of meats, fish, and taro leaves) may also be placed inside. Leaves—ti, banana, even ginger—cover the pig followed by wet burlap sacks (to create steam). The whole is topped with a canvas tarp and left to steam for the better part of a day.

OPENING THE IMU

This is the moment everyone waits for: The imu is unwrapped like a giant present and the imu keepers gingerly wrestle out the steaming pig. When it's unwrapped, the meat falls moist and smoky-flavored from the bone, looking just like Southern-style pulled pork, but without the barbecue sauce.

WHICH LUAU?

Most resort hotels have luau on their grounds that include hula, music, and, of course, lots of food and drink. Each island also has at least one "authentic" luau. For lists of the best luau on each island, visit the Hawaii Visitors and Convention Bureau website at ⊕ *www.gohawaii.com*.

MEA AI ONO:
GOOD THINGS TO EAT.

LAULAU
Steamed meats, fish, and taro leaf in ti-leaf bundles: fork-tender, a medley of flavors; the taro resembles spinach.

LOMI LOMI SALMON
Salt salmon in a piquant salad or relish with onions and tomatoes.

POI
Poi, a paste made of pounded taro root, may be an acquired taste, but it's a must-try during your visit.

Consider: The Hawaiian Adam is descended from *kalo* (taro). Young taro plants are called "keiki" (children). Poi is the first food after mother's milk for many Islanders. *Ai*, the word for food, is synonymous with poi in many contexts.

Not only that, locals love it. "There is no meat that doesn't taste good with poi," the old Hawaiians said.

But you have to know how to eat it: with something rich or powerfully flavored. "It is salt that makes the poi go in," is another adage. When you're served poi, try it with a mouthful of smoky kalua pork or salty *lomi lomi* salmon. Its slightly sour blandness cleanses the palate. And if you don't like it, smile and say something polite. (And slide that bowl over to a local.)

Laulau

Lomi lomi salmon

Poi

E HELE MAI AI! COME AND EAT!

Local-style Hawaiian restaurants tend to be inconveniently located in well-worn storefronts with little or no parking, outfitted with battered tables and clattering Melmac dishes, but they personify aloha, invariably run by local families who welcome tourists who take the trouble to find them.

Many are cash-only operations and combination plates, known as "plate lunches," are a standard feature: one or two entrées, two scoops of steamed rice, one scoop of macaroni salad, and—if the place is really old-style—a tiny portion of coarse Hawaiian salt and some raw onions for relish.

Most serve some foods that aren't, strictly speaking, Hawaiian, but are beloved of *kamaaina* (locals), such as salt meat with watercress (preserved meat in a tasty broth), or *akubone* (skipjack tuna fried in a tangy vinegar sauce).

Weddings and Honeymoons

There's no question that Hawaii is one of the country's foremost honeymoon destinations. Romance is in the air here, and the white-sand beaches, turquoise water, swaying palm fronds, soft Hawaiian music, balmy tropical breezes, and perpetual sunshine put people in the mood for love. It's easy to understand why Hawaii is a popular wedding destination as well, especially as the cost of airfare is often discounted, and new resorts and hotels entice visitors. You can plan a traditional ceremony in a place of worship followed by a reception at an elegant resort, or you can go barefoot on the beach and celebrate at a luau. There are almost as many wedding planners in the Islands as real estate agents, which makes it oh-so-easy to wed in paradise and then, once the knot is tied, stay for the honeymoon as well.

THE BIG DAY

Choosing the perfect place: When selecting a location, remember that you really have two choices to make: the ceremony location and where to have the reception, if you're having one. For the former, there are beaches, bluffs overlooking beaches, gardens, private residences, resort lawns, and, of course, places of worship. As for the reception, there are these same choices, as well as restaurants and even a luau. If you decide to go outdoors, remember the seasons—yes, Hawaii has seasons. If you're planning a summer wedding outdoors, be sure you have a backup plan (such as a tent) in case it rains. Also, if you're planning an outdoor wedding at sunset—which is very popular—be sure you match the time of your ceremony to the time the sun sets at that time of year. If you choose an indoor spot, always ask for pictures of the location when you're planning. You don't want to plan a pink wedding, say, and wind up

in a room that's predominantly red. Or maybe you do. The point is, it should be your choice.

Finding a wedding planner: If you're planning to invite more than an officiant and your loved one to your wedding ceremony, seriously consider an on-island wedding planner who can help select a location; help design the floral scheme and recommend a florist and photographer; help plan the menu and choose a restaurant, caterer, or resort; and suggest Hawaiian traditions to incorporate into your ceremony. And more: Will you need tents, a cake, music? Maybe transportation and lodging? Many planners have relationships with vendors providing packages—which mean savings.

If you're planning a resort wedding, most have on-site wedding coordinators; however, there are many independents around the Islands and even planners who specialize in certain types of ceremonies—by locale, size, religious affiliation, and so on. A simple "Hawaii weddings" internet search will reveal dozens. What's important is that you feel comfortable with your coordinator. Ask for references and call them. Share your budget. Get a proposal—in writing. Ask how long they've been in business, how much they charge, how often you'll meet with them, and how they select vendors. Request a detailed list of the exact services they'll provide. If your idea of your wedding doesn't match their services, try someone else. If you can afford it, you might want to meet the planner in person.

Getting your license: The good news about marrying in Hawaii is that there is no waiting period, no residency or citizenship requirement, and no blood test or shots required. You can apply and pay the fee online; however, the couple must appear together in person before a marriage-license agent to receive the marriage license (the permit to get married). You'll need proof of age—the legal age to marry is 18. (If you're 19 or older, a valid driver's license will suffice; if you're 18, a certified birth certificate is required.) Upon approval, a marriage license is immediately issued and costs $60 plus a $5 portal fee. After the ceremony, your officiant will mail the marriage certificate (proof of marriage) to the state. Approximately four months later, you will receive a copy in the mail. Applications are good for one year.

Also—this is important—the person performing your wedding must be licensed by the Hawaii Department of Health, even if he or she is a licensed officiant. Be sure to ask.

Wedding attire: In Hawaii, basically anything goes, from long, formal dresses with trains to white bikinis. Floral sundresses or even a simple *pareau* (wrap) are fine, too. For men, tuxedos are not the norm; a pair of solid-colored slacks with a nice aloha shirt is. In fact, it's traditional in Hawaii for the groom to wear a beautiful white-on-white aloha shirt (they do exist) with slacks or long shorts and a colored sash around the waist. If you're planning a wedding on the beach, barefoot is the way to go.

If you decide to marry in a formal dress and tuxedo, you're better off making your selections on the mainland and hand-carrying them aboard the plane. Yes, it can be a pain, but ask your wedding-gown retailer to provide a special carrying bag. After all, you don't want to chance losing your wedding dress in a wayward piece of luggage. And when it comes to fittings, again, that's something to take care of before you arrive in Hawaii.

Local customs: The most obvious traditional Hawaiian wedding custom is the lei exchange, in which the bride and groom take turns placing a lei around the neck of the other—with a kiss. Traditional lei for both bride and groom are created of fragrant and rare *maile,* a green leafy garland that drapes around the neck and is open at the ends. *Maile* should be ordered in advance and can be expensive. Check with your florist well ahead, especially if your wedding coincides with the timing of local events such as graduation or hula festivals. Brides often also wear a *haku* lei—a circular floral headpiece. Other Hawaiian customs include the blowing of the conch shell, hula, chanting, and Hawaiian music.

THE HONEYMOON

Do you want Champagne and strawberries delivered to your room each morning? A breathtaking swimming pool in which to float? A five-star restaurant in which to dine? Then a resort is the way to go. If, however, you prefer the comforts of a home, try a bed-and-breakfast. A small inn is also good if you're on a tight budget or don't plan to spend much time in your room. On the other hand, perhaps you want your own private home in which to romp freely—or just laze around recovering from the wedding festivities. Do you want your own kitchen so you can whip up a gourmet meal for your loved one? In that case, a private vacation-rental home or resort condo is the answer. That's another beautiful thing about Hawaii: the lodging accommodations are almost as plentiful as the beaches, and there's one that will perfectly match your tastes and your budget.

Big Island's Best Farmers' Markets

The Big Island boasts a wealth of farmers' markets, all providing at the very least a good place to pick up fresh produce, jarred goods such as jams and salsas, and local homemade Hawaiian treats. Not surprisingly, locally grown mango, papaya, pineapple, lychee, passion fruit, coconut, and guava are available in abundance at good prices, but you can also find delicious avocados, organic peppers, fantastic goat cheese, and, of course, world-class coffee. Local artisan gifts abound, too.

Hawaii's farmers are experimenting with dozens of varieties of less common fruits such as dragon fruit, poha berries, and bilimbis. Due to state government restrictions, these fruits generally can't leave the island, so this is your only chance to sample them.

ON THE WEST SIDE

Hawi Farmers' Market. Fresh produce, seasonal fruit, plants, and craft items along with live entertainment are on tap at the Kohala Village Hub in North Kohala. It's open Saturday from 8 am to 12:30 pm.

Kamuela Farmers' Market. Check out the crafts sold here at the Pukalani Stables before heading to Waimea's more expensive stores. Produce, flowers, plants, and baked goods are also available. It's open 7 to noon every Saturday.

Keauhou Farmers' Market. Live music and plenty of local color permeate this down-home farmers' market held every Saturday from 8 to noon in the parking lot of the Keauhou Shopping Center.

Kona Farmers' Market. Wednesday through Sunday from 7 am until 4 pm, this market by the beach features fresh fruit, veggies, wind chimes, and other souvenirs.

Naalehu Farmers' Market. On a trip to South Point, stock up on local produce and freshly baked pastries at this market held in front of the Shaka restaurant in Naalehu. It's open every Wednesday and Saturday from 8 to noon. Get there early.

Pure Kona Green Markets. This popular market features coffee, baked goods, and local honey and jams. Located at Amy B. H. Greenwell Ethnobotanical Garden in Captain Cook, it runs Friday and Sunday from 9 am to 2 pm.

ON THE EAST SIDE

Hamakua Harvest Farmers' Market. This good old-fashioned farmers' market in the midst of the quaint old plantation town of Honokaa is a good stop during a drive up the Hamakua Coast. It opens at 9 am on Sunday.

Hilo Farmers' Market. Although it's open every day, the biggest and best of the farmers' markets on the island features big market days on Wednesday and Saturday from 7 am to 3 pm. They boast the best flowers on the island.

Kaimu Farmers' Market. Packed with vendors offering local produce, prepared foods, coffee, and clothing, this market is held at Kaimu Beach Park in Lower Puna every Saturday from 8 am until noon. There's live music, too. Wednesday after 5 pm brings the famous Kalapana Night Market with live music and adult beverages.

Makuu Farmers' Market. Along with food and produce, this market in Puna sells Hawaiian crafts, plants, jewelry, shells, books, and secondhand clothing. It's along the Keaau/Pahoa Highway and is open Sunday 7:30 am to noon.

Volcano Farmers' Market. In Volcano Village near Hawaii Volcanoes National Park, this market sells local produce, fresh flowers, prepared foods, and baked goods. It's held in the Cooper Center from 6 to 10 am on Sunday.

Top 5 Big Island Outdoor Adventures

Getting outdoors for active adventure is one of the top reasons people come to the Big Island. There are endless options here for spending time outside and enjoying the land, the ocean, or the highest points of mountains and volcanoes. Here are a few of our favorites.

BIKE KULANI (KE ALA O KULANIHAKOI) TRAILS

Newly added to the state Na Ala Hele trail system, and also known as Kulani Trails, this bit of mountain biking heaven is for advanced cyclists only. Stands of 80-foot eucalyptus. Giant *hapuu* tree ferns. The sweet song of honeycreepers overhead. Add a single track of rock and root—no dirt here—and we're talking technical. Did we mention this is a rain forest near Hilo? That explains the perennial slick coat of slime on every possible surface, but it's all part of the fun.

GO HORSEBACK RIDING ABOVE WAIPIO VALLEY

The Valley of the Kings on the Hamakua Coast owes its relative isolation and off-the-grid status to the 2,000-foot-high cliffs bookending the valley. While the beautiful valley is currently closed to all except residents while the road undergoes repairs, one can still take in the glorious sights with a horseback ride above the valley on private property that wends through coconut orchards and even by the famed Hamakua ditch. Here, those photo ops abound.

HIKE THROUGH A STEAMING CRATER AT HAWAII VOLCANOES NATIONAL PARK

When lava returns to Halemaumau Crater, Hawaii Volcanoes National Park's summit caldera, it ensures a gentle and self-contained crater eruption. Viewing is best at night after 9 pm to commune with the glow and avoid the crowds. By day, you can walk the floor of Halemaumau, along a spot far away from the active lava lake. Kilauea Iki Crater, in the center of the national park, last erupted spectacularly in 1959, the cones shooting astonishing 1,900-foot lava fountains into the air. One of the park's best hikes, the Kilauea Iki Trail is a 4-mile loop that takes you down the crater walls and across an otherworldly landscape of a solidified lava lake dotted with steaming vents and alien-looking fumaroles. You climb up the crater wall along a zigzagging trail, ending back at the crater overlook.

SNORKEL AT KEALAKEKUA BAY

Yes, the snorkeling here is outstanding. Visibility reaches depths of 80 feet, and you'll spot colorful creatures swimming among jagged pinnacles and pristine coral habitats. But, to be real, the draw here is the Hawaiian spinner dolphins that come to rest in the bay during the daytime. While it's enticing to swim with wild dolphins, getting too close can disrupt their sleep cycles; it's now illegal here. Observe from a distance and respect their space while still enjoying a fantastic experience communing with nature.

WITNESS WATERFALLS ON THE HILO SIDE

The east side of the Big Island—also called the Hilo side (as opposed to the west-facing Kona side)—is essentially a rain forest, with an average rainfall of 130 inches a year. It's no wonder Hilo is nicknamed the City of Rainbows—and all that rain means tons of waterfalls. Some of our favorites include Boiling Pots (Peepee Falls) and Rainbow Falls, both easy to access from main roads just above downtown Hilo. Akaka Falls State Park on the Hamakua Coast offers some towering cascades.

What to Read and Watch

HAWAIIAN MYTHOLOGY BY MARTHA BECKWITH

This exhaustive work of ethnology and folklore was researched and collected by Martha Beckwith over decades and published when she was 69. *Hawaiian Mythology* is a comprehensive look at the Hawaiian ancestral deities and their importance throughout history.

HAWAII'S STORY BY HAWAII'S QUEEN BY LILIUOKALANI

This poignant book by Queen Liliuokalani chronicles the 1893 overthrow of the Hawaiian monarchy and her plea for her people. It's an essential read to understand the political undercurrent and the push for sovereignty that exists in the Islands more than 125 years later.

LETTERS FROM HAWAII BY MARK TWAIN

In 1866, when Samuel Clemens was 31, he sailed from California and spent four months in Hawaii. He eventually mailed 25 letters to the *Sacramento Union* newspaper about his experiences. Along the way, Twain sheds some cultural biases as he visits Kilauea Volcano, meets with Hawaii's newly formed legislators, and examines the sugar trade.

SHOAL OF TIME: A HISTORY OF THE HAWAIIAN ISLANDS BY GAVAN DAWS

Perhaps the most popular book by this best-selling Honolulu author is *Shoal of Time*. Published in 1974, the account of modern Hawaiian history details the colonization of Hawaii and everything that was lost in the process.

MOLOKAI BY ALAN BRENNERT

The writer's debut novel, set in the 1890s, follows a Hawaiian woman who contracts leprosy as a child and is sent to the remote, quarantined community of Kalaupapa on the island of Molokai,

where she then lives. The Southern California–based author was inspired to write the book during his visits to Hawaii.

HAWAII SAYS "ALOHA" BY DON BLANDING

First published in 1928, this volume of enchanting, rhyming verse about Hawaii evokes the rich details about the Islands that mesmerized the author in the 1920s and for the rest of his life. Blanding also illustrated this and many other books and was later named Hawaii's poet laureate.

THE DESCENDANTS

Based on the book by local author Kaui Hart Hemmings, the film adaptation starring George Clooney and directed by Alexander Payne was filmed on Oahu and Kauai. It spotlights a contemporary, upper-class family in Hawaii as they deal with family grief and landholdings in flux.

BLUE HAWAII

The 1961 musical features the hip-shaking songs and moves of Elvis Presley, who plays tour guide Chadwick Gates. Elvis famously sings "Ke Kali Nei Au," or "The Hawaiian Wedding Song," at the iconic and now-shuttered Coco Palms Resort on Kauai. (The resort has remained closed since 1992 following Hurricane Iniki.)

MOANA

The release of *Moana* in 2016 was celebrated by many in Hawaii and the Pacific for showcasing Polynesian culture. The now-beloved animated movie, which tells the story of the demigod Maui, features the voice talents of Aulii Cravalho and Dwayne Johnson. In 2018, *Moana* was rerecorded and distributed in Olelo Hawaii, or the Hawaiian language, with Cravalho reprising her role. It marked the first time a Disney movie was available in Hawaiian.

Chapter 2

TRAVEL SMART

Updated by
Karen Anderson

★ MAJOR CITIES
Kailua-Kona, Hilo

POPULATION:
205,294 (Big Island);
1,440,196 (Hawaii)

LANGUAGES:
English, Hawaiian

$ CURRENCY:
U.S. dollar

AREA CODE:
808

⚠ EMERGENCIES:
911

DRIVING:
On the right

ELECTRICITY:
120–220 v/60 cycles; plugs have two or three rectangular prongs

TIME:
Two or three hours behind California, five or six hours behind New York, depending on time of year

WEB RESOURCES:
GoHawaii.com
Hawaii.com
LoveBigIsland.com

AIRPORTS:
Ellison Onizuka Kona International Airport (KOA); Hilo International Airport (ITO)

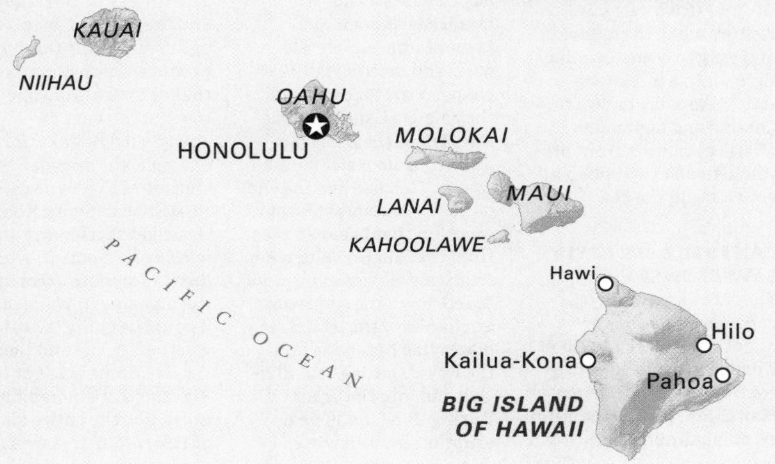
KAUAI
NIIHAU
OAHU
HONOLULU
MOLOKAI
MAUI
LANAI
KAHOOLAWE
PACIFIC OCEAN
Hawi
Hilo
Kailua-Kona
Pahoa
BIG ISLAND OF HAWAII

Know Before You Go

GREEN GECKOS

With their green bodies and tails, bright circular spots, and funny little toes, Madagascar gold-dust day geckos have proliferated on the Big Island since the early 1990s. As its name suggests, the day gecko comes out during the day, while other species of geckos come out at night.

DRIVING ON THE BIG ISLAND

The Big Island is, well, *big*, which means the average drive to get from Point A to Point B can take time. If you're on the Kona side and are planning a day trip to Hawaii Volcanoes National Park, the round trip could take at least five hours of drive time. Conversely, if you're in Hilo and want to check out the island's best sand beaches, you must drive across "the Saddle" or travel upcountry through Waimea to the South Kohala resort beaches, which are a minimum 1½-hour drive away. Many visitors make the mistake of trying to cram too many sights into a week-long stay. Take a day or two to unwind and appreciate the offerings right in front of you instead of spending all your time in the car.

CAN I STILL SEE ACTIVE LAVA FLOWS?

The short answer is: it depends. Eruptions are historically intermittent at Kilauea volcano. Recently confined within Halemaumau Crater at the summit, an on-again, off-again eruption has taken place sporadically from late 2020 to late 2023 and into the foreseeable future. During this time span, the level of the lava lake has risen within view of visitor observation points at the summit, putting on a spectacular show including towering lava fountains inside the crater. Prior to 2020, visible lava at the summit had taken a two-year absence after a months-long eruption in 2018.

This infamous Kilauea eruption of 2018 destroyed bays, beaches, and hundreds of homes in Lower Puna outside the park, and dramatically changed the landscape of the Kilauea Caldera inside the park as the lava lake drained from Halemaumau Crater. This marked the end of the continuous 35-year eruption that began in 1983 from the Puu Oo Vent, when relatively slow-moving lava oozed down the southwestern flanks of the island into places like Kalapana and the Royal Gardens subdivision and into the ocean. During Puu Oo's 35-year eruption, lava viewing, whether by land, boat, or air, was a sight to behold. The lava lake at the summit awed visitors nightly for 10 straight years with an otherworldly glow that lit up the Kilauea Caldera.

Although most of the recent lava viewing has been limited to Halemaumau Crater, there was a short-lived eruption of Mauna Loa in 2022, the mountain's first eruption since 1984. Fortunately, the flow headed down an uninhabited section of the Northeast Rift Zone and stopped short of crossing the Saddle Road.

Whether or not there is visible lava at any given time at Kilauea volcano, Hawaii Volcanoes National Park always presents a wealth of fascinating sights, from the summit to the shore.

WEATHER

Of all the islands in the Hawaiian Islands chain, the Big Island is the most diverse in terms of weather. The variety of elevations and the vast expanse of differing topography produce weather patterns that can vary from one town to the next on any given day. Take, for example, the seaside enclave of Puako near Kawaihae in South Kohala. It can get searing hot and windy one moment, while just a 15-minute drive up the highway in Waimea, it could be chilly "sweater weather" in the middle of the day. Some areas of the Big Island are incredibly rainy, like the entire district of Hilo; other areas stay relatively arid, such as the resort zones in South Kohala. At the higher elevations, such as in Volcano, it can get downright bone-chilling, with temperatures dropping into the low 40s on some nights. Pack accordingly and bring layers.

POPULAR ACTIVITIES

The Big Island is well known for deep-sea fishing and is also a golfer's island. It's also popular for snorkeling, kayaking, stand-up paddleboarding, and scuba diving; the visibility is amazing. If you book a nighttime manta-ray dive, you will likely see some majestic manta rays up close in Keauhou Bay. In winter, you might see the spouts of migrating humpback whales just off the coast. All year-round, spinner dolphins make their home close to shore. Turtle-watching is another entertaining pursuit at beaches such as Punaluu Black Sand Beach in Kau.

FESTIVALS YEAR-ROUND

From the Kona Brew Fest and the Merrie Monarch Festival to the Kona Coffee Cultural Festival, King Kamehameha Day Celebration events, Waimea Cherry Blossom Heritage Festival, and many more, festivals happen year-round and can be a highlight of a trip. One of the most prestigious annual events in the state of Hawaii, the Merrie Monarch Festival takes place in Hilo in mid-April and attracts thousands internationally for hula competitions.

BEACH TREKS

Because of its rocky shorelines and lava-laden coasts, the Big Island of Hawaii has fewer sand beaches than Maui or Oahu. Fortunately, some of the Big Island's best beaches are also some of the best beaches in Hawaii. To protect your feet, reef walkers are essential for getting in and out of the water over potentially rocky entries, or for walking along the shoreline and exploring tide pools. Pack a rash guard that is lightweight and can protect you from harmful UV rays. Reef-safe sunscreen is also essential.

INSECTS, PESTS, AND MOSQUITOES

It's the tropics, so don't be surprised if you encounter an extra-large flying cockroach at night or the occasional mosquito buzzing around you during the day. Pack insect repellent and anti-itch spray. A rare but emerging disease in Hawaii, rat lungworm disease can be contracted by accidental consumption of a slug or slug residue hidden in lettuce or other types of vulnerable produce. Never eat fruit that you pick up off the ground. Think twice about eating locally grown lettuce unless it was grown hydroponically.

VACATION RENTAL ORDINANCE

In 2019, the County of Hawaii passed a new piece of legislation that regulates non-hosted vacation rentals that operate outside of the resort zones. To continue

to operate in these zones, the owners of non-hosted vacation rentals had to obtain nonconforming-use permits (among other requirements) from the county. Fortunately, there are plenty of permitted vacation rentals in most areas across the Big Island, contrary to Internet rumors. Hosted rentals (owner-occupied) are exempt from this ordinance if the owner or site manager resides on the property. You can book directly from the owner or through the traditional online platforms.

TRAVELING WITH YOUNGER KIDS

Traveling with young children can be a challenge, especially when it comes to keeping them entertained. Luckily, there are lots of kid-friendly places to go on the Big Island. A great home base for family vacations, Waikoloa Beach Resort is the island's most kid-friendly vacation destination. Queens' Market-Place offers daily free activities for the family, plus there are quick-bite eateries for easy family fare. Whether it's the giant waterslide or the waterfall swimming pools at the Hilton Waikoloa Village or a family-friendly 9-hole putting course at the Kings' Shops, the entire Waikoloa Beach Resort area offers lots of fun stuff for the *keiki* (children).

Getting Here and Around

Air

Flying time to the Big Island is about 10 hours from New York; eight hours from Chicago; five hours from Los Angeles and other west coast cities; and 15 hours from London, not including layovers. Some of the major airline carriers serving Hawaii fly direct to the Big Island, allowing you to bypass connecting flights out of Honolulu and Maui. If you're a more spontaneous traveler, island-hopping flights depart daily every 90 minutes or so.

Serving Kona are Air Canada, Alaska Airlines, American Airlines, Delta Airlines, Hawaiian Airlines, Japan Airlines, Mokulele, Southwest, United Airlines, Virgin Atlantic, and Westjet. Hawaiian Airlines, Mokulele, Southwest, and United fly into Hilo. Airlines schedule flights seasonally, meaning the number of daily flights—and sometimes the carriers themselves—vary according to demand.

Should you wish to visit neighbor islands, Hawaiian Airlines, Mokulele, and Southwest offer regular service. Prices for interisland flights have increased quite a bit in recent years. Mokulele also serves Waimea. Planning ahead is your best bet.

Big Island Air, in addition to offering air tours of the Big Island, offers charter service between all the Islands onboard a Cessna Caravan. Nine passengers can ride comfortably, and the plane has plenty of room for luggage.

Although the Big Island's airports are smaller and more casual than Oahu's Honolulu International, during peak times they can get quite busy. Allow extra travel time getting to airports during morning and afternoon rush-hour traffic periods. TSA screening can often back up, depending on how many departures are taking place at any given time. Plan to arrive at the airport 90 minutes before departure for interisland or domestic flights. If your interisland flight is part of an international itinerary, then you must check in to your interisland flight at least two hours prior.

Plants and plant products are restricted by the U.S. Department of Agriculture upon both entering and leaving Hawaii. When you leave the Islands, both checked and carry-on bags will be screened and tagged at the airport's agricultural inspection stations. Pineapples and coconuts with the packer's agricultural inspection stamp pass freely; papayas must be treated, inspected, and stamped. All other fruits are banned for export to the U.S. mainland. Flowers pass except for gardenias, rose leaves, jade vines, and maunaloa. Also banned are insects, snails, soil, cotton, cacti, sugarcane, and all berry plants.

Pet policies vary by airline. If specific pre- and post-arrival requirements are met, animals may qualify for a 30-day or five-day-or-less quarantine; this includes service animals. The provision allows for direct release of the pet at a number of airports around the Islands (Kona, on the Big Island; also Honolulu, Lihue, and Kahului on other Islands) if all requirements are met upon inspection. Hilo Airport does not have a direct-release program.

AIRPORTS

Daniel K. Inouye International Airport (HNL) on Oahu is the main gateway for most domestic and international flights into Hawaii. From Honolulu, interisland flights to the Big Island depart regularly from early morning through mid-evening. From Honolulu, the travel time is about 35 minutes. From Maui, it's about 20 minutes.

Those flying to the Big Island regularly land at one of two fields. Ellison Onizuka Kona International Airport at Keahole, on the west side, serves Kailua-Kona, Keauhou, the Kohala Coast, North Kohala, Waimea, and points south. There are Visitor Information Program (VIP) booths by all baggage-claim areas to assist travelers. Additionally, the airport offers news and lei stands, Laniakea by Centerplate (a café), and a small gift and sundries shop. A modernization project joined the two terminals (previously separate) so that baggage and passenger screening can be streamlined and retail options enhanced.

Hilo International Airport is more appropriate for those planning visits based on the east side of the island. VIP booths are across from the Centerplate Coffee Shop near the departure lobby and in the arrival areas at each end of the terminal. In addition to the coffee shop, services include a Bank of Hawaii ATM, a gift shop, newsstands, and lei stands.

Waimea-Kohala Airport, called Kamuela Airport by residents, is used primarily for private flights between islands but offers daily flights via Mokulele Airlines.

AIRPORT TRANSFERS

Check with your hotel to see if it runs an airport shuttle. If you're not renting a car, you can choose from multiple taxi companies serving the Hilo Airport. The approximate taxi rate is $3 for the initial 1/8th mile, plus $3 for each additional mile, with surcharges for waiting time (40¢ per minute) and baggage ($1 per bag) for up to six people. Call or calculate online for fares to popular destinations. The local Hele-On county bus also services the Hilo airport.

At the Kona airport, taxis are available. SpeediShuttle also offers transportation between the airport and hotels, resorts, and condominium complexes from Waimea to Keauhou. Uber and Lyft have designated pickup areas at the Kona and Hilo airports.

 ## Bus

Although public transportation isn't very practical for the average vacationer, depending on where you're staying, you can take advantage of the affordable Hawaii County Mass Transit Agency's Hele-On Bus, which travels several routes throughout the island. Mostly serving local commuters, the Hele-On Bus is currently free until December 2025 when the program will be reevaluated. To catch a ride, just wait at a scheduled stop for the next bus. A one-way journey between Hilo and Kona takes about four hours. There's regular service in and around downtown Hilo, Kailua-Kona, Waimea, North and South Kohala, Honokaa, and Pahoa. Nevertheless, some routes are served only once a day, so if you are planning on using the bus, study up carefully before assuming the bus serves your area.

Visitors staying in Hilo can take advantage of the Transit Agency's Shared Ride Taxi program, which provides door-to-door transportation in the area. A one-way fare is $2, and a book of 15 coupons can be purchased for $30. Visitors to Kona can also take advantage of free trolleys operated by local shopping centers.

 ## Car

It's essential to rent a car when visiting the Big Island. As the name suggests, it's a very big island, and it takes a while to get from one destination to another.

Despite the drive time, when you circle the island by car, you are treated to miles

Getting Here and Around

and miles of wondrous vistas of every possible description. In addition to using standard compass directions such as east and west, Hawaii residents often refer to places as being either *mauka* (toward the mountains) or *makai* (toward the ocean).

It's difficult to get lost along the main roads of the Big Island. Although their names may challenge the visitor's tongue, most roads are well marked; in rural areas look for mile marker numbers. Free publications containing basic road maps are given out at car rental agencies, but if you are doing a lot of driving, invest about $4 in the standard Big Island map available at local retailers. GPS might be unreliable in remote areas.

Driving the roads on the Big Island can be dangerous, as there's no margin for error to avoid a head-on collision. Distracted drivers are all too common. Most roads and main highways are two lanes with no shoulders; if there is a shoulder to access, it might be riddled with rocks, debris, and potholes. Speeding and illegal passing are frequent occurrences along winding, remote roads. In addition, most roads are not well lit at night. Fatalities can happen at a moment's notice, whether on the main highway from the airport to the resorts, on the Saddle Road, on the upper road from Waimea to Hawi, or on the Hawaii Belt Road that wraps around the island. During Ironman week, cyclists pose additional potential hazards on all roads in West Hawaii. Use extreme caution when driving on the Big Island, and of course, do not drive after drinking.

For those who want to travel from the west side to the east side, or vice versa, the rerouted and repaved Saddle Road, known as the Daniel K. Inouye Highway, is a nice shortcut across the middle of the island. This is especially convenient if you are staying on the west side of the island and wish to visit the east side. Hazardous conditions such as fog, wet asphalt, and speeding are common.

Turning right on a red light is legal, except where noted. Hawaii has a strict seat-belt law that applies to both drivers and passengers. The fine for not wearing a seat belt is $102. Mobile phone use is strictly limited to talking on a hands-free mobile device, and only for those over 18. Many police officers drive their own cars while on duty, strapping the warning lights to the roof. Because of the color, locals call them "blue lights."

GASOLINE

You can count on having to pay more at the pump for gasoline on the Big Island than almost anywhere on the U.S. mainland except for California. Prices average over $5 per gallon but tend to be higher in Kailua-Kona and cheaper in Hilo. Gas stations can be few and far between in rural areas, and it's not unusual for them to close early. If you notice that your tank is getting low, don't take any chances: keep your tank filled.

ISLAND DRIVING TIMES

Before you embark on your day trip, it's a good idea to know how long it will take you to get to your destination. Some areas, like downtown Kailua-Kona and Waimea, can become congested at certain times of day. For those traveling to South Kona, a bypass road between Keauhou and Captain Cook alleviates congestion considerably during rush hour. In general, you can expect the following average driving times.

PARKING

Parking can be limited in Historic Kailua Village. A few municipal lots near Alii Drive offer convenient parking on an honor system. (You'll be ticketed if you

Island Driving Times

Kailua-Kona to Kealakekua Bay	14 miles/25 min
Kailua-Kona to Kohala Coast	32 miles/40 min
Kailua-Kona to Waimea	40 miles/1 hr
Kailua-Kona to Hamakua Coast	53 miles/1 hr, 40 min
Kailua-Kona to Hilo	75 miles/2 hrs
Kohala Coast to Waimea	16 miles/20 min
Kohala Coast to Hamakua Coast	29 miles/55 min
Hilo to Volcano	30 miles/40 min

don't pay.) There is one free county lot downtown. In Hilo, you'll find plenty of free parking along the scenic bayfront.

RENTALS

Should you plan to sightsee around the Big Island, it is best to rent a car. Because the island has more than 260 miles of coastline—and attractions as varied as Hawaii Volcanoes National Park, Akaka Falls State Park, Puuhonua O Honaunau National Historical Park, and Puukohola Heiau National Historic Site—ideally you should split up your stay between the east and west sides. Even if all you want to do is relax at your resort, you may want to hop in the car to check out one of the island's popular restaurants or beaches.

While on the Big Island, you can rent anything from an economy vehicle to a sports car to a motorcycle. Rates are usually better if you reserve through a rental agency's website, and most sites allow you to reserve for free. It's wise to make reservations in advance and make sure that a confirmed reservation guarantees you a car, especially if visiting during

peak seasons or for major events. It's not uncommon to find several car categories sold out during the Merrie Monarch Festival in Hilo in April or the Ironman World Championship triathlon in Kailua-Kona in October.

If exploring the island on two wheels is more your speed, Big Island Motorcycle Company rents motorcycles and mopeds.

Rates begin at about $62 a day for an economy car with air-conditioning, automatic transmission, and unlimited mileage. This does not include the airport concession fee, general excise tax, rental vehicle surcharge, or vehicle license fee. When you reserve a car, ask about cancellation penalties and drop-off charges should you plan to pick up the car in one location and return it to another. Many rental companies in Hawaii offer coupons for discounts at various attractions.

In Hawaii, you must be 21 years of age to rent a car, and you must have a valid driver's license and a major credit card. Those under 25 pay a daily surcharge of $27 to $30. Request car seats and extras such as GPS when you book. Hawaii's Child Restraint Law requires that all children three years and younger be in an approved child safety seat in the back seat of a vehicle. Children ages four to seven must be seated in a rear booster seat or child restraint such as a lap and shoulder belt. Car seats and booster rentals range from $8 to $10 per day.

In Hawaii, a mainland driver's license is valid for a rental for up to 90 days.

Because the roads on the Big Island can be two-lane, narrow, and winding in places, allow plenty of time to return your vehicle so that you can make your flight. Traffic can be heavy during morning and afternoon rush hours, especially in the

Getting Here and Around

Car Rental Resources

Automobile Associations

American Automobile Association	☎ 315/797–5000	⊕ www.aaa.com

Local Agencies

AA Aloha Cars-R-Us	☎ 800/655–7989	⊕ www.hawaiicarrental.com
Big Island Motorcycle Co.	☎ 866/886–2011	⊕ bigislandmotorcyclecompany.com
Car Rentals Hawaii by Harper	☎ 800/488–6624	⊕ www.carrentalshawaii.com
Hawaii Drive-O Discount Car Rentals		⊕ www.hawaiidrive-o.com

Major Agencies

Alamo	☎ 844/354–6962	⊕ www.alamo.com
Avis	☎ 808/327–3000	⊕ www.avis.com
Budget	☎ 800/214–6094	⊕ www.budget.com
Dollar	☎ 800/800–5252	⊕ www.dollar.com
Enterprise	☎ 808/331–2509	⊕ www.enterprise.com
Hertz	☎ 808/329–3566	⊕ www.hertz.com
National Car Rental	☎ 888/826–6890	⊕ www.nationalcar.com
Thrifty	☎ 808/331–0531	⊕ www.thrifty.com

Kailua-Kona area. ■ TIP→ **Give yourself about three and a half hours before departure time to return your vehicle.**

CAR RENTAL INSURANCE

Everyone who rents a car wonders whether the insurance that the rental companies offer is worth the expense. No one—including us—has a simple answer. It all depends on how much regular insurance you have, how comfortable you are with risk, and whether or not money is an issue.

If you own a car and carry comprehensive car insurance for both collision and liability, your personal auto insurance probably covers a rental, but call your auto insurance company to confirm. If you don't have auto insurance, then you will need to buy the collision- or loss-damage waiver (CDW or LDW) from the rental company. The CDW allows you to walk away from most incidents, so it might be worth the peace of mind. Some credit cards offer CDW coverage, but it's usually supplemental to your own insurance and rarely covers SUVs, minivans, and luxury models. If your coverage is secondary, you may still be liable for loss-of-use costs from the car-rental company (again, read the fine print). But no credit card insurance is valid unless you use that card for *all* transactions, from reserving to paying the final bill.

■ TIP→ **Diners Club offers primary CDW coverage on all rentals reserved and paid for with the card. This means that Diners Club's company—not your own car insurance—pays in case of an accident. It doesn't mean that your car insurance**

company won't raise your rates once it discovers you had an accident.

You may also be offered supplemental liability coverage. The car-rental company is required to carry a minimal level of liability coverage insuring all renters, but it's rarely enough to cover claims in a really serious accident if you're at fault. Your own auto-insurance policy will protect you if you own a car; if you don't, you have to decide whether or not you are willing to take the risk.

U.S. rental companies sell CDWs and LDWs for about $15 to $25 a day; supplemental liability is usually more than $10 a day. The car-rental company may offer you all sorts of other policies, but they're rarely worth the cost. Personal accident insurance, which is basic hospitalization coverage, is an especially egregious rip-off if you already have health insurance.

ROAD CONDITIONS
Roads on the Big Island are generally well marked with street signs and can be easily accessed. Most of the roads are two-lane highways with limited shoulders—and yes, even in paradise, there is traffic, especially during the morning and afternoon rush hours and before and after school. Several lighted intersections in downtown Kailua-Kona and Hilo are notorious for backed-up traffic no matter the time of day, so give yourself extra time if you need to catch a flight. Jaywalking and bike riding are common, so pay careful attention, especially while driving along Alii Drive. Also use caution during heavy downpours, especially if you see signs warning of flash floods and falling rocks. Stay clear of ponding or rising water on roadways and heed emergency weather advisories not to cross flooded roads.

Ride-Sharing

Both Uber and Lyft have designated pickup sites at the Hilo and Kona airports. Those who plan on traveling long distances may find that regular taxis are a bit cheaper, and you may have a longer wait for Uber and Lyft pickups beyond the airports.

2

Travel Smart GETTING HERE AND AROUND

Essentials

Beaches

Don't believe anyone who tells you that the Big Island lacks beaches. It's just one of the myths about Hawaii's largest island. Because of the distance between beaches along with the rugged lava shorelines, getting to a beach can be slightly less convenient than on Maui or Oahu. That said, there are plenty of those perfect white-sand stretches you think of when you hear "Hawaii," plus the added bonus of black- and green-sand beaches, thanks to the relative young age of the island and its active volcanoes. New beaches appear and disappear at times, created and/or destroyed by volcanic activity or surf.

Hawaii's largest coral reef systems lie off the Kohala Coast. Waves have battered them over millennia to create abundant white-sand beaches on the northwest side of the island. Black- and green-sand beaches lie in the southern regions and along the coast nearest the volcano. On the eastern side of the island, beaches tend to be of the rocky-coast–surging-surf variety, but there are still a few worth visiting, and this is where the Hawaii shoreline is at its most picturesque.

Dining

Between star chefs and myriad local farms, the Big Island restaurant scene has become a destination for foodies. Food writers praise chefs of the Big Island for their ability to turn the local bounty into inventive blends inspired by the island's cultural heritage.

Resorts along the Kohala Coast have long invested in culinary programs offering memorable dining experiences that include inventive entrées, spot-on wine pairings, and customized chef's table options. But great food on the Big Island doesn't begin and end with the resorts. A handful of chefs have retired from the fast-paced hotel world and opened their own small bistros in upcountry Waimea or other places off the beaten track. Unique and wonderful restaurants have cropped up in Hawi, Kainaliu, and Waikoloa Village, and on the east side of the island in Hilo.

In addition to restaurants, festivals devoted to island products draw attendees to learn about everything from breadfruit and mango to avocado, chocolate, and coffee. Agritourism has turned into a fruitful venture for farmers as farm tours afford the opportunity to meet with and learn from local producers. Some tours conclude with a meal of items sourced from the same farms. Whether a tour includes Puna goat farms churning creamy, savory goat cheese, or farms in Waimea producing row after row of bright tomatoes, or high-tech aquaculture operations at the Natural Energy Lab of Hawaii Authority (NELHA), visitors can see exactly where their next meal comes from.

HOURS AND PRICES

Though it might seem at first glance like the Big Island's dining scene consists of either pricey restaurants or fast-casual eateries, there is a fairly large middle ground of good restaurants that cater to both local and visiting families. Tipping is similar to elsewhere in the country: 15%–20% of the bill or $1 per drink at a bar. Bills for large parties generally include an 18% tip, as do bills at some resort restaurants, so check before leaving extra.

⇨ *Restaurant prices are for a main course at dinner or if dinner is not served, at lunch, excluding 4.7% excise tax.*

What It Costs in U.S. Dollars

$	$$	$$$	$$$$
RESTAURANTS			
under $20	$20–$30	$31–$40	over $40

RESERVATIONS

In general, restaurants on the Big Island don't require reservations, but at the height of tourist season, it's a good idea to call ahead, especially if you're bringing a large party or booking a special-occasion dinner.

WHAT TO WEAR

There isn't a single place on the Big Island that requires formal attire. There are a handful of restaurants where you might feel out of place in your beach attire, but resort wear is acceptable at even the most upscale restaurants.

WITH KIDS

Keiki (kids') menus are offered at many restaurants on the Big Island, the exceptions being a small handful of fine-dining restaurants that don't necessarily cater to families.

⊕ Health and Safety

HEALTH

The Hawaii State Department of Health recommends that you drink 16 ounces of water per hour to avoid dehydration when hiking or spending time in the sun. Use zinc-based sunblock, wear UV-reflective sunglasses, and protect your head with a visor or hat for shade. If you're not acclimated to warm, humid weather, allow time for rest stops and refreshments. When visiting freshwater streams, be aware of the tropical disease leptospirosis, which is spread by animal urine and carried into streams and mud. Symptoms include fever, headache, nausea, and red eyes. If left untreated, it can cause liver and kidney failure, respiratory failure, internal bleeding, and even death. To avoid this, don't swim or wade in freshwater streams or ponds if you have open sores and don't drink from any freshwater streams or ponds. Wash all locally grown leafy vegetables thoroughly to protect yourself against rat lungworm disease, which is rare but extremely serious.

The Islands have their share of bugs and insects that enjoy the tropical climate as much as visitors do. Most are harmless but annoying. When planning to spend time outdoors in hiking areas, wear long-sleeve shirts and pants and use mosquito repellent. In damp or rocky places, you may encounter the dreaded local centipede. Blue or brown in color, centipedes can grow as long as eight inches. If surprised, they might sting, which can be painful and the sting can last for days. If you are stung by a centipede, wash the site of your bite thoroughly to prevent infection. When camping, shake out your sleeping bag before climbing in, and check your shoes in the morning, as centipedes like warm, moist places. If you're planning on hiking or traveling in remote areas, always carry a first-aid kit and appropriate medications for sting reactions.

SAFETY ISSUES

Hawaii is generally a safe tourist destination, but it's still wise to stick to the same commonsense safety precautions you would normally follow in your own hometown. Hotel and visitor-center staff can provide information should you decide to head out on your own to more remote areas. Because some of the models and colors are obvious, rental cars are magnets for break-ins, so don't leave any valuables in them, not even in a locked trunk. Thieves watch areas such

Essentials

as beach parking lots and can pop your hood and be gone in 60 seconds. Avoid poorly lighted areas, beach parks, and isolated areas after dark as a precaution. When hiking, stay on marked trails, no matter how alluring the temptation might be to stray. Changing weather conditions can cause landscapes to become muddy and slippery, so staying on marked trails lessens the possibility of a fall or getting lost. This is especially true on the wetter, windward side. Heed warnings about dangerous currents in rivers and swimming holes.

Ocean safety is of the utmost importance when visiting any island destination. Visitors often get into trouble because the beach looks benign and they can't wait to get in the water, so they throw caution to the wind and jump in. Avoid swimming if the conditions seem rough or dangerous. Most beaches on the Big Island do not have lifeguards. Unfortunately, most of the drowning deaths that occur in Hawaii are visitors. Winter brings higher, more dangerous surf, so exercise caution. Don't swim alone; follow the international signage posted at beaches, which alerts swimmers to strong currents, man-of-war or box jellyfish, sharp coral, high surf, sharks, and dangerous shore breaks. At coastal lookouts along cliff tops, heed the signs indicating that waves can inundate the ledges. If there are lifeguards, ask about present conditions; if the red flags are up, or if a high surf advisory has been issued by the National Weather Service indicating swimming and surfing are risky, don't go in. Waters that look calm on the surface can harbor strong currents and undertows, and sometimes people who were "just wading" have been dragged out to sea and never seen again. When in doubt, don't go out!

Women traveling alone are generally safe in Hawaii, but always follow the same safety precautions you would use in any major destination. When booking hotels, request rooms closest to the elevator, and always keep your hotel room door and balcony doors locked. Stay away from isolated areas after dark. If you stay out late at a bar, use caution when exiting and returning to your car or lodging.

Internet

Most hotels, resorts, B&Bs, condo complexes, and vacation rentals offer high-speed access in rooms or on-site. You should check with your accommodation in advance to confirm that access is complimentary; also ask if the signal is strong in every room. In some cases, there could be a daily charge posted to your room. The latest unhappy trend is for the major hotels to charge a resort fee, a mandatory daily fee that is supposed to cover Wi-Fi and parking. It may range from $25 to $40.

Lodging

Our recommendation is to stay on both sides of the island. Each offers a different range of accommodations, restaurants, and activities. Consider staying at one of the upscale resorts along the Kohala Coast or in a condo in Kailua-Kona for half of your trip. Then, shift gears and check into a romantic bed-and-breakfast on the Hamakua Coast, South Kona, Hilo, or near the volcano. If you've got children in tow, opt for a vacation home or a stay at one of the island's many family-friendly hotels. On the west side, explore the island's most pristine beaches or try some of the fine-dining restaurants; on the east side, hike through rain forests, witness majestic waterfalls, or go for a plate lunch.

Where to Stay on the Big Island

	LOCAL VIBE	PROS	CONS
Kailua-Kona	A bustling little village; Alii Drive brims with hotels and condo complexes.	Plenty to do, day and night; everything within easy walking distance of most hotels; many grocery stores in the area.	More traffic than anywhere else on the island; limited number of beaches; traffic noise on Alii Drive.
South Kona and Kau	Kealakekua Bay and Captain Cook have many B&Bs and vacation rentals; a few more are farther south in the Kau district.	Kealakekua Bay is popular for kayaking and snorkeling; Captain Cook and Kainaliu have some good restaurants and coffee farms.	Few sandy beaches; not as many restaurant options; Kau is quite remote.
The Kohala Coast	Home to most of the Big Island's major resorts. Blue sunny skies prevail here. Has the island's best beaches.	Beautiful beaches; high-end shopping and dining; lots of activities for adults and children.	Pricey; long driving distances to Volcano, Hilo, and Kailua-Kona.
Waimea	Though it seems a world away, upcountry Waimea is only about a 15- to 20-minute drive from the Kohala Coast.	Striking scenery; *paniolo* (cowboy) culture; home to some exceptional local restaurants.	Can be cool and rainy year-round; nearest beaches are a 20-minute drive away.
The Hamakua Coast	A nice spot for those seeking peace, tranquility, and an alternative to the tropical-beach-vacation experience.	Close to Waipio Valley; foodie and farm tours in the area; good spot for honeymooners seeking low-key vibe.	Beaches are an hour's drive away; convenience shopping is limited, as are lodging options.
Hilo	Hilo is on the wet and lush eastern side of the Big Island. It's less touristy than the west side but retains much local charm.	Proximity to waterfalls, rain forest hikes, museums, zoo, and botanical gardens; also many good restaurants.	The best white-sand beaches are on the other side of the island; noise from coqui frogs can be distracting at night.
Puna	Puna doesn't attract as many visitors as other regions, so you'll find good deals on rentals here.	A few black-sand beaches; off the beaten path and fairly wild; lava has flowed into the sea here in years past.	Few dining and entertainment options; no resorts or resort amenities; noisy coqui frogs at night.
Hawaii Volcanoes National Park and Vicinity	There are any number of enchanting B&B inns in fern-shrouded Volcano Village, near the park.	Great for hiking, nature tours, and bike riding; close to Hilo and Puna.	Just a few dining options; not much nightlife; can be cold and wet.

Essentials

Some locals like to say that the east is "more Hawaiian," but we argue that King Kamehameha himself made Kailua-Kona his final home during his sunset years. Another reason to try a bit of both: your budget. You can justify splurging on a stay at a Kohala Coast resort for a few nights because you'll spend the rest of your time paying far less at a cozy cottage in Volcano or a vacation rental on Alii Drive. And although food at the resorts is very expensive, you don't have to eat every meal there. Condos and vacation homes can be ideal for a family trip or for a group of friends looking to save money and live like *kamaainas* (local residents) for a week or two. Many of the homes also have private pools and hot tubs, lanai, ocean views, and more—you can go as budget or as high-end as you like.

If you choose a B&B, inn, or out-of-the-way hotel, explain your expectations fully to the proprietor and ask plenty of questions before booking. Be clear about your travel and location needs. Some places require stays of two or three days.

B&BS AND INNS

B&Bs and locally run inns offer a nice alternative to hotels or resorts in terms of privacy and location. Guests enjoy the perks of a hotel (breakfast and cleaning service) but without the extras that drive up rates.

Be sure to check property websites and call to ask questions. There are still a few "B&Bs" that are just dumpy rooms in someone's house, and you don't want to end up there. One of the premier B&Bs on Hawaii Island, Holualoa Inn occupies a historic coffee estate in the artists' village of Holualoa just above Kailua-Kona.

CONDOS AND VACATION RENTALS

Renting a condo or vacation home gives you much more living space than the average hotel, plus the chance to meet residents when you stroll the neighborhood. You'll also likely pay lower nightly rates than at a hotel and have the option of cooking or barbecuing rather than eating out. When booking, remember that most properties are individually owned, with rates and amenities that differ substantially depending on the place. Some properties are handled by rental agents or agencies, while many are handled through the owner.

The booking agencies may specialize in various lodging types or locations, so be sure to call and ask questions before booking. Big Island Villas lists condos attached to a number of resorts. Hawaiian Beach Rentals is an excellent source for high-end homes. Keauhou Property Management has condos along the Kona Coast, as do Kona Coast Vacations and Knutson and Associates. Kona Hawaii Vacation Rentals is known for affordable Kailua-Kona condos. Kolea Vacations lists high-end condos in Waikoloa, and Kona Vacation Rentals focuses on luxury Kohala Coast condos. Hawaii Vacation Rentals has some properties in Puako, near the Kohala Coast resorts. South Kohala Management handles everything from family-friendly condos to larger homes in the Kohala Coast resort areas.

HOTELS AND RESORTS

The resorts—most clustered on the Kohala Coast or north of the airport—are expensive, no two ways about it. That said, some may offer free nights with longer stays (fifth or seventh night free) and sometimes team with airlines or consolidators to offer package deals that may include a rental car, spa treatments, golf, and other activities. Some hotels allow children to stay for free. Ask about specials when you book, and check websites as well—some resorts have Internet-only deals.

PRICES

Many resorts charge daily resort fees of $25 to $40 for things like parking, Internet, daily newspaper service, beach gear, and activities. Most condos and vacation rental owners charge an additional cleaning fee. Always ask about hidden fees as well as specials and discounts when you book. Look online for great package deals.

⇨ *Prices in the hotel reviews are the lowest cost of a standard double room in high season, which generally include taxes and service charges but not any optional meal plans.*

What It Costs in U.S. Dollars

	$	$$	$$$	$$$$
HOTELS				
	under $200	$200–$280	$281–$380	over $380

RESERVATIONS

You'll almost always be able to find a room on the Big Island, but you might not get your first choice if you wait until the last minute. Make reservations six months to a year in advance if you're visiting during the peak seasons (summer, Christmas holiday, and spring break). Major festivals and events affect availability, too: during the week after Easter Sunday, for example, the week-long Merrie Monarch Festival is in full swing, and most of Hilo's rooms are booked. Kailua-Kona is packed in mid-October during the week leading up to the Ironman World Championship triathlon.

📷 Packing

Hawaii is casual: sandals, bathing suits, and comfortable, informal clothing are the norm. Year-round, clothing of cotton or rayon proves very comfortable. Beach-going women love to wear the *pareu,* or sarong. Men will look right at home in T-shirts and board shorts.

One of the most important items to pack is sunscreen. Some traditional sunscreens are harming coral reefs; statewide legislation now bans the sale of sunscreens that contain oxybenzone and octinoxate. So if you do want to use reef-safe sunscreen, buy products that are zinc-based or reef approved. Even better? Buy a long-sleeved rash guard, available at all major retailers. That way, you have no gunky lotions or harmful chemicals to deal with while out enjoying the reefs. Hats and sunglasses offer important sun protection, too. Both are easy to find in island shops if you don't bring them with you. All major hotels in Hawaii (and most small ones) provide beach towels.

The aloha shirt is accepted dress in Hawaii for business and most social occasions. Shorts are acceptable daytime attire, along with a T-shirt or polo shirt. There's no need to buy expensive sandals on the mainland—here you can get flip-flops (called "slippers" by locals) for under $5. Golfers should remember that many courses have dress codes requiring a collared shirt; call courses for details. If you're not prepared, you can buy appropriate clothing at resort pro shops.

If your vacation plans include Hilo, you'll want to pack a compact umbrella and a light poncho. And if you'll be visiting Hawaii Volcanoes National Park, make sure you pack appropriately, as weather ranges from hot and dry along the shore to chilly, foggy, and rainy at the 4,000-foot summit. Sturdy boots are recommended if you'll be hiking or camping in the park.

Groceries are expensive in Hawaii, and sticker shock at the grocery store is

Essentials

guaranteed. Pack some light-weight snacks, spreads, and non-perishable food items in your check-in luggage. You'll be glad you brought that $6 bag of trail mix or $3 bag of microwave lentil soup with you from the mainland when you discover that the same exact item in Hawaii is more than twice the price. For bulk shopping, there's a Costco in Kailua-Kona.

🌐 Passport

All international visitors to the United States are required to have a valid passport that is valid for six months beyond your expected period of stay.

🎟 Performing Arts

A handful of local playhouses, half a dozen or so movie houses (including those that play foreign and independent films), and plenty of musical entertainment can keep fans of the arts happy.

Free hula shows take place at shopping centers in Keauhou and Waikoloa Beach Resort. And don't forget the luau. Featuring highly skilled cultural dancers and musical performers, the quintessential Hawaiian luau showcases an array of traditional fare, tropical beverages, and sometimes even an authentic imu (underground oven) for cooking the pig.

👜 Shopping

Dozens of shops in Kailua-Kona offer souvenirs from far-flung corners of the globe as well as many local coffee and foodstuffs to take home as gifts. Housewares and artworks made of local materials (lauhala, coconut, koa, and milo wood) fill the

shelves of small boutiques and galleries throughout the island. Upscale shops in the resorts along the Kohala Coast carry high-end clothing and accessories, as do a few boutiques scattered around the island. Galleries and gift shops, many showcasing the work of local artists, fill historical buildings in Waimea, Kainaliu, Holualoa, Hilo, Volcano, and Hawi.

HOURS

In general, stores on the Big Island open around 10 am and close by 6 pm. Hilo's Prince Kuhio Plaza stays open until 7 pm Monday through Saturday and 6 pm on Sunday. In Historic Kailua Village and in Keauhou, most shopping plazas geared to tourists remain open until 9. Grocery stores such as KTA grocery stores are usually open until 8.

📍 Spas

High prices are the norm at the island's resort spas, but a handful of unique experiences are worth every penny. Beyond the resorts, the Big Island is also home to independent massage therapists and day spas that offer similar treatments for lower prices, albeit usually in a slightly less luxurious atmosphere. Spa visits provide obvious relaxation benefits; in addition, the Big Island's spas have done a fantastic job incorporating local traditions and ingredients into their menus. Massage artists work with coconut or kukui (candlenut) oil; hot-stone massages are conducted with volcanic stones, and ancient healing techniques such as lomilomi—a massage technique with firm, constant movement—are staples at every island spa.

$ Taxes

Businesses on the Big Island of Hawaii collect a 4.7120% general excise tax on all purchases, including food and services. A hotel transient accommodations tax of 13.25% (10.25% to the state; 3% to the county), combined with the excise tax, totals a 17.96% rate added to your room bill. Even vacation rentals and B&Bs are required to collect this tax. A $5-per-day road tax is also assessed on each rental vehicle, in addition to an airport concession recovery tax and other fees that are not technically taxes but are tacked on to the base rate.

⊘ Time

Hawaii is on Hawaii Standard Time, five hours behind New York, two hours behind Los Angeles, and 10 hours behind London.

When the U.S. mainland switches to Daylight Savings Time, Hawaii does not, so add an extra hour of time difference between the Islands and U.S. mainland destinations.

ⓢ Tipping

Tipping is not only common, but expected. Hawaii is a major vacation destination, and many people who work at the hotels and resorts rely on tips to supplement their wages. Give $1 to bartenders and bellhops and $2 to cleaners, but tip more in an expensive luxury resort. Tip 15%–20% in restaurants, salons, and for taxi or rideshare service.

Tipping Guide for the Big Island	
Bartender	$1–$5 per round of drinks, depending on the number of drinks
Bellhop	$1–$5 per bag, depending on the level of the hotel
Coat check	$1–$2 per coat
Hotel cleaner	$2–$5 a day (in cash, preferably daily since cleaning staff may be different each day you stay)
Hotel concierge	$5 or more, depending on the service
Hotel doorstaff	$1–$5 for help with bags or hailing a cab
Hotel room service waitstaff	$1–$2 per delivery, even if a service charge has been added
Porter at airport or train station	$1 per bag
Restroom attendants	$1 or small change
Skycap at airport	$1–$3 per bag checked
Spa personnel	15%–20% of the cost of your service
Taxi driver	15%–20%
Tour guide	10%–15% of the cost of the tour, per person
Valet parking attendant	$2–$5, each time your car is brought to you
Waitstaff	15%–20%, with 20% being the norm at high-end restaurants; nothing additional if a service charge is added to the bill

Essentials

Visa

Except for citizens of Canada and Bermuda, most visitors to the United States must have a visa. If you are from one of the 40 designated members of the Visa Waiver Program, then you only require an Electronic System for Travel Authorization (ESTA) as long as you are staying for 90 days or less. You must have an e-passport to use the Visa Waiver Program.

⦿ Visitor Information

Before you depart for your trip, visit Hawaii Tourism Authority's website (⊕ www.gohawaii.com) for a plethora of helpful advice and to download a free official vacation planner.

The Hawaii Island Chamber of Commerce has links to dozens of museums, attractions, B&Bs, restaurants and parks on its website. The Kona-Kohala Chamber of Commerce lists local activities, lodging, shopping, dining, and more under its Visitors tab.

🗓 When to Go

Long days of sunshine and mild year-round temperatures make the Big Island an all-seasons destination. Most resort areas are at sea level, with average afternoon temperatures of 75°F–80°F during December and January; in August and September the temperature can reach 90°F along the coast. Higher "upcountry" elevations have cooler and often misty conditions. Most trade winds drop their precipitation on the north and east side of the island, while the south and west sides remain warmer and drier. Rainfall can be higher in summer months; winter brings higher surf and windier conditions.

Many travelers head here from mid-November to mid-April. Christmas holiday and spring break are very busy. Summer is also a popular time to visit. September and February can be great months for a trip, as crowds are smaller and accommodation prices reduced. You can see humpback whales off the western coast of the Big Island from November to May. Key festivals and events also draw crowds (⇨ see On the Calendar).

State holidays include March 26, the birthday of Prince Jonah Kuhio Kalanianaole, who led the effort to set aside homelands for Hawaiian people. June 11 honors the Hawaiian Kingdom's first monarch, Kamehameha I. May 1 isn't an official holiday but marks a time when people celebrate May Day and the flower lei. Statehood day is the third Friday in August; Hawaii became the 50th state on August 21, 1959.

On the Calendar

February

Waimea Cherry Blossom Heritage Festival, first weekend in February. A celebration of Japanese culture takes place in conjunction with cherry blossom viewing in Waimea. See the Facebook page for information. ☎ 808/961–8706. ⊕ facebook.com/p/Waimea-Cherry-Blossom-Heritage-Festival-100064661262713.

March

Kona Brewers Festival, second weekend of March. A celebration of suds, hops, craft beers, and home brews is held on the grounds of the Courtyard by Marriott King Kamehameha's Kona Beach Hotel in Kailua-Kona. ☎ 808/987–9196 ⊕ www.konabrewersfestival.com.

April

Merrie Monarch Festival, mid-April. The most prestigious hula competition in the world attracts dancers from around the globe at this popular weeklong event in Hilo. ☎ 808/935–9168 ⊕ www.merriemonarch.com.

May

Kau Coffee Festival, mid-May. While Kona coffee gets all the attention, this festival near Ka Lae (South Point) sets the record straight about the excellence of coffee grown in the Kau District. ⊕ www.kaucoffeefestival.com.

June

King Kamehameha Day Celebration Parade in Kailua-Kona, Saturday closest to June 11. Traditional Hawaiian equestrian units are the star attraction of this annual floral parade in Historic Kailua Village. ⊕ www.konaparade.org.

July

Parker Ranch Independence Day Rodeo, July 4. Witness Hawaiian paniolos (cowboys) in action at the rodeo grounds in Waimea. ☎ 808/885–7311 ⊕ www.parkerranch.com.

September

Big Island Slack Key Guitar Festival, late August. The free music festival at Courtyard by Marriott King Kamehameha's Kona Beach Hotel features the island's top slack-key players. ☎ 808/226–2697 ⊕ www.slackkeyfestival.com.

October

Ironman World Championship, usually second Saturday in October. The Super Bowl of triathlons attracts tens of thousands of visitors to Kailua-Kona to watch the swim-bike-run competition that starts and ends near the pier. ⊕ www.ironman.com/im-world-championship.

November

Kona Coffee Cultural Festival, mid-November. Nearly 50 events over a 10-day period celebrate Kona's rich coffee heritage. ☎ 808/990–6511 ⊕ www.konacoffeefest.com.

Hawaiian Vocabulary

Although an understanding of Hawaiian is by no means required on a trip to the Aloha State, a *malihini,* or newcomer, will find plenty of opportunities to pick up a few of the local words and phrases. Traditional names and expressions are widely used in the Islands. You're likely to read or hear at least a few words each day of your stay.

Simplifying the learning process is the fact that the Hawaiian language contains only seven consonants—H, K, L, M, N, P, W, and the silent *'okina,* or glottal stop, written '—plus one or more of the five vowels. All syllables, and therefore all words, end in a vowel. Each vowel, with the exception of a few diphthongized double vowels, such as *au* (pronounced "ow") or *ai* (pronounced "eye"), is pronounced separately. Thus *'Iolani* is four syllables (ee-oh-la-nee), not three (yo-la-nee). Although some Hawaiian words have only vowels, most also contain some consonants, but consonants are never doubled.

Pronunciation is simple. Pronounce *A* "ah" as in *father, E* "ay" as in *weigh; I* "ee" as in *marine; O* "oh" as in *no; U* "oo" as in *true.*

Consonants mirror their English equivalents, with the exception of *W.* When the letter begins any syllable other than the first one in a word, it is usually pronounced as a *V. 'Awa,* the Polynesian drink, is pronounced "ava," *'ewa* is pronounced "eva."

Almost all long Hawaiian words are combinations of shorter words; they are not difficult to pronounce if you segment them. *Kalaniana'ole,* the highway running east from Honolulu, is easily understood as *Kalani ana 'ole.* Apply the standard pronunciation rules—the stress falls on the next-to-last syllable of most two- or three-syllable Hawaiian words—and Kalaniana'ole Highway is as easy to say as Main Street.

Now about that fish. Try *humu-humu nuku-nuku āpu a'a.*

The other unusual element in Hawaiian language is the *kahakō,* or macron, written as a short line (ˉ) placed over a vowel. Like the accent (ˊ) in Spanish, the kahakō puts emphasis on a syllable that would normally not be stressed. The most familiar example is probably *Waikīkī.* With no macrons, the stress would fall on the middle syllable; with only one macron, on the last syllable, the stress would fall on the first and last syllables. Some words become plural with the addition of a macron, often on a syllable that would have been stressed anyway. No Hawaiian word becomes plural with the addition of an *S,* since that letter does not exist in the language.

Note that Hawaiian diacritical marks are not printed in this guide.

PIDGIN

You may hear Pidgin English, the unofficial language of Hawaii. It is a Creole language, with its own grammar, evolved from the mixture of English, Hawaiian, Japanese, Portuguese, and other languages spoken in 19th-century Hawaii, and it is heard everywhere.

GLOSSARY

What follows is a glossary of some of the most commonly used Hawaiian words. Hawaiian residents appreciate visitors who at least try to pick up the local language.

'a'ā: rough, crumbling lava, contrasting with *pāhoehoe,* which is smooth.

'ae: yes.

aikane: friend.

āina: land.

akamai: smart, clever, possessing savoir faire.

akua: god.

ala: a road, path, or trail.

ali'i: a Hawaiian chief, a member of the chiefly class.

aloha: love, affection, kindness; also a salutation meaning both greetings and farewell.

'ānuenue: rainbow.

'a'ole: no.

'apōpō: tomorrow.

'auwai: a ditch.

auwē: alas, woe is me!

'ehu: a red-haired Hawaiian.

'ewa: in the direction of 'Ewa plantation, west of Honolulu.

hala: the pandanus tree, whose leaves (*lau hala*) are used to make baskets and plaited mats.

hālau: school.

hale: a house.

hale pule: church, house of worship.

hana: to work.

haole: foreigner. Since the first foreigners were Caucasian, *haole* now means a Caucasian person.

hapa: a part, sometimes a half; often used as a short form of *hapa haole,* to mean a person who is part-Caucasian.

hau'oli: to rejoice. *Hau'oli Makahiki Hou* means Happy New Year. *Hau'oli lā hānau* means Happy Birthday.

heiau: an outdoor stone platform; an ancient Hawaiian place of worship.

he mea iki or **he mea 'ole:** you're welcome.

holo: to run.

holoholo: to go for a walk, ride, or sail.

holokū: a long Hawaiian dress, somewhat fitted, with a yoke and a train. It was worn at court, and at least one local translates the word as "expensive muumuu."

holomū: a post–World War II cross between a *holokū* and a mu'umu'u, less fitted than the former but less voluminous than the latter, and having no train.

honi: to kiss; a kiss. A phrase that some tourists may find useful, quoted from a popular hula, is *Honi Ka'ua Wikiwiki:* Kiss me quick!

honu: turtle.

ho'omalimali: flattery, a deceptive "line," bunk, baloney, hooey.

huhū: angry.

hui: a group, club, or assembly. A church may refer to its congregation as a *hui* and a social club may be called a *hui.*

hukilau: a seine; a communal fishing party in which everyone helps to drive the fish into a huge net, pull it in, and divide the catch.

hula: the dance of Hawaii.

iki: little.

ipo: sweetheart. Commonly seen as "ku'uipo," or "my sweetheart."

ka: the. This is the definite article for most singular words; for plural nouns, the definite article is usually *nā.* Since there is no S in Hawaiian, the article may be your only clue that a noun is plural.

Hawaiian Vocabulary

kahuna: a priest, doctor, or other trained person of old Hawaii, endowed with special professional skills that often included prophecy or other supernatural powers.

kai: the sea, saltwater.

kalo: the taro plant from whose root *poi* (paste) is made.

kamā'aina: literally, a child of the soil; it refers to people who were born in the Islands or have lived there for a long time.

kanaka: originally a man or humanity, it is now used to denote a male Hawaiian or part-Hawaiian, but is occasionally taken as a slur when used by non-Hawaiians. *Kanaka maoli* is used by some Native Hawaiian rights activists to embrace part-Hawaiians as well.

kāne: a man, a husband. If you see this word (or *kane*) on a door, it's the men's room.

kapa: also called by its Tahitian name, *tapa*, a cloth made of beaten bark and usually dyed and stamped with a repeat design.

kapakahi: crooked, cockeyed, uneven. You've got your hat on *kapakahi*.

kapu: keep out, prohibited. This is the Hawaiian version of the more widely known Tongan word *tabu* (taboo).

kēia lā: today.

keiki: a child; *keikikāne* is a boy, *keikiwahine* a girl.

kōkua: to help, assist. Often seen in signs like "Please *kōkua* and throw away your trash."

kona: the leeward side of the Islands, the direction (south) from which the *kona* wind and *kona* rain come.

kula: upland.

kuleana: a homestead or small plot of ground on which a family has been installed for some generations without necessarily owning it. By extension, *kuleana* is used to denote any area or department in which one has a special interest or prerogative. You'll hear it used this way: "If you want to hire a surfboard, see Moki; that's his *kuleana*."

kupuna: grandparent; elder.

lā: sun.

lamalama: to fish with a torch.

lānai: a porch, a balcony, an outdoor living room.

lani: heaven, the sky.

lauhala: the leaf of the *hala*, or pandanus tree, widely used in handicrafts.

lei: a garland of flowers.

lōlō: feeble-minded, crazy.

luna: a plantation overseer or foreman.

mahalo: thank you.

mahina: moon.

makai: toward the ocean.

mālama: to take care of, preserve, protect

malihini: a newcomer to the Islands.

mana: the spiritual power that the Hawaiians believe inhabits all things and creatures.

manō: shark.

manuahi: free, gratis.

mauka: toward the mountains.

mauna: mountain.

mele: a Hawaiian song or chant, often of epic proportions.

Mele Kalikimaka: Merry Christmas (a transliteration from the English phrase).

Menehune: a Hawaiian pixie. The Menehune were a legendary race of little people who accomplished prodigious work, such as building fishponds and temples in the course of a single night.

moana: the ocean.

mu'umu'u: the voluminous dress in which the missionaries enveloped Hawaiian women. Culturally sensitive locals have embraced the Hawaiian spelling but often shorten the spoken word to "mu'u." Most English dictionaries include the spelling "muumuu."

nani: beautiful.

nui: big.

'ohana: family.

'ono: delicious.

pāhoehoe: smooth, unbroken, satiny lava.

palapala: document, printed matter.

pali: a cliff, precipice.

pānini: prickly pear cactus.

paniolo: a Hawaiian cowboy, a rough transliteration of *español,* the language of the Islands' earliest cowboys.

pau: finished, done.

pilikia: trouble. The Hawaiian word is much more widely used here than its English equivalent.

pū: large conch shell used to trumpet the start of luau and other special events.

puka: a hole.

pule: prayer, blessing. Often performed before a meal or event.

pupule: crazy, like the celebrated Princess Pupule. This word has replaced its English equivalent in local usage.

pu'u: volcanic cinder cone.

tūtū: grandmother

waha: mouth.

wahine: a female, a woman, a wife, and a sign on the ladies' room door; the plural form is *wāhine.*

wai: freshwater, as opposed to saltwater, which is *kai.*

wailele: waterfall.

wikiwiki: to hurry, hurry up (since this is a reduplication of *wiki,* quick, neither *W* is pronounced as a *V*).

2

Travel Smart

HAWAIIAN VOCABULARY

Great Itineraries

Best of the Big Island in a Week

Experiencing the best of the Big Island requires some drive time, plus some downtime.

DAY 1: HISTORIC KAILUA VILLAGE

Start your first day in Kailua-Kona with a stroll around Historic Kailua Village. Eat breakfast at one of the oceanfront restaurants along Alii Drive. Stroll the seaside village's many gift stores, art galleries, and boutiques. Historic landmarks include royal **Hulihee Palace** and the oldest Christian church in Hawaii, **Mokuaikaua Church.** In the afternoon, take a ride on the *Atlantis X* **submarine,** or take a sunset dinner sail with **Body Glove Cruises.**

Logistics: The village is walkable. There are paid and free lots behind the shops on the mountain side of Alii Drive.

DAY 2: BEST KOHALA BEACHES

Head north to the beautiful sand beaches of the Kohala Coast. Check out **Anaehoomalu Bay** in Waikoloa Beach Resort. Not only can you rent beach amenities including kayaks or stand-up paddleboards, you'll also be near Queens' MarketPlace with its restaurants and shops, as well as retail and dining destinations at the Kings' Shops. For lunch, try Lava Lava Beach Club, right on the beach at Anaehoomalu Bay. Head north to Kawaihae and visit **Puukohola Heiau National Historic Site,** where King Kamehameha I oversaw the building of a great temple. On the way back, make a stop at **Hapuna Beach State Recreation Area.**

Logistics: Parking is easy at Waikoloa Beach Resort. It's a 35-mile, 40-minute drive from Kailua-Kona via Queen Kaahumanu Highway.

DAY 3: KEALAKEKUA BAY

In South Kona, **Kealakekua Bay State Historical Park** attracts visitors to this marine conservation district frequented by spinner dolphins. The **Captain James Cook Monument,** a white obelisk on a wharf across the bay at Kaawaloa Flats, marks near where the navigator was slain in 1779. Guided kayak tours are available, and snorkeling is excellent. In the afternoon, visit **St. Benedict Painted Church**, plus **Puuhonua O Honaunau National Historical Park.** On your way back north, stop at **Greenwell Farms** in Kealakekua for a Kona coffee farm tour.

Logistics: Take the lower bypass road from Keauhou or the upper road from Kailua-Kona, and head down Napoopoo Road to the end. It's a 34-mile, 30-minute round-trip from Kailua-Kona.

DAY 4: HAWAII VOLCANOES NATIONAL PARK

It's a long drive from Kailua-Kona to **Hawaii Volcanoes National Park,** so leave early to get to the park by 10 am. Begin at the **Kilauea Visitor Center,** where you can review maps, buy trail-guide booklets, or talk to the rangers. Stroll along a boardwalk to the sulfur banks and steam vents. Along the way, stop at **Volcano Art Center** to view fantastic local art. Drive to the Steaming Bluffs and walk to an overlook with views of Halemaumau Crater and Kilauea Caldera. Then drive down Chain of Craters Road to visit **Thurston Lava Tube** and the adjacent **Kilauea Iki Trail.** Afterward, stop by **Volcano House** and eat lunch or dinner at The Rim.

Logistics: The park is open 24/7, but entrance fees are charged during normal visiting hours. It's 90 miles (2½ hours) from Kailua-Kona.

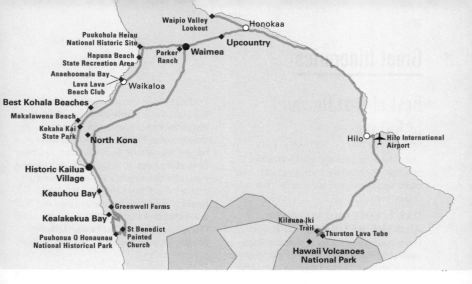

DAY 5: WAIMEA AND UPCOUNTRY

At the foothills of Maunakea, this small upcountry town is home to **Parker Ranch,** one of the country's largest privately owned cattle ranches. You can book several activities in town, including horseback riding and tours of two historic homes. Waimea has great restaurants, including Merriman's and Big Island Brewhaus. Not far from Waimea, **Waipio Valley** is a beautiful destination. The nearby town of **Honokaa** still feels like a slice of the old sugar plantation days.

Logistics: Waimea can be reached via the upper road (Highway 190) from Kailua-Kona, or up Kawaihae Road from the lower highway near the Kohala Coast resorts. Distance from Kailua-Kona: 39 miles one way.

DAY 6: KEAUHOU BAY

Keauhou is just south of Kailua-Kona on Alii Drive. Here you'll find lots of recreational activities, including tennis, golf, and stand-up paddleboarding. **Keauhou Shopping Center** has movie theaters, restaurants, and cafés. Some of the island's most popular activities are the nighttime manta ray tours with operators that depart nightly from Keauhou Harbor.

Tips

■ Book manta ray or kayaking tours in advance, as they are popular.

■ Plan your time at Hawaii Volcanoes National Park carefully so you can see what you want.

Logistics: You'll need your car to drive around the area, or you can take the Kona Trolley from town. It's 5 miles one way on Alii Drive.

DAY 7: NORTH KONA

Two of the best beaches near Kailua-Kona take some time to get to. **Kekaha Kai State Park,** also known as **Mahaiula,** is accessed down a long gravel road that winds through a lava field on the way to a wonderful white-sand beach. About a 20-minute walk south across a lava field from Kekaha Kai State Park, **Makalawena Beach** is a gem and worth the hike; be sure to pack water, a shade umbrella, food, and sunscreen.

Logistics: On Wednesday, the park is closed. Distance from Kailua-Kona: 13 miles one way.

Great Itineraries

Best of East Hawaii in 5 Days

The east side of the Big Island offers spectacular scenery, hidden attractions, must-see destinations, and Hilo's thriving downtown.

DAY 1: VOLCANO VILLAGE AND THE NATIONAL PARK

From your home base at **Volcano House** or your cozy nearby vacation rental, drive to small, artsy Volcano Village for breakfast at **Lava Rock Cafe.** Explore **Kilauea Kreations** for local souvenirs and handmade Hawaiian quilts, and check out **2400 Fahrenheit** gallery for handblown glass; **Volcano Garden Arts** offers more locally crafted items. Notice the old homes and lodges, including historic **Kilauea Lodge,** tucked away in the residential neighborhoods. Arrive at Hawaii Volcanoes National Park by 11 am, so you can explore the steam vents, sulfur banks, **Thurston Lava Tube,** and **Kilauea Iki Trail,** a 2-mile (one way) trek into the still-steaming crater. Have dinner at **The Rim** at Volcano House, which features views of Halemaumau Crater. After dinner, visit the arcade and bowling alley at **Kilauea Military Camp.**

Logistics: Distance traveled: 4–5 miles round-trip via Hawaii Belt Road from the park to Volcano Village, and Crater Rim Drive inside the park.

DAY 2: HAWAII VOLCANOES NATIONAL PARK

Head to **Kilauea Visitor Center** to talk to the rangers and to learn about ranger-led programs. Visit **Devastation Trail**, an area strewn with cinder that descended from towering lava fountains in 1959. One of the park's most fascinating hikes is **Mauna Ulu Trail** (2½-mile round-trip) off **Chain of Craters Road.** Purchase a trail guide at the visitor center about the Mauna Ulu lava flow of 1969–74. Allow about two hours for the hike, which has stellar views of Mauna Loa and Maunakea. Afterward, continue driving Chain of Craters Road to its end and take in the view of the sea arch from the viewing station. After lunch back at **Volcano House,** wander along the Earthquake Trail and Waldron Ledge just outside the hotel. Don't miss **Volcano Art Center,** which presents works by Hawaii artists.

Logistics: Distance and time traveled: about 40 miles round-trip, starting in park via Chain of Craters Road.

DAY 3: HILO AND VICINITY

From Volcano, take a 40-minute drive to Hilo and have breakfast at a local restaurant. Wander around the Hilo bayfront to visit the many galleries, cafés, and shops, including **Sugar Coast Candy**. If you are in Hilo on a Wednesday or Saturday, the **Hilo Farmers Market** is in full swing with Hawaii-made products like honey, mochi, goat cheese, and crafts. Across the way on Banyan Drive, **Liliuokalani Gardens** offers a serene Japanese setting with arched bridges and gazebos. Take in a planetarium show at the **Imiloa Astronomy Center**. Afterward, head back to town (2 miles away) for lunch and more exploring. Then drive up the road a mile above town and visit **Rainbow Falls** and, a bit farther up, **Boiling Pots**. Take a walk by Reeds Bay along Banyan Drive, shaded by a canopy of 50 enormous banyan trees, followed by a first-rate dinner at **Hilo Bay Cafe**.

Logistics: You'll need a car to travel between sights, though you can walk around downtown Hilo. Distance and time traveled: 30 miles, 45 minutes one way. Car, via Highway 11 starting in Volcano.

DAY 4: HAMAKUA COAST, HONOKAA, WAIPIO VALLEY

The longest drive of your itinerary takes you back through Hilo to the opposite side of the island on the Hamakua Coast. It's a 22-minute drive from Hilo to **Akaka Falls State Park** on the Hamakua Coast, with its two cascading waterfalls. Then drive to the historic town of **Honokaa** and browse the galleries and shops downtown. Afterward, follow the signs to the awesome **Waipio Valley** lookout at the end of the Hamakua Heritage Corridor. At this writing, the road down to the valley is closed to all but valley residents, farmers, and property owners due to hazardous road conditions. On your way back to Hilo, stop at **Laupahoehoe Point Beach Park** for breathtaking ocean views. Treat yourself to dinner in Hilo before driving back to Volcano.

Logistics: Distance and time traveled: 78 miles; 1 hour, 50 minutes one way, starting in Volcano. Car, via Highway 19.

DAY 5: LOWER PUNA AND PAHOA

It's a 31-mile drive east from Volcano to the Big Island's most offbeat destination, **Pahoa**. It's in the Puna District, known for its wild, jagged, black lava coastline. This funky, historic village, developed during the sugar plantation era, has escaped destruction twice: in 2014 and more recently in 2018, when an eruption destroyed entire neighborhoods in Lower Puna. Explore the hippie boutiques and cafés of Pahoa Town; eat lunch in town. Near Pahoa, you can explore the lava molds of expired tree trunks at **Lava Tree State Monument.** On the nearby coast, explore the striking, new **Pohoiki Black Sand Beach,** formed when hot lava from the 2018 eruption flowed into the ocean and was pulverized. Note that this beach is for viewing, not swimming. Head back to your home base for dinner.

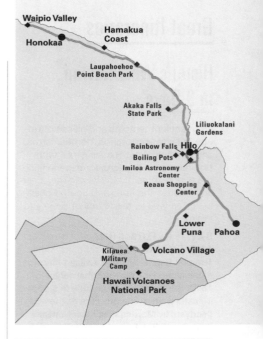

Tips

■ Even on sunny mornings, bring a light, hooded jacket and umbrella: rain showers can happen anytime.

■ Affordable, local-style "plate lunch" eateries are abundant on the east side: try one!

■ Plan your time carefully if you want to hike in the Waipio Valley; this is a long driving day.

Logistics: Gas up for the round trip to this destination. Distance and time traveled: 31 miles, 42 minutes one way, starting from Volcano. Car, via Highway 11 and Highway 130.

Great Itineraries

Historic West Hawaii in 3 Days

From ancient temples and places of refuge to historic churches, homes, farms, and ranches, West Hawaii is rich with fascinating destinations for experiencing the bygone eras of old Hawaii. This itinerary includes the Kona and South Kohala areas, as well as the towns of Hawi and Waimea.

DAY 1: KAILUA-KONA AND SOUTH KONA

The first capital of the Hawaiian Kingdom established by King Kamehameha I in 1812, the town of Kailua-Kona is steeped in history. Stroll the grounds of the **Courtyard by Marriott King Kamehameha's Kona Beach Hotel**, the site where the king spent his last years at **Kamakahonu**, the royal compound. Inside the hotel, historic artifacts and exhibits are displayed in the lobby. A reconstructed temple, **Ahuena Heiau**, sits sentry at the entrance to Kailua Bay by the pier. Kamehameha I met with advisers here and passed away here in 1819. Nearby, **Hulihee Palace** is one of three royal palaces in the state and the US. Docents lead guided tours, which showcase antique koa furnishings and artifacts of the day. Across the street, **Mokuaikaua Church** is the first Christian church in the state of Hawaii. It features a history room documenting the arrival of the first missionaries to Hawaii.

Drive south on Highway 11 to Kona Historical Society in upcountry Kealakekua on Mamalahoa Highway. The destination includes the **H. N. Greenwell Store Museum** (check opening hours). This area is a peaceful place to linger awhile, as there are coffee farm tours and tastings at the adjacent **Greenwell Farms.** A few miles further south on Mamalahoa Highway,

the **Kona Coffee Living History Farm** in Captain Cook highlights farm life in the 1920s on a still-active coffee farm. Your next stop is **Puuhonua O Honaunau National Historical Park**, overlooking Honaunau Bay. This ancient sacred site offers self-guided walking tours through the royal compounds that once served as a refuge for lawbreakers and warriors fleeing battle.
■ TIP→ **Before heading to the historical park, stop at ChoiceMart in Captain Cook and buy picnic items. The oceanfront picnic grounds at the park include barbecues, picnic tables, tide pools, and hiking trails.**

Logistics: You can walk around Kailua-Kona but will need a car for South Kona sites. When traveling south from Keauhou to Captain Cook, take the bypass road. Distance and time traveled: 44 miles round-trip, 35 minutes one way, starting in Kailua-Kona. Car, via Highway 11.

DAY 2: SOUTH KOHALA

Pack your bags for a beach day while you also explore some ancient sites of old Hawaii. While in downtown Kailua-Kona, have breakfast and drive to nearby Honokohau Harbor. At the farthest end of the parking lot, a beach access trail takes you to a sandy cove inside **Kaloko-Honokohau National Historical Park.** Swim the pristine bay or walk the boardwalk to see ancient petroglyphs. Drive north on Queen Kaahumanu Highway and grab a tasty to-go lunch at **Pine Tree Cafe** before heading to the popular **Hapuna Beach State Recreation Area** for the afternoon. After spending time at this white-sand beach, explore the nearby **Puukohola Heiau National Historic Site**, home to the last major temple built by Kamehameha I. Ruins of the massive temple are still intact, and there's a small bay where black-tipped reef sharks pass over a submerged temple. For dinner, head back south down the highway to the **Shops at Mauna Lani**, where restaurants offer options for dinner. **Queens' Marketplace** in Waikoloa has a food court with locally owned eateries.

Logistics: A car is needed. Distance and time traveled: 44 miles round-trip, 35 minutes one way, starting in Kailua-Kona. Car, via Queen Kaahumanu Highway.

DAY 3: NORTH KOHALA AND WAIMEA

Start your day with breakfast at the **Kings' Shops**, where early-morning fare is served at several places at this lakeside retail and dining center in Waikoloa Beach Resort. Head north past the harborside town of Kawaihae to **Lapakahi State Historical Park**, site of an ancient fishing village revealing remnants of canoe houses, dwellings, and temples. Farther up the highway before the town of Hawi, turn west at the Upolu Airport turnoff and drive left of the airfield to King Kamehameha I's birthplace, marked by a plaque. Park your car and hike south down the dirt road about a mile to the mysterious ruins of **Mookini Heiau**, which dates to AD 480 and was known for human sacrifices. An eerie vibe emanates from the moss-laden rock walls on the windswept cliffs above the ocean. During winter, this is a great spot to watch migrating humpback whales. Drive into the artists' town of Hawi and eat lunch, then browse the galleries and stores. Continue past Hawi to the town of Kapaau, home to the original **King Kamehameha statue**; it towers above the highway on the grounds of the Kohala Information Center.

Take the scenic Kohala Mountain Road (Highway 250) to Waimea, in the heart of *paniolo* (cowboy) country. Two historic homes on **Parker Ranch** host visitor tours. Mana Hale, a home built of koa wood

Tips

- You can drive this loop itinerary in either direction, starting in Waimea if you wish.

- Remember: "Kona" is the district, "Kailua-Kona" is the town, even though many people incorrectly use the terms interchangeably.

- Respectful behavior is essential at sacred historic sites.

by John Parker Palmer in 1879, sits just below a "Hawaiian Victorian" manor house built in 1862. The manor house was the family home of six generations of Parkers, the last of whom was actor Richard Smart, who outfitted it with art, family portraits, and treasures from his world travels. The houses can be toured on weekdays (check schedule). Another historic site in Waimea, **Anna Ranch Heritage Center**, offers tours of the historic home that belonged to the legendary female equestrian and rancher Anna Lindsey Perry-Fiske. Before heading back home, eat dinner at one of Waimea's acclaimed restaurants.

Logistics: This day involves some scenic driving. Factor about 35 miles from Waikoloa Beach Resort to Kapaau, and 22 miles from Kapaau to Waimea. It's about a 15-minute drive from Waimea to the Kohala Coast resorts, and an hour or so drive from Waimea back to Kailua-Kona.

Best Tours

A guided tour can be a hassle-free way to see lots of attractions on the Big Island (and other islands) without having to worry about the logistics and details yourself. Taking a tour can also be a great way to make new friends. Tour operators offer all kinds of itineraries to Hawaii, from general trips that include a variety of sights and experiences to more focused trips that hone in on anything from biking to nature. Keep in mind that Hawaii is a popular destination, and trips can book up well in advance.

GENERAL-INTEREST TOURS

If you want to cover the ground efficiently while seeing a variety of sights, a general-interest tour is a good bet. These trips can include several islands. Often, visits to Hawaii Volcanoes National Park are included.

Aloha Hawaiian Vacations. Among other trips to the Hawaiian Islands, this company offers an all-inclusive, six-day adventure to the Big Island that includes a luau, beachfront buffets, half-day expeditions, a rental car, bellman tips, and all taxes. ⊠ Kailua-Kona ☎ 800/256–4211 ⊕ www.aloha-hawaiian.com ⊠ From $4,000.

Globus. On its Grand Hawaii Vacation, Globus visits the main Hawaiian Islands, including the Big Island. Guests visit the Kona Coffee Living History Farm and the world's most active volcano, Kilauea. This very popular tour sells out quickly. Check online as tours to the Big Island frequently change, and some years only interisland cruises are available. ⊠ Honolulu ☎ 866/755–8581 ⊕ www.globusjourneys.com ⊠ From $5,359.

Road Scholar. Focusing on travelers over age 50, this nonprofit organization leads all-inclusive learning adventures, including cultural and educational tours of Hawaii; other tours are adventure-focused. Several multi-island tour packages include stays on the Big Island, where participants can explore such places as Hawaii Volcanoes National Park and the Imiloa Astronomy Center in Hilo. ⊠ Honolulu ☎ 800/454–5768 ⊕ www.roadscholar.org ⊠ From $5,999.

Trafalgar. Offering a wide range of Hawaii tour itineraries and pricing, Trafalgar is great for visitors who want to see a lot of Hawaii without having to arrange all the fly-drive-hotel details themselves. On most of its Big Island legs, the company takes you to Hawaii Volcanoes National Park, with stops along the way, and then gives you a free day to enjoy snorkeling, whale-watching, or manta ray dives. ⊠ Honolulu ☎ 844/602–9662 ⊕ www.trafalgar.com ⊠ From $3,419.

YMT Vacations. Billing itself as the best choice in affordable travel, YMT offers a 12-day, four-island tour and an 11-day Hawaiian Islands cruise and tour. ⊠ Honolulu ☎ 877/322–6185 ⊕ www.ymtvacations.com ⊠ From $2,799.

ADVENTURE STUDY

A tour of Kilauea Volcano—the most active volcano on Earth—is even better when led by an actual geologist, volcanologist, retired ranger, or even botanist.

Friends of Hawaii Volcanoes National Park. With tours tailored to small groups or individuals, the Friends of Hawaii Volcanoes National Park offers custom tours with specialist guides who help you make fascinating discoveries and learn details about geologic features such as lava tubes, fissures, and craters. Tours last four to eight hours. Another option is to join the Friends and participate in their regular programs. ⊠ Hilo ☎ 808/985–7373 ⊕ fhvnp.org ⊠ From $400 for group of 1–6 people.

BIKING

If you're a bicycling enthusiast, you've got exciting options on the Big Island.
■TIP→ **Most airlines accommodate bikes as luggage, provided they're dismantled and boxed.**

Bicycle Adventures. Take a six-day Hawaii tour that includes biking, hiking, snorkeling, stargazing, and manta ray viewing. Accommodations, meals, and park admissions are included. ⊠ *Kailua-Kona* ☎ *800/443–6060* ⊕ *www.bicycleadventures.com* ✈ *From $4,513*.

BIRD-WATCHING

Because of its isolated location, nearly 2,500 miles from any major landmass, Hawaii's unique habitats have spawned many unusual species of birds that have evolved through the centuries. Although countless bird species have been lost due to mosquito-borne diseases, introduced predators, or loss of habitat, some native birds still thrive, mostly in the Hakalau National Wildlife Refuge on the slopes of Maunakea, where their natural forest habitats have been restored and protected. Birders from around the world come here and to other parts of the island to spot such endangered birds as the Hawaiian honeycreeper (iiwi)—and you can, too, with the help of expert guides.

Hawaii Forest and Trail. This company offers exclusive daylong bird-watching tours to a cloud-misted native habitat on the slopes of Maunakea and to dryland or rain forest destinations on the Big Island. Expert guides help you search native forests for amakihi, iiwi, elepaio, *apapane*, and the endangered *akiapolaau*.

The Hakalau Forest tour offers outstanding opportunities to spot the rarest endemic birds, allowing exclusive access to the highly restricted Hakalau National Wildlife Refuge. You may even see such thrilling sights as the highly endangered, bright orange *akepa* juvenile being fed by its parents. Walking sticks, binoculars, rain ponchos, and meals are provided. ⊠ *Kailua-Kona* ☎ *808/331–8505* ⊕ *www.hawaii-forest.com* ✈ *From $235*.

Victor Emanuel Nature Tours. The company has multiday trips that include the Big Island, led by well-known birding experts such as Brendan Mulrooney and Erik Bruhnke. Focusing on off-the-beaten path destinations and habitats, the tours offer birders the chance to spot such indigenous species as the amakihi, *apapane*, elepaio, and the iconic iiwi honeycreeper, as well as endemic birds such as the omao, palila, and *akepa* honeycreepers. Tour prices include interisland flights and are offered in both spring and fall. ⊠ *Honolulu* ☎ *800/328–8368* ⊕ *www.ventbird.com* ✈ *From $7,995*.

ECOTOURS

Backroads. This outfit offers a 6-day adventure trek exploring Hawaii Volcanoes National Park and the Kohala Coast. Snorkeling, biking, swimming, and kayaking are on the agenda. ☎ *800/462-2848* ⊕ *www.backroads.com* ✈ *From $4,099 per person*.

Sierra Club Outings. With this company, tours include a service-project component, such as restoring critical bird habitats or beautifying gardens. Book early because most itineraries sell out fast. ⊠ *Honolulu* ☎ *415/977–5522* ⊕ *www.sierraclub.org/outings* ✈ *From $2,801*.

Contacts

Air

MAJOR AIRLINE CONTACTS Air Canada. ✉ Honolulu ☎ 888/247–2262 ⊕ www.aircanada.com. **Alaska Airlines.** ✉ Honolulu ☎ 800/252–7522 ⊕ www.alaskaair.com. **American Airlines.** ✉ Honolulu ☎ 800/433–7300 ⊕ www.aa.com. **Delta Airlines.** ✉ Honolulu ☎ 800/221–1212 for U.S. reservations ⊕ www.delta.com. **Hawaiian Airlines.** ✉ Honolulu ☎ 800/367–5320 ⊕ www.hawaiianair.com. **Japan Airlines.** ✉ Honolulu ☎ 800/525–3663 ⊕ www.jal.com. **Southwest Airlines.** ✉ Honolulu ☎ 800/435–9792 ⊕ www.southwest.com. **United Airlines.** ✉ Honolulu ☎ 800/864–8331 for U.S. reservations, 800/241–6522 arrival and departure information ⊕ www.united.com. **Virgin Atlantic.** ✉ Honolulu ☎ 800/862–8621 ⊕ www.virginatlantic.com. **Westjet.** ✉ Honolulu ☎ 888/937–8538 ⊕ www.westjet.com.

AIRPORTS Daniel K. Inouye International Airport (HNL). ✉ 300 Rodgers Blvd., Honolulu ☎ 808/836–6413 ⊕ hawaii.gov/hnl. **Ellison Onizuka Kona International Airport at Keahole (KOA).** ✉ 73-200 Kupipi St., Kailua-Kona ☎ 808/327–9520 ⊕ hawaii.gov/koa. **Hilo International Airport (ITO).** ✉ 2450 Kekuanaoa St., Hilo ☎ 808/961–9300 ⊕ hawaii.gov/ito. **Waimea-Kohala Airport (MUE).** ✉ Waimea-Kohala Airport Rd., Waimea (Hawaii County) ☎ 808/887–8126 ⊕ hawaii.gov/mue.

AIRPORT TRANSFERS SpeediShuttle. ✉ 74555 Honokohau St., D10, Kailua-Kona ☎ 877/242–5777, 808/242–7777 ⊕ www.speedishuttle.com.

CHARTER CONTACTS Big Island Air. ✉ 73-103 Uu St., Kailua-Kona ☎ 808/329–4868 ⊕ www.bigislandair.com.

INTERISLAND CONTACTS Mokulele Airlines. ✉ Honolulu ☎ 866/260–7070 ⊕ www.mokuleleairlines.com.

Bus

Hele-On Bus. ✉ Kailua-Kona ☎ 808/961–8744 ⊕ www.heleonbus.org.

🛏 Lodging

Big Island Villas. ✉ Waimea (Hawaii County) ☎ 808/936–3870, 808/443–6991 ⊕ www.bigislandvillas.com. **Hawaiian Beach Rentals.** ✉ Honolulu ☎ 844/261–0464 ⊕ www.hawaiianbeachrentals.com. **Hawaii Vacation Rentals.** ✉ Waimea (Hawaii County) ☎ 808/882–7000 ⊕ www.vacationbigisland.com. **Keauhou Property Management.** ✉ Keauhou ☎ 808/326–7053 ⊕ www.konacondo.net. **Knutson and Associates.** ✉ Kailua-Kona ☎ 808/329–1010 ⊕ www.konahawaiirentals.com. **Kolea Vacations.** ✉ Waikoloa ☎ 808/987–4519 ⊕ www.waikoloavacationrentals.com/kolea-rentals. **Kona Coast Vacations.** ✉ Kailua-Kona ☎ 808/329–2140 ⊕ www.konacoastvacations.com. **Kona Vacation Rentals.** ✉ Kailua-Kona ☎ 808/334–1199 ⊕ www.konarentals.com. **South Kohala Management.** ✉ Waimea (Hawaii County) ☎ 808/883–8500 ⊕ www.southkohala.com.

 Visitor Information

Hawaii Island Chamber of Commerce. ✉ 1321 Kinoole St., Hilo ☎ 808/935–7178 ⊕ www.hicc.biz. **Island of Hawaii Visitors Bureau.** ✉ 68-1330 Mauna Lani Dr., Puako ✚ In Shops at Mauna Lani ☎ 808/885–1655 ⊕ www.gohawaii.com/islands/hawaii-big-island. **Kona-Kohala Chamber of Commerce.** ✉ 75-5737 Kuakini Hwy., #208, Kailua-Kona ☎ 808/329–1758 ⊕ www.kona-kohala.com.

Chapter 3

KAILUA-KONA

3

Updated by
Kristina Anderson

◉ Sights	🍴 Restaurants	🛏 Hotels	👜 Shopping	🍸 Nightlife
★★★★★	★★★☆☆	★★★☆☆	★★★☆☆	★★☆☆☆

WELCOME TO KAILUA-KONA

TOP REASONS TO GO

★ **Hulihee Palace:** Now a museum, this lovely oceanfront palace dates to the 19th century.

★ **Kamakahonu and Ahuena Heiau:** This compound, a National Historic Landmark, served as the seat of government for King Kamehameha and housed his personal *heiau*, or temple.

★ **Kailua-Kona Village:** Once a sleepy fishing village, today Kailua-Kona hosts lively restaurants, shops, and historic sites.

★ **Mokuaikaua Church:** Built in 1836 of sand, lime, and coral mortar, this church's steeple reaches 112 feet, making it a Kailua landmark.

★ **Herb Kane Artwork:** An incredible collection by this iconic artist is on display in the lobby of the King Kamehameha Kona Beach Hotel.

★ **Laaloa Beach Park:** This small but gorgeous beach has a storied history of sands that disappear as magically as they reappear.

Kailua-Kona is the closest thing the Big Island has to a "city" on the leeward coast and is the population center closest to the Big Island's major resorts. One of the island's two airports, Ellison Onizuka Kona International Airport, is 7 miles north of the town center. The town is also where the first Christian missionaries landed in 1820 and changed life in the Islands forever. Beautiful beaches, historical sites, and the hilly Kona coffee belt draw visitors.

1 Kailua-Kona. Formerly a quaint fishing town, Kailua-Kona is now a charming tourist area dotted with historical sites such as Hulihee Palace and Ahuena Heiau, final home of King Kamehameha I (Kamehameha the Great). Development is centered along Alii Drive by the waterfront, where most of the area's condo complexes, restaurants, and shops are; it's highly walkable. Because of the concentration of establishments, this can be one of the more congested parts of the Big Island.

2 Holualoa. This artsy town nestled in the upcountry only 3 miles from town is home to artisans, painters, sculptors, and woodworkers. Large numbers of vintage buildings here house studios, galleries, and coffee shops. It's a great place to stroll the galleries and then try a farm tour, complete with a cup of Kona coffee, as plantations and estates are nearby.

3 North Kona. Some of the most stellar Big Island beaches and historical sites, including Kekaha Kai State Park and Kaloko-Honokohau National Historical Park, are in North Kona, which is largely undeveloped with the exception of the luxurious Four Seasons Hualalai resort. While the area's expansive black lava plains are the dominant feature, beautiful white-sand beaches are scattered along the coastline.

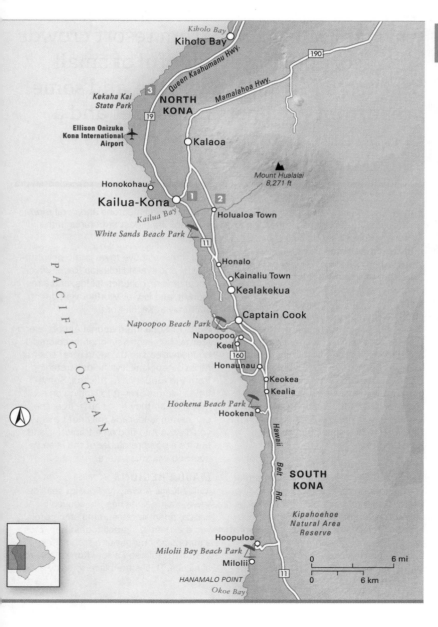

More laid-back than the tonier Kohala Coast to the north, the Kona Coast and its largest town, Kailua-Kona, are great if you want to get away from resort crowds and resort pricing. A handful of small beaches, a fun surf town vibe, and some oceanfront hot spots for sunset and a mai tai are just a few good reasons to spend time here.

Except for the rare deluge, the sun shines year-round. Mornings offer cooler weather, smaller crowds, and more birds singing in the banyan trees; you'll see tourists and locals out running on Alii Drive, the town's main drag, by about 5 am every day. Afternoons sometimes bring clouds and light rain, but evenings often clear up so you can enjoy cool drinks, brilliant sunsets, gentle trade breezes, and lazy hours spent gazing out over the ocean. Though there are better beaches north of town on the Kohala Coast, Kailua-Kona is home to a few gems, including a beginner's snorkeling beach (Kahaluu Beach Park) and a tranquil bay perfect for kids (Kamakahonu Beach, in front of the Courtyard King Kamehameha's Kona Beach Hotel).

In the heart of town are several important historical sites within an easy stroll of downtown hotels and condos. Hulihee Palace, vacation home of Hawaiian Royalty, is beautifully restored with antique furnishings and art; Ahuena Heiau, which was the seat of government of Kamehameha I is one of Kona's most iconic sights; and Mokuaikaua Church built in 1836 of solid limestone and coral mortar is one of the oldest structures in the state.

Just 3 miles above town is the delightful artists' enclave of Holualoa Town, which hosts several galleries, cafés, and a restaurant, and is well worth a visit during your stay in Kailua-Kona.

North of Kona International Airport, along Mamalahoa Highway, brightly colored bougainvillea stands out in relief against miles of jet-black lava fields stretching from the mountain to the sea. Sometimes visitors liken it to landing on the moon when they first see it. True, the dry, barren landscape may not be what you'd expect to find on a tropical island, but it's a good reminder of the island's evolving volcanic nature.

MAJOR REGIONS

Kailua-Kona. A lively and quaint seaside town, Kailua-Kona has the souvenir shops, open-air restaurants, and hotels you'd expect in a small tourist hub, plus a surprising number of historic sites, including Hulihee Palace, Kona's only royal palace. This is the place to enjoy a mai tai at sunset at one of the town's ocean-front restaurants. It's also fun to cruise Alii Drive and people-watch as locals and visitors enjoy this splendid spot.

Holualoa. With its roots firmly planted in Kona coffee culture, the village of Holu-aloa and its thriving arts community is a draw for visitors and residents alike. The town hosts monthly Friday night strolls and an annual Christmas street fair. So many vintage buildings, including the old original post office, now serve as gal-leries, shops, and cafés. There's even a gallery dedicated to carved *ipu* (gourds), which are used in traditional Hawaiian hula ceremonies.

North Kona. In this rather barren area, vast lava fields turn off onto some of the island's most beautiful beaches. It's also where you'll find the Four Seasons Resort Hualalai, one of the Big Island of Hawaii's superluxurious resorts and the billionaire enclave, Kukio.

Planning

Planning Your Time

Three-quarters of a day is enough to get a taste of Kailua-Kona, as most of the sights are in or near the downtown area. Still, if you add in a beach trip (Magic Sands Beach offers a small patch of white sand and some shore breaks for body boarding), it's tempting to while away an entire day or more here.

You are only about five minutes to the lovely and underrated Kaloko-Honokahau National Historical Park. Enjoy a nice lunch or schooner at the Harbor House, which faces the local fishing fleet, then walk to the back entrance of the park. It's free, and trails lead you around to canoe *hales* (workshop/shed) and two restored ancient fishponds. You'll see

local families on the beach here because the gentle waters are nice for kids.

Consider spending a morning exploring Holualoa Village, which is a short drive up *mauka* (toward the mountain) from town. You can stroll numerous galleries and shops based in quaint historic buildings, meet the artists directly and have a snack or lunch at the Holualoa Cafe. Because you'll already be in the heart of Kona coffee country, book your Kona coffee farm tour (some are free) to witness the operations of a real plantation that excels in growing, processing, and packaging of the world's finest coffee.

Getting Here and Around

AIR
The Big Island of Hawaii has two major airports—one on the east side and one serving the west side. Ellison Onizuka Kona International Airport (KOA) is the busiest, with the most direct flights from the mainland United States and frequent connections from Honolulu. Staffed booths provide visitor information. Renovations, including a newly opened international terminal and new shops, are ongoing. Even with its modernizations, the airport still welcomes most visitors the old-fashioned way—with a trip down a ramp as opposed to a jetway.

The town closest to Kona International Airport (it's about 7 miles away), Kail-ua-Kona is a convenient home base from which to explore the island.

BUS AND TROLLEY
The Hele-On Bus (⊕ *www.heleonbus. org*) offers some service around the immediate Kailua-Kona area, but other routes run less frequently and aren't useful or recommended for tourists with limited time. The price is right—the fare is free.

The Kona Trolley runs 9 am to 9 pm from the Kona Commons Shopping Center to the Outrigger Keauhou Resort & Spa at the south end of Alii Drive. The fare is $2, and $1 for students, seniors, and the disabled.

CAR

It's essential to rent a car when you're visiting this part of the Big Island. There is no organized or easy bus service beyond the immediate Kailua-Kona area, so you'll need transportation if you want to explore even a bit.

The easiest place to park your car in Kailua-Kona is at the free public lot behind town. When you enter Kailua-Kona via Palani Road, turn left onto Kuakini Highway, drive for a half block, and turn right into the small marked parking lot. Walk *makai* (toward the ocean) on Likana Lane a half block to Alii Drive, and you'll be in the heart of Kailua-Kona. When this lot is full, there are quite a few paid lots near the junction of Hualalai Road and Alii Drive.

Beaches

There are a few good sandy beaches in and near Kailua-Kona. Nevertheless, the coastline is generally rugged black lava rock, so don't expect long stretches of white sand. The beaches in town get lots of use by local residents, and visitors enjoy them, too. Excellent opportunities for snorkeling, scuba diving, swimming, kayaking, and other water sports are easy to find.

Just slightly north of town, Old Airport Beach Park and Kohanaiki Beach Park come with a lot more space, and Kohanaiki has an appealing surf break, popular with locals. Camping is allowed with a permit.

Hotels

Downtown Kailua-Kona offers tons of lodging options. In addition to hotels, oceanfront Alii Drive is lined with condos and vacation homes. All the conveniences are here, and there are grocery stores and big-box retailers nearby for those who need to stock up on supplies. Kailua-Kona has a smattering of beaches—Laaloa (Magic Sands), Kahaluu, and Kamakahonu (at the pier) among them. The downside to staying here is the drive 30 to 45 minutes up the road to the Kohala Coast to visit Hawaii's signature white-sand beaches. But you'll also pay about half what you would at any of the major resorts, not to mention that Kailua-Kona offers a bit more local charm, a walkable downtown, and more shops and dining choices.

There are no large resorts along the Kona Coast (other than the Four Seasons Resort Hualalai in North Kona), but there are plenty of outstanding bed-and-breakfasts and vacation rentals along Alii Drive and a few sprinkled through nearby residential neighborhoods (make sure they are permitted). Three large hotel properties serve the downtown Kailua-Kona and Keauhou areas—the Outrigger Kona Resort & Spa, the Royal Kona Resort, and the Courtyard by Marriott King Kamehameha's Kona Beach Hotel. All have pools, bars, spas, and restaurants on-site. Two smaller properties—Pacific 19 and the Holiday Inn Express—are very decent and well located.

⇨ *Hotel prices in the reviews are the lowest cost of a standard double room in high season. Restaurant prices in the reviews are the average cost of a main course at dinner, or if dinner is not served, at lunch. Hotel and restaurant reviews have been shortened. For full information, see Fodors.com.*

What It Costs in U.S. Dollars			
$	$$	$$$	$$$$
HOTELS			
under $200	$200–$280	$281–$380	over $380
RESTAURANTS			
under $20	$20–$30	$30–$40	over $40

Restaurants

While all the hotels in the area offer an on-site, upscale restaurant or two, the majority of establishments in Kailua-Kona tend to be family owned and feature locally sourced seafood, meat, and produce. A handful of restaurants offer Hawaiian plate specialties and Asian fusion, Japanese, and Thai cuisine. If you want a mai tai at sunset, you've come to the right place. Just about every restaurant hosts a nightly happy hour. Prices are slightly lower than at the Kohala resorts, and Kailua-Kona eateries offer greater diversity, plus some amazing oceanfront views of crashing surf and gleaming sunsets.

Check some of the nearby shopping centers for decent food as well. Excellent pizza, sushi, deli food, and burgers can all be found in the centers such as Crossroads, Kona Commons, and Lanihau Centers.

Two brewpubs are located in an industrial area just adjacent to town. Kona Brewing Company showcases a popular restaurant that offers great pizza and salads; Ola Brew has less in the way of full meals, but if you order one of their homebrews, plenty of tapas and appetizers will tempt you.

Tours

Kona Historical Society Walking Tour
SELF-GUIDED TOURS | The society, based in Kealakekua, sells a 24-page *Historic Kailua Village Map* booklet with a map and more than 40 historical photos. You can take a self-guided walking tour to learn more about the village's fascinating past. Order the booklet online before you travel so you have it in hand for your visit to Kailua-Kona. ⊠ *81-6551 Mamalahoa Hwy., Kealakekua* ☎ *808/323–3222* ⊕ *konahistorical.org* ⊡ *$4.*

Kailua-Kona

Kailua-Kona is about 7 miles south of the Kona airport.

The largest town on the Kona Coast, Kailua-Kona offers plenty to accommodate the needs of locals and visitors, but it also has some significant historic sites. Scattered among the shops, restaurants, and condo complexes of Alii Drive are Ahuena Heiau, a temple complex restored by King Kamehameha the Great and the spot where he spent his last days (he died here in 1819); the last royal palace in the United States (Hulihee Palace); and a battleground dotted with the graves of ancient Hawaiians who fought for their way of life and lost. It was also in Kailua-Kona that Kamehameha's successor, King Liholiho, broke with the ancient *kapu* (roughly translated as "forbidden," it was the name for the strict code of conduct that islanders were compelled to follow) system by publicly sitting and eating with women. The following year, on April 4, 1820, the first Christian missionaries came ashore here, changing life in the Islands forever.

GETTING HERE AND AROUND
Most first-time visitors to the island are startled by the seemingly endless black lava fields that make up the airport area

and immediate surroundings. But just a 10-minute drive on Queen Kaahumanu Highway heading south takes you into the seaside town of Kailua-Kona and nearby retail centers. To get to town, take a right onto Palani Road and a left on Kuakini, and find one of the free lots along Kuakini Highway. You can park and walk right to the village and the seawall. You can also get to the restaurant row area by taking Kuakini Highway and turning right into the Coconut Grove Marketplace's parking lot (fee applies). From there, you can walk to oceanfront establishments such as Humpy's Big Island Alehouse and Island Lava Java. Alii Drive, the town's main street, runs north and south along the water and is popular for walking, with plenty of shops and restaurants. Sunsets here are spectacular.

◉ Sights

Courtyard King Kamehameha's Kona Beach Hotel
HOTEL | Even if you're not staying here, make time to stroll through the expansive lobby of this Kailua-Kona fixture to view impressive displays of Hawaiian artifacts, including feathered helmets, capes, ancient hula instruments, and battle weapons. Portraits of Hawaiian royalty adorn the walls. You'll also see mounted marlin from Hawaii International Billfish tournaments (Kailua Pier used to be the weigh-in point, and these "grander" marlin weighed 1,000 pounds or more). One of the best collections of works by Hawaiian artist Herb Kane is on display in the breezeway. Activities in Hawaiian arts and crafts are conducted regularly by on-site cultural staff, and there are nice gift shops, shave ice, and cafés scattered throughout the small mall. ⊠ 75-5660 Palani Rd., Kailua-Kona ☏ 808/329-2911, 800/367-2111 ⊕ marriott.com.

Glyph Gallery
ART GALLERY | More than 30 artists and craftspeople are represented in this small but lovely gallery. They feature original works as well as archival giclée pieces. If you are looking for Big Island artists, a stop at Glyph is a must. ⊠ 76-5933 Mamalahoa Hwy, Holualoa ☏ 808/769–1150 ⊕ glyphartgallery.com.

★ Holualoa
TOWN | Hugging the hillside above the Kona Coast, the tiny, artsy village of Holualoa might contain more artists per square foot than any other town in Hawaii. Painters, woodworkers, jewelers, gourd makers, silk screeners, photographers, and potters work in their studios in back and sell their wares up front. Look for frequent town-wide events such as art strolls and block parties (the annual Christmas light stroll is a favorite) and relax with a cup of coffee in one of the cafés or galleries. Formerly the exclusive domain of coffee plantations, Holualoa still boasts quite a few coffee farms offering free tours and inviting cups of Kona. The town is 3 miles up winding Hualalai Road from Kailua-Kona. ⊠ Holualoa ⊕ www.holualoahawaii.com.

Holualoa Kona Coffee Company
FARM/RANCH | There is a lot going on at this USDA-organic-certified coffee farm and processing facility, from growing the beans to milling and drying. The processing plant next door to the farm demonstrates how the beans are roasted and packaged. A flock of 50 geese welcomes visitors and "provides fertilizer" for the plantation at no charge. Holualoa also processes beans for 200 coffee farms in the area. Enjoy a cup of their finest as you peruse the gift shop after the tour. ⊠ 77-6261 Old Mamalahoa Hwy., Holualoa ☏ 808/322–9937, 800/334–0348 ⊕ konalea.com ☜ Free ⊗ Closed Fri.–Sun.

Hula Daddy Kona Coffee
FARM/RANCH | On a walking tour of this 20-acre working coffee farm (by advance reservation only), visitors can witness the workings of a small plantation, pick and pulp their own coffee beans, watch a roasting demonstration, and savor a

tasting. Lee and Karen Patterson have perfected their coffee over many years, winning local cupping competitions. The gift shop carries whole beans and logo swag including bags, T-shirts, and mugs. Coffee brewing workshops and one-on-one tours with a master roaster are also offered. ✉ 74-4944 Mamalahoa Hwy., Holualoa ☎ 808/327–9744 ⊕ www. huladaddy.com ⌨ $30 ⊘ Closed Sat. and Sun.

★ Hulihee Palace

CASTLE/PALACE | On the National Register of Historic Places, this lovely two-story oceanfront home, surrounded by jewel-green grass and elegant coconut palms and fronted by an elaborate wrought-iron gate, is one of only three royal palaces in America (the other two are in Honolulu). The royal residence was built by Governor John Adams Kuakini in 1838, a year after he completed Mokuaikaua Church. During the 1880s, it served as King David Kalakaua's summer palace.

Built of lava rock and coral lime mortar, it features vintage koa furniture, weaving, European crystal chandeliers, giant four-poster beds, royal portraits, tapa cloth, feather work, and Hawaiian quilts. After the overthrow of the Hawaiian monarchy in 1893, the property fell into disrepair. Set to be torn down for a hotel, it was rescued in 1920 by the Daughters of Hawaii, a nonprofit organization dedicated to preserving the culture and royal heritage of the Islands. The organization oversees and operates the site to this day; visitors see it on a guided tour. ✉ 75-5718 Alii Dr., Kailua-Kona ☎ 808/329–1877 ⊕ www.daughtersofhawaii.org ⌨ $22 includes guided tour.

Kailua Pier

MARINA/PIER | Though most fishing and sail charters use Honokohau Harbor in Kailua-Kona, this pier dating from 1918 is still a hub of ocean activity where outrigger canoe teams practice and race, shuttles transport cruise ship passengers to and from town, and tour boats depart from the docks. Old photos depict cattle being wrangled from the pier to steamers bound for slaughterhouses. Along the seawall, children and old-timers cast their lines and hope for the best. For youngsters, a bamboo pole and hook are easy to come by, and plenty of locals are willing to give pointers. September brings the world's largest long-distance outrigger canoe race, and in October, elite athletes line up on the beach next to the pier to swim 2.4 miles in the first leg of the internationally famous Ironman World Championship triathlon. ✉ Alii Dr., Kailua-Kona ⊹ Across from Courtyard King Kamehameha's Kona Beach Hotel.

★ Kamakahonu and Ahuena Heiau

HISTORIC SIGHT | In the early 1800s, King Kamehameha the Great built a large royal compound at Kamakahonu, the bay fronting what is now the Courtyard King Kamehameha's Kona Beach Hotel; today it is one of the most revered and historically significant sites in all of Hawaii. Kamakahonu, meaning "eye of the turtle," was named for a prominent turtle-shaped rock there, covered in cement when the hotel and pier were built. The Ahuena Heiau, an impressive heiau (temple), was dedicated to Lono, the Hawaiian god of peace and prosperity. It was also used as a seat of government. The compound features a scaled-down replica of the temple and is a National Historic Landmark. You can't go inside the heiau, but you can view it from the beach or directly next door at the hotel's luau grounds. ✉ 75-5660 Palani Rd., Kailua-Kona ☎ ⊕ www. nps.gov/places/kamakahonu.htm.

Kuamoo Battlefield and Lekeleke Burial Grounds

HISTORIC SIGHT | In 1819, an estimated 300 Hawaiians were killed on this vast lava field; their burial mounds are still visible at the south end of Alii Drive (called the "End of the World" by locals). After the death of his father, King Kamehameha, the newly crowned King Liholiho ate at a table with women, breaking

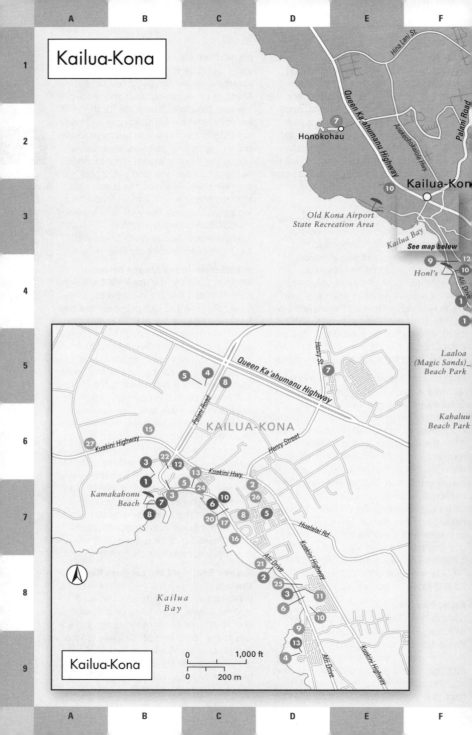

Kailua-Kona

Queen Ka'ahumanu Highway

Hina Lani St

Palani Road

Honokohau

Kailua-Kona

Old Kona Airport
State Recreation Area

Kailua Bay

See map below

Honl's

Alii Drive

Kailua-Kona

Queen Ka'ahumanu Highway

Henry St

Palani Road

KAILUA-KONA

*Laaloa
(Magic Sands)
Beach Park*

*Kahaluu
Beach Park*

Kuakini Highway

Henry Street

Kuakini Hwy.

*Kamakahonu
Beach*

Hualalai Rd.

Kuakini Highway

Alii Drive

*Kailua
Bay*

Kuakini Highway

Alii Drive

| 0 | | 1,000 ft |
| 0 | 200 m | |

KEY

1 *Sights*
1 *Restaurants*
1 *Quick Bites*
1 *Hotels*

Sights ▼

1 Courtyard King Kamehameha's Kona Beach Hotel **B6**
2 Glyph Gallery **H4**
3 Holualoa **H4**
4 Holualoa Kona Coffee Company **H5**
5 Hula Daddy Kona Coffee **G1**
6 Hulihee Palace **C7**
7 Kailua Pier **B7**
8 Kamakahonu and Ahuena Heiau **B7**
9 Kuamoo Battlefield and Lekeleke Burial Grounds **G7**
10 Mokuaikaua Church **C7**
11 St. Peter's by the Sea Chapel **G6**

Restaurants ▼

1 Bianellis Kona **G6**
2 Big Island Grill **C7**
3 Big Kahuna Beach Grill **B7**
4 Don's Mai Tai Bar & Restaurant at Royal Kona Resort **D9**
5 The Fish Hopper **C7**
6 Foster's Kitchen **D8**
7 Harbor House **E2**
8 Hayashi's You Make the Roll **C7**
9 Huggo's **D8**
10 Humpy's Big Island Alehouse **D8**
11 Island Lava Java **D8**
12 Jackie Rey's Ohana Grill **F4**
13 Kalikala Cuisine **C7**
14 Kenichi Pacific **G6**
15 Kona Brewing Co. **B6**
16 Kona Inn Restaurant **C7**
17 Kona Taeng on Thai **C7**
18 La Bourgogne **G4**
19 Magics Beach Grill **G5**
20 Pancho and Lefty's Cantina & Restaurante **C7**
21 Papa Kona Restaurant & Bar **D8**
22 Quinn's Almost by the Sea **B6**
23 Sunset Kai Lanai **G6**
24 Sushi Cocoro & Udon Noodle **C7**
25 Thai Rin **D8**
26 TK Noodle House **D7**
27 Umekes Fish Market Bar & Grill **A6**
28 The View Restaurant Bar & Grill **G6**

Quick Bites ▼

1 Da Poke Shack **F4**
2 Kai Eats & Drinks **D8**
3 Kanaka Kava **D8**
4 Kona Coffee & Tea **C5**
5 Kona Crust **C5**
6 Los Habaneros **G6**
7 Poi Dog Deli **D5**
8 Sack N Save Kona **C5**
9 Tea-licious Cafe **F4**
10 Ultimate Burger **E3**

Hotels ▼

1 Aston Kona by the Sea **F4**
2 Castle Kona Bali Kai **G4**
3 Courtyard by Marriott King Kamehameha's Kona Beach Hotel **B6**
4 Hale Hualalai Bed and Breakfast **G1**
5 Holiday Inn Express and Suites Kailua-Kona, an IHG Hotel **D7**
6 Holualoa Inn **H4**
7 Holua Resort at Mauna Loa Village **G7**
8 Kanaloa at Kona by Outrigger **G6**
9 Kona Coast Resort **G6**
10 Kona Tiki Hotel **F4**
11 Outrigger Kona Resort and Spa at Keauhou Bay **G6**
12 Pacific 19 Kona **B6**
13 Royal Kona Resort **D9**

Holualoa Town

Holualoa Rd.

Mamalahoa Highway

Kuakini Highway

Alii Drive

Mamalahoa Highway

Honalo

Kainaliu Town

Mamalahoa Bypass Rd.

Kealakekua

Captain Cook

0   1 mi
0   1 km

G   H   I

Mokuaikaua Church in Kailua-Kona, completed in 1837, was the first Christian church in the Hawaiian Islands.

the ancient *kapu* (taboo) system. Chief Kekuaokalani, his cousin and co-heir, held radically different views about religious traditions and unsuccessfully challenged Liholiho's forces in battle here. It's a great place to watch the surf, especially when a large swell is in, creating splashes as large as three-story buildings. ⊠ *Alii Dr., Kailua-Kona.*

★ Mokuaikaua Church

CHURCH | Site of the first Christian church in the Hawaiian Islands, this solid lava-rock structure, completed in 1837, is mortared with burned lime, coral, and kukui (candlenut) oil and topped by an impressive 112-foot steeple. The ceiling and interior were crafted of timbers harvested from a forest on Hualalai and are held together with wooden pegs, not nails. Inside, behind a panel of gleaming koa wood, rests a model of the brig *Thaddeus* as well as a koa-wood table crafted by Henry Boshard, pastor for 43 years. The sanctuary is still undergoing renovations, but if you attend Sunday services, they are glad to give you a tour. ⊠ *75-5713 Alii Dr., Kailua-Kona* ☎ *808/329–0655* ⊕ *www.mokuaikaua. org* ⊠ *Free.*

St. Peter's by the Sea Chapel

CHURCH | This tiny oceanfront Roman Catholic chapel by Kahaluu Beach Park, with its crisp white-and-blue trim and old-fashioned steeple, sits next to the site of an ancient *heiau* (temple), now marked by a dry-stack rock wall. This is not the church's original location, however. In 1912, it was dismantled and carried here piece by piece from a site across from Magic Sands Beach. Masses are not currently being held here, and the chapel is not open to the public, although you may certainly take photographs of the exterior. ⊠ *78-6684 Alii Dr., Kailua-Kona* ✛ *Just north of mile marker 5, by Kahaluu* ⊕ *catholichawaii.org.*

Beaches

Honl's

BEACH | This tiny but scenic white-sand-beach park is best known as the birthplace of boogie boarding. That's because boogie board inventor Tom Moray first tried his foam creation out right here in 1971. The Honl's nickname honors a family that once resided here, but its official name is Waiaha, which means "gathered waters." Lots of rocks limit easy access, but it's worth a stop for the history alone. **Amenities:** parking (no fee); picnic tables; showers; toilets. **Best for:** body boarding, swimming, sunbathing. ⊠ *75-5907 Alii Drive, Kailua-Kona* ✛ *South of Royal Kona Resort* ☞ *Free.*

Kahaluu Beach Park

BEACH | Shallow and easily accessible, this salt-and-pepper beach is one of the Big Island's most popular swimming and snorkeling sites, thanks to the fringing reef that helps keep the waters calm, visibility high, and reef life—especially *honu* (green sea turtles) and colorful fish—plentiful. Kahaluu was a favorite of the Hawaiian royal family, too. Because it is so protected, it's great for first-time snorkelers. Avoid areas marked off for coral regrowth and be sure to use reef-safe sunscreen. Outside the reef, very strong rip currents can run, so caution is advised. Listen to lifeguard instructions. Never hand-feed the unusually tame reef fish here; it upsets the balance of the reef.

Experienced surfers find good waves beyond the reef, and scuba divers like the shore dives—shallow ones inside the breakwater, deeper ones outside. Snorkel equipment and boards are available for rent nearby, and surf schools operate here. A community group has provided reef-safe sunscreen dispensers on-site. **Amenities:** food and drink; lifeguards; parking (small fee); showers; toilets. **Best for:** snorkeling; surfing; swimming. ⊠ *78-6720 Alii Dr., Kailua-Kona* ✛ *5½ miles*

south of Kailua-Kona, across from Beach Villas ☎ *808/961–8311* ☞ *Free.*

★ Kamakahonu Beach

BEACH | FAMILY | This beach is where King Kamehameha spent his final days—the replica of the Ahuena Heiau sits on a platform across from the sand. Adjacent to Kailua Pier, the scenic crescent of white sand is one of the few beaches in downtown Kailua-Kona. The water here is almost always calm and the beach clean, making this a perfect spot for kids. For adults, it's a great place for swimming, stand-up paddleboarding (SUP), watching outrigger teams practice, or enjoying a lazy beach day, but it can get crowded on weekends. Snorkeling can be good north of the beach, and snorkeling, SUP, and kayaking equipment can be rented nearby. There's lots of grass and shade. **Amenities:** food and drink; showers; toilets; water sports. **Best for:** snorkeling; swimming. ⊠ *75-5660 Palani Rd., at Alii Dr., Kailua-Kona* ☞ *Free.*

Laaloa (Magic Sands) Beach Park (*White Sands Beach*)

BEACH | Towering coconut trees provide some shade and lend a touch of tropical beauty to this pretty little beach park, which may well be the Big Island's most intriguing stretch of sand. A migratory beach of sorts, it can disappear when strong surf washes away the small white-sand parcel (hence the name "Magic Sands"). Then suddenly, all the sand can reappear within days. You'll know you've found it when you see the body and board surfers. It's often quite crowded, no matter what time of year. Large shore breaks here can be dangerous, so always listen to lifeguard instruction. **Amenities**: lifeguards; parking (no fee); showers; toilets. **Best for:** sunset; surfing. ⊠ *77-6470 Alii Dr., Kailua-Kona* ✛ *4½ miles south of Kailua-Kona* ☎ *808/961–8311* ☞ *Free.*

Old Kona Airport State Recreation Area

BEACH | FAMILY | Hugging the long shoreline adjacent to the runway that served

Kona's airport until 1970, this beach is flat, generally clean, and speckled with black rocks and coral bits. Mostly calm waters make for good snorkeling, and a few accessible small coves of white sand offer safe water entry and tide pools for children. Shady areas are good for picnics or admiring the Kona skyline, complete with a whale (in season) and a cruise ship or two. A well-tended community garden, jogging trail, and dog park opposite the runway are worth checking out. Just north, an offshore surf break known as Old A's is popular with local surfers. It's usually not crowded, but this area can get busy on weekends. **Amenities:** parking (no fee); showers; toilets. **Best for:** sunset; walking. ⊠ *Kailua-Kona* ✢ *North end of Kuakini Hwy.* ☎ *808/961–8561* ⌦ *Free.*

Restaurants

Bianellis Kona

$ | **ITALIAN** | **FAMILY** | With indoor and outdoor seating, this easygoing Italian restaurant in a Keauhou shopping center serves gourmet pizzas and a tasty selection of pasta dishes, calzones, sandwiches, and salads. Everything is made from scratch, and they even have dairy-free cheese and gluten-free options. **Known for:** excellent wine selection; online ordering available; take-and-bake pizzas. ⑤ *Average main: $14* ⊠ *Keauhou Shopping Center, 78-6831 Alii Dr., Kailua-Kona* ☎ *808/322–0377* ⊕ *www.bianellis.com.*

Big Island Grill

$ | **HAWAIIAN** | **FAMILY** | This beloved local-style restaurant serves huge portions of pork chops, diet-busting *loco moco* (meat, rice, and eggs smothered in gravy), fresh poke, and an assortment of fish specialties at very reasonable prices. Get there early, as they are open only until 2 pm. **Known for:** authentic local vibe; succulent Kalbi short ribs; large saimin portions. ⑤ *Average main: $15* ⊠ *75-5702 Kuakini Hwy., Kailua-Kona* ☎ *808/326–1153* ⊙ *Closed Sun. and Mon. No dinner.*

★ Big Kahuna Beach Grill

$ | **AMERICAN** | **FAMILY** | From its upstairs, open-air dining room decorated with kitschy surfer chic, this restaurant invites customers to enjoy views of the pier and a bustling corner of Alii Drive. Fortunately, an excellent, extensive menu makes it well worth a stop; fresh fish plates including fish tacos are a sure bet. **Known for:** clam chowder; five types of eggs Benedict; full bar menu of island-style cocktails. ⑤ *Average main: $15* ⊠ *75-5663 Palani Rd., Kailua-Kona* ☎ *808/731–5055* ⊕ *bigkahunabeachgrill.com.*

Don's Mai Tai Bar & Restaurant at Royal Kona Resort

$$ | **HAWAIIAN** | The largest open-air tiki bar in Kona has the absolute best view of Kailua Bay in town. This is the perfect spot to relax with a *pupu* (appetizer) such as the coconut-crusted shrimp or "Hapa" poke bowl, or to dig into something more substantial like the kiawe wood–smoked prime rib. **Known for:** 10 types of mai tais; worthy desserts and dessert coffees; Hawaiian performers weekly. ⑤ *Average main: $25* ⊠ *Royal Kona Resort, 75-5852 Alii Dr., Kailua-Kona* ☎ *808/329–3111* ⊕ *www.royalkona.com.*

The Fish Hopper

$$ | **SEAFOOD** | **FAMILY** | In the heart of Historic Kailua Village, the open-air Hawaii location of the popular Monterey, California restaurant offers an expansive menu for breakfast, lunch, and dinner in a vintage building with a bayfront view. Inventive fresh-fish specials as well as simple fish-and-chips are among the local favorites. **Known for:** award-winning clam chowder; good lunch menu; signature Volcano flaming cocktail. ⑤ *Average main: $24* ⊠ *75-5683 Alii Dr., Kailua-Kona* ☎ *808/326–2002* ⊕ *www.fishhopperkona.com.*

★ Foster's Kitchen

$$ | **AMERICAN** | Ocean breezes flow through this open-air restaurant on Alii Drive, known for a quality menu infused with Cajun and island influences. Almost

The Plate Lunch Tradition

To experience island history firsthand, take a seat at one of Hawaii's popular "plate lunch" eateries and order a segmented paper plate piled with rice, macaroni salad, and maybe some "pig and poi" or *lomi lomi* salmon. On the sugar plantations, Native Hawaiians and immigrant workers from many different countries ate together in the fields, sharing food from their *kau kau* kits, the utilitarian version of the Japanese bento lunch box. From this melting pot came the vibrant language of pidgin and its equivalent in food: the plate lunch.

At beach parks and events, you might see a few tiny kitchens-on-wheels, another excellent venue for sampling plate lunch. These food trucks are descendants of the lunch wagons that began selling meals to plantation workers in the 1930s. Try the deep-fried chicken *katsu* (rolled in Japanese panko bread crumbs and spices). The marinated beef teriyaki is another good choice, as is miso butterfish. The noodle soup, saimin, with its Japanese fish stock and Chinese red-tinted barbecue pork, is a distinctly local medley. Koreans have contributed spicy barbecue *kalbi* ribs, often served with chili-laden kimchi. Portuguese bean soup and tangy Filipino adobo stew are also favorites. The most popular Hawaiian contribution to the plate lunch is the *laulau*, a mix of meat or fish and young taro leaves, wrapped in more taro and ti leaves, and steamed.

all dishes are made to order and feature non-GMO, hormone-free, or USDA-certified organic ingredients. **Known for:** scratch-made food and cocktails; live entertainment nightly; great happy hour prices. ⑤ *Average main: $23* ⊠ *75-5805 Alii Dr., Kailua-Kona* ☎ *808/326–1600* ⊕ *www.fosterskitchen.com.*

★ Harbor House

$ | **AMERICAN** | On the docks at Kona's sleepy harbor, this open-air restaurant is an authentic place to grab a beer and a bite after a long day of fishing, beach-going, or diving. The venue is nothing fancy, but it's one of the best spots in Kona for fresh-fish sandwiches, a variety of fried fish-and-chip combos, and even burgers. **Known for:** chilled schooners of Kona Brewing Co. lager; fresh fish right off the incoming boats; fun waterfront dining on the way to or from the airport. ⑤ *Average main: $16* ⊠ *Honokohau Harbor, 74-425 Kealakehe Pkwy., Suite 4, Kailua-Kona* ☎ *808/326–4166* ⊕ *harborhouserestaurantkona.com.*

★ Hayashi's You Make the Roll

$ | **JAPANESE** | Tiny and locally owned, this sushi shack in the heart of town has gained an incredible following and specializes in "reverse" (rice on the outside, nori on the inside) rolls, filled with three or four ingredients of your choice. It's super popular and gets crazy crowded, so expect a long wait—but it's worth it. (Wait times can exceed an hour or more, but they let you know how long before you order.) The restaurant also makes fantastic party platters that you can order in advance. **Known for:** affordable take-out sushi rolls; small, low-key location; local favorite. ⑤ *Average main: $10* ⊠ *75-5725 Alii Dr., Suite D101, Kailua-Kona* ☎ *808/326–1322* ⊙ *Closed Sun. No dinner.*

Huggo's

$$$ | **HAWAIIAN** | A Kona icon since 1969, family-owned Huggo's is one of the few restaurants in town with prices and atmosphere comparable to the splurge

restaurants at the Kohala Coast resorts. Dinner offerings sometimes fall short, considering the prices, but the *pupus* (appetizers) and small plates are usually a good bet. **Known for:** fine dining at the water's edge; next-door bar with toes-in-the sand dining; nightlife hot spot. [$] *Average main: $40* ⊠ *75-5828 Kahakai Rd., off Alii Dr., Kailua-Kona* ☎ *808/329–1493* ⊕ *www.huggos.com.*

Humpy's Big Island Alehouse

$ | AMERICAN | This place is usually packed for a reason: the more than 36 craft brews on tap, plus an upstairs and downstairs bar with plenty of outdoor seating. Take in the oceanfront view with amazing sunsets while chowing down on stone-baked pizza, fresh salads, fish-and-chips, fish tacos, burgers, stone-baked subs, and lots of appetizers. **Known for:** largest selection of craft beer on the island; great steamed clams; good nightlife (for Kona). [$] *Average main: $18* ⊠ *Coconut Grove Marketplace, 75-5815 Alii Dr., Kailua-Kona* ☎ *808/324–2337* ⊕ *humpys-kona.com.*

Island Lava Java

$$ | AMERICAN | With cocktail bars both upstairs and downstairs, oceanfront Island Lava Java serves eggs Benedict for breakfast; fresh fish tacos for lunch; and pasta, Big Island beef, and seafood for dinner, plus towering, fresh bistro salads. There are also pizzas, sandwiches, and plenty of choices for both vegetarians and meat eaters. **Known for:** large portions using mostly local organic ingredients; bar with extensive cocktail menu; 100% Kona coffee. [$] *Average main: $20* ⊠ *Coconut Grove Marketplace, 75-5801 Alii Dr., Kailua-Kona* ☎ *808/327–2161* ⊕ *www.islandlavajava.com.*

Jackie Rey's Ohana Grill

$$$ | AMERICAN | FAMILY | The brightly decorated, open-air restaurant located in a nondescript office center, is a favorite lunch and dinner destination for visitors and residents, thanks to generous portions and a nice variety of chef's specials, steaks, and seafood dishes. Try the Mochiko-crusted fresh catch with Molokai sweet potatoes, vegetables, ginger lime beurre blanc along with Namasu relish. **Known for:** strong local following; great-value lunch menu; $5 happy hour. [$] *Average main: $36* ⊠ *Pottery Terrace, 75-5995 Kuakini Hwy., Kailua-Kona* ☎ *808/327–0209* ⊕ *www.jackiereys.com.*

Kalikala Cuisine

$ | AMERICAN | They specialize in breakfast and great views. This covered, outdoor establishment sits directly across from the Kailua seawall, so even if you have to wait, the view alone is worth it. **Known for:** tropical ambience; long waits; food cooked to order. [$] *Average main: $17* ⊠ *75-5695 Alii Dr., Kailua-Kona* ☎ *808/327–5254.*

Kenichi Pacific

$$$ | JAPANESE | With black lacquer tables and lipstick-red banquettes, Kenichi offers a more sophisticated dining atmosphere than normally found in Kona shopping centers. This is the place residents go when they feel like splurging on top-notch sushi, sashimi, steak, and Asian-fusion cuisine. **Known for:** upscale dining at far less than resort prices; happy hour discounts on sushi; cheaper lounge menu of small plates. [$] *Average main: $36* ⊠ *Keauhou Shopping Center, 78-6831 Alii Dr., Suite D-125, Kailua-Kona* ☎ *808/322–6400* ⊕ *www.kenichipacific.com* ⊗ *Closed Mon. No lunch.*

★ Kona Brewing Co.

$ | AMERICAN | FAMILY | An ultrapopular destination with an outdoor patio, Kona Brewing offers an excellent, varied menu, including famous brews; pulled-pork quesadillas; gourmet pizzas; and a killer spinach salad with Gorgonzola cheese, strawberries, and macadamia nuts. The sampler tray, a good value, offers four of the 10 available microbrews. **Known for:** Longboard Lager and other famous brews made on-site; live music; growlers of to-go beer from taps. [$] *Average main: $16* ⊠ *74-5612 Pawai Pl., Kailua-Kona*

✛ Off Kaiwi St. at end of Pawai Pl.
☎ 808/329–2739 ⊕ www.konabrewingco.
com.

★ Kona Inn Restaurant

$$ | AMERICAN | This open-air restaurant in a vintage 1920s-era building at the historical Kona Inn Shopping Village offers a beautiful oceanfront setting on Kailua Bay. The view and the bar are Kona signature icons, and it's a great place when you first land in Kona to have a mai tai along with some appetizers or to enjoy a calamari sandwich, clam chowder, or salad at lunch. **Known for:** sunset-watching spot; nice bar and lounge at all times; inconsistent food at dinner. Ⓢ *Average main: $25* ✉ *Kona Inn Shopping Village, 75-5744 Alii Dr., Kailua-Kona* ☎ *808/329–4455* ⊕ *konainnrestaurant.com.*

Kona Taeng on Thai

$ | THAI | A hidden gem, the open-air eatery is on the second floor of an oceanfront shopping center. Patrons can watch the scene below on bustling Alii Drive while enjoying freshly prepared Thai specialties, including plenty of vegetarian options and delicious Thai iced tea. **Known for:** uncrowded, spacious layout; lunch specials; large portions. Ⓢ *Average main: $13* ✉ *Kona Inn Shopping Center, 75-5744 Alii Dr., #208, 2nd fl., Kailua-Kona* ☎ *808/329–1994.*

La Bourgogne

$$$$ | FRENCH | A nondescript office building, just to the south of town, is home to this quiet, country-style bistro with dark wood walls and private booths. This popular, longtime local favorite offers such classics as escargots, frogs legs, filet mignon with a Cabernet Sauvignon sauce, and slow-roasted lavender rabbit with a Chardonnay sauce. **Known for:** reservations needed well ahead of time; great cassoulet; good wines by the glass. Ⓢ *Average main: $125* ✉ *77-6400 Nalani St., Kailua-Kona* ☎ *808/329–6711* ⊕ *labourgognehawaii.com* ☽ *Closed Sun. and Mon. No lunch.*

Magics Beach Grill

$$$ | HAWAIIAN | In a vintage building dating from 1965, Magics offers an exhilarating oceanfront location overlooking the famous Disappearing Sands Beach, also known as Magic Sands. From fried *ulu* (breadfruit) wedges in umami truffle oil aioli to firecracker fish tacos and mushroom pasta, the eclectic menu features intriguing choices using locally sourced ingredients with contemporary island flair. **Known for:** sunset beach views; ube margarita; great happy hour 2–4 pm. Ⓢ *Average main: $33* ✉ *77-6452 Alii Dr., Kailua-Kona* ☎ *808/662–4427* ⊕ *magicsbeachgrill.com.*

Pancho and Lefty's Cantina & Restaurante

$ | MEXICAN | Across the street from the Kona Inn Shopping Village, in Kailua Village, this upstairs cantina is a nice perch for enjoying nachos and margaritas (try the hibiscus margarita) on a lazy afternoon, or for watching the passersby on Alii Drive. Try the *molcajete*—a type of bowl—loaded with marinated chicken, steak, and shrimp and a sauce crafted of chiles and topped with jack cheese. **Known for:** popular happy hour hangout; better for snacks than a full meal; homemade salsa. Ⓢ *Average main: $15* ✉ *75-5725 Ali'i Dr., Kailua-Kona* ☎ *808/326–2171* ⊕ *panchoandleftyskona.com.*

Papa Kona Restaurant & Bar

$ | AMERICAN | Simply unbeatable proximity to the ocean is part of the draw of this lively restaurant in the heart of town: you just can't get any closer to the water without getting wet—and sometimes you do! It's popular to come here for sunset for drinks and appetizers such as the poke stack or the avocado fries. **Known for:** specialty craft cocktails; large portions; great spot for brunch. Ⓢ *Average main: $18* ✉ *The Waterfront Row, 75-5770 Alii Dr., 1st floor, Kailua-Kona* ☎ *808/300–0044* ⊕ *papakonarestaurant. com.*

★ Quinn's Almost by the Sea

$ | **AMERICAN** | **FAMILY** | With the bar in the front and the dining patio in the back, Quinn's may seem like a bit of a dive at first glance, but this venerable Kona classic serves the best darn cheeseburger and fries in town. Make your already-large burger a "monster" for an additional $4.50. **Known for:** strong cocktails; comfort food like meatballs; old Kona vibe. ⑤ *Average main: $15* ⊠ *75-5655 Palani Rd., Kailua-Kona* ☎ *808/329–3822* ⊕ *www.quinnsalmostbythesea.com* ⊙ *Closed Wed.*

Sunset Kai Lanai

$$ | **HAWAIIAN** | **FAMILY** | Perched above a shopping center with sweeping panoramic views, this open-air restaurant has lots to offer besides spectacular views from every table in the house. The slow-roasted rack of ribs is the star of the show, and the locally sourced fish-and-chips is a close second. Be sure to try the famous Key lime pie or Mighty Dozen doughnut holes with some 100% Kona coffee. **Known for:** limited parking for such a popular place; excellent happy hour pricing; the best views in town. ⑤ *Average main: $22* ⊠ *Keauhou Shopping Center, 78-6831 Alii Dr., Suite 1000, Kailua-Kona* ☎ *808/333–3434* ⊙ *Closed Mon.*

Sushi Cocoro & Udon Noodle

$ | **JAPANESE** | A tiny hidden gem in the heart of downtown, this authentic little place offers excellent sushi at affordable prices. The Japanese-born chefs serve such offerings as six-piece rolls for under $6. **Known for:** Red Hot Lava roll; inexpensive sushi combos for two; BYOB welcome. ⑤ *Average main: $12* ⊠ *75-5699 Alii Dr., Kailua-Kona* ☎ *808/331–0601.*

Thai Rin

$ | **THAI** | **FAMILY** | Everything is cooked to order at this low-key oceanfront restaurant with an excellent selection of Thai food at decent prices. The menu brims with choices, including five curries, a green-papaya salad, and deep-fried fish. **Known for:** great views with both indoor and outdoor seating; appetizer platters for sharing; convenient to village shops. ⑤ *Average main: $18* ⊠ *75-5799 Alii Dr., Kailua-Kona* ☎ *808/329–2929* ⊕ *www.thairin.com* ⊙ *Takeout only on Tues.*

TK Noodle House

$ | **ASIAN FUSION** | **FAMILY** | Former resort chef TK Keosavang serves inventive Asian fusion cuisine with the emphasis on noodles. Generous portions are beautifully plated, like the crispy pork belly sauté with Chinese greens and garlic sauce, and noodle soups and abundant salads don't disappoint. **Known for:** ample parking; seafood yentafo soup; lunch specials. ⑤ *Average main: $18* ⊠ *75 Hanama Pl., Kailua-Kona* ⊹ *Near Big Island Grill* ☎ *808/327–0070* ⊕ *www.cheftk.com.*

★ Umekes Fish Market Bar & Grill

$ | **HAWAIIAN** | **FAMILY** | Locals flock to this downtown Kailua-Kona restaurant for good reason: the poke is the most *onolicious* (super delicious) in town, and the many other seafood, pork, and beef offerings are just as stellar. Poke does not get more authentic than this, and you can get it by the bowl or the pound. **Known for:** daily specials using the freshest fish; locally sourced ingredients; authentic Kona experience. ⑤ *Average main: $18* ⊠ *74-5599 Pawai Pl., Kailua-Kona* ☎ *808/238–0571* ⊕ *umekesrestaurants.com.*

The View Restaurant Bar & Grill

$ | **AMERICAN** | Tucked away at the Kona Country Club at the far end of Alii Drive, this hideaway is the place to go for happy hour, appetizers, and ocean breezes. Oh, and did we mention the view? **Known for:** good bar menu; old Kona–style building; wonderful view. ⑤ *Average main: $16* ⊠ *78-7000 Alii Dr., Kailua-Kona* ☎ *808/731–5033* ⊙ *No dinner.*

☕ Coffee and Quick Bites

★ Da Poke Shack

$$ | **HAWAIIAN** | This tiny place is the real deal. Yes, your tab might be a bit high,

but it will be worth it because authentic, always-fresh poke doesn't get better than this. **Known for:** freshly caught fish; local ingredients; Spicy Garlic Sesame bowl. $ *Average main: $20* ✉ *76-6246 Ali'i Drive, Suite 101, Kailua-Kona* ☎ *808/329–7653* ⊕ *dapokeshack.com.*

Kai Eats & Drinks

$ | **AMERICAN** | **FAMILY** | With its ocean-front location close enough for diners to feel the salt spray, Kai's is a fun, casual dining experience. Just pick a table, then order and pay online; they bring your meal to your table. In the morning, you can fill your paper coffee cup with limitless amounts of coffee at the self-serve station. **Known for:** easy online ordering or take-out options; no waiting; great breakfast spot. $ *Average main: $15* ✉ *75-5776 Alii Drive, Kailua-Kona* ☎ *808/900–3328 text only* ⊕ *kaieatsanddrinks.com.*

Kanaka Kava

$ | **HAWAIIAN** | This is a popular local hangout, and not just because the kava drink makes you mellow. The Hawaiian proprietors, who have a certified organic farm in Hamakua, also serve traditional Hawaiian food, including fresh poke, bowls of healthy organic greens, *opihi* (limpets), and traditional Hawaiian *laulau* (pork or chicken wrapped in taro leaves and steamed). **Known for:** kava served in coconut cups; pulled kalua pork; squid luau (the leaf from a taro plant). $ *Average main: $12* ✉ *Coconut Grove Marketplace, 75-5803 Alii Dr., Space B6, Kailua-Kona* ☎ *808/327–1660* ⊕ *www.kanakakava.bar/bar-1.*

Kona Coffee & Tea

$ | **CAFÉ** | All of this family-owned coffee company's businesses—growing, roasting, brewing, and serving their authentic Kona coffee—operate within a 10-mile radius of the farm. At their homey little café, they offer a staggering array of coffee drinks, along with upscale deli items such as lox and a veggie focaccia sandwich; breakfast goodies include acai bowls. **Known for:** small-batch, estate-grown coffee; Kona coffee tastings every Wednesday; Hawaiian-made food treats for sale. $ *Average main: $8* ✉ *Kona Coast Shopping Center, 74-5588 Palani Rd., Kailua-Kona* ☎ *808/329–6577* ⊕ *www.konacoffeeandtea.com.*

Kona Crust

$ | **PIZZA** | It's quite simply the best New York–style pizza in Kona. At this small, no-frills shop, the proprietors take great care to obtain the highest-quality ingredients for their pizzas, including large gourmet olives, banana peppers, and even meats sourced directly from Fontanini in New York. **Known for:** authentically sourced ingredients; homemade drizzles; pizza by the slice. $ *Average main: $5* ✉ *74-5586 Palani Rd., Kailua-Kona* ☎ *808/731–7553* ⊕ *konacrust.com.*

Los Habaneros

$ | **MEXICAN** | **FAMILY** | Hidden in the corner of Keauhou Shopping Center adjacent to the movie theater, Los Habaneros serves up fast, decent Mexican food for good prices. Favorites are usually combos, which can be anything from enchilada plates to chiles rellenos. **Known for:** before- or after-beach stop; margaritas, tequila shots, and Mexican beer; homemade sopas (soups). $ *Average main: $9* ✉ *Keauhou Shopping Center, 78-631 Alii Dr., Kailua-Kona* ☎ *808/324–4688* ⊕ *haberoskona.com* ⊘ *Closed Sun.*

★ Poi Dog Deli

$ | **AMERICAN** | With vintage memorabilia and a bluesy soundtrack as a background, this cool deli in a tiny strip mall has a lot more to offer than the average sandwich shop. Yes, there are gourmet sandwiches, salads, and wraps, but Poi Dog's wide-ranging menu extends to an impressive list of wines, craft beers, ales, and pilsners from all over the world. **Known for:** salads featuring house-made Cajun croutons and house dressings; house-made soups; Ranch House Reuben. $ *Average main: $10* ✉ *75-1022 Henry St., Kailua-Kona* ✛ *Across from*

Walmart ☎ 808/329–2917 ⊕ poidogdeli. com.

Sack N Save Kona

$ | **HAWAIIAN** | Locals know the seafood counter at Sack N Save Kona is the place to get delicious, affordable poke. Sample and then choose from a variety of freshly made poke salad selections. **Known for:** grocery store with convenient hours; no waiting; variety of freshly caught and previously frozen selections. ⑤ *Average main: $8* ⊠ *Lanihau Center, 75-5595 Palani Rd, Kailua-Kona* ☎ *808/326–2729* ⊕ *foodland.com.*

Tea-licious Cafe

$ | **CAFÉ** | Known for home-baked pastries, gourmet loose-leaf teas, and high-end coffees, this sweet, cozy spot is a lovely destination not far from the beach. Try the brie, apple, and fig jam combo on freshly baked baguette or one of the signature salads. **Known for:** European-style specialties; Italian sodas; flaky Portuguese tart. ⑤ *Average main: $7* ⊠ *75-159 Lunapule Rd., Kailua-Kona* ☎ *808/209–8282* ⊕ *tealiciouskona.com.*

Ultimate Burger

$ | **BURGER** | **FAMILY** | Located in the Crossroads shopping complex in Kailua-Kona, this excellent burger joint may look like a chain, but it's an independent, locally owned and operated eatery that serves 100% organic, grass-fed Big Island beef. Be sure to order a side of seasoned Big Daddy fries served with homemade aioli dipping sauce. **Known for:** organic, hormone-free ingredients; supporting local farmers and ranchers; locally made buns. ⑤ *Average main: $8* ⊠ *Kona Commons Shopping Center, 74-5450 Makala Blvd., Kailua-Kona* ☎ *808/329–2326* ⊕ *www. ultimateburger.net.*

Hotels

Aston Kona by the Sea

$$$$ | **APARTMENT** | **FAMILY** | Complete modern kitchens, tiled lanai, and washer-dryer units are found in every suite of this comfortable oceanfront condo complex with a welcoming entry lobby and a reception area that feels like a hotel. **Pros:** lobby and activities desk; near delis and convenience stores; ocean-fed saltwater pool next to the property. **Cons:** no beach access (2 miles away); not walking distance to Kailua Village; individually owned units, so prices may vary. ⑤ *Rooms from: $678* ⊠ *75-6106 Alii Dr., Kailua-Kona* ☎ *808/327–2300, 877/997–6667* ⊕ *www. astonhotels.com* ⌁ *86 units* ⍾ *No Meals.*

Castle Kona Bali Kai

$$$ | **APARTMENT** | **FAMILY** | These slightly older condominium units, spread out among three low-rises on the ocean side of Alii Drive, are situated at Kona's most popular surfing spot, Banyans, and also just a couple of minutes' drive from Kailua Village and within walking distance of popular Laaloa (Magic Sands) Beach Park. **Pros:** convenience mart and beach-gear rental nearby; choice of different views among the units; views of surfers on the water. **Cons:** mountain-view rooms close to noisy street; oceanfront rooms don't have a/c; older-looking concrete buildings. ⑤ *Rooms from: $319* ⊠ *76-6246 Alii Dr., Kailua-Kona* ☎ *808/329–9381, 800/535–0085* ⊕ *www.castleresorts.com* ⌁ *64 units* ⍾ *No Meals.*

Courtyard by Marriott King Kamehameha's Kona Beach Hotel

$$$$ | **HOTEL** | **FAMILY** | Right on the beach in the heart of Historic Kailua Village, this landmark hotel built in 1975 offers good vibrations and authentic local hospitality—all for less than the price of a Kohala Coast resort. **Pros:** easy access to shops and restaurants; deep historical ambience includes Hawaiian artifacts; on-site restaurant and poolside bar. **Cons:** most rooms have partial ocean views; some rooms face the parking lot; often sold out. ⑤ *Rooms from: $435* ⊠ *75-5660 Palani Rd., Kailua-Kona* ☎ *808/329–2911* ⊕ *marriott.com* ⌁ *452 rooms* ⍾ *No Meals.*

Kona Condo Comforts

Visitors choosing to stay in a condo rather than a resort or hotel will find a range of useful accommodations in the area.

Safeway Kona at the brand-new Niumalu Marketplace (✉ 75-971 Henry St., Kailua-Kona ☎ 808/339–9155) offers an excellent inventory of groceries and produce, although prices can be steep. Delivery and curbside pickup are available.

Longs Drugs at Lanihau Center (✉ 75-5595 Palani Rd., Kailua-Kona ☎ 808/329–1632) is the place to stock up on personal care items, rubber slippers, a snorkel, and sunscreen. They also have a good selection of liquor at competitive prices.

For pizza, **Kona Crust** in the Kona Coast Shopping Center (✉ 74-5586 Palani Rd., Kailua Kona ☎ 808/731–7553) is the best bet; order online and pick up. Otherwise, for delivery, try **Domino's** (☎ 808/329–9500).

Hale Hualalai Bed and Breakfast

$ | B&B/INN | In cool, upcountry Holualoa, Hale Hualalai offers two exceptionally large suites with exposed beams, whirlpool tubs, and private lanai, but perhaps most memorable are the breakfasts ($15 per person)—owner Ricky Brewster was a chef at Four Seasons Hualalai Resort's Beach Tree restaurant. **Pros:** sunset views; tastefully decorated house; rental SUVs available. **Cons:** not for kids; not a central location; frequently booked. ⓢ Rooms from: $175 ✉ 74-4968 Mamalahoa Hwy., Holualoa ☎ 808/464–7074 ⊕ www.hale-hualalai.com ⇨ 2 suites ⦿ No Meals.

Holiday Inn Express and Suites Kailua-Kona, an IHG Hotel

$$ | HOTEL | FAMILY | While the location feels more parking lot than island paradise, this practical and comfortable hotel (one of Kona's newest) isn't far from the ocean and still offers lots of pluses, from nicely appointed rooms to a fitness center. **Pros:** convenient downtown location; 24-hour business center; free high-speed Wi-Fi. **Cons:** most rooms don't have views; no landscaping; parking lot views on lower level. ⓢ Rooms from: $271 ✉ 75-146 Sarona Rd., Kailua-Kona

☎ 808/329–2599 ⊕ www.ihg.com ⇨ 75 rooms ⦿ Free Breakfast.

★ Holualoa Inn

$$$$ | B&B/INN | Six spacious rooms and suites—plus two vintage one-bedroom cottages perfect for honeymooners—are available at this 30-acre coffee-country estate, a few miles above Kailua Bay in the heart of the artists' village of Holualoa. **Pros:** walking distance from art galleries and cafés; everything necessary for hosting a wedding or event; luxurious, Zen-like vibe. **Cons:** not kid-friendly; unheated swimming pool; books up far in advance. ⓢ Rooms from: $635 ✉ 76-5932 Mamalahoa Hwy., Holualoa ☎ 808/324–1121, 800/392–1812 ⊕ www.holualoainn. com ⇨ 8 units ⦿ Free Breakfast.

Holua Resort at Mauna Loa Village

$$$$ | RESORT | FAMILY | Tucked away by Keauhou Bay amid a plethora of coconut trees, this well-maintained enclave of blue-roofed villas offers lots of amenities, including a 27-court tennis and pickleball center, swimming pools, hot tubs, a fitness center, waterfalls, and covered parking. **Pros:** manicured gardens; upscale feeling; walking distance to major resort restaurants. **Cons:** no beach; partial ocean views; no on-site restaurant. ⓢ Rooms from: $499 ✉ 78-7190 Kaleiopapa St., Kailua-Kona ☎ 808/324–1550 ⊕ www. shellhospitality.com ⇨ 73 units ⦿ No Meals.

Kanaloa at Kona by Outrigger

$$$ | **APARTMENT** | **FAMILY** | The 16-acre grounds provide a peaceful and verdant background for this low-rise condominium complex bordering the Keauhou-Kona Country Club and within a five-minute drive of the nearest beaches, Kahaluu and Laaloa (Magic Sands). **Pros:** walking distance from Keauhou Bay; three pools with hot tubs; shopping center and restaurants nearby. **Cons:** no elevators; no front desk; remote customer support; air-conditioning available only by paying a daily fee. ⑤ Rooms from: $329 ✉ 78-261 Manukai St., Kailua-Kona ☎ 808/322–7222, 800/688–7444 ⊕ www.outrigger. com ⇨ 63 units ⦿ No Meals.

Kona Coast Resort

$$$$ | **RESORT** | **FAMILY** | Just below Keauhou Shopping Center, this timeshare resort offers furnished condos on 21 acres with pleasant ocean views and a host of on-site amenities, including two swimming pools, dry sauna, beach volleyball, a cocktail bar, barbecue grills, a hot tub, tennis courts, a fitness center, hula classes, equipment rentals, and children's activities. **Pros:** all rooms updated in 2018; good amenities for kids; away from the bustle of downtown Kailua-Kona. **Cons:** some units have parking lot views; not on the beach; time-share salespeople. ⑤ Rooms from: $499 ✉ 78-6842 Alii Dr., Keauhou ☎ 808/324–1721 ⊕ extraholidays.com ⇨ 268 units ⦿ No Meals.

★ Kona Tiki Hotel

$$$ | **HOTEL** | This small, oceanfront, walk-up hotel about a mile south of downtown Kailua Village, with modest, pleasantly decorated rooms on the ocean, is probably the best deal in town. **Pros:** friendly staff; oceanfront lanai on every room; free parking. **Cons:** no A/C; no TV in rooms; parking can be a challenge.

⑤ Rooms from: $299 ✉ 75-5968 Alii Dr., Kailua-Kona ☎ 808/329–1425 ⊕ www. konatikihotel.com ⇨ 16 rooms ⦿ No Meals.

Outrigger Kona Resort and Spa at Keauhou Bay

$$$ | **RESORT** | **FAMILY** | What the hotel's concrete architecture lacks in intimacy, it makes up for with its beautifully manicured grounds, historical sense of place, stylish interiors, and stunning location on Keauhou Bay. Many rooms have great views of the bay and feel like they're right on the water, and each is decorated in a modern Polynesian style. **Pros:** cool pool that's great for kids; manta rays on view nightly; resort style at lower price. **Cons:** no beach; long walk from parking area; Wi-Fi can be spotty. ⑤ Rooms from: $324 ✉ 78-128 Ehukai St., Keauhou ☎ 808/930–4900 ⊕ outrigger.com ⇨ 484 rooms ⦿ No Meals.

Pacific 19 Kona

$$$ | **HOTEL** | Stocked with a plethora of adventure gear (for sale) such as snorkels, coolers, and sunscreen along with drinks and snacks in each room's "macro" bar, Kona's newest hip boutique hotel caters to the younger, more adventurous traveler. **Pros:** air-conditioning; bikes, yoga, beach chairs included; live music Fri. and Sat.. **Cons:** no TVs; no free parking; only partial ocean views. ⑤ Rooms from: $327 ✉ 75-5646 Palani Rd, Kailua-Kona ☎ 808/334–8050 ⊕ pacific19.com ⇨ 122 rooms ⦿ No Meals.

Royal Kona Resort

$$$ | **HOTEL** | **FAMILY** | This iconic Kona hotel is a great option: the location is central; the bar, lounge, pool, and restaurant are right on the water; and the rooms feature comfortable, contemporary Hawaiian decor with Polynesian accents. **Pros:** convenient location by shops and restaurants; waterfront pool; restaurant and bar with great views. **Cons:** can be crowded; $25 per day parking fee; grounds have dated feel. ⑤ Rooms from: $292 ✉ 75-5852 Alii Dr., Kailua-Kona

☏ *808/329–3111, 800/774–5662* ⊕ *www. royalkona.com* ⇥ *430 rooms* ❍❙ *No Meals.*

Nightlife

BARS

The Mask-Querade Bar

BARS | Hidden away in an unassuming strip mall, this friendly establishment is one of the Big Island's most venerable gay bars. Drag shows, darts, hot DJs, live music, karaoke, drink specials, fiestas, and Sunday barbecues are included in the roster of weekly events. ⊠ *Kopiko Plaza, 75-5660 Kopiko St., Kailua-Kona* ⊹ *Below Longs Drugs* ☏ *808/329–8558* ⊕ *www.themask-queradebar.com.*

Oceans Sports Bar and Grill

BARS | A popular gathering place, this sports bar in the back of the Coconut Grove Marketplace has a pool table and an outdoor patio, along with dozens of TVs screening the big game (whatever it happens to be that day). It really gets hopping on the weekends and for karaoke. There's good happy hour pricing and taco specials three days a week. ⊠ *Coconut Grove Marketplace, 75-5811 Alii Dr., Kailua-Kona* ☏ *808/327–9494* ⊕ *oceanssportsbar.com.*

★ Ola Brew Co

BREWPUBS | There's an enticing and creative array of beers, ales, ciders, and hard seltzers at this employee-owned brewing company. Ola Brew is committed to community investment and support of local farmers and merchants. Take a barstool at a picture window facing the main brewing operation and enjoy a fresh on-tap draft and an appetizer. There's plenty of outdoor seating as well. The taproom menu features reasonably priced tacos, salads, flatbreads, and poke bowls. Ask about their brewery tours. Popular local bands entertain on a regular basis. ⊠ *74-5598 Luhia St., Kailua-Kona* ☏ *808/339–3599* ⊕ *www.olabrewco.com* ⊙ *Kitchen closed Sun.*

CLUBS

★ Huggo's on the Rocks

COCKTAIL BARS | Nothing says "Kona casual" like this toes-in-the-sand establishment right on the water, next door to their famous flagship restaurant. Jazz, island, and classic-rock bands perform here nightly, and it's tradition to dance in the sand at least once before leaving the island. Try a signature tropical cocktail such as the Big Bamboocha Mai Tai crafted with Kuleana Hui Hui, Kuleana Nanea, and Lemon Hart 151 rums, plus appetizers such as poke bowls, *kalua* (earth oven–baked) pork nachos, or Kona fish tacos. Happy hour is one of the best in town as is the location. All beers—draft or bottles—are $6. Fish tacos and sliders are only $5. ⊠ *75-5824 Kahakai Rd., at Alii Dr., Kailua-Kona* ☏ *808/329–1493* ⊕ *huggosontherocks.com.*

Laverne's Sports Bar

DANCE CLUB | They call themselves Kona's "dive" bar, but we're not sure we agree. It's fun and kitschy, and locals know this is the best place to dance and drink in Kailua-Kona. With 32 TVs, there's not a sports event you will miss, either. Sometimes Hawaiian and island music headliners perform here, such as local recording artists Anuhea or Rebel Souljahz. Local musicians with followings also draw their "groupies." After 10, DJs spin tunes on the ocean-breeze-cooled dance floor, located upstairs with killer views of the water. The food is decent and includes full meals, such as cheeseburgers or fish-and-chips. They also serve breakfast. ⊠ *Coconut Grove Marketplace, 75-5819 Alii Dr., Kailua-Kona* ☏ *808/331–2633* ⊕ *laverneskona.com.*

Performing Arts

FESTIVALS

Aloha Shirt Festival

ARTS FESTIVALS | Hawaii's "wearable arts" are showcased at this unique festival held every September at the Outrigger Kona Resort and Spa. From vintage displays of all kinds, to fashion runway shows (tickets required) and pop-up vendors and exhibits, this fun event also includes a few paid workshops, a lei contest, live entertainment, and even a special festival rate for the Feast & Fire Luau. ⊠ *Keauhou* ⊕ *alohashirtfestival. com.*

★ King Kamehameha Day Celebration Parade

FESTIVALS | Each summer, on the Saturday nearest to King Kamehameha Day (June 11), at least 100 regal riders on horseback parade through Historic Kailua Village, showing off the colorful flora and aloha spirit of Hawaii. This spectacular free event is one of the highlights of summer. The traditional royal *pau* riders (women dressed in long skirts) include a queen and princesses representing the major Hawaiian Islands. A cultural festival with live music and a *houlaulea* (local fundraiser) always follow on the historic grounds of Hulihee Palace, Hawaii Island's only royal palace. ⊠ *Historic Kailua Village, Alii Dr., Kailua-Kona* ⊕ *www.konaparade.org* 🎫 *Free.*

★ Kona Brewers Festival

FESTIVALS | The lively festival held every March showcases island-based brewers and chefs at the popular BREW block in Kona's "Old" Industrial Area. A "trash" fashion show, a 10K fun run, live music, and community fundraisers are all part of the fun. The festival has raised more than $1.5 million for local causes. Save the date and get tickets online starting in January, as this event always sells out. ⊠ *BREW block, Pawai Pl., Kailua-Kona* ☎ *808/331–3033* ⊕ *www.konabrewersfestival.com* 🎫 *From $50.*

★ Kona Coffee Cultural Festival

FESTIVALS | Held over 10 days in early November, the longest-running food festival in Hawaii celebrates world-renowned Kona coffee. The highly anticipated Kona-side festival includes coffee contests, serious cupping (tasting) competitions, a lecture series, label contests, farm

tours, and a colorful community parade featuring the newly crowned Miss Kona Coffee. Throughout locations in town and at many Kona coffee plantations, you can meet growers and sample estate coffees. ⊠ *Kailua-Kona* ☎ *808/323–2006* ⊕ *www.konacoffeefest.com.*

LUAU AND POLYNESIAN REVUES

Feast & Fire Luau at the Outrigger Kona Resort and Spa

CULTURAL FESTIVALS | FAMILY | On the graceful grounds of the Outrigger Kona Resort and Spa, this popular luau (Mondays and Thursdays) takes you on a journey of song and dance, celebrating the culture and history of the Islands. The excellent buffet is a feast of local favorites, including *kalua* (earth oven–baked) pig, poi, ahi poke, chicken long rice, fish, and mango chutney. Generous mai tai refills are a plus, and a highlight is the dramatic fire-knife dance finale. ⊠ *Sheraton Kona Resort and Spa at Keauhou Bay, 78-128 Ehukai St., Kailua-Kona* ☎ *808/930–4900* ⊕ *outrigger.com* 🎫 *$200.*

★ Island Breeze Luau

CULTURAL FESTIVALS | With traditional dancing showcasing the interconnected Polynesian roots of Hawaii, Samoa, Tahiti, and New Zealand, the "We Are *Ohana* (family)" luau is not a hokey, tourist-trap event; these performers take their art seriously, and it shows. The historic oceanfront location—on the Courtyard King Kamehameha's Kona Beach Hotel's luau grounds and directly next to the king's former royal compound and Ahuena Heiau—adds to the authenticity of the event, which takes place daily except Monday and Saturday. The bounty of food includes *kalua* (earth oven–baked) pig. It's one of the best-priced luaus in town. The hotel validates parking. ⊠ *75-5660 Palani Rd., Kailua-Kona* ☎ *866/482–9775* ⊕ *www.islandbreezeluau.com* 🎫 *$169.*

Voyagers of the Pacific

CULTURAL FESTIVALS | The Royal Kona Resort lights its torches for a spectacular show and oceanfront buffet four times a week (Monday–Wednesday and Friday); this may just be the best luau deal in town. The entire Polynesian Triangle is represented through song and dance by seasoned professional performers who love sharing their dance traditions with visitors. Traditional luau fare is served along with succulent pork cooked in an authentic underground *imu* (oven), and an open bar offers mai tais and other tropical concoctions. An exciting Samoan fire-knife dancer caps off the show.

■ TIP→ **Book online for the best prices and early bird special.** ☒ *Royal Kona Resort, 75-5852 Alii Dr., Kailua-Kona* ☏ *808/329–3111* ⊕ *www.royalkona.com* ☒ *$169.*

Shopping

ARTS AND CRAFTS

★ Hula Lamps of Hawaii

CRAFTS | Located near Costco in the Kaloko Light Industrial complex, this one-of-a-kind shop features the bronze creations of artist Charles Moore. Inspired by the vintage hula-girl lamps of the 1930s, Moore creates art pieces (both dancing and nondancing) sought by visitors and residents alike. Mix and match with an array of hand-painted lampshades. Check out the specials online and in the shop. ☒ *73-5613 Olowalu St., Suite 2, Kailua-Kona* ♦ *Near Costco on upper road* ☏ *808/326–9583* ⊕ *www.hulalamps.com.*

★ Kimura Lauhala Shop

CRAFTS | Originally a general store built in 1914, this shop features handmade products crafted by local lauhala weavers, who use the leaves of the hala tree. Among the offerings are hats, baskets, containers, and mats, many of which are woven by the proprietors. Owner Alfreida Kimura-Fujita was born in the house behind the shop, and her daughter Renee is also an accomplished weaver. ☒ *77-996 Hualalai Rd., Holualoa* ☏ *808/324–0053* ⊙ *Closed Sun.–Tues.*

BOOKSTORES

Kona Stories

BOOKS | FAMILY | With more than 10,000 titles, this bookstore also sells Hawaiiana, children's toys, and whimsical gifts. Special events, such as readings, *keiki* (children's) storytime and book signings, are held weekly. ☒ *Keauhou Shopping Center, 78-6831 Alii Dr., Kailua-Kona* ♦ *Located near KTA in the shopping center* ☏ *808/324–0350* ⊕ *www.konastories.com.*

CLOTHING AND SHOES

Honolua Surf Company

CLOTHING | FAMILY | Surfer chic apparel, compliments of Roxy, Billabong, Hurley, and even Honolua's private label, is for sale here for both men and women. This is a great place to shop for a bikini or board shorts, or to pick up a cool, retro-design T-shirt or Hawaii-style embroidered hoodie. There are also plenty of beach accessories, including hats, sunglasses, and sunscreen, plus a section dedicated to kids. ☒ *Kona Inn Shopping Village, 75-5744 Alii Dr., Kailua-Kona* ☏ *808/329–1001* ⊕ *www.honoluasurf.com.*

Macy's

DEPARTMENT STORE | Located in a large shopping center by itself, this small but upscale Macy's features name brands and island-influenced clothing for men, women and children, plus designer handbags, shoes, jewelry, and housewares, along with top-quality luggage if you find yourself needing to take more than you have room for. It's the best place in Kona to find high-quality, name-brand aloha shirts. They always have great sales and are beloved by local residents. ☒ *Makalapua Center, 74-5475 Kamakaeha Av, Kailua-Kona* ☏ *808/329–6300* ⊕ *macys.com.*

Mermaids Swimwear

CLOTHING | Local residents know that Mermaids is one of the best places in Kona to buy fashion-forward ladies' swimwear, cover-ups, sandals, hats, sunglasses, and other stylish beach accessories. Although on the pricey side, the swimwear is mostly name brand and high quality. There's a beautiful selection of *pareau* (sarongs), which are island-style wraps in tropical prints and colors. The owner's husband, Tony, is a famous surfboard maker whose World Core surf shop is just around the corner. ⊠ *Kona Inn Shopping Village, 75-5744 Alii Dr., Kailua-Kona* ☎ *808/329–6677.*

Olivia Clare Boutique

CLOTHING | From tropical dresses to jumpers to swimsuits, this stylish boutique—a favorite of residents—carries a wide variety of Hawaiian-themed accessories and jewelry as well. Their selection of high-quality men's aloha shirts might be some of the best offered on the island. You can also find hats, purses, sunglasses, and a complete line of body and bath items. ⊠ *74-5606 Pawai Place, Kailua-Kona* ☎ *808/731–5022* ⊕ *oliviaclareboutique.com.*

FOOD AND WINE

★ Kona Wine Market

WINE/SPIRITS | Near Costco, this long-time local wine store carries both local and imported varietals (with more than 600 high-end wines), specialty liquors, Champagnes, 150 craft beers, gourmet foods, and cigars. There are even some accessories for home brewers. As a bonus, the market delivers wine and gift baskets to hotels and homes, and it offers complimentary tastings Fridays from 3 to 6. ⊠ *73-5613 Olowalu St., Kailua-Kona* ☎ *808/329–9400* ⊕ *www.konawinemarket.com.*

★ Mrs. Barry's Kona Cookies

FOOD | Since 1980, Mrs. Barry and her family have been making and serving yummy homemade cookies, including macadamia nut, white chocolate–macadamia nut, oatmeal raisin, and coffee crunch. Packaged in beautiful gift boxes or bags, the cookies make excellent gifts. She even makes cookie treats for the family dog. Stop by on your way to

Costco or the airport and pick up a bag or two or three—or just ask Mrs. Barry to ship your stash instead. ⊠ *73-5563 Maiau St., Kailua-Kona* ⊹ *By Costco in the Kaloko Light Industrial Area* ☎ *808/329–6055* ⊕ *www.konacookies.com.*

Westside Wines

WINE/SPIRITS | Tucked away in a small downtown Kona retail center below Longs, this nifty gourmet wine and spirits shop offers restaurant-quality "wine list" wines at affordable prices. It's also the place to find large-format craft beers, Champagne from France, single-malt whiskies, organic vodka, small-batch bourbon, rye whiskey, fresh bread, and artisan cheeses from around the world. George Clooney's Casamigos tequila is the store's house tequila. A certified wine specialist, proprietor Alex Thropp was one of the state's top wholesale wine reps for decades. Wine tastings take place Friday and Saturday afternoons from 3 to 6. ⊠ *75-5660 Kopiko St., #4, Kailua-Kona* ⊹ *Below Longs Drugs in Kopiko Plaza* ☎ *808/329–1777* ⊗ *Closed Sun.*

GALLERIES

Dovetail Gallery and Design

ART GALLERY | Woodworker Gerald Ben and his wife, Renee, own this fine gallery that specializes in contemporary and abstract pieces while supporting the Holualoa arts community. It features a variety of art, including woodworking, sculpture, ceramics, photography, and painting. ⊠ *76-5942 Mamalahoa Hwy., Holualoa* ☎ *808/322–4046* ⊕ *dovetailgallery.net* ⊗ *Closed Sun. and Mon.*

Kona Art Gallery

ART GALLERY | Gary and Elizabeth Theriault showcase a variety of local art here, including Gary's Big Island life photos and Elizabeth's hand-painted drums and rattles. The gallery owners also feature other artists' work, including Hawaiian *ipus* (gourds used as instruments in hula), exotic wood items, paper sculptures, quilts, and jewelry, at their sweet cottage gallery. ✉ *76-5938 Mamalahoa Hwy., Holualoa* ☎ *808/322–5125* ☽ *Closed Sun. and Mon.*

M.Field Gallery

ART GALLERY | Mike Field's iconic, high-graphic artwork is on display at this small, quaint gallery. An active waterman raised in Hawaii, Mike captures the island lifestyle of canoe paddling, surfing, and sailing as well as island plants and landscapes. T-shirts and other inexpensive items are also for sale here. ✉ *76-5936 Mamalahoa Hwy., Holualoa* ☎ *808/315–8114* ⊕ *mfield.com* ☽ *Closed Sun. and Mon.*

MARKETS

Alii Gardens Marketplace

MARKET | **FAMILY** | The outdoor stalls at this mellow, parklike market offer tropical flowers, produce, soaps, kettle corn, coffee, coconut postcards, cookies, jewelry, koa wood, clothing, antiques and collectibles, handmade lei, silk flowers, and kitschy crafts. The made-on-site barbecue is a real hit. A food kiosk also serves shave ice, fish tacos, coconut water, fresh-fruit smoothies, and hamburgers. Free parking and Wi-Fi are available. ✉ *75-6129 Alii Dr., Kailua-Kona* ⊹ *1½ miles south of Kona Inn Shopping Village* ☎ *808/937–8844* ⊕ *facebook.com/aliigardensmarketplace* ☽ *Closed Mon.*

Keauhou Farmers Market

MARKET | **FAMILY** | Held in the parking lot at Keauhou Shopping Center, this cheerful market is the place to go on Saturday morning for live music, local produce (much of it organic), goat cheese, honey, island-raised meat, flowers, macadamia nuts, fresh-baked pastries, Kona coffee, and plenty of local color. ✉ *Keauhou Shopping Center, 78-6831 Alii Dr., Kailua-Kona* ⊕ *www.keauhoufarmersmarket. com.*

Kona Farmers' Market

MARKET | **FAMILY** | An awesome flower vendor creates custom arrangements while you wait at this touristy farmers' market near the ocean. There are more than 40 vendors with souvenirs and crafts for sale, as well as some of the best prices on fresh produce, lei, and orchids in Kona. The market is held in a parking lot at the corner of Hualalai Road and Alii Drive from 7 to 4. ✉ *75-7544 Alii Dr., Kailua-Kona* ☽ *Closed Mon. and Tues.*

MUSIC

Just Ukes

MUSIC | As the name suggests, this place is all about ukuleles—from music books to T-shirts and accessories like cases and bags. The independently owned shop carries a variety of ukuleles ranging from low-priced starter instruments to high-end models made of koa and mango. ✉ *Ali'i Gardens Marketplace, 75-6129 Ali'i Dr., Kailua-Kona* ☎ *808/769–5101* ⊕ *justukes.com.*

SHOPPING CENTERS

Coconut Grove Marketplace

SHOPPING CENTER | This meandering oceanfront marketplace includes gift shops, cafés, restaurants (including Outback Steakhouse, Humpy's Big Island Alehouse, Thai Rin, Lava Java, Foster's Kitchen, and Gecko Girlz), sports bars, sushi, boutiques, crystal stores, Jack's Diving Locker, a running shop, and several art galleries. At night, locals gather to watch outdoor sand volleyball games held in the courtyard or grab a beer and enjoy live music. Directly adjacent is Alii Sunset Plaza, which is served by the same large paid parking lot. (Parking may be validated by some retailers.) ✉ *75-5795–75-5825 Alii Dr., Kailua-Kona* ⊕ *www.thecoconutgrovemarketplace. com.*

Kaloko Light Industrial Park

SHOPPING CENTER | Located south of the airport, this large retail complex includes Costco, the best place to stock up on food if you're staying at a vacation rental. Kona Wine Market features curated wines and beers, while Mrs. Barry's Kona Cookies sells beautifully packaged, delicious "souvenirs." ✉ *Off Hwy. 19 and Hina Lani St., Kailua-Kona* ⊹ *Near Kona airport.*

Keauhou Shopping Center

SHOPPING CENTER | About 5 miles south of Kailua Village, this large neighborhood shopping center includes KTA Superstore, Longs Drugs, Kona Stories bookstore, and a multiplex movie theater. Kenichi Pacific, an upscale sushi restaurant, and Peaberry & Galette, a café that serves excellent crepes, are favorite eateries, joined by Bianelli's Pizza. You can also grab a quick bite at Los Habaneros, Subway, or L&L Hawaiian Barbecue. ✉ *78-6831 Alii Dr., Kailua-Kona* ☎ *808/322–3000* ⊕ *www.keauhoushoppingcenter.com.*

Kona Commons

SHOPPING CENTER | This downtown center features a Ross Dress for Less (for suitcases, shoes, swimsuits, and aloha wear) and Hawaiian Island Creations (for a great selection of surf gear, clothing, and accessories). There's also an Old Navy, Island Naturals, Vitamin Shoppe, Office Max, and a number of other smaller clothing retailers. Food and drink options include fast-food standbys like Dairy Queen, Subway, and Panda Express, as well as Ultimate Burger, for local beef and delicious house-made fries, and Genki Sushi, where the goods are delivered via conveyor belt. ■**TIP**→ **Across the street, Target has fresh-flower lei for a fraction of the cost of local florists.** ✉ *75-5450 Makala Blvd., Kailua-Kona* ⊕ *www.konacommons.com.*

Kona Inn Shopping Village

SHOPPING CENTER | Originally a hotel, the Kona Inn was built in 1928 to accommodate a new wave of wealthy travelers arriving by steamer and was booked months in advance. As hotels and resorts opened along the Kona and Kohala Coasts, it was transformed into a low-rise, outdoor shopping village with shops and island-style eateries. Although quite a few longtime shops did not survive the pandemic, new ones are expected to take their place. Broad lawns with coconut trees on the ocean side provide a lovely setting for an afternoon picnic. The iconic Kona Inn is best for drinks and appetizers. ✉ *75-5744 Alii Dr., Kailua-Kona.*

Kona Marketplace

SHOPPING CENTER | On the *mauka* (mountain) side of Alii Drive, near Hulihee Palace, this small retail enclave in Historic Kailua Village includes galleries, T-shirt/souvenir shops, and Sam's Hideaway bar. Local favorite Hayashi's You Make the Roll offers outstanding sushi to go. ✉ *75-5744 Alii Dr., Kailua-Kona.*

Activities

SPAS

A Ala Hawaii Oceanfront Massage and Spa

SPA | With oceanfront views of Kailua Bay, this sweet spa offers a full menu of massage treatments as well as scrubs, wraps, facials, and waxing. It's a convenient place to get pampered before hitting the village shops or restaurants. Bonus: listening to waves crash as you relax to a massage is a pretty nice deal. ✉ *Kona Inn Shopping Village, 75-5744 Alii Dr., Suite 245, Kailua-Kona* ☎ *808/937–9707* ⊕ *www.oceanfrontmassage.com* ✉ *Massages from $129, facials from $150.*

Hoola Spa at the Sheraton Kona Resort & Spa at Keauhou Bay

SPA | The hotel's oceanfront spa offers a menu of tropical delights with combination options that let you mix and match for a heavenly—and affordable—treatment. The private outdoor lanai lets you melt into dreamland as you listen to waves lapping at the rocks inches away. After your treatment, rinse off with hot steam and cool water in the complimentary shower/steam room. The spa has Hawaii's first Himalayan Salt Room, a natural therapy for spa-going guests. Couples' treatments take place outside on the secluded balcony and start with a private whirlpool bath followed by a side-by-side massage. ⊠ *Sheraton Kona Resort & Spa, 78-128 Ehukai St., Kailua-Kona* ☎ *808/930–4848* ⊕ *www. hoolaspa.com.*

The Lotus Center

SPA | Tucked away on the first floor of the Royal Kona Resort, the Lotus Center provides a convenient option for massage treatments, facials, and waxing. There's also a chiropractor on the premises. Ocean-side massage is available on a private patio outside the treatment rooms. Alternative offerings include acupuncture, yoga, Reiki, crystal-energy sessions, and biofeedback. Ask about discounted packages. ⊠ *Royal Kona Resort, 75-5852 Alii Dr., Kailua-Kona* ☎ *808/334–0445* ⊕ *www.konaspa.com* ⊠ *Massages from $79, facials from $89.*

North Kona

The North Kona district is characterized by vast lava fields, dotted with turnoff points from Highway 19 leading to some of the most beautiful beaches in the world. Most lava flows here originate from the last eruptions of Hualalai, in 1800 and 1801, although some flows by the resorts (primarily Mauna Lani, to the north) hail from Mauna Loa. The stark black lavascapes contrast spectacularly with luminous azure waters framed by coconut palms and white-sand beaches. Some of the turnoffs will take you to state parks with parking lots and bathrooms, while others are simply a park-on-the-highway-and-hike-in adventure.

GETTING HERE AND AROUND

Head north from Kona International Airport and follow Highway 19 along the coast. Take caution driving at night between the airport and where resorts begin on the Kohala Coast; it's extremely dark, and there are few road signs, street lights, or traffic lights on this two-lane road. Wild donkeys and goats may appear on the roadway without warning, not to mention speeders.

Sights

★ Kaloko–Honokohau National Historical Park

NATIONAL PARK | FAMILY | The trails at this sheltered 1,160-acre coastal park near Honokohau Harbor, just north of Kailua-Kona, are popular with walkers and hikers, and the park is a good place to observe Hawaiian archaeological history and intact ruins. These include a *heiau* (temple), house platforms, ancient fishponds, and numerous petroglyphs along a boardwalk. The park's wetlands provide refuge to waterbirds such as the endemic Hawaiian stilt and coot. Two beaches here are good for swimming, sunbathing, and sea turtle spotting: Aiopio, a few yards north of the harbor, is small and calm, with protected swimming areas (good for kids); Honokohau Beach, also north of the harbor, is a ¾-mile stretch with ruins of ancient fishponds. Of the park's three entrances, the middle one leads to a visitor center with helpful rangers and lots of information. Local docents with backgrounds in geology or other subjects give nature walks. To go directly to the beaches, take the harbor road north of the Gentry retail center, park in the gravel lot, and follow the signs. ⊠ *74–425 Kealakehe Pkwy., off Hwy. 19 near airport, Kailua-Kona* ✛ *3 miles south of Kona International Airport* ☎ *808/329–6881* ⊕ *www.nps.gov/kaho* ⊠ *Free.*

Mountain Thunder

FARM/RANCH | FAMILY | This coffee producer offers hourly "bean-to-cup" tours, including a tasting and access to the processing plant, which shows dry milling, sizing, coloring, sorting, and roasting. For $10, take the lava tube/nature walk in the cloud forest ecosystem. There's a small retail store where you can purchase

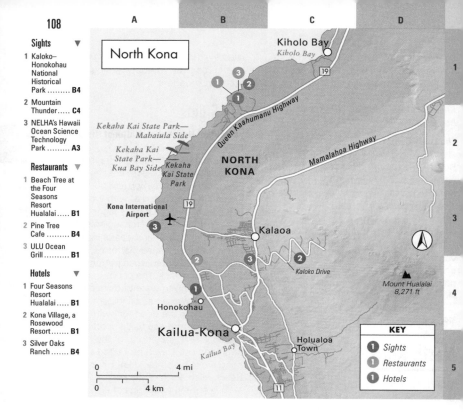

coffee and souvenirs. Remember that afternoon rains are common at this elevation, so bring an umbrella and sturdy shoes. ⊠ *73-1944 Hao St., Kailua-Kona* ☎ *808/325–5566* ⊕ *www.mountainthunder.com* ⊠ *Free; nature walk $10.*

NELHA's Hawaii Ocean Science Technology Park

OTHER ATTRACTION | Just south of Kona International Airport, a big building with a large photovoltaic (solar) panel installation resembles a top-secret military station, but it's actually the site of the Natural Energy Lab of Hawaii Authority's (NELHA) Hawaii Ocean Science Technology (HOST) Park. Here, scientists, researchers, and entrepreneurs make use of a cold, deep-sea pipeline to develop and market everything from desalinated, mineral-rich drinking water

and super-nutritious algae products to energy-efficient air-conditioning systems to environmentally friendly aquaculture techniques. Seahorses, abalone, *kampachi* (a type of yellowtail), Dungeness crab, and Maine lobsters are raised here, too. Farm tours are available directly through tenants Big Island Abalone, Ocean Rider Sea Horse Farm, and Sea Salts of Hawaii. ⊠ *73-4485 Kahilihili St., Kailua-Kona* ☎ *808/329–8073* ⊕ *kcshi.org* ⊠ *$53* ⊘ *Closed Sat. and Sun.*

⏏ Beaches

Kekaha Kai State Park—Kua Bay Side

BEACH | **FAMILY** | On the northernmost stretch of the park's coastline, this lovely beach fronts an absolutely beautiful bay with crystal-clear, deep aquamarine water. It's peaceful in summer, but the

Beautiful Kua Bay in North Kona is known for its white sand and clear, aquamarine water.

park's paved entrance, amenities, and parking lot make the beach very accessible and, as a result, often crowded. Fine white sand sits in stark contrast to old black lava flows, and there's little shade—bring umbrellas. Rocky shores on either side protect the beach from afternoon winds and offer some fabulous snorkeling spots. Gates open daily from 8 to 7. In winter, surf can get rough, and often the sand washes away. **Amenities:** parking (no fee); showers; toilets. **Best for:** surfing; swimming. ⊠ *Hwy. 19, north of mile marker 88, Kailua-Kona* ✛ *Across from Veterans Cemetery* ⊕ *dlnr.hawaii. gov/dsp* ✉ *Free.*

★ **Kekaha Kai State Park—Mahaiula Side**
BEACH | It's slow going down a 1.8-mile, bumpy but partially paved road off Highway 19 to this beach park, but the lovely beaches are worth it when you reach the end. Very low-profile rentals may have some trouble making the drive. This state park encompasses three beaches: from south to north, Mahaiula, Makalawena,

and Kua Bay, which has its own entrance. Mahaiula and Makalawena are classically beautiful expanses of white sand with dunes. Makalawena has great swimming and body boarding. (⚠ **Makalawena, sandwiched between the two state parks, is private property and falls under the jurisdiction of Kamehameha Schools Bishop Estates.**) Watch out for rough surf and strong currents, especially in winter. From Makalawena, a 4½-mile trail leads to Kua Bay. If you're game, work your way on foot to the top of Puu Kuili, a 342-foot-high cinder cone with a fantastic coastline view. But be prepared for the heat and bring water, as there are no services of any kind in the park. Gates at the highway entrance close promptly at 7, so you must leave the lot by about 6:30. **Amenities:** toilets. **Best for:** swimming. ⊠ *Hwy. 19, Kailua-Kona* ✛ *Turnoff is about 2 miles north of Kona International Airport* ☎ *808/974–6200* ⊕ *dlnr.hawaii. gov/dsp* ✉ *Free.*

🍴 Restaurants

Beach Tree at the Four Seasons Resort Hualalai

$$$ | MODERN ITALIAN | FAMILY | Beautifully designed, this venue provides a relaxed and elegant setting for alfresco dining near the sand, with its boardwalk-style deck and enormous vaulted ceiling. The menu features brick-oven pizzas, gnocchi with Keahole lobster, seafood entrées, steak, and farm-fresh salads. **Known for:** Ohana Table four-course dinner; 60 wines by the glass; upscale resort atmosphere. ⑤ *Average main: $35* ⊠ *Four Seasons Resort Hualalai, 72-100 Kaupulehu Dr., Kailua-Kona* ☎ *808/325–8000* ⊕ *www.fourseasons.com/hualalai.*

Pine Tree Cafe

$ | HAWAIIAN | FAMILY | This low-key, no-frills café offers local plate lunch options and classics such as *loco moco* (meat, rice, and eggs smothered in gravy), alongside new inventions like crab curry bisque. The prices are very affordable, and the portions are huge. **Known for:** early-morning breakfast; fresh fish; popular with locals. ⑤ *Average main: $10* ⊠ *Kohanaiki Plaza, 73-4354 Mamalahoa Hwy. (Hwy. 11)* ☎ *808/327–1234* ⊕ *pinetreecafehi.com.*

★ ULU Ocean Grill

$$$$ | MODERN HAWAIIAN | Casual elegance takes center stage at the resort's flagship oceanfront restaurant, one of the most upscale restaurants on the Big Island. Diverse menu choices include roasted beet salad, flame-grilled prime New York steak, Kona lobster, shrimp pad Thai, and more. **Known for:** sushi lounge; ingredients sourced from 160 local purveyors; impressive wine list. ⑤ *Average main: $45* ⊠ *Four Seasons Resort Hualalai, 72-100 Kaupulehu Dr., Kailua-Kona* ☎ *808/325–8000* ⊕ *www.fourseasons.com* ☾ *No lunch.*

🛏 Hotels

★ Four Seasons Resort Hualalai

$$$$ | RESORT | FAMILY | Beautiful views everywhere, polished wood floors, custom furnishings and linens, and fine Hawaiian artwork make this oceanfront resort a peaceful, opulent retreat. **Pros:** beautiful location; gourmet restaurants; renowned service. **Cons:** not the best beach among the resorts; quite pricey; 20-minute drive to Kailua-Kona. ⑤ *Rooms from: $1,340* ⊠ *72-100 Kaupulehu Dr., Kailua-Kona* ☎ *808/325–8000, 888/340–5662* ⊕ *www.fourseasons.com/hualalai* ⇨ *243 rooms* ⦿ *No Meals.*

★ Kona Village, a Rosewood Resort

$$$$ | HOTEL | Years after being destroyed by a tsunami, one of Kona's most beloved resorts has reopened, completely remodeled, yet retaining much of what made the original so special. **Pros:** commitment to sustainability; good wedding destination; freestanding rooms. **Cons:** remote location; not all hales have views; pricey. ⑤ *Rooms from: $1,695* ⊠ *72-300 Maheawalu Drive, Kailua-Kona* ☎ *808/865–2545* ⊕ *rosewoodhotels.com* ⇨ *150 rooms* ⦿ *Free Breakfast.*

Silver Oaks Ranch

$$ | HOUSE | FAMILY | Three private cottages set on a 10-acre working ranch afford total privacy, with a few more amenities than a vacation house or condo. **Pros:** washer and dryer in each cottage; deck with ocean views; great for animal lovers. **Cons:** five-night minimum stay; rural location; no online booking. ⑤ *Rooms from: $250* ⊠ *73-4570 Mamalahoa Hwy., just south of Kaloko Dr., Kailua-Kona* ☎ *808/325–2000* ⊕ *www.silveroaksranch.com* ⇨ *3 cottages* ⦿ *No Meals.*

Chapter 4

SOUTH KONA

4

Updated by
Kristina Anderson

⊙ Sights	🍴 Restaurants	🛏 Hotels	🛍 Shopping	🍸 Nightlife
★★★★★	★★★☆☆	★★★☆☆	★★☆☆☆	★☆☆☆☆

WELCOME TO SOUTH KONA

TOP REASONS TO GO

★ **Puuhonua O Honaunau National Historical Park:** Step back into ancient Hawaii and visit an authentic "place of refuge," where transgressors of the *kapu* (law) were forgiven their sins or crimes.

★ **St. Benedict's Painted Church:** In 1899, a priest transformed a simple chapel into a colorful interpretation of the New Testament imbued with tropical flair.

★ **Kona Coffee Living History Farm:** Learn how Japanese immigrants farmed Kona coffee at this fully restored, working farm.

★ **Hookena Beach Park:** This scenic, idyllic beach park boasts soft sand and wonderful swimming.

★ **Kealakekua Bay State Historical Park:** Stunning and pristine, the bay is blessed with the clearest water on the island.

★ **Kona Coffee Belt:** Stretching about 30 miles long, this special agricultural area was established by hard-working pioneers whose descendants nurture their crop in hundreds of small estates.

Take the famous "five mile" hill heading south from Kailua-Kona and you'll reach the storied and breathtaking South Kona region of the island. Comprised of upcountry villages and towns and coastal regions steeped in rich history, South Kona introduces the visitor to the confluence of many diverse cultures, in addition to Hawaiian, that blend into a cohesive local community here—Japanese, Filipino, Chinese and Portuguese, to name just a few. Although the towns are small, each is worth a quick stop. Have a coffee while you stroll the shops and cafes in charming historical buildings, some dating to the late-1800s. Merging with the upper road from Holualoa, this stretch was the original road to Volcano, and you can still get there from here in about two hours.

1 Honalo and Kainaliu. Former plantation towns, these charming streetscapes host cafes, shops, antique shops and even the famed Aloha Theatre, all housed in vintage buildings.

2 Kealakekua. The classic 1933 song, "My Little Grass Shack in Kealakekua, Hawaii" put this tiny town on the map. It's the gateway to beautiful Kealakekua Bay.

3 Captain Cook. The historic town of Captain Cook is home to the Manago Hotel, the oldest operating hotel in the state. A farmers market takes place on Sundays; an excellent grocery store (owned by the descendants of the first general store here) serves the community.

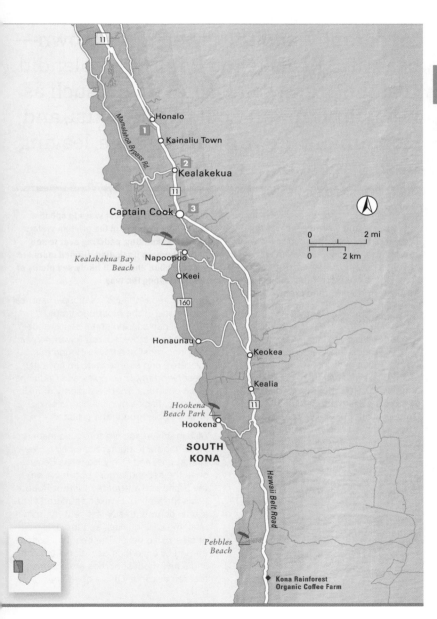

Honalo

1 Kainaliu Town

2 Kealakekua

11

Captain Cook 3

Kealakekua Bay Beach Napoopoo

Keei

160

Honaunau Keokea

Kealia

11

Hookena Beach Park Hookena

SOUTH KONA

Hawaii Belt Road

Pebbles Beach

◆ Kona Rainforest Organic Coffee Farm

Mamalahoa Bypass Rd

11

0   2 mi

0   2 km

The gateway to the mountainous Kona coffee belt, South Kona is home to rural farming communities, jaw-dropping topography, and the jewel in the crown—beautiful Kealakekua Bay. Here, splendid coastlines and small rural towns such as Kainaliu, Captain Cook, Kealakekua, and Honaunau take you back in time, leaving busy streets behind.

This magnificent area stretches halfway to the Big Island's southernmost tip. The winding upcountry road takes you straight to the Honaunau Valley, the heart of coffee country, where fertile plantations (some open for tours and tastings), simple farmhouses, and breathtaking views offer a taste of what Hawaii was like before the resorts took over.

South Kona is quiet and relatively rural. Much of the farmland is in leasehold status, which explains why this part of the Big Island has remained rather untouched by development. Tour one of the coffee farms to find out what the big deal is about Kona coffee, and enjoy a free sample while you're at it. A 20-minute drive off the highway from Captain Cook leads to beautiful Kealakekua Bay, where Captain James Cook arrived in 1778, dying here not long after. Hawaiian spinner dolphins visit the bay, now a Marine Life Conservation District, nestled alongside high green cliffs that jut dramatically out to sea. The bay is normally extremely calm and offers superb snorkeling, although not a lot of good access points.

■ TIP→ **One of the best ways to spend a morning is to kayak in the pristine waters of Kealakekua Bay, paddling over to see the spot where Cook died. Guided tours are your best bet, and you'll likely see plenty of dolphins along the way.**

Puuhonua o Honaunau National Historical Park is one of the most underrated national parks in the state, so it's generally not very crowded. You'll want to plan to spend most of a day exploring this evocative and serene park, an ancient, preserved temple complex and traditional place of refuge. There are plenty of hiking trails too. Pack a picnic lunch to enjoy after a stroll through the grounds.

Also in this region are the Honaunau Valley (home to numerous small coffee plantations) and lovely Hookena Beach, once the second largest port town on the island and a favorite of writer Robert Louis Stevenson. Hookena suffered virtual abandonment early last century from tsunami, earthquakes, and the decline of steamship travel. The beautiful beach, framed by a glorious *pali* (elongated cliff) and a few modest homes are about all that remain. Today it is a quiet county park.

At the edge of the district boundary dividing South Kona and Kau is the authentic fishing village of Milolii. Residents revere their privacy and independence as they practice traditional cultural activities in this isolated spot. Visit respectfully.

MAJOR REGIONS

Honalo and Kainaliu. In the first towns you encounter to the south heading upcountry from Kailua Town, a ribbon of funky old stores, clothing boutiques, coffee bars, and bistros lines the road, and a handful of galleries and antiques shops have sprung up. Browse around the Deja Vu shop, Oshima's Surf and Skate, and Kimura's, founded in 1927, to find fabrics and Japanese goods beyond tourist trinkets. Pop into a local café for everything from burgers to New York–style deli fare. Peek into the 1932-vintage Aloha Theatre, where a troupe of community-theater actors might be practicing a Broadway revue.

Kealakekua. This small town has a few banks, shops, eateries, and a post office. The only hospital in the region is located here as well. The meandering road to Kealakekua Bay is home to a historic painted church, as well as numerous coffee-tasting spots, and several reasonably priced B&Bs with incredible views. If you're feeling exceptionally strong, you could hike the steep trail (trailhead is at the top of Napoopoo Road) to the north end of the bay, but be forewarned: the hike back up is extremely strenuous and there are no services in this area.

Captain Cook. Gas stations, grocery stores, banks, a couple of restaurants, and a post office serve the local residents. Captain Cook encompasses the coastal regions as well, which include Puuhonua o Honaunau National Historical Park and Honaunau Bay. Visitors may get confused by the large geographic area of Captain Cook, which is actually an official postal code designation. Until you cross into the Kau district, it's all considered Captain Cook.

Planning

Getting Here and Around

Upcountry South Kona, elevation 1,400 feet, is about 9 miles from Kailua-Kona town, and is mainly served by a 25–35 mph, single-lane highway. The beach areas must be accessed by side roads that take you back down to sea level. Some are steep; others winding.

Plenty of free parking is available throughout South Kona.

To get to Kealakekua Bay, follow the signs off Highway 11 and park at Kealakekua Bay State Historical Park. It's not much of a beach (it used to be before Hurricane Iniki washed it away in 1992), but it provides access to the water and beautiful views across the bay. Parking is extremely limited. Use caution if waters are rough; it can be difficult to exit the water due to the large boulders.

CAR

Unfortunately, the west side of the Big Island has very few public transportation options. Bus service does run and is free but it does not stop at any of the points of interest for visitors and is mostly used by commuters. Sometimes visitors use taxis or drivers, but these can get expensive rather quickly. If you want to get the most out of your visit to South Kona, you will need to rent a car.

Parking is free at all the beach venues in South Kona, although the national park does charge an entrance fee. These sites have attracted an increasing number of visitors in recent years, and parking can get very congested, especially on weekends and during school holidays. Your best bet is to get an early start to beat the crowds and the heat.

Traffic can be an issue in South Kona due to the mostly single-lane rural roads. Give yourself extra time to accommodate school traffic in the mornings and afternoons. Roadworks and frequent accidents can also delay or stop traffic altogether. The Alii Drive bypass road, connecting the south end of Alii Drive to South Kona, does provide relief, especially during rush hour. And the view isn't half bad either.

Hotels and Restaurants

South Kona has only one hotel—the venerable Manago Hotel, founded in 1917. It began with tatami mats on the floor, catering to travelers taking the long trek to Volcano, which in those days was quite the journey. The entire establishment feels like stepping back in time. The present-day owners are original descendants of the founders Kinzo and his picture bride, Osame. A small restaurant serving homestyle meals is a favorite with residents and visitors alike.

The majority of travelers wishing to stay in South Kona opt for either a bed-and-breakfast, vacation rental, hostel, or homestay. When regulations on short-term rentals went into effect islandwide in 2018, many operators of standalone holiday homes in rural areas were unable to stay in business and had to close. That said, quite a few still operate illegally, so when considering an unhosted vacation home, make sure the place is legal—check for permit and tax ID numbers. As of this writing, Hawaii County also intends to introduce regulation on hosted rentals, in which the owner lives on-site, but final regulation of those units may still be while off.

One hostel operation—Pineapple Park Hostel in Captain Cook—offers good rates and lots of availability.

Numerous delightful bed-and-breakfasts in various price ranges and locales are scattered throughout the region and make a perfect home base for exploring this beautiful and unique region of the island.

⇨ *Hotel prices in the reviews are the lowest cost of a standard double room in high season. Restaurant prices in the reviews are the average cost of a main course at dinner, or if dinner is not served, at lunch.*

What It Costs in U.S. Dollars			
$	$$	$$$	$$$$
HOTELS			
under $200	$200–$280	$281–$380	over $380
RESTAURANTS			
under $20	$20–$30	$31–$40	over $40

South Kona

Sights

Big Island Bees
FARM/RANCH | FAMILY | At this meticulously run family operation, artisanal honey is produced slowly and organically. They focus on three varietals: Lehua, Macadamia Nut, and Wilelaiki (Christmasberry). You can take a secured, screened tour of the bee hives, see how the queen lives and is cared for, and enjoy free samples of honey. Reservations are required for the tour, but you can peruse the museum and shop free of charge. ✉ *82-1140 Meli Rd, #102, Captain Cook* ☎ *808/328–1315* ⊕ *bigislandbees.com* 🎟 *$30.*

★ Captain James Cook Monument
MONUMENT | On February 14, 1779, famed English explorer Captain James Cook was killed here during an apparent misunderstanding with local residents, and this 27-foot-high obelisk marks the spot where he died. He had chosen Kealakekua Bay as a landing place in November 1778. Arriving during the celebration of Makahiki, the harvest season, Cook was welcomed at first.

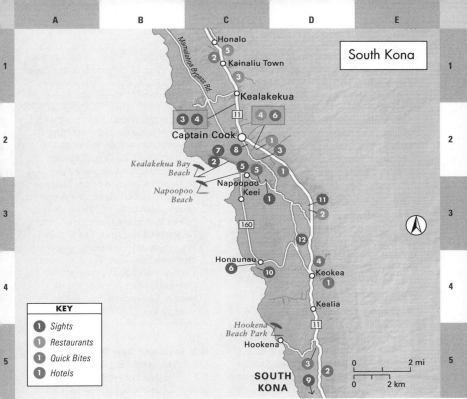

South Kona

Sights ▼
1 Big Island Bees **C3**
2 Captain James Cook Monument................ **C2**
3 Greenwell Farms......... **C2**
4 H. N. Greenwell Store Museum **C2**
5 Hikiau Heiau **C2**
6 Honaunau Bay **C4**
7 Kealakekua Bay State Historical Park **C2**
8 Kona Coffee Living History Farm **C2**
9 Kona RainForest Farms.................... **D5**
10 Puuhonua O Honaunau National Historical Park **C4**
11 Royal Kona Coffee Center and Coffee Mill.............. **D3**
12 St. Benedict's Painted Church **D3**

Restaurants ▼
1 Black Rock Pizza......... **C2**
2 Kaaloa's Super J's Authentic Hawaiian Food **D3**
3 Keei Cafe at Hokukano **C1**
4 Manago Hotel Restaurant................ **C2**
5 Teshima's Restaurant............... **C1**

Quick Bites ▼
1 The Coffee Shack **D2**
2 Kaya's Coffee **C1**
3 Kealia Ranch Store..... **D5**

Hotels ▼
1 Aloha Guest House **D4**
2 Horizon Guest House ... **D5**
3 Kaawa Loa Plantation................. **C2**
4 Kane Plantation Guesthouse.............. **D4**
5 Luana Inn **C3**
6 Manago Hotel **C2**

Some Hawaiians saw him as an incarnation of the god Lono. Cook's party sailed away in February 1779, but a freak storm forced his damaged ship back to Kealakekua Bay. Believing that no god could be thwarted by a mere rainstorm, the Hawaiians were not so welcoming this time. The theft of a longboat brought Cook and an armed party ashore to reclaim it. Shots were fired, daggers and spears were thrown, and Cook fell, mortally wounded.

A trail leading to the site is accessible from the top of Napoopoo Road, but caution is advised. The very strenuous trail gains an elevation of about 1,500 feet and is recommended for advanced hikers only. ✉ *Captain Cook.*

★ Greenwell Farms
FARM/RANCH | FAMILY | Depending on the season, the 20-minute walking tour of this working farm takes in various stages of coffee production, including a look at the 100-year-old coffee trees. The Greenwell family played a significant role in the cultivation of the first commercial coffee in the Kona area (as well as the first grocery store). No reservations are required, unless you are booking for a private party, which does have a cost. You can also book a master brewing class. ✉ *81-6581 Mamalahoa Hwy., Kealakekua ✛ Ocean side, between mile markers 112 and 111* ☎ *808/323–2295* ⊕ *www. greenwellfarms.com* ✉ *Free.*

Hikiau Heiau
HISTORIC SIGHT | This stone platform, once an impressive temple dedicated to the god Lono, was built by King Kalaniopuu. When Captain Cook arrived in 1778, ceremonies in his honor were held here. It's still considered a religious site, so visit with respect and do not walk on the platform. There are small pathways nearby, and the heiau is tended to by lineal descendants of people who lived in the area. ✉ *Captain Cook ✛ Bottom of Napoopoo Rd. at bay* ✉ *Free.*

Hawaii Cherries

Don't scratch your head too much when you see signs advertising "cherries" as you drive around South Kona. They aren't about the cherries used in cherry pie; these signs refer to coffee cherries. Coffee beans straight off the tree are encased in fleshy, sweet red husks that make them look like bright little cherries. These husks are removed in the pulping process, and then the beans are sun-dried. Farmers who don't process their own coffee can sell 100-pound bags of just-picked cherries to the roasters.

H. N. Greenwell Store Museum
HISTORY MUSEUM | Established in 1850, the homestead of Henry N. Greenwell served as cattle ranch, sheep station, store, post office, and family home all in one. Now, all that remains is the 1875 stone structure, which is listed on the National Register of Historic Places. It houses a fascinating museum with exhibits on ranching and coffee farming. It's also headquarters for the Kona Historical Society, which archives and preserves the history of the Kona district. An interesting aside: today, direct descendants of Henry Greenwell operate a popular South Kona grocery store, ChoiceMart, bringing their ancestors' legacy full circle. ✉ *81-6551 Mamalahoa Hwy., mile marker 112, Kealakekua* ☎ *808/323–3222* ⊕ *www. konahistorical.org* ✉ *$5* ⊙ *Closed Wed. and Fri.–Sun.*

Honaunau Bay
BODY OF WATER | FAMILY | Not technically a beach, this beautiful small bay is an underwater wonderland. Living in and

Continued on page 122

HAWAII'S PLANTS 101

Tropical hibiscus

Hawaii is a bounty of rainbow-colored flowers and plants. The evening air is scented with their fragrance. Just look at the front yard of almost any home, travel any road, or visit any local park and you'll see a spectacular array of colored blossoms and leaves. What most visitors don't know is that many of the plants they are seeing are not native to Hawaii; rather, they were introduced during the last two centuries as ornamental plants, or for timber, shade, or fruit.

Hawaii boasts nearly every climate on the planet, excluding the two most extreme: arctic tundra and arid desert. The Islands have wine-growing regions, cactus-speckled ranchlands, icy mountaintops, and the rainiest forests on earth.

The lush lowland valleys along the windward coasts are predominantly populated by non-native trees including yellow- and red-fruited **guava**, silver-leafed **kukui**, and orange-flowered **tulip trees**.

The colorful **plumeria flower**, very fragrant and commonly used in lei making, and the giant multicolored **hibiscus flower** are both used by many women as hair adornments, and are two of the most common plants found around homes and hotels. The umbrella-like **monkeypod tree** from Central America provides shade in many of Hawaii's parks including Kapiolani Park in Honolulu. Hawaii's largest tree, found in Lahaina, Maui, is a giant **banyan tree**, which survived the devastating fire there in 2023 despite major damage. Its canopy and massive support roots cover about two-thirds of an acre. The native **ohia tree**, with its brilliant red brush-like flowers, and the **hapuu**, a giant tree fern, are common in Hawaii's forests and are also used ornamentally in gardens.

Naupaka, Limahuli Garden

Bougainvillea

Guava

Monkeypod

Banyan

Ohia lehua*

Tulip tree

Plumeria

Pandanus

Hibiscus

Anthurium

Kukui

Hapuu

*Endemic to Hawaii

DID YOU KNOW?

As many as 6,000 plant species are found in the Hawaiian Islands, but only about 1,400 are native. Of these, 366 are so rare, they are endangered. Hawaii's endemic plants evolved from ancestral seeds arriving in the Islands over thousands of years as baggage with birds, floating on ocean currents, or drifting on winds from continents thousands of miles away. Once here, these plants evolved in isolation, creating many new species known nowhere else in the world.

Kealakekua Bay is generally considered the best snorkeling spot on the Big Island.

among a wide stretch of lovely coral gardens, yellow tangs, coronet fish, triggerfish, eels, eagle rays, and even Hawaiian green sea turtles make daily appearances. Access is via a lava rock step. Due to its easy access, this spot has seen much overuse in recent years and can get very crowded. Only a few parking spots are available outside the bay as it's also an active fishing launch area. Please visit with the utmost respect to other users of the bay, including residents, canoe club members, fishermen, and others. Please do not stand on coral, use toxic sunscreen, or chase or herd dolphins ($500 fines for violators). Early is best for all conditions—there will be fewer humans and more fish. ⊠ *Honaunau Beach Road, Captain Cook.*

★ Kealakekua Bay State Historical Park
STATE/PROVINCIAL PARK | One of the most beautiful spots in the state, this underwater marine reserve has dramatic cliffs that surround super deep, crystal clear, turquoise water chock-full of stunning coral pinnacles and tropical fish. The federally protected dolphins that frequent the sanctuary should not be disturbed, as they use the bay to sleep and escape predators. There's very little sand at west-facing Napoopoo Beach, but this is a nice place to enter the water and swim (when the water is calm) as it's well protected from currents. There are no lifeguards, but there are bathrooms, a pavilion, shower, and limited parking. The Captain James Cook Monument, marking where the explorer died, is at the northern edge of the bay. Stay at least 300 feet from the shoreline along the cliffs, which have become unstable during recent earthquakes. A limited number of tour operators offer snorkeling and kayaking tours nearby. ⊠ *Beach Rd., off Government Rd. from Puuhonua Rd. (Hwy. 160), Captain Cook* ⊕ *dlnr.hawaii. gov/dsp* ⊠ *Free.*

★ Kona Coffee Living History Farm
FARM/RANCH | On the National Register of Historic Places, this perfectly preserved farm was completely restored by the Kona Historical Society. It includes a

Kona Coffee

The Kona coffee belt, some 16 miles long and about a half-mile wide, has been producing smooth, aromatic coffee for more than a century. The slopes of massive Mauna Loa at this elevation provide the ideal conditions for growing coffee: sunny mornings; cloudy, rainy afternoons; and rich, rocky, volcanic soil. More than 600 farms, most just 3 to 7 acres in size, grow the delicious—and luxurious, at generally more than $40 per pound—gourmet beans. Only coffee from the North and South Kona districts can be called Kona (labeling requirements are strict and fiercely defended), and Hawaii is the only state in the United States that produces commercially grown coffee.

The caffeine goodness began in 1828, when the Reverend Samuel Ruggles, an American missionary, brought a cutting over from the Oahu farm of Chief Boki, Oahu's governor. That coffee plant was a strain of Ethiopian coffee called Arabica, which is still produced today, although a Guatemalan strain of Arabica introduced in the late 1800s is produced in far higher quantities.

In the early 1900s, the large Hawaiian coffee plantations subdivided their lots and began leasing parcels to local tenant farmers, a practice that continues today. Many tenant farmers were Japanese families. In the 1930s, local schools switched summer vacation to "coffee vacation," August to November, so that children could help with the coffee harvest, a practice that held until 1969.

When coffee trees are flowering, the white blossoms are fondly known as "Kona snow." Once ripened, coffee is harvested as "cherries"—beans encased in a sweet, red shell. Kona coffee trees are handpicked several times each season to guarantee the ripest product. The cherries are shelled, their parchment layer sun-dried and removed, and the beans roasted to perfection. Today most farms—owned and operated by Japanese-American families, West Coast mainland transplants, and descendants of Portuguese and Chinese immigrants—control production from cultivation to cup.

1913 farmhouse first homesteaded by the Uchida family and is surrounded by coffee trees, a Japanese bathhouse, a *kuriba* (coffee-processing mill), and a *hoshidana* (traditional drying platform). Caretakers still grow, harvest, roast, and sell the coffee exactly as they did more than 100 years ago. All admission proceeds directly help the nonprofit's educational efforts. ■ TIP→ **Call ahead to confirm hours, as they have been limited and varied.** ⊠ *82-6199 Mamalahoa Hwy., mile marker 110* ☎ *808/323–2006* ⊕ *www.konahistorical.org* 🎫 *$20* ⊙ *Closed Sat. and Sun.*

Kona Rainforest Farms

FARM/RANCH | At this family-owned business, the commitment to growing 100% organic coffee starts even before the plants are in the ground, with organic mulch and naturally developed fertilizers that they also sell throughout Hawaii. No pesticides or commercial fertilizers are used on the 80-acre farm. Because it's such an exacting process, only 2% of Kona coffee can claim to be 100% certified organic. They process coffee from cherry to roasted on a solar-powered mill. The farm does private tours (with tastings) by appointment only and even

The 2022 Eruption of Mauna Loa

After slumbering for 38 years, Mauna Loa erupted suddenly on the evening of November 27, 2022. Like nearly all of her past eruptions, this one began as fissures in the summit caldera, Mokuaweoweo, and quickly migrated to a rift zone, "choosing" the Northeast Rift Zone side within hours. This direction induced a sigh of relief in thousands of residents of the Southwest Rift Zone, as lava flowing their direction could have immediately impacted infrastructure. The spectacular eruption lasted about 25 days, covered 8,900 acres and produced 40 billion gallons of lava. About 30 feet of lava inundated 6,000 feet of the Mauna Loa Observatory road and buried some power lines, the only impact to infrastructure.

---

offers a guesthouse should you wish to stay a little longer than a day. ■ **TIP→ The property can be accessed only by four-wheel-drive vehicles.** ✉ *87-2854 Mamalahoa Hwy., Captain Cook* ☎ *808/328–1941* ⊕ *www.mawahocoffee.com* ✉ *Free* ☞ *Tours by appointment only.*

★ Puuhonua O Honaunau National Historical Park *(Place of Refuge)*

NATIONAL PARK | This breathtaking, 420-acre National Historical Park has the best preserved *puuhonua* (place of refuge) in the state, and an aura of ancient sacredness and serenity still imbues the place. Providing a safe haven for noncombatants, *kapu* (taboo) breakers, defeated warriors, and others, the puuhonua offered protection and redemption for anyone who could reach its boundaries, by land or sea. The oceanfront, 960-foot stone wall built more than 400 years ago still stands and is one of the park's most prominent features. A number of ceremonial temples, including the restored Hale o Keawe Heiau (circa 1700), have served as royal burial chambers. Bring a picnic to the oceanfront park, where there are tables and bathrooms. The 2.25-mile, 1871 Trail takes you past incredible lava features and historic sites. This treasure of a park is a must-see for every visitor to the Big Island. ✉ *Rte. 160, Honaunau* ✛ *About 20 miles south* of *Kailua-Kona* ☎ *808/328–2288* ⊕ *www. nps.gov/puho* ✉ *$20 per vehicle.*

Royal Kona Coffee Center and Coffee Mill

FACTORY | FAMILY | Come here to learn how growers create the perfect cup of Kona coffee through a multilayered process, with coffee cherries getting pulped, sorted, and dried in preparation for roasting, both by hand and with machinery. Take an easy, self-guided tour of this mill by following the descriptive plaques around the property. Then stop off at the coffee center to see coffee-making relics, peruse the gift shop, and watch an informational film. Visitors can also enjoy the beautiful views and stroll through a real lava tube on the grounds. ✉ *83-5427 Mamalahoa Hwy.* ✛ *Next to the tree house* ☎ *808/328–2511* ⊕ *www. royalkonacoffee.com* ✉ *Free* ☉ *Closed Sat. and Sun.*

St. Benedict's Painted Church

CHURCH | Between 1899 and 1902, Belgian-born priest and self-taught artist Father John Velge painted the walls, columns, and ceiling of this Roman Catholic church with religious scenes in the colorful style of Christian folk art found throughout the South Pacific. The tiny chapel evokes the European Gothic cathedral tradition and is listed on the Hawaii State Register of Historic Places and the National Register of Historic

St. Benedict's Roman Catholic Church was painted by Father John Velge, the parish's priest in the early 20th century.

Places. It's closed to tours Saturday through Monday, but masses held these days welcome all; call to check times. ✉ 84-5140 Painted Church Rd., off Hwy. 160, Captain Cook ☎ 808/328–2227 ⊕ thepaintedchurchhawaii.org 🎫 Free, donations welcome.

 Beaches

Hookena Beach Park

BEACH | FAMILY | The 2½-mile road to this secluded little gem feels like you're venturing off the beaten path, through an area rich in history. Remnants of an old steamship pier testify to its former role as a thriving port town, complete with (now gone) post office, church, and stores. A favorite of writer Robert Louis Stevenson, Hookena suffered virtual abandonment after tsunami, earthquakes, and the decline of steamship travel. Today, though much quieter, it's still an active Hawaiian fishing village, beloved by residents and tended to by a county-community partnership. The beach has a soft mix of dark brown and gray sand and is backed by steep emerald embankments and a dramatic sloping *pali* (cliff) that make for picturesque tropical vistas. The bay is usually calm, tranquil, and clear with small surf. The park caretakers oversee beach concessions, camping permits, and security. You can rent equipment, beach chairs, and umbrellas. **Amenities:** food and drink; parking (no fee); showers; toilets; water sports. **Best for:** snorkeling; swimming. ✉ Hookena Beach Rd., Hwy. 11, between mile markers 101 and 102, Captain Cook ☎ 808/961–8311 ⊕ www.hookena.org 🎫 Free.

★ Napoopoo Beach

BEACH | Gorgeous and undeveloped, this area in the state historical park offers extraordinary vistas and protected swimming. The shoreline is rocky, but the area is surrounded by high green cliffs, creating calm conditions for superb swimming, snorkeling, and diving (beware of jellyfish). Protected Hawaiian spinner dolphins come to rest and escape predators during the day. Captain James Cook

first landed in Hawaii here in 1778, but a year later he was killed in a skirmish with Hawaiians, now marked by a monument on the bay's north end. Rocky but walkable trails lead to Hikiau Heiau, a sacred place for the Hawaiian people. Please proceed respectfully and do not walk on it or enter it. Parking is very limited. Be aware of the off-limits area (in case of rockfalls) marked by orange buoys. **Amenities:** parking (no fee); showers; toilets. **Best for:** snorkeling; swimming. ⊠ *Kealakekua Bay State Historical Park, Napoopoo Rd. off Hwy. 11, just south of mile marker 111* ☎ *808/961–9544* ⊕ *dlnr. hawaii.gov/dsp* ⊴ *Free.*

🍴 Restaurants

Black Rock Pizza

$ | PIZZA | Diners at their original location in Captain Cook enjoy lovely sunsets from the open air lanai while indulging in such house specialties as the Kanak Attack—a lively mix of sausage, *kalua* pork, meatballs, roasted red pepper, and smoked mozzarella—or the more traditional Kau Ono, infused with spinach, goat cheese, and Italian sausage on a base of garlic and olive oil. All sauces and doughs are completely handcrafted, while an impressive array of salads make a great combo. **Known for:** 12 taps including local beer and seltzers; lunch specials; gluten-free pizza options. ⑤ *Average main: $16* ⊠ *82-6127 Mamalahoa Hwy, Captain Cook* ☎ *808/731–6162* ⊕ *blackrock.pizza.*

★ Kaaloa's Super J's Authentic Hawaiian Food

$ | HAWAIIAN | It figures that the best *laulau* (pork or chicken wrapped in taro leaves and steamed) in West Hawaii can be found at a roadside hole-in-the-wall rather than at an expensive resort luau; in fact, this humble family-run eatery was featured on the Food Network's *The Best Thing I Ever Ate.* Plate lunches to go include tender chicken or pork *laulau,*

steamed for up to 10 hours. **Known for:** tasty kalua pig and cabbage; friendly and welcoming proprietors; *lomi lomi* salmon. ⑤ *Average main: $9* ⊠ *83-5409 Mamalahoa Hwy., between mile markers 106 and 107, Honaunau* ☎ *808/328–9566* ⊙ *Closed Sun.*

Keei Cafe at Hokukano

$$ | ECLECTIC | This nicely appointed restaurant with a warm, woodsy vibe serves delicious dinners with Brazilian, Asian, and European flavors, highlighting fresh ingredients from local farmers. Favorites are the pork chops, Brazilian seafood chowder, peanut-miso salad, and pasta primavera smothered with a basil-pesto sauce. **Known for:** most upscale restaurant in South Kona; live dinner music; cash only. ⑤ *Average main: $20* ⊠ *79-7511 Mamalahoa Hwy., Kealakekua* ✛ *½ mile south of Kainaliu* ☎ *808/322–9992* ▭ *No credit cards* ⊙ *Closed Sun. and Mon. No lunch.*

★ Manago Hotel Restaurant

$ | HAWAIIAN | FAMILY | The historic Manago Hotel is like walking into a time warp, complete with a vintage neon sign, old-timey TV room, high school trophies on the shelves, and old photos on the walls. Their T-shirts brag (and it's not false advertising) that the restaurant has the best grilled pork chops in the world; the fresh fish and New York steak are excellent as well. **Known for:** one of the only places in Kona serving opelu, a local fish; mains come with a variety of side dishes; local hospitality. ⑤ *Average main: $12* ⊠ *82-6155 Mamalahoa Hwy., Captain Cook* ☎ *808/323–2642* ⊕ *www. managohotel.com* ⊙ *Closed Mon.*

Teshima's Restaurant

$ | JAPANESE | FAMILY | Its modest exterior and interior belie the fantastic South Kona experience Teshima's brings; it has been a *kamaaina* (local) favorite since 1929 for a reason. Locals gather at this small landmark restaurant whenever they're in the mood for fresh sashimi, puffy shrimp tempura, or *hekka* (beef and vegetables cooked in an iron pot). **Known for:** excellent tempura combos; long-standing family-owned establishment; authentic local flavor. $ *Average main: $15* ✉ *79-7251 Mamalahoa Hwy., Honalo* ☎ *808/322–9140* ⊕ *www.teshimarestaurant.com.*

 Coffee and Quick Bites

The Coffee Shack

$ | **AMERICAN** | Visitors enjoy stopping here before or after a morning of snorkeling at Kealakekua Bay, and for good reason: the views of the Honaunau Coast from this roadside restaurant are nothing short of drop-dead stunning. This place is best for breakfast or a quick bite, as overpriced mains can miss; but if you're in the mood for a Hawaiian smoothie, iced honey-mocha latte, or scone, it's worth the stop. **Known for:** house-baked luau bread; its own brand of Kona coffee; popular spot with limited parking. $ *Average main: $12* ✉ *83-5799 Mamalahoa Hwy., Captain Cook* ☎ *808/328–9555* ⊕ *www.coffeeshack.com* ☽ *Closed Wed.*

Kaya's Coffee

$ | **CAFÉ** | Authentic organic everything is on the menu here. This bakery and café serves a variety of coffee, baked goods, sandwiches, kombucha, teas, and salads, and it's all 100% organic. **Known for:** vegan and vegetarian; local gathering spot; comfy seating. $ *Average main: $7* ✉ *79-7300 Mamalahoa Hwy,, Captain Cook* ☎ *808/322–8800* ⊕ *kayascoffee.com.*

Kealia Ranch Store

$ | **HAWAIIAN** | **FAMILY** | Part of a huge working cattle ranch—McCandless Ranch, founded in 1915—this homey country store offers bargain-priced shave ice delectably made with a traditional machine. You can order it with a variety of syrups and even add ice cream at the bottom of your cup. **Known for:** huge portions; traditionally made shave ice; locally made crafts. $ *Average main: $5* ✉ *86-4181 Mamalahoa Hwy., Captain Cook* ☎ *808/328–8744* ☽ *Closed Sat.–Mon.*

Hotels

Aloha Guest House

$$ | **B&B/INN** | In the hills above Puuhonua O Honaunau National Historical Park, this guesthouse offers quiet elegance, complete privacy, and beautiful ocean views from every room. **Pros:** eco-conscious option; delicious full breakfast; kitchenette in common area. **Cons:** remote location up a bumpy 1-mile dirt road; 40 minutes from downtown; four-wheel drive recommended. $ *Rooms from: $250* ✉ *Old Tobacco Rd., off Hwy. 11, near mile marker 104, Honaunau* ☎ *808/328–8955* ⊕ *www.alohaguesthouse.com* ⇥ *5 rooms* ⦿ *Free Breakfast.*

Horizon Guest House

$$$$ | **B&B/INN** | Surrounded by McCandless Ranch on 40 acres in South Kona, this place may seem remote, but it's actually just a short drive from some of the best water attractions on the island, including Puuhonua O Honaunau, Kealakekua Bay, and Hookena Beach. **Pros:** private and quiet; heated pool with Jacuzzi; lovely ocean views. **Cons:** not on the beach; 40 minutes from Kailua-Kona; pricier option considering the location. $ *Rooms from: $400* ✉ *86-3992 Mamalahoa Hwy., between mile markers 101 and 100, Captain Cook* ☎ *808/938–7822* ⊕ *www.horizonguesthouse.com* ⇥ *4 suites* ⦿ *Free Breakfast.*

★ Kaawa Loa Plantation

$$ | **B&B/INN** | On a 5-acre coffee farm above Kealakekua Bay, proprietors Mike Martinage and Greg Nunn operate a grand yet very reasonably priced B&B in a plantation-style home featuring a 2,000-square-foot wraparound veranda with excellent views of the bay and the

entire Honaunau Coast. **Pros:** gracious and friendly hosts; excellent breakfast; Hawaiian steam room. **Cons:** not within walking distance of bay; some rooms share a bath; slightly steep turnoff. ⑤ *Rooms from: $209* ⊠ *82-5990 Napoopoo Rd., Captain Cook* ☏ *808/323–2686* ⊕ *www.kaawaloaplantation.com* ↝ *5 rooms* ⑪ *Free Breakfast.*

Kane Plantation Guesthouse

$$$ | B&B/INN | The former home of the late legendary artist Herb Kane, this luxury boutique guesthouse occupies a 16-acre avocado farm overlooking the South Kona coastline. **Pros:** sauna, hot tub, and massage therapy room; upscale amenities; beautiful artwork. **Cons:** not on the beach; off the beaten track; 25 minutes to downtown. ⑤ *Rooms from: $335* ⊠ *84-1120 Telephone Exchange Rd., off Hwy. 11, Honaunau* ✛ *¼ mile past mile marker 105, south of Captain Cook* ☏ *808/328–2416* ⊕ *www.kaneplantation-hawaii.com* ↝ *3 suites* ⑪ *Free Breakfast.*

Luana Inn

$$$$ | B&B/INN | This B&B, with its rare location within walking distance to splendid Kealakekua Bay, offers three high-luxury rooms with kitchenettes in the main house that share the pool-patio area, as well as two suites with more room and privacy in the detached Ohana Cottage. **Pros:** nice pool; Jacuzzi spa at sunset; tranquility and privacy. **Cons:** no breakfast; two- or three-night minimums; not oceanfront. ⑤ *Rooms from: $450* ⊠ *82-5856 Napoopoo Rd., Captain Cook* ☏ *808/731–6634* ⊕ *www.luanainn.com* ↝ *5 units* ⑪ *No Meals.*

★ Manago Hotel

$ | HOTEL | If you are on a budget but still want to be near attractions such as Kealakekua Bay and Puuhonua O Honaunau National Historical Park, this 42-room historical hotel is a good option. **Pros:** authentic local color; rock-bottom prices; terrific on-site restaurant. **Cons:** not the best sound insulation between rooms; older decor; some rooms have highway noise. ⑤ *Rooms from: $91* ⊠ *81-6155 Mamalahoa Hwy., Captain Cook* ☏ *808/323–2642* ⊕ *www.managohotel.com* ↝ *64 rooms* ⑪ *No Meals.*

Nightlife

The HI Dive Bar

BARS | What this watering hole lacks in decor, it makes up for in friendliness. Knock one or two back with a fun *pupu* menu, including street tacos or pork sliders. There's also more for the hungrier bar patron, like Mike's special chili, Reuben sandwiches, or hot dogs. They also offer comedy and open mic nights. Happy hour prices and portions are generous. ⊠ *Mango Court, 79-7460 Mamalahoa Hwy., Kealakekua* ☏ *808/498–0993.*

Korner Pocket Sports Bar & Grill

BARS | A favored haunt of the South Kona crowd, Korner Pocket is tucked into the back of an office plaza and looks like a dive at first glance. But don't let appearances fool you. They serve fantastic, affordable food, ranging from scrumptious burgers to a killer prime rib. The fish taco is a reliable bet. Popular local bands frequently perform, with no cover, and everyone gets up to dance. You can also play pool. It's one of the only places open late in South Kona. ⊠ *81-970 Halekii St., Kealakekua* ☏ *808/322–2994* ⊕ *kornerpocketkona.com.*

 Performing Arts

Aloha Theatre

THEATER | FAMILY | A local community theater group stages musicals and plays at this charming 1930s-vintage theater in Kainaliu. The theater also hosts concerts and film festivals. ⊠ *79-7384 Mamalahoa Hwy., Kainaliu* ☏ *808/322–9924* ⊕ *apachawaii.org.*

4

South Kona SOUTH KONA

Shopping

ANTIQUES

Deja Vu Old and New

ANTIQUES & COLLECTIBLES | Hawaiiana of all kinds, old and new (as the name suggests) is showcased in this clean, tiny antique shop. They carry vintage aloha shirts and clothing, vinyl LPs, jewelry, posters, toys, and more. You're bound to find an easily packable, special souvenir to take home. The owner is fun to talk with because he is so honest about his collections and what you are getting if you buy something. ⊠ *79-7401 Mamalahoa Hwy., Kealakekua* ☎ *808/345–6787* ☉ *Closed Sun.*

CLOTHING

Paradise Found

CLOTHING | Carrying contemporary silk and rayon clothing for women, and aloha shirts for men, this venerable shop is in Kainaliu, near the Aloha Theatre, but there's also a branch at Keauhou Shopping Center. You can even buy 100% Kona coffee at the stores, which is grown on their family farm. ⊠ *79-7406 Mamalahoa Hwy., Kainaliu* ☎ *808/322–2111 Kainaliu location, 808/324–1177 Keauhou location* ⊕ *paradisefoundboutique.com.*

LOCAL SPECIALTIES

Mahina Mele Market

SKINCARE | Small on space but huge on sustainable quality, this shop carries the owners' full line of proprietary organic skincare products created mostly of botanicals grown on their farm. The store also stocks the organic macadamia nuts and coffee grown on 60 acres the proprietors own and manage in South Kona. ⊠ *Mango Court, 79-7460 Mamalahoa Hwy., Suite A-103, Kealakekua* ☎ *808/217–7622* ⊕ *konarosecoffee.com.*

MARKETS

ChoiceMART

FOOD | This gem of a supermarket carries standard groceries and a surprisingly good selection of specialty items for such a small store. They also have excellent organic and Hispanic food aisles. Fresh poke is available by the pound at the butcher counter. This is probably the best place on the island for fresh fish, as the owner once fished with all his current suppliers and still maintains those connections. Grass-fed meats are plentiful too. Prices can be on the high side at times, balanced with good prices on other items. ⊠ *82-6066 Mamalahoa Hwy., Captain Cook* ☎ *808/323–3994* ⊕ *choicemarthawaii.com.*

Pure Kona Green Market

MARKET | **FAMILY** | A favorite in Captain Cook, this Sunday farmers' market runs from 9 to 2 and offers great hot breakfast and lunch items, live music, produce from local farms, and artists selling their work. A limited version is open on Fridays. ⊠ *Amy B. H. Greenwell Ethnobotanical Garden Grounds, 82-6160 Mamalahoa Hwy., Captain Cook.*

🏃 Activities

SPAS

Mamalahoa Hot Tubs and Massage

SPA | Tucked into a residential neighborhood above Kealakekua, this welcome alternative to the large Kohala Coast resort spas feels like a secret hideaway, aglow with tiki torches. Hawaiian lomilomi and hot-stone massages are offered at affordable prices, and couple's massage is also available. ■ **TIP→ Soaking tubs, enclosed in their own thatched gazebos with roof portholes for stargazing, are great for a couple's soak.** ⊠ *81-1016 St. John's Rd., Kealakekua* ☎ *808/323–2288* ⊕ *www.mamalahoa-hottubs.com* ✍ *Hot tubs, from $50; Massage from $210* ☉ *Closed Sun.–Tues.*

THE KOHALA COAST AND WAIMEA

Updated by
Kristina Anderson

◉ Sights	🍴 Restaurants	🛏 Hotels	👜 Shopping	🍸 Nightlife
★★★★★	★★★★★	★★★★★	★★★★☆	★★☆☆☆

WELCOME TO
THE KOHALA COAST AND WAIMEA

TOP REASONS TO GO

★ **Hapuna Beach State Recreation Area:** With soft sand and clear blue water, Hapuna is a ½-mile strand of exquisite loveliness that often makes lists of the world's best beaches.

★ **Puukohala Heiau National Historic Site:** A massive temple structure dating to the 18th century, this was Kamehameha the Great's homage to the war god in order to unify the Hawaiian Islands.

★ **Parker Ranch:** The largest working cattle ranch in Hawaii features historic homes open to the public for tours.

★ **Kaunaoa Beach:** Framed by snow-topped mountains and coconut palms, this magnificent crescent beach is recognizable on many a postcard of Hawaii.

★ **Anaehoomalu Bay:** This beautiful bay, ideal for swimming and snorkeling, is easily accessible and presents the perfect tropical beach setting.

The Kohala Coast in the island's northwest is where you'll find the majority of the Big Island's luxury resorts, not to mention most of its gorgeous white-sand beaches (some off the beaten path and worth exploring), golf courses, and top restaurants. It's not called the "Gold Coast" for nothing. In contrast, North Kohala has low-key, artsy former sugar towns; hilly upcountry Waimea is ranching country.

1 Waikoloa. Home to several major resorts, this region also boasts golf, lots of shopping, and excellent beaches.

2 Mauna Lani. Known as a five-star destination for its resorts, with lavish spas and championship golf courses, the area is home to intriguing historical sites such as petroglyph fields.

3 Mauna Kea and Hapuna. This area has two resorts and two spectacular beaches, including Kaunaoa Beach—a gorgeous, white-sand crescent fronting a sheltered bay—and Hapuna Beach—considered by some to be the island's finest sunset-watching spot.

4 Kawaihae. An important commercial hub, Kawaihae is not a manicured resort area, but some excellent eateries are a draw, and the working harbor is the jumping-off point for tourist boats on weekends, not to mention commercial fishermen and competitive paddlers. The harbor has been key since the days of King Kamehameha.

5 Hawi and Kapaau. These onetime sugar towns on the far north end of the island thrived during the plantation days, but when the sugar business dried up, they turned to artists, who were keen to preserve the town's past. Today, artsy shops and lovingly restored buildings offer a splash of authentic old Hawaiian character.

6 Waimea. Unlike any other part of the Big Island, the rolling green hills and open pastureland lend a pastoral quality to this appealing upcountry town known for good dining. It was once dominated by the Parker family and their ranch, still one of the largest privately owned ranches in the United States.

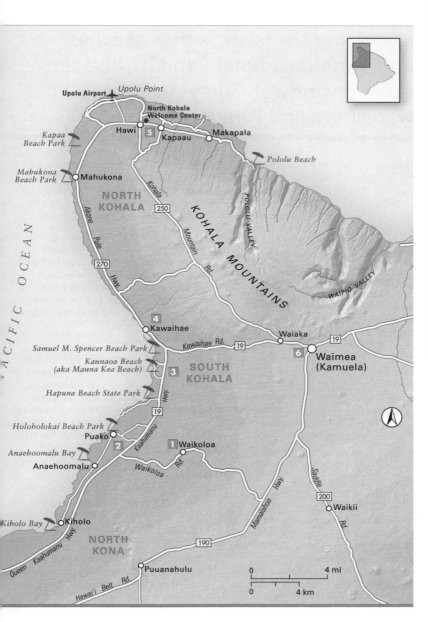

If you had only a weekend to spend on the Big Island, this is probably where you'd want to be. The Kohala Coast is a mix of the island's best beaches and swankiest hotels, and it's also not far from ancient valleys and temples, waterfalls, and funky artist enclaves.

This area is home to almost all of the Big Island's megaresorts. Dotting the coastline are manicured lawns and golf courses, restaurants, and destination spas. But the real attractions here are the area's glorious beaches. On a clear day, you can see Maui, and during the winter months, numerous glistening humpback whales cleave the waters just offshore. Many visitors to the Big Island check in here and rarely leave the Kohala Coast. If you're looking to be pampered and lounge on the beach or by the pool all day with an umbrella drink in hand, this is where you need to be. You can still see the rest of the island since most of the hiking and adventure-tour companies offer pickups at the Kohala Coast resorts, and many hotels have connections to car rental agencies (though the number of cars is limited, and you will need to book ahead).

Rounding the northern tip of the island, the arid coast shifts rather suddenly to green villages and hillsides, leading to lush Pololu Valley in North Kohala, where the hot sunshine along the coast gives way to cooler temperatures. In this area are Hawi and Kapaau, quaint sugar-plantation towns turned artsy villages. New galleries are interspersed with charming reminders of old Hawaii—wooden boardwalks, quaint local storefronts, ice cream shops, delicious neighborhood restaurants, friendly locals, and a delightfully slow pace. There's great shopping for everything from antiques and designer beachwear to authentic Hawaiian crafts.

A short drive from the resorts, Waimea's upcountry, pastoral countryside is sprinkled with well-tended vintage homes with picket fences and flower beds. There's a gentle *paniolo* (Hawaiian cowboy) vibe throughout the town, which boasts a number of excellent restaurants worth seeking out.

MAJOR REGIONS

Kohala Coast. Sometimes referred to as the "Gold Coast" of the Big Island, the stunning Kohala Coast pairs stark black lava fields with azure oceans and white-sand beaches. It's home to all the major resorts: Waikoloa, Mauna Lani, and Mauna Kea and Hapuna boast five-star resorts, spas, golf, and restaurants. Kawaihae, in contrast, is a small working harbor town with some restaurants and amenities. In North Kohala, the tiny towns of Hawi and Kapaau round out the island's northern tip. Having survived the decline of the sugar business, today they evoke a low-key, artsy, historical spirit.

Waimea. Situated at an elevation of 2,600 feet, cool upcountry Waimea has splendors that include mists, rainbows, sun, and verdant hills. Ranchlands sprawl across the cool upland meadows of the area, known as cowboy country. The town has some excellent restaurants.

Planning

Planning Your Time

Two days (or three, if your schedule allows) is sufficient time for experiencing each unique side of Kohala—one day for the resort perks, including the beach, the spa, the golf, and the restaurants; one day for hiking and admiring the waterfalls and valleys of North Kohala, coupled with a wander around Hawi and Kapaau. In addition, don't miss a quick drive up to explore the rustic town of Waimea, with its restaurants, galleries, and bucolic scenery.

Diving and snorkeling are primo along the Kohala Coast, so bring or rent equipment. If you're staying at a resort, it will usually have all the equipment you could possibly want. Or rent gear at the local dive shop in Kawaihae. If you're feeling adventurous, rent a four-wheel-drive vehicle and head to one of the unmarked beaches along the Kohala Coast—you may end up with a beach to yourself.

The best way to explore the valleys of North Kohala is with a hiking tour. Look for one that includes lunch, maybe a zip line, and a dip in one of the area's waterfall pools.

Getting Here and Around

AIR
The Kohala Coast and Waimea are most accessible from the Ellison Onizuka Kona International Airport. South Kohala is a roughly 30-minute drive from the airport, while it's double that to either Hawi or Waimea.

CAR
While some resort guests enjoy staying put at a single property for their entire trip, others appreciate having a rental car to sightsee and explore the island's wide diversity at their own pace. There are many rental options at the airport, but if you change your mind midtrip and want to rent a car, the rental companies operate satellite offices from the Fairmont Orchid Hotel, the Hilton Waikoloa Village, and Waikoloa Village itself.

Beaches

Most of the Big Island's best white, sandy beaches lie on the Kohala Coast, home to the majority of the island's world-class resorts. Simply incomparable beauty, enchanting contrasts of sun-baked black lava with light sands, stands of coconut trees, active reefs, and shimmering, clear water all combine to create the beaches that the world wants to visit. The island's west side tends to be calmer too, but the surf still gets rough in winter. Most of Hawaii's beaches are public property, and the resorts are required to provide public access, so don't be frightened off by a guard shack and a fancy sign. Most resorts have public parking, although it's very limited. Resort beaches aside, there are some beautiful beach parks and some real hidden gems, accessible only by boat, four-wheel drive, or a 15- to 20-minute hike. It's well worth the effort to get to at least one of these.

Hotels

If you are a resort kind of traveler, it doesn't get better than the famous Kohala Coast. Several resort properties offer options for most lifestyles, tastes, and budgets. Most resorts have adjacent condo complexes that offer short-term rentals, too. You may also find housing developments in the Waikoloa, Puako, and the Kawaihae areas with condos and vacation homes for rent, primarily through local property management companies. But some owners handle rentals themselves, through platforms such as VRBO and Airbnb. Relatively recent short-term rental regulations here mean travelers need to check that the property they are considering is operating legally. Check the listings for mandatory operating permits, parking, taxes, and cleaning fees/deposits. Nothing in this area will be far from beaches, restaurants, the airport, and good weather.

The rolling hills and emerald pastures of Waimea present a sharp contrast to the hot, arid beachfront resorts. Just a 20-minute drive up a small hill takes you into this peaceful ranching locale, with its charming residential areas and easy proximity to attractions along the Hamakua Coast and North Kohala. Bed-and-breakfasts and short-term rental options are great choices, as you can enjoy chilly evenings (lots of fireplaces up here) and then have your morning coffee with views of misty hills, and still have lots of time to snorkel at Kohala beaches.

⇨ *Hotel prices in the reviews are the lowest cost of a standard double room in high season. Restaurant prices in the reviews are the average cost of a main course at dinner, or if dinner is not served, at lunch. Hotel and restaurant reviews have been shortened. For full information, see Fodors.com.*

What It Costs in U.S. Dollars			
$	$$	$$$	$$$$
HOTELS			
under $200	$200–$280	$281–$380	over $380
RESTAURANTS			
under $20	$20–$30	$31–$40	over $40

Restaurants

The restaurants along the Kohala Coast range from fine-dining, oceanfront experiences to quick food-court choices and beach shacks serving hot dogs and sandwiches. The resorts hire some of the best chefs in the world to design and prepare their cuisine, and the menu prices reflect that star quality. Hawaii Regional Cuisine, farm-to-table fare, and Asian fusion are popular resort cuisine styles. That said, some resort offerings are overpriced and will disappoint. Nevertheless, affordable local choices are just a short distance away in Kawaihae and Waimea.

Waikoloa

25 miles north of Ellison Onizuka Kona International Airport.

Waikoloa is a region known for its two large resort properties (one a bit outlandish), excellent golf, and eclectic shopping at both the Kings' Shops and Queens' MarketPlace. Sushi, local grills, food courts, small markets, and pricey restaurants all combine to give you abundant eating choices in Waikoloa. The natural gem here is the stunning, classically tropical Anaehoomalu Bay, once the site of royal fishponds and today an ideal spot to soak up some sun, explore along the trails, or try windsurfing. Waikoloa Village, a few miles inland and up the hill to the northeast, offers golf and rental condos for a fraction of the cost of the big resorts.

☺ Beaches

★ Anaehoomalu Bay

BEACH | FAMILY | This gorgeous, expansive stretch of white sand, fringed with coconut palms, fronts the Waikoloa Beach Marriott and is a perfect spot for swimming, windsurfing, snorkeling, and diving. Unlike some Kohala Coast beaches near hotel properties, this one is very accessible to the public and offers plenty of free parking. The bay is well protected, so even when the surf is rough or the trade winds are blasting, it's fairly calm here. (Mornings are calmest.) Snorkel gear, kayaks, and body boards are available for rent at the north end.

■ TIP→ **Locals will appreciate your efforts to use the proper name (pronounced *ā'-nāe-ho'o-mā'lu*) rather than simply its nickname, "A-Bay."**

Behind the beach are two ancient Hawaiian fishponds, Kuualii and Kahapapa, that once served ancient Hawaiian royalty. A walking trail follows the coastline to the Hilton Waikoloa Village next door, passing by tide pools, ponds, and a turtle sanctuary where sea turtles can often be spotted sunbathing on the sand. Footwear is recommended for the trail. **Amenities:** food and drink; parking (no fee); showers; toilets; water sports. **Best for:** snorkeling; sunset; swimming; walking. ✉ *69-275 Waikoloa Beach Dr., Waikoloa* ✛ *Just south of Waikoloa Beach Marriott; turn left at Kings' Shops* 🗪 *Free.*

Kiholo State Park Reserve

BEACH | One of the state park system's newest treasures, Kiholo Bay is still in the planning stage, so facilities are sparse (portable toilets, for example) and not yet complete. The brilliant turquoise waters of this stunning bay, set against stark black lava fields, are a cooling invitation on a warm Kohala day. The shore is rocky and the water's a bit cold and hazy due to freshwater springs, but tons of green sea turtles are in residence year-round. Swimming and snorkeling are excellent when the tide is calm. Thanks to the eruptions of Mauna Loa, what was once the site of King Kamehameha's gigantic fishpond is now several freshwater ponds encircling the bay, with a lava-rock island in the middle. Bring plenty of drinking water. Gates are locked promptly at the times indicated;

weekend camping is allowed with fee and permit. Community group Hui Aloha Kiholo helps the state manage the park. **Amenities:** parking (no fee); toilets. **Best for:** snorkeling; swimming; walking. ✉ *Hwy. 19 between mile markers 82 and 83, Waikoloa* ✛ *Just south of the lookout* ☎ *808/974–6200* ⊕ *dlnr.hawaii.gov/dsp* 🗪 *Free.*

🍴 Restaurants

★ A-Bay's Island Grill

$$ | **MODERN HAWAIIAN** | Beachy yet upscale, this restaurant has an in-house beer sommelier who advises on the perfect pairing with your food choice, which can range from fresh catch, steak, burgers, and sandwiches to crab cakes and escargots. Many dishes incorporate Hawaiian touches. **Known for:** fish tacos; patio seating available; great tapas menu. ⑤ *Average main: $20* ✉ *Kings' Shops, 250 Waikoloa Beach Dr., Waikoloa* ☎ *808/209–8494* ⊕ *www.a-bays.com.*

Hawaii Calls Restaurant and Lounge

$$$$ | **HAWAIIAN** | **FAMILY** | The only full-service restaurant at the Waikoloa Beach Marriott offers a farm-to-table, island-inspired menu. Photos of surf breaks from around the world adorn the walls of this casual, spacious open-air restaurant, which has plenty of patio seating with sunset views. **Known for:** weekly special nights, including lobster night and prime rib and crab night; good breakfast buffet; famous Kuu Alii mai tai. ⑤ *Average main: $41* ✉ *Waikoloa Beach Marriott Resort and Spa, 69-275 Waikoloa Beach Dr., Waikoloa* ☎ *808/886–6789* ⊕ *www. waikoloabeachmarriott.com.*

KPC (Kamuela Provision Company)

$$$$ | **MODERN HAWAIIAN** | The breezy lanai has the most spectacular view of the leeward coast of any restaurant on the Big Island, and it's the perfect accompaniment to the elegant yet down-to-earth Hawaii Regional Cuisine and specialty cocktails. Entrées are on

Kohala Coast

Pololu Valley Beach

POLOLU VALLEY

MOUNTAINS

WAIPIO VALLEY

250   19

Waiaka

Rd.

Waimea
(Kamuela)

190

Mamalahoa

Hwy.

200   Saddle   Rd.

Waikii

0		4 mi
0		4 km

the pricey side, but the Chinese-style mahimahi with mung bean, jade pesto, and ginger scallion sizzle is a winner, and the broiled Keahole lobster does not disappoint. **Known for:** specialty cocktails, such as the mango mojito; the island's best sunset dinner spot; chef's specials nightly. ⑤ *Average main: $55* ⊠ *Hilton Waikoloa Village, 69-425 Waikoloa Beach Dr., Waikoloa* ☎ *808/886–1234* ⊕ *www. hiltonwaikoloavillage.com* ۞ *No lunch.*

★ Lava Lava Beach Club Restaurant
$$ | HAWAIIAN | FAMILY | Dig your toes into the sand and enjoy one of the most happening, entertaining, and memorable bar/restaurants on the Kohala Coast. There's something for everybody here, whether you want cocktails and *pupus* (appetizers) for sunset or a fine-dining experience; highlights include macadamia-nut-and-arare-crusted fresh island fish, baby back ribs, and the chef's signature gazpacho topped with macadamia nut pesto. **Known for:** live entertainment; great Parmesan lava tots and coconut shrimp; signature Sandy Toes cocktail. ⑤ *Average main: $30* ⊠ *69-1081 Kuualii Pl., Waikoloa* ☎ *808/769–5282* ⊕ *lavalava-beachclub.com/bigisland.*

Pueo's Osteria
$$$ | ITALIAN | Perched in a shopping center in Waikoloa Village, this late-night destination also serves dinner from 5 until 9 pm: *pueo* means "owl" in Hawaiian, and refers to the restaurant's "night owl" concept. Renowned executive chef James Babian (Four Seasons Hualalai, Fairmont Orchid) serves multiregional Italian offerings that combine farm-fresh ingredients with fine imported Italian products like prosciutto from Parma. **Known for:** inventive cocktails; late-night bar menu until 11 pm; Tuscan-inspired dining room. ⑤ *Average main: $33* ⊠ *68-1820 Waikoloa Rd., #1201, Waikoloa* ☎ *808/339–7566* ⊕ *www.pueososteria. com* ۞ *No lunch.*

Roy's Waikoloa Bar and Grill
$$$ | MODERN HAWAIIAN | FAMILY | One of celebrity chef Roy Yamaguchi's Hawaii restaurants, this reliable, albeit pricey, place overlooks the lake at the Kings' Shops. Despite the restaurant's boxy interior, the food is good; the three-course, prix-fixe meal is a sure bet, as is blackened ahi. **Known for:** great appetizers to share; extensive list of wines by the glass; Hawaiian fusion cuisine. ⑤ *Average main: $40* ⊠ *Kings' Shops at Waikoloa Village, 69-250 Waikoloa Beach Dr., Waikoloa* ☎ *808/886–4321* ⊕ *www. roysrestaurant.com* ۞ *No lunch.*

Sansei Seafood Restaurant and Sushi Bar
$$ | JAPANESE | FAMILY | Creative sushi and contemporary Asian cuisine take center stage at this entertaining restaurant at Queens' MarketPlace, where you can make a meal out of appetizers and sushi rolls or feast on great entrées from both land and sea. Though it has tried-and-true mainstays, the menu is consistently updated to include options such as Hawaiian ahi carpaccio and Japanese yellowtail nori aioli poke. **Known for:** sushi bar specials; panko-encrusted ahi sashimi roll; karaoke on the weekends. ⑤ *Average main: $20* ⊠ *Queens' MarketPlace, 201 Waikoloa Beach Dr., Suite 801, Waikoloa* ☎ *808/886–6286* ⊕ *www.sanseihawaii.com* ۞ *Closed Tues. and Wed.*

☕ Coffee and Quick Bites

Island Fish and Chips
$ | AMERICAN | FAMILY | Hidden lakeside at the Kings' Shops, this little takeout place is a best-kept secret in the Waikoloa Beach Resort. The combo baskets brim with tempura fresh-catch fish, chicken, shrimp, and more. **Known for:** breakfast options such as loco moco laden with tempura fish fillet; local ownership since 2000; great fish-and-chips to go. ⑤ *Average main: $15* ⊠ *Kings' Shops, 69-250 Waikoloa Beach Dr., #D3, Waikoloa* ☎ *808/886–0005.*

Kohala Condo Comforts

Renting a resort condo is a great way to relax near the beach with many of the comforts of home. The upside is that you get all the pluses of being near a resort with all the privacy of your own place. Most condos have kitchens or a place to barbecue, so you'll want to stock up on groceries.

The nearest full-service market is **KTA Super Stores** (✉ 68-3916 Paniolo Ave., Waikoloa Village ☎ 808/883–1088), no more than a half hour from the resorts.

Even closer are both the **Kings' Shops** (✉ 250 Waikoloa Beach Dr., Waikoloa ☎ 808/886–8811) and the **Queens' MarketPlace** (✉ 201 Waikoloa Beach Dr., Waikoloa ☎ 808/886–8822) in the Waikoloa Beach Resort. There is a small general store with a liquor department and several nice restaurants at the Kings' Shops. Across the street, Queens' MarketPlace also has a food court and sit-down restaurants, as well as a gourmet market where you can get pizza baked to order.

Waikoloa Shrimp Company
$$ | **HAWAIIAN** | Fashioning itself after Hawaii's iconic shrimp trucks, this little place in the Queens' MarketPlace food court specializes in island-style fare, including garlic shrimp, teriyaki chicken, and *kalua* pig and cabbage. They are one of the few quick bites open in the food court and can get quite busy, but everything is made to order, so come with patience. **Known for:** several varieties of Kauai-style shrimp; mac nut pie; classic plate lunches. ⑤ *Average main: $20* ✉ 69-201 Waikoloa Beach Dr., Unit F6, Waikoloa ⊕ www.waikoloashrimpco.com.

Hotels

Aston Shores at Waikoloa
$$$$ | **RESORT** | **FAMILY** | Villas with terra-cotta-tile roofs are set amid landscaped lagoons and waterfalls at the edge of the championship Waikoloa Village Golf Course. **Pros:** good prices for the area; free parking; kid-friendly option with a pool and in-room kitchens. **Cons:** no restaurants on-site; daily resort fee; older decor in some rooms. ⑤ *Rooms from: $395* ✉ 69-1035 Keana Pl., Waikoloa ☎ 808/886–5001, 800/922–7866 ⊕ www.

aquaaston.com ⤵ 120 suites ⦿ No Meals.

Fairway Villas Waikoloa by Outrigger
$$$ | **RESORT** | **FAMILY** | These large and comfy town houses and condominiums, located just off the fairway of the Waikoloa Beach Course, are a short walk from Anaehoomalu Bay. Designed in the style of plantation-era homes, the villas are decorated with rattan furniture and tropical themes and come complete with top-notch appliances in fully equipped kitchens. **Pros:** good location for beach, shopping, dining, and golf; infinity pool; well-equipped kitchens. **Cons:** no ocean views; lots of guest rules and regulations; expensive cleaning fees. ⑤ *Rooms from: $281* ✉ Waikoloa Beach Resort, 69-200 Pohakulana Pl., Waikoloa ☎ 808/886–0036 ⊕ www.outrigger.com ⤵ 70 units ⦿ No Meals.

Hilton Waikoloa Village
$$$$ | **RESORT** | **FAMILY** | Gondola trams glide by, pint-size guests zoom down the 175-foot waterslide, a bride poses on the grand staircase, a fire-bearing runner lights the torches along the seaside path at sunset—these are some typical scenes at this 62-acre megaresort. **Pros:** family-friendly saltwater lagoon; lots of

restaurant and activity options, including two golf courses; close to retail shopping. **Cons:** gigantic and crowded; $48 per night resort fee; restaurants are pricey. ⑤ *Rooms from: $448* ✉ *69-425 Waikoloa Beach Dr., Waikoloa* ☎ *808/886–1234, 800/445–8667* ⊕ *www.hiltonwaikoloavillage.com* ⤳ *1,241 rooms* ⑩ *No Meals.*

★ Kolea at Waikoloa Beach Resort

$$$$ | **RESORT** | **FAMILY** | These modern, impeccably furnished condos offer far more high-end amenities than the average condo complex, including both an infinity pool and a sand-bottom children's pool at its oceanside Beach Club, a fitness center, and a hot tub. **Pros:** can walk to beach; close to activities; resort amenities of nearby Hilton. **Cons:** pricey for not being directly on the beach; no on-property restaurants; limited view from some units. ⑤ *Rooms from: $496* ✉ *Waikoloa Beach Resort, 69-1000 Kolea Kai Circle, Waikoloa* ☎ *808/987–4519* ⊕ *www.kolea. com* ⤳ *53 units* ⑩ *No Meals.*

★ Lava Lava Beach Club Cottages

$$$$ | **HOUSE** | **FAMILY** | Spend the day swimming at the beach just steps away from your private lanai and fall asleep to the sound of the ocean at one of four artfully decorated, one-room cottages on the sandy beach at Anaehoomalu Bay. These cottages are among the few beachfront rentals you will find anywhere on the island. **Pros:** one of the island's few beachfront rentals; fully air-conditioned; fun, Hawaii-themed decor. **Cons:** beach is public, so there may be people in front of cottage; quite expensive; noise, music from nearby restaurant. ⑤ *Rooms from: $699* ✉ *69-1081 Kuualii Pl., Waikoloa* ☎ *808/769–5282* ⊕ *www. lavalavabeachclub.com* ⤳ *4 cottages* ⑩ *No Meals.*

Waikoloa Beach Marriott Resort and Spa

$$$$ | **RESORT** | **FAMILY** | Encompassing 15 acres replete with ancient fishponds, historic trails, and petroglyph fields, the Marriott offers rooms with sleek modern

beds, bright white linens, Hawaiian art, and private lanai. **Pros:** more low-key than the Hilton Waikoloa; sunset luau Wednesday and Saturday; sand-bottom pool for kids. **Cons:** some rooms lack views; expensive daily parking charge; resort fee of $40 per day. ⑤ *Rooms from: $637* ✉ *69-275 Waikoloa Beach Dr., Waikoloa* ☎ *808/886–6789, 800/228–9290* ⊕ *www. marriott.com* ⤳ *297 rooms* ⑩ *No Meals.*

Nightlife

BARS

Kona Tap Room

BARS | A favorite after-work spot for employees from the surrounding hotels, this sports bar lounge in the Hilton Waikoloa Village offers friendly bartenders, free Wi-Fi, and pool tables. Enjoy tropical cocktails, craft beers, light fare, and live music from 8 to 10 nightly. ✉ *Hilton Waikoloa Village, 425 Waikoloa Beach Dr., Waikoloa* ☎ *808/886–1234* ⊕ *www. hiltonwaikoloavillage.com.*

 Performing Arts

LUAU AND POLYNESIAN REVUES

Legends of Hawaii Luau at Hilton Waikoloa Village

CULTURAL FESTIVALS | **FAMILY** | Presented outdoors at the Kamehameha Court, the aptly subtitled "Our Big Island Story" features song and a fire-knife dance as well as a delicious buffet with Big Island–grown luau choices and more familiar fare and tropical drinks. Pay a small fee and upgrade to Alii seating for a front-row vantage; unlimited cocktails, beer, and wine; and your own buffet station. A children's station has kid favorites. Delicious desserts such as *haupia* (coconut pudding) cream puffs and Kona-coffee cheesecake top it all off. ✉ *Hilton Waikoloa Village, 69-425 Waikoloa Beach Dr., Waikoloa* ☎ *808/886–1234* ⊕ *www. hiltonwaikoloavillage.com* ▧ *$190.*

Hawaiian Music on the Big Island

It's easy to forget that Hawaii has its own style of music until you step off a plane onto the Islands—and then there's no escaping it. It's a unique blend of the strings and percussion imported by early Portuguese settlers and the chants and rituals of the ancient Hawaiians, reflecting the unique mixed heritage of this special place. Hawaiian music today includes Island-born tunings of acoustic guitar—slack key and steel guitar—along with the ukulele and vocals.

This is one of the few folk music traditions in the United States that is fully embraced by the younger generation, with no prodding from their parents or grandparents. A good many radio stations on the Big Island play Hawaiian/"island"/reggae music, and concerts performed by Island favorites like Makana or L. T. Smooth are filled with fans of all ages.

The best introduction is one of the annual festivals: the free **Hawaiian Slack Key Guitar Festival** (Labor Day weekend), with a handful of greats performing at the Outrigger Kona Resort and Spa; the **Great Waikoloa Ukulele Festival** (March), which features prominent players and everything ukulele; and the **KWXX Hoolaulea** (September), a popular Island music jam with big names performing on four stages in downtown Hilo.

You can also catch live performances most nights at a handful of local bars and clubs, including **Big Kahuna**, **Huggo's on the Rocks, Laverne's,** and the **Kona Brewing Co.** in Kailua-Kona; **Korner Pocket** in Kealakekua; and **Cronies Bar and Grill** in Hilo.

Wherever you go on the island, sweet Hawaiian music fills the air.

Waikoloa Beach Marriott Resort and Spa Sunset Luau

CULTURAL FESTIVALS | In a setting overlooking the white sands of Anaehoomalu Bay, this Polynesian luau includes a spectacular Samoan fire-dance performance as well as traditional music and dances from Pacific Island cultures. Making use of island ingredients such as Waipio Valley poi, Keahole shrimp, and Pulehu steaks, the menu by executive chef Jayson Kanekoa treats guests to authentic island flavors. Probably the most affordable luau on the island, they also offer an open bar. ⊠ *Waikoloa Beach Marriott Resort and Spa, 69-275 Waikoloa Beach Dr., Waikoloa* 🕾 *808/886–8111* ⊕ *www.waikoloabeachresort.com* 🍴 *$159.*

MAGIC

★ Kona Kozy's Comedy and Magic Show

MAGIC | Paul "Kona Kozy" Kozak, a veteran Las Vegas and New York comedy club entertainer, brings a world-class magic show to the Kohala Coast. Every show is different but, guaranteed, each one is hilarious. Held within his fine-art tiki gallery, the shows will truly have you asking "How'd he do that?" for days afterward. Kozy knows his stuff: he once did a command performance for Prince Charles and Princess Diana. The show is for ages 18 and up; there are two shows nightly. ⊠ *Queens' MarketPlace, 69-201 Waikoloa Beach Dr., Suite E3, Waikoloa* 🕾 *808/430–1957* ⊕ *konakozy.com* 🍴 *$79.*

Shopping

ARTS AND CRAFTS

Hawaiian Quilt Collection

CRAFTS | The iconic Hawaiian quilt is a work of art that is prized and passed down through generations. At this store, the oldest quilt retailer in Hawaii, you'll find everything from hand-quilted purses and bags to wall hangings and blankets. More than likely, a friendly Hawaiian *tutu* (grandma) will be in the shop talking story. You can even get a take-home kit and sew your own Hawaiian quilt. ✉ *Queens' MarketPlace, 69-201 Waikoloa Beach Dr., #305, Waikoloa* ☎ *808/886–0494* ⊕ *www.hawaiian-quilts.com.*

CLOTHING

Blue Ginger

CLOTHING | The Waikoloa branch of this fashion veteran offers really sweet matching aloha outfits for the entire family in tropical batik prints. Handbags, shoes, robes, jewelry, and lotions are also sold here. ✉ *Queens' Market-Place, 69-201 Waikoloa Beach Dr., #K2, Waikoloa* ☎ *808/886–0022* ⊕ *www. blueginger.com.*

Reyn Spooner

CLOTHING | The dressy clothing available here has been a tradition in Hawaii since 1959 and remains popular among locals and visitors alike. The store offers rayon, cotton, and silk aloha shirts for both men and boys, men's shorts, and clothing for women and girls. Prices may be high, but you're buying the best. ✉ *Queens' MarketPlace, 69-201 Waikoloa Beach Dr., Waikoloa* ☎ *808/886–1162* ⊕ *www. reynspooner.com.*

GALLERIES

★ Lava Light Galleries

ART GALLERY | C.J. Kale is an accomplished, award-winning photographer famous for capturing extraordinary images of lava flowing through the curl of a wave. Not a believer in using any photo manipulation or special effects, Kale produces work that is as authentic as it gets. He and gallery partners Linda and Don Hurzeler showcase their fine images of the beauty of Hawaii and other scenic places around the world. ✉ *Queens' MarketPlace, 69-201 Waikoloa Beach Dr., #F-13, Waikoloa* ☎ *808/756–0778* ⊕ *www.lavalightgalleries.com.*

JEWELRY AND ACCESSORIES

Maui Divers

JEWELRY & WATCHES | Among the fine jewelry at this boutique is a wide selection of high-end pearl jewelry, including Tahitian black pearls, South Sea white and golden pearls, and chocolate Tahitian pearls. It also sells freshwater pearls in the shell, black coral (the Hawaii state gemstone), and diamonds. Creations in 14-karat gold showcasing Hawaii themes such as traditional heirloom designs and flora and fauna are also on display. Prices are high but so is the quality. ✉ *Queens' MarketPlace, 69-201 Waikoloa Beach Dr., #J-11, Waikoloa* ☎ *808/886–4817* ⊕ *www. mauidivers.com.*

★ Na Hoku

JEWELRY & WATCHES | In business since 1924 and the oldest and largest jeweler in Hawaii, this impressive retailer specializes in crafting stunning pieces that reflect the beauty of the islands. You will see sand, sun, and sea in their signature Wave collection—pendants set with diamonds and inlaid with shimmering blue iridescent opal. If you can't afford gold and diamonds, consider one of their charming Puka Bead build-a-bracelet creations, an affordable option. ✉ *Kings' Shops, 69-250 Waikoloa Beach Dr., Waikoloa* ☎ *808/886–7566* ⊕ *nahoku.com.*

SHOPPING CENTERS

Kings' Shops

SHOPPING CENTER | Lakeside restaurants and cafés, surf shops, designer boutiques, a nine-hole putting green, a farmers' market, a weekly Polynesian fire-knife show, and free morning petroglyph tours are just a few of the reasons to visit this conveniently located outdoor shopping center. Probably the best large center on the Kohala Coast, its roster of stores includes Martin & MacArthur, Tori Richard, and island jewelers Na Hoku, as well as high-end retailers Tiffany & Co. and Michael Kors. Gourmet offerings abound at A-Bay's Island Grill, Foster's Kitchen, and the more casual Island Fish & Chips. Shuttles run from the resorts to the center daily from noon to 8, although A-Bay's stays open until midnight, a rarity on the coast. ⊠ *Waikoloa Beach Resort, 250 Waikoloa Beach Dr., Waikoloa* 🕾 *808/339–7145* ⊕ *www.kingsshops. com.*

Queens' MarketPlace
SHOPPING CENTER | The largest shopping complex on the Kohala Coast houses fashionable clothing stores, jewelry boutiques, galleries, gift shops, and restaurants such as Sansei Seafood Restaurant & Sushi Bar, Kuleana Rum Shack, and Romano's Macaroni Grill. Island Gourmet Markets, Starbucks, and an affordable food court are other options. Waikoloa Luxury Cinemas offers the ultimate movie experience and includes a restaurant called Bistro at the Cinemas, which is a worth a stop even if you don't hit a show with dinner. ⊠ *Waikoloa Beach Resort, 201 Waikoloa Beach Dr., Waikoloa* 🕾 *808/886–8822* ⊕ *www.queensmarketplace.net.*

Activities

SPAS
Kohala Spa at the Hilton Waikoloa Village
SPA | Naupaka (a flowering shrub) grows in abundance along the shores of Hawaii Island, and Kohala Spa pays it tribute with the 80-minute Signature Naupaka White Flower Ritual. This feast for the senses incorporates a foot massage with awa root and Hawaiian ginger, followed by warmed body compressions with healing herbs and a full-body massage, blending essential oils. Locker rooms

are outfitted with a wealth of beauty and bath products, and the spa's retail facility sells signature Coco-Mango lotions, body washes, and shampoos. An open-air, seaside cabana provides a tropical spot for a massage overlooking the Pacific, while the fitness center has the latest machines and plentiful classes. ⊠ *Hilton Waikoloa Village, 69-425 Waikoloa Beach Dr., Waikoloa* 🕾 *808/886–2828* ⊕ *www. kohalaspa.com* 🖼 *Massages from $165; Wiki massage from $105.*

Mandara Spa at the Waikoloa Beach Marriott Resort
SPA | Overlooking the hotel's main pool and with a distant view of the ocean, Mandara offers a complete spa menu, with lomilomi massage, scrubs, wraps, and numerous facial options. Mandara, which operates spas all over the world, uses Elemis products and incorporates local ingredients like lime and ginger in the scrubs and warm coconut milk in the wraps. Try the Tropical Hawaiian Body Scrub Experience, exfoliating with a selection of Hawaii's natural ingredients. The facility's stunning design fuses contemporary and traditional Asian motifs. A glam squad awaits you at the full-service salon. ⊠ *Waikoloa Beach Marriott Resort and Spa, 69-275 Waikoloa Beach Dr., Waikoloa* 🕾 *808/886–8191* ⊕ *www.mandaraspa.com* 🖼 *Massages from $205, facials from $270.*

Mauna Lani

8 miles north of Waikoloa.

Mauna Lani is known for its expensive resorts, but it's so much more. In addition to soothing trade winds, black lava landscapes, and turquoise seas, the region offers numerous historical sites, including ancient fishponds, petroglyphs, and historical trails that invite lovers of history and culture to explore numerous spots along this stunning coast.

◉ Sights

Holoholokai Beach Park and Petroglyph Trail

TRAIL | While mostly rocky topography makes swimming and snorkeling a bit difficult here, this little park is still scenic and relaxing. Take the short trail over to the petroglyph trail; interpretive signs will guide you. There are showers, picnic tables, and restrooms; public parking is limited. ⊠ *Holoholokai Beach Park Rd., Waimea (Hawaii County)* ⊹ *Near the end of N. Kaniku Dr.* ☎ *808/657–3293* 🎫 *Free.*

🍴 Restaurants

Binchotan Bar and Grill

$$ | **ASIAN FUSION** | In a sophisticated setting that includes open-air patio seating, this restaurant offers contemporary Asian dishes made with meats, prawns, peppers, and more grilled over an open flame in the traditional style. Blending locally sourced ingredients with Japanese and Hawaiian influences, Binchotan creates a menu that pays homage to multiple cultures. **Known for:** Robatayaki Experience (chef's selection of grilled items); okonomiyaki (savory Japanese-style pancakes) featuring Kona lobster and macadamia nut shrimp; reservations strongly recommended. ⑤ *Average main: $28* ⊠ *Fairmont Orchid Hawaii, 1 N. Kaniku Dr., Waimea (Hawaii County)* ☎ *808/885–5778* ⊕ *www.fairmont.com* ⊘ *Closed Tues. and Wed. No lunch.*

Brown's Beach House at the Fairmont Orchid Hawaii

$$$$ | **MODERN HAWAIIAN** | Sitting right on the resort's sandy Pauoa Bay, the Fairmont's signature restaurant Brown's Beach House offers beautiful sunset dining and innovative cuisine. Attention to detail is evident in the sophisticated menu, which may include crab-crusted Kona *kampachi* or other dishes with fresh fish, roasted duck breast, or Kona coffee–crusted venison, as well as local produce and ingredients. **Known for:** Dungeness crab and lobster tail; tiki torches and live Hawaiian music beneath starry skies; reservations highly recommended. ⑤ *Average main: $56* ⊠ *Fairmont Orchid Hawaii, 1 N. Kaniku Dr., Waimea (Hawaii County)* ☎ *808/885–2000* ⊕ *www.fairmont.com* ⊘ *No lunch.*

★ CanoeHouse

$$$$ | **MODERN HAWAIIAN** | One of the most romantic settings on the Kohala Coast, this landmark, oceanfront restaurant showcases traditional Hawaiian flavors, artful presentations, and locally grown or raised products. The progressive menu spotlights standout entrées such as roasted beef tenderloin, dry-rubbed New York Steak, Keahole lobster, fish caught locally, shellfish, island-fresh greens, and local goat cheese. **Known for:** memorable sunsets with tiki torches; customized dining program by the chef offered at the Captain's Table; reservations essential far in advance. ⑤ *Average main: $56* ⊠ *Mauna Lani, Auberge Resorts Collection, 68-1400 Mauna Lani Dr., Waimea (Hawaii County)* ☎ *808/885–6622* ⊕ *aubergeresorts.com/maunalani* ⊘ *No lunch.*

★ Knead & Bake

$ | **PIZZA** | This authentic little pizzeria with tables inside and outdoors might just make the best hand-tossed pizza on the Kohala Coast, if not the whole island. The New York–born owner does not scrimp and has even imported special pizza ovens and dough machines from New York, as well as Fontanini-brand ingredients, to give his pizzas that extra pizzazz. **Known for:** fresh local ingredients; innovative pizza toppings; good prices. ⑤ *Average main: $19* ⊠ *Shops at Mauna Lani, 68-1330 Mauna Lani Dr., Waimea (Hawaii County)* ☎ *808/731–4490* ⊕ *kneadandbake.com.*

Tommy Bahama Restaurant and Bar

$$$ | **MODERN HAWAIIAN** | **FAMILY** | Upstairs at the Shops at Mauna Lani, this breezy, open-air restaurant offers an excellent roster of appetizers, including seared-scallop sliders and coconut-crusted crab cakes, as well as meat and fish mains and decadent desserts. The chef here has freedom to cook up his own daily specials, and the seared ahi is a standout. **Known for:** the chain's reliable cuisine and relaxed vibe; popular cocktail bar and lounge; house-baked breads and specialty butters. ⑤ *Average main: $38* ✉ *The Shops at Mauna Lani, 68-1330 Mauna Lani Dr., Suite 102, Waimea (Hawaii County)* ☎ *808/881–8686* ⊕ *www.tommybahama.com.*

Coffee and Quick Bites

Mauna Lani Coffee Company

$ | CAFÉ | The staff at this little place take pride in learning customers' names and treating you like a "regular." All the coffee favorites are here, from espresso to latte to a good old-fashioned cup of Kona. Homemade pastries are available, and they open at 6 am for the early birds. **Known for:** variety of blended frappes; outdoor seating; free Wi-Fi and outlets. ⑤ *Average main: $8* ✉ *The Shops at Mauna Lani, 68-1330 Mauna Lani Dr., #300, lower level, Waimea (Hawaii County)* ☎ *808/731–4000* ⊕ *maunalanicoffeeco. com.*

🛏 Hotels

★ Fairmont Orchid Hawaii

$$$$ | RESORT | FAMILY | This first-rate resort overflows with tropical gardens, cascading waterfalls, a sandy beach cove, a meandering pool, a lagoon for the kids, and all the luxury amenities. **Pros:** oceanfront location; excellent pool; aloha hospitality. **Cons:** central pool can get very crowded; $48 resort fee; not the best beach among Kohala Coast resorts. ⑤ *Rooms from: $847* ✉ *1 N. Kaniku Dr., Waimea (Hawaii County)* ☎ *808/885–2000, 800/845–9905* ⊕ *www.fairmont. com* ⇌ *540 rooms* ⊙ *No Meals.*

★ Mauna Lani, Auberge Resorts Collection

$$$$ | RESORT | Popular with honeymooners and anniversary couples for decades, this elegant Kohala Coast classic is still one of the island's most beautiful resorts, highlighted by a breathtaking, open-air lobby with cathedral-like ceilings, Zen-like koi ponds, and illuminated sheets of cascading water. **Pros:** beautiful design; award-winning spa; many Hawaiian cultural programs. **Cons:** no luau; limited dining selection on-site; $50 resort fee. ⑤ *Rooms from: $1,099* ✉ *68-1400 Mauna Lani Dr., Waimea (Hawaii County)* ☎ *808/885–6622, 808/657–3293* ⊕ *aubergeresorts.com/maunalani* ⇌ *338 rooms* ⊙ *No Meals.*

Mauna Lani Point and the Islands at Mauna Lani

$$$$ | RESORT | Surrounded by the emerald greens of a world-class oceanside golf course, the private, independent, luxury condominiums at Islands at Mauna Lani offer spacious two-story suites, while Mauna Lani Point's villas are closer to the beach. **Pros:** friendly front desk; stellar views; extra-large units. **Cons:** quite pricey; individually owned units vary in decor and amenities; some units are a distance from the barbecue/pool area. ⑤ *Rooms from: $691* ✉ *Mauna Lani Point, 68-1050 Mauna Lani Point Dr., Waimea (Hawaii County)* ☎ *808/885–5022, 800/642–6284* ⊕ *www.classicresorts.com* ⇌ *66 units* ⊙ *No Meals.*

🍸 Nightlife

BARS

Luana Lounge

COCKTAIL BARS | The contemporary lounge in the Fairmont Orchid has a large terrace and an impressive water view. Serving signature sushi and classic rolls, the Luana is a favorite of locals too. Bartenders are skilled at mixology, and service is impeccable. The crowd is mellow, so it's a nice place for an early evening cocktail or after-dinner liqueur. Happy hour is from 4 to 5 with all drinks discounted; live music begins at sunset and continues until 9. ✉ *Fairmont Orchid Hawaii, 1 N.*

Kaniku Dr., Waimea (Hawaii County)
☎ *808/885–2000* ⊕ *www.fairmont.com.*

 Performing Arts

LUAU AND POLYNESIAN REVUES
Hawaiiloa Luau
CULTURAL FESTIVALS | Slickly produced and well choreographed, this gorgeous show incorporates both traditional and contemporary music and dance, along with an array of beautiful costumes. It tells the tale of Hawaiiloa, the great navigator from Tahiti, and of the celestial object—Hokulea, "Star of Gladness"—that guided him to the islands later named Hawaii. Presented under the stars at the Fairmont Orchid Hawaii on Saturdays, the luau offers several stations with a variety of Hawaiian and Hawaii Regional Cuisine dishes, and there's an open full bar for mai tais and other tropical libations. ⊠ *Fairmont Orchid Hawaii, 1 N. Kaniku Dr., Waimea (Hawaii County)* ☎ *808/885–2000, 808/326–4969* ⊕ *fairmont.com/orchid-hawaii* ⊠ *$189.*

 Shopping

SHOPPING CENTERS
The Shops at Mauna Lani
SHOPPING CENTER | This pleasant complex offers Hawaiian and tropical apparel, a hair salon, and lots of dining choices. Pizza does not get better than at Knead & Bake, where you can dine in or order online for pickup. A small market lets you stock up on basics, and coffee, smoothie, and sandwich shops are still around, as well as a couple of nice surf shops, jewelry stores, and upscale clothing boutiques. Tommy Bahama Restaurant and Bar is especially favored by locals for a *pau hana* (after work) cocktail and *pupu* (appetizer). ⊠ *68-1330 Mauna Lani Dr., Waimea (Hawaii County)* ☎ *808/885–9501* ⊕ *www.shopsatmaunalani.com.*

 Activities

SPAS
Auberge Spa at Mauna Lani Resort
SPA | Available only to hotel guests, the spa is a one-of-a-kind experience with a mix of traditional standbys (lomilomi massage, moisturizing facials) and innovative treatments influenced by ancient traditions and incorporating local products. Deep tissue, Swedish, and the Mailani scalp and foot massage round out the offerings. The hibiscus and papaya body exfoliation will leave your skin glowing. The spa incorporates the exclusive line of signature products by goop in their treatments, and a small retail store helps you take some home with you. ⊠ *Mauna Lani Resort, 68-1365 Pauoa Rd., Waimea (Hawaii County)* ☎ *808/885–6622* ⊕ *www.aubergeresorts.com* ⊠ *Massages from $225, facials from $225, body scrub from $240.*

★ Spa Without Walls at the Fairmont Orchid Hawaii
SPA | This spa ranks among the best massage facilities on the island, partially due to the superlative setting—private massage areas are situated amid the resort's waterfalls, freshwater pools, and meandering gardens. In addition, the Fairmont Orchid is one of the few resorts on the island to offer beachside massage. Splurge on the 110-minute Alii Royal Experience, combining a detox treatment called Awa Earth and Fire with the Kahinu, a warm coconut oil applied on the forehead and scalp, then blending into a neck and shoulder massage. Add a fragrant herbal wrap or a coffee-and-vanilla scrub. Where else can you relax to the sounds of cascading waterfalls while watching tropical yellow tangs swim beneath you through windows in the floor? ⊠ *Fairmont Orchid Hawaii, 1 N. Kaniku Dr., Waimea (Hawaii County)* ☎ *808/887–7540* ⊕ *www.fairmont.com/orchid-hawaii* ⊠ *Massages from $270, facials from $275, body treatments from $300.*

Continued on page 152

BIRTH OF THE ISLANDS

How did the volcanoes of the Hawaiian Islands come to be here, in the middle of the Pacific Ocean? The ancient Hawaiians believed that the volcano goddess Pele's hot temper was the key to the mystery; modern scientists contend that it's all about plate tectonics and one very hot spot.

Plate Tectonics and the Hawaiian Question: The theory of plate tectonics says that the Earth's surface is comprised of plates that float around slowly over the planet's hot interior. The vast majority of earthquakes and volcanic eruptions occur near plate boundaries—the San Francisco earthquakes in 1906 and 1989, for example, were the result of activity along the nearby San Andreas Fault, where the Pacific and North American plates meet. Hawaii, more than 1,988 miles from the nearest plate boundary, is a giant exception. For years scientists struggled to explain the island chain's existence—if not a fault line, what caused the earthquakes and volcanic eruptions that formed these islands?

Kilauea erupting on the Big Island of Hawaii

What's a Hot Spot? In 1963, J. Tuzo Wilson, a Canadian geophysicist, argued that the Hawaiian volcanoes must have been created by small concentrated areas of extreme heat beneath the Pacific Plate. Wilson hypothesized that there is a hot spot beneath the present-day position of Hawaii Island (the "Big Island") and its heat produced a persistent source of magma. Magma is produced by rising-but-solid mantle rock that melts when it reaches about 100 km. At that depth, the lower pressure can no longer stop the rock from melting, and the magma rises to erupt onto the sea floor, forming an active seamount. Each flow caused the seamount to grow until it finally emerged above sea level as an island volcano. Plausible so far, but why then, is there not one giant Hawaiian island?

THE JOURNEY OF PELE

Holo Mai Pele, often told through hula, is the Hawaiian story of how volcano goddess Pele sends her sister Hiiaka on an epic quest from the Big Island to fetch her lover Lohiau, living on Kauai. Overcoming many obstacles, Hiiaka reaches full goddess status and falls in love with Lohiau herself. When Pele finds out, she destroys everything dear to her sister, killing Lohiau and burning her sister's ohia groves. Each time lava flows from a volcano, ohia trees sprout shortly after, in a constant cycle of destruction and renewal.

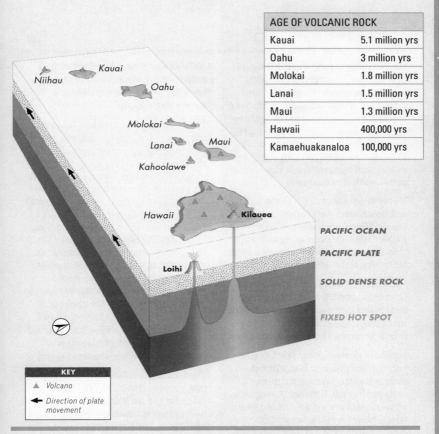

AGE OF VOLCANIC ROCK	
Kauai	5.1 million yrs
Oahu	3 million yrs
Molokai	1.8 million yrs
Lanai	1.5 million yrs
Maui	1.3 million yrs
Hawaii	400,000 yrs
Kamaehuakanaloa	100,000 yrs

PACIFIC OCEAN

PACIFIC PLATE

SOLID DENSE ROCK

FIXED HOT SPOT

KEY
▲ Volcano
← Direction of plate movement

Volcanoes on the Move: Wilson further suggested that the movement of the Pacific Plate itself eventually carries the island volcano beyond the hot spot. Cut off from its magma source, the island volcano becomes dormant. As the plate slowly moved to the northwest, one island volcano would become extinct just as another would develop over the hot spot. After several million years, there is a long volcanic trail of islands and seamounts across the ocean floor. The oldest islands are those farthest from the hot spot. The exposed rocks of Kauai, for example, are about 5.1 million years old, but those on the Big Island are less than half a million years old, with new volcanic rock still being formed.

An Island on the Way: Off the coast of the Big Island of Hawaii, another volcano is still submerged but erupting. Geologists long believed it to be a retired seamount volcano, but in the 1970s they discovered both old and new lava on its flanks, and in 1996 it erupted with a vengeance. It is believed that thousands of generations from now, it will be the newest addition to the Hawaiian archipelago, so in July 2021 was given the name Kamaehuakanaloa, "the red child of Kanaloa."

Hawaii Beach Safety

Hawaii's world-renowned, beautiful beaches can be extremely dangerous at times due to large swells and strong currents—so much so that the state rates wave hazards using three signs: a yellow square (caution), a red stop sign (high hazard), and a black diamond (extreme hazard). Signs are posted and updated three times daily or as conditions change.

Never swim alone or dive into unknown water or shallow breaking waves. If you're unable to swim out of a rip current by swimming sideways, tread water and wave your arms in the air to signal for help.

Even in calm conditions, this is still the ocean, and there are other dangerous things in the water to be aware of, including razor-sharp coral, jellyfish, eels, and rarely, sharks, to name a few.

Signs are posted along beaches when jellyfish are present. Box jellyfish swarm Hawaii's leeward shores 9 to 10 days after a full moon. Portuguese man-of-wars are usually found when winds blow from the ocean onto land. Reactions to a sting range from usually mild (burning sensation, redness, welts) to severe (breathing difficulties). Rinse the affected area with rubbing alcohol and apply ice. Seek first aid if you experience a severe reaction.

The chances of a shark bite in Hawaiian waters are very low; sharks attack swimmers or surfers three or four times per year. Of the 40 species of sharks found near Hawaii, tiger sharks (recognized by their blunt snouts and vertical bars on their sides) are considered the most dangerous because of their size and indiscriminate feeding behavior. To reduce your shark-attack risk, avoid swimming at dawn, dusk, and night, when some shark species may move inshore to feed. Avoid murky waters, harbor entrances, areas near stream mouths, channels, or steep drop-offs. Heed high-surf and brown-water advisories. Storm runoff attracts these apex predators who feast on fish feeding closer to shore.

The website ⊕ *safebeachday. com* provides beach hazard maps for the main islands, as well as current weather and surf advisories, and listings of closed beaches; ⊕ *hioceansafety.com* has good advice for beachgoers.

Mauna Kea and Hapuna

6 miles north of Mauna Lani.

Every visitor to the Big Island should put Hapuna Beach State Recreation Area on your itinerary, especially if you're not staying at the Westin Hapuna Beach Resort, located beachfront. This glorious stretch of white-sand beauty will not fail to take your breath away, no matter what the season or time of day. Sheer enchantment also defines the luminous waters and curve of white sand at Kaunaoa, also called Mauna Kea Beach, but it's more difficult to access due to the Mauna Kea Beach Hotel's control of the parking area.

Beaches

★ **Hapuna Beach State Recreation Area**
BEACH | FAMILY | One of Hawaii's most breathtaking beaches, Hapuna is a ½-mile-long stretch of white perfection, with turquoise water that is calm in summer, so it's good for kids, with just enough rolling waves to make

Hapuna Beach State Recreation Area protects the island's largest white-sand beach. At the northern end sits the Westin Hapuna Beach Resort.

bodysurfing and body boarding fun. Watch for the undertow; in winter it can be very rough. There is excellent snorkeling around the jagged rocks that border the beach on either side, but high surf brings strong currents. Known for awesome sunsets, this is one of the island's best places to see the "green flash" as the sun dips below a clear horizon.

Parking is ample, although the lot can fill up by midday and the beach can get crowded on weekends and holidays. Plenty of picnic tables and lots of grass overlooking the beach offer shady respite on a hot day. Lifeguards are on duty during peak hours. **Amenities:** lifeguards; parking (fee); showers; toilets; water sports. **Best for:** sunset; surfing; swimming; walking. ⊠ *Hwy. 19 near mile marker 69, Mauna Kea* ✛ *Just south of the Westin Hapuna Beach Resort* ☎ *808/961–9544* ⊕ *dlnr.hawaii.gov/dsp/ parks* ⧉ *$10 parking fee per vehicle.*

★ **Kaunaoa Beach** (*Mauna Kea Beach*)
BEACH | FAMILY | Hands down one of the most beautiful beaches on the island, if

not the whole state, Kaunaoa features a short crescent of pure white sand framed by coconut palms. The beach, which fronts the Mauna Kea Beach Hotel, slopes very gradually, and there's great snorkeling along the rocks. Classic Hawaii postcard views abound, especially in winter, when snow tops Maunakea to the east. When conditions permit, waves are good for body and board surfing also. Currents can be strong in winter, so be careful. Get a cocktail at the beach cabana and enjoy the sunset. ■ **TIP➜ Public parking is limited to a few spaces, so arrive before 10 am or after 4 pm. If the lot is full, head to nearby Hapuna Beach, where there's a huge parking lot ($10 per vehicle). Try this spot again another day—it's worth it! Amenities:** parking (no fee); showers; toilets; water sports. **Best for:** snorkeling; sunset; swimming; walking. ⊠ *62-100 Mauna Kea Beach Dr., Mauna Kea* ✛ *Entry through gate to Mauna Kea Beach Hotel* ⧉ *Free.*

Waialea Bay

BEACH | This hidden gem just off to the north of Puako Beach Drive is popular with locals and offers good swimming in a protected, sandy setting. Snorkeling is fairly good here due to the presence of lots of rocky lava formations; turtles are everywhere. It's a Marine Life Conservation District, which regulates certain activities. Summer finds it calm and pristine; winter can be rough and unswimmable. **Amenities**: none. **Best for**: snorkeling, sunbathing, swimming. ⊠ *Puako Beach Road, veer right, then left at pole 69, Puako.*

 Restaurants

Hau Tree

$$ | **MODERN HAWAIIAN** | Though it sits on a patio by the pool, this casual beachside restaurant and beach bar with gazebo is not just for *pupus* and cocktails. The island-infused dinner menu features excellent entrées, such as the Korean-style short ribs or the Kona Kanpachi Nicosia salad, plus plentiful seafood dishes and greens from local farms. **Known for:** famous Fredrico cocktail; great sunset views; reasonable prices for a resort restaurant. Ⓢ *Average main: $27* ⊠ *Mauna Kea Beach Hotel, 62-100 Mauna Kea Beach Dr., Mauna Kea* ☎ *808/882–5707* ⊕ *www.maunakeabeachhotel.com.*

★ Manta at the Mauna Kea Beach Hotel

$$$$ | **MODERN HAWAIIAN** | Perched on the edge of a bluff overlooking the sparkling waters of Kaunaoa Beach, the resort's flagship restaurant is a compelling spot for a romantic meal at sunset, especially at one of the outside tables. The culinary team's take on Hawaii Regional Cuisine highlights locally sourced, sustainable fish, chicken, and beef. **Known for:** beachfront balcony dining; exhibition kitchen; Sunday brunch with prime rib, smoked salmon, and omelet station. Ⓢ *Average main: $50* ⊠ *Mauna Kea Beach Hotel, 62-100 Mauna Kea Beach Dr., Mauna Kea* ☎ *808/882–5707* ⊕ *www.maunakeabeachhotel.com* ⊘ *Closed Sun. and Mon.*

★ Meridia

$$$$ | **MEDITERRANEAN** | This open-air restaurant at the Westin Hapuna Beach Resort has high ceilings and a lanai that overlooks the pool and the sandy-white shores of gorgeous Hapuna Beach. The focus is on the freshest seafood, and the small-plate appetizers and main course options also showcase a bounty of Big Island ingredients infused with Mediterranean influences. **Known for:** reservations essential; almond-crusted ahi; fantastic location (including for sunset viewing). Ⓢ *Average main: $53* ⊠ *The Westin Hapuna Beach Resort, 62-100 Kaunaoa Dr., Mauna Kea* ☎ *808/880–1111* ⊕ *www.meridiarestaurant.net* ⊘ *No lunch.*

 Hotels

Mauna Kea Beach Hotel, Autograph Collection

$$$$ | **RESORT** | The grande dame of the Kohala Coast has long been regarded as one of the state's premier vacation resort hotels, and it borders one of the world's finest white-sand beaches, Kaunaoa. **Pros:** good dining options; premier tennis center; no resort fees. **Cons:** some oceanfront rooms are noisy; $35 daily valet parking fee; 27 miles from airport. Ⓢ *Rooms from: $999* ⊠ *62-100 Mauna Kea Beach Dr., Mauna Kea* ☎ *808/882–7222, 866/977–4589* ⊕ *www.maunakeabeachhotel.com* ⟡ *252 rooms* ⦿ *No Meals.*

The Westin Hapuna Beach Resort

$$$$ | **RESORT** | **FAMILY** | Known for its direct access to the Big Island's largest white-sand beach, this massive hotel has enormous columns and a terraced, open-air lobby with a rotunda ceiling, curved staircases, and skylights. **Pros:** extra-large rooms, all ocean-facing; helpful staff; 18-hole championship golf course.

Cons: fitness center a five-minute walk from the hotel; $35/day parking fee; 30 miles from Kailua-Kona. ⓢ *Rooms from: $766* ✉ *62-100 Kaunaoa Dr., Mauna Kea* ☎ *808/880–1111, 866/774–6236* ⊕ *www. marriott.com* ⇌ *249 rooms* ⎮⊙⎮ *No Meals.*

Performing Arts

LUAU AND POLYNESIAN REVUES

⭐ **Mauna Kea Beach Luau**

CULTURAL FESTIVALS | FAMILY | On the oceanfront North Side Luau Grounds, you can indulge in the best of island cuisine—a traditional feast of *kalua* (earth oven–baked) pig roasted in an *imu* (oven), island fish, *lomi lomi* salmon, and sashimi—while enjoying entertainment by renowned local performers. The luau, originally premiering in 1960 for *Newsweek* magazine and going strong ever since, includes an amazing fire-knife dance, spirited chanting, and traditional hula. *Keiki* (children) can learn the *hukilau* (a traditional song and dance), and you can relax right on the beach, under the stars. If you choose one luau during your visit to the Big Island, this should be the one, and it's surprisingly affordable. ∎TIP→ **You can elect to see only the show for a reasonable fee.** ✉ *Mauna Kea Beach Hotel, Autograph Collection, 62-100 Mauna Kea Beach Dr.* ☎ *808/882–5810, 808/882–7222* ⊕ *www.maunakeabeach-hotel.com* ✉ *$180, $130 show only.*

🏃 Activities

SPAS

Hapuna Spa by Mandara

SPA | At this resort spa, luxury awaits visitors who select from a menu of body treatments and massages, the most popular being the traditional Hawaiian lomilomi massage. Another option is to splurge on the dramatic Fire and Ice Massage, which incorporates heated basalt stones counterbalanced by ice-cool gels to gently detoxify and soothe the body.

An outdoor, covered treatment lanai is the spot for couples to enjoy fresh tropical breezes and ocean sounds and have a massage in tandem. ✉ *The Westin Hapuna Beach Resort, 62-100 Kaunaoa Dr., Mauna Kea* ☎ *808/880–3335* ⊕ *marri-ott.com* ✉ *Massages from $205.*

Mauna Kea Spa by Mandara

SPA | Mandara blends European methods and indigenous treatments to create the ultimate spa experience. Though this resort facility is on the smaller side, the excellent treatments are up to the international company's exacting standards. Try the Mandara Signature Facial or the coconut poultice massage, which uses heated, scented herbs to relax muscles and release tension. Traditional Hawaiian lomilomi is also available. ✉ *Mauna Kea Beach Hotel, Autograph Collection, 62-100 Mauna Kea Beach Dr., Mauna Kea* ☎ *808/882–5630* ⊕ *www.mandaraspa. com* ✉ *Massages from $205, facials from $250.*

Kawaihae

6 miles north of Hapuna.

This no-frills industrial harbor, where in 1793 the first cattle landed in Hawaii, is a hub of commercial and community activity. It's also where King Kamehameha and his men launched their canoes when they set out to conquer the neighboring islands. Kawaihae is especially busy on weekends, when paddlers, surfers, tourist charters, and local fishing boats share the waters. Second in size only to Hilo Harbor, the port serves interisland cargo carriers and often shelters the *Makalii*, one of three traditional Hawaiian sailing canoes. Kawaihae Village has several restaurants with nice sunset views.

Sights

⭐ Puukohola Heiau National Historic Site

HISTORIC SIGHT | Quite simply, this is one of the most historic and commanding sites in all of Hawaii: here, in 1810, on top of Puukohola (Hill of the Whale), Kamehameha the Great built the war *heiau*, or temple, that would serve to unify the Hawaiian Islands, ending 500 years of warring chiefdoms. The oceanfront, fortresslike site is foreboding and impressive. A paved ½-mile looped trail runs from the visitor center to the main temple sites. An even older temple, dedicated to the shark gods, lies submerged just offshore, where sharks can be spotted swimming, usually first thing in the morning. A museum displays ancient Hawaiian weapons, including clubs, spears, a replica of a bronze cannon that warriors dragged into battle on a Hawaiian sled, and three original paintings by artist Herb Kane. This underrated park is often very uncrowded. Rangers are available to answer questions, or you can take a free audio tour on your smartphone. Plan about an hour to see everything. ⊠ *62-3601 Kawaihae Rd., Kawaihae* ☎ *808/882-7218* ⊕ *www.nps.gov/puhe* ⧉ *Free.*

Beaches

Spencer Park at Ohaiula Beach

BEACH | FAMILY | Popular with local families because of its reef-protected waters, this white-sand beach is probably the safest beach in West Hawaii for young children. It's also generally safe for swimming year-round, which makes it a reliable spot for a lazy day at the beach. There is a little shade, plus a volleyball court and pavilion, and the soft sand is perfect for sand castles. It tends to get crowded with families and campers on weekends, but the beach is mostly clean. You won't see a lot of fish if you're snorkeling here, but in winter you can often

catch sight of a breaching whale or two. The beach park lies just below Puukohola Heiau National Historic Site. **Amenities:** lifeguards (weekends and holidays only); parking (no fee); showers; toilets. **Best for:** sunset; swimming. ⊠ *Hwy. 270, Kawaihae* ✛ *Toward Kawaihae Harbor, just after road forks from Hwy. 19* ☎ *808/961-8311* ⧉ *Free.*

 Restaurants

⭐ Seafood Bar and Grill

$$ | SEAFOOD | Upstairs in a historical building, this seafood tiki bar has been a hot spot for years, known for a dynamite and well-priced bar menu with tasty pupus, signature seafood dishes such as the coconut shrimp and poke burger, and even a prime rib special on Tuesday. Don't let the kitschy retro appearance fool you; this place is frequented by legacy celebrities whose names you know or whose records you've bought. **Known for:** funky tiki theme; seafood quesadilla; excellent service. ⑤ *Average main: $23* ⊠ *61-3642 Kawaihae Harbor (Hwy. 270), Kawaihae* ☎ *808/880-9393* ⊕ *www.seafoodbarandgrill.com* ⊗ *Closed Sat.*

☕ Coffee and Quick Bites

Anuenue Ice Cream and Shave Ice

$ | HAWAIIAN | FAMILY | Shave ice and ice cream in every imaginable flavor can be found at the ideal spot, close to the resort coast beaches. Prepare to wait in line for 15–20 minutes as you ponder your options, but don't fret: it's worth it. **Known for:** lilikoi shave ice; Kona fudge ice cream; creative use of local flavors. ⑤ *Average main: $6* ⊠ *Kawaihae Harbor Shopping Center, 61-3665 Akoni Pule Hwy., Kawaihae* ☎ *808/882-1109.*

Kohala Burger and Taco

$ | AMERICAN | This little spot offers epic cheeseburger plates (using grass-fed beef) and even has a 1950s-style malt shop. They also serve a local favorite, the pineapple whip, perfect for a cool break on a hot day. **Known for:** Mexican food on the menu; one of few eateries in Kawaihae; freshly prepared meals. $ *Average main: $10 ⊠ Kawaihae Shopping Center, 61-3665 Akoni Pule Hwy., Kawaihae* ☎ *808/880–1923* ⊕ *kohalaburgerandtaco. com* ⊗ *Closed Sat.–Mon. No dinner.*

Nightlife

★ Blue Dragon Tavern and Cosmic Musiquarium

BARS | Across from the harbor in Kawaihae, you can dine and dance to live music under the stars and palms at this wildly popular tavern, with central uncovered atrium (offering a clue about how often it rains here—nearly never). The fare is of the burger, fish-and-chips, and fish taco variety and is decent in both price and quality. The grog offerings are super fun, with inventive cocktails such as the Dancing Dragon, an elixir with house-made sangria infused with peach and raspberry liqueurs and tropical juices. Sometimes the bands are great and sometimes not, but it's so much fun to come here you really won't mind. ⊠ *61-3616 Kawaihae Rd., Kawaihae* ☎ *808/882–7771* ⊕ *www.bluedragontavern.com* ⊗ *Closed Mon.–Wed.*

Shopping

GALLERIES

Harbor Gallery

ART GALLERY | Since 1990, this classy gallery has been enticing visitors with a vast collection of paintings and sculptures by more than 200 Big Island artists. There are also antique maps and prints, wooden bowls, paddles, koa furniture, jewelry, and glasswork. The shop hosts two annual wood shows and actively supports the local arts community. ⊠ *Kawaihae Harbor Shopping Center, 61-3665 Akoni Pule Hwy., Kawaihae* ☎ *808/882–1510* ⊕ *www.harborgallery.biz.*

SHOPPING CENTERS

Kawaihae Harbor Shopping Center

SHOPPING CENTER | This almost-oceanfront shopping plaza houses the exquisite Harbor Gallery, which represents many Big Island artists. Try the Big Island–made ice cream and shave ice (the best in North Hawaii) at local favorite Anuenue. Also here are Kohala Burger and Taco, Mountain Gold Jewelers, and Kohala Divers. ⊠ *61-3665 Akoni Pule Hwy., Kawaihae.*

SPORTING GOODS

Kohala Divers

SPORTING GOODS | **FAMILY** | If you plan to dive or snorkel a lot, you can save by buying your own top-quality gear at this friendly shop. It also carries cute clothing, sun-protection wear for adults and kids, souvenirs, lotions, sunscreens, toys, and beach gear. Snorkel rentals (mask, snorkel, fins, and defogger) are $10 per day or $35 weekly. This is the premier dive shop in this area, where you can also book your dive tour at the counter. (If you are not certified, they do that too.) ⊠ *Kawaihae Harbor Shopping Center, 61-3665 Akoni Puli Hwy., Kawaihae* ☎ *808/882–7774* ⊕ *kohaladivers.com.*

Hawi and Kapaau

18 miles north of Kawaihae.

These North Kohala towns have an interesting history, and today they are full of lovingly restored vintage buildings housing fun and funky shops and galleries, as well as eateries worth a stop for a quick bite. Near the birthplace of King Kamehameha, the towns thrived during the plantation days, once bustling with hotels, saloons, and theaters—even a railroad. They took a hit when "Big Sugar" left the island, but both are blossoming again, thanks to strong local communities, tourism, athletic events, and an influx of artists keen on honoring the towns' past. Hawi is internationally known as the turnaround point for the cycling portion of the Ironman World Championship triathlon event.

Sights

Keokea Beach Park

CITY PARK | A pavilion welcomes visitors to this 7-acre county beach park fronting the rugged shore in North Kohala. This is a popular local spot for picnics, fishing, and surfing. You're likely to spot some sea life from shore as well. It's a nice rest stop on your way to Pololu Valley. ■TIP→ **Enjoy the scenery, but don't try to swim here—the water is very rough. Be careful on the hairpin curve going down.** ⊠ *Hwy. 270, Kapaau* ✢ *On the way to Pololu Valley, near mile marker 27* ☞ *Free.*

King Kamehameha Statue

MONUMENT | A statue of Kamehameha the Great, the famous king who united the Hawaiian Islands in the early 19th century, stands watch over his descendants in North Kohala. The 8½-foot-tall figure wears the king's sacred feather *kihei*, *mahiole*, and *kaei* (cape, helmet, and sash). This is actually the original of the statue fronting the Judiciary Building on King Street in Honolulu. Cast in Florence in 1880, it was lost at sea. A replica was commissioned and shipped to Honolulu, but the original statue was later found in a Falklands Island junkyard. It now stands in front of the old Kohala Courthouse in Kapaau, next to the highway on the way toward Pololu Valley. Every year on King Kamehameha Day (June 11), Kohala residents honor their most famous son with a celebration that involves a parade and draping the statue in dozens of handmade floral lei. ⊠ *54-3900 Kapaau Rd., Kapaau.*

Lapakahi State Historical Park

HISTORIC SIGHT | A self-guided, 1-mile walking tour leads through the ruins of the once-prosperous fishing village of Koaie, which dates as far back as the 15th century. Displays illustrate early Hawaiian fishing and farming techniques, salt gathering, games, and legends. Because the shoreline near the state park is an officially designated Marine Life Conservation District (and part of the site itself is considered sacred), swimming is not allowed nor are swim gear or sunscreen. Portable restrooms are available but not drinking water. ■TIP→ **Gates close promptly at 4 pm, and they mean business!** ⊠ *Hwy. 270 at mile marker 14, between Kawaihae and Mahukona, Kapaau* ☏ *808/327–4958* ⊕ *www.hawaiistateparks.org* ☞ *Free.*

Mookini Heiau

HISTORIC SIGHT | Dating from as early as AD 480, this parallelogram-shaped structure is a stunning example of a *luakini heiau*, used for ritualized human sacrifice to the Hawaiian war god Ku. The isolated National Historic Landmark within Kohala Historical Sites State Monument is so impressive in size and atmosphere that it's guaranteed to give you what locals call "chicken skin" (goose bumps). The place feels haunted, and even more so if you are the only visitor and the skies are dark and foreboding. Visit with utmost care and respect. Nearby is Kapakai Royal Housing Complex, the birthplace of Kamehameha the Great. Although it is now under the care of the National Park Service, family descendants still watch over the site. ■TIP→ **Don't drive out here if it's been raining; even with a four-wheel drive, you could easily get stuck.** ⊠ *Coral Reef Pl./Upolu Point Rd., off Upolu Airport Rd. and Hwy. 270 (Akoni Pule Hwy.), Hawi* ✢ *Turn at sign for Upolu Airport, near Hawi, and hike or drive 1½ miles southwest* ☏ *808/961–9540* ⊕ *www.nps. gov* ☞ *Free* ☺ *Closed Weds.*

Beaches

Mahukona Beach Park

BEACH | Snorkelers and divers often make exciting discoveries in the clear waters of this park, now a swimming hole and an

Pololu Valley Beach is one of the island's most beautiful, but you may want to enjoy it from the lookout at the top; it's a steep 15-minute climb down to reach the light-gray sand.

underwater museum of sorts. Amazingly, it's also home to a dormant, submerged shield volcano of the same name with a summit of 9,500 feet, showcasing just how deep it gets right offshore. Long ago, when sugar was the economic staple of Kohala, this harbor was busy with boats waiting to make overseas shipments. Now remnants of shipping machinery, train wheels and parts, and what looks like an old boat are easily visible in the clear water. There's no actual beach here, but a ladder off the old dock makes getting in the water easy. Venture out only on tranquil days, though, when the water is calm; conditions can get windy and the ocean choppy.

A popular place with locals, Mahukona is busy on weekends. A camping area on the south side of the park has picnic tables and an old covered pavilion. A trail also leads to nearby Lapakahi State Park, about a ½-mile hike. **Amenities:** showers; toilets. **Best for:** snorkeling; swimming. ⊠ *Hwy. 270 between mile markers 14*
and 15, Hawi* ✛ *About 7 miles south of Hawi* ☏ *808/961–8311* ☞ *Free.*

Pololu Valley Beach

BEACH | At the tip of North Kohala, this is one of the Big Island's most scenic beaches. Rain and erosion over millennia have created a stunning, deep-cut windward valley with a windswept gray-sand beach that is piled with large, round boulders and driftwood and backed by ironwood trees and sheer green cliffs. The trail is steep and rocky; it can also be muddy and slippery, so use caution. A Pololu Trail Steward program stations local "stewards" at the trailhead to share historical and cultural perspectives of the valley. Please visit with respect for the land and for all area residents. This is not a safe swimming beach even though locals swim, body board, and surf here. Rip currents and usually rough surf pose a real hazard. Because this is an isolated area far from emergency help, extreme caution is advised. **Amenities:** none. **Best for:** solitude. ⊠ *Hwy. 270 at end of road, Kapaau* ☞ *Free.*

Restaurants

Bamboo Restaurant and Gallery

$$ | **HAWAIIAN** | In the heart of Hawi, this popular restaurant provides a historical setting in which to enjoy a menu brimming with Hawaiian country flair. Most of the entrées feature fish and chicken prepared several ways, although if the kitchen gets busy, you might get a mediocre plate. **Known for:** fresh catch with ginger, cilantro, and peanuts; passion fruit margaritas; weekend entertainment. ⓢ *Average main: $25* ✉ *55-3415 Akoni Pule Hwy., Hawi* ☎ *808/889–5555* ⊕ *www.bamboorestauranthawaii.com* ⊙ *Closed Mon. No dinner Sun.*

Mi Ranchito

$ | **MEXICAN** | Hawaii is not usually known for good Mexican food, but this tiny, cash-only café on the ground floor of a vintage building is definitely one of the exceptions. Quality ingredients and a decent menu are on tap at this friendly establishment decorated with charming touches of Mexico. **Known for:** large portions; outstanding chiles rellenos; BYOB policy. ⓢ *Average main: $13* ✉ *55-3419 Akoni Pule Hwy., Hawi* ☎ *808/756–4636* ▤ *No credit cards* ⊙ *Closed Sun.*

ⓒ Coffee and Quick Bites

Kohala Coffee Mill and Tropical Dreams

$ | **CAFÉ** | If you're looking for something sweet—or savory—this busy café in downtown Hawi serves breakfast (bagels, espresso machine–steamed eggs), and lunch (hot dogs, burgers, chili, salads) until 6. Sit outside and watch the world go by as you enjoy locally made ice cream that is *ono* (delicious), as well as other sweet treat specialties. **Known for:** vegan soup; sometimes crowded; outstanding local coffee. ⓢ *Average main: $6* ✉ *55-3412 Akoni Pule Hwy., Hawi* ☎ *808/889–5577* ⊙ *No dinner.*

🛏 Hotels

★ Hawaii Island Retreat at Ahu Pohaku Hoomaluhia

$$$$ | **B&B/INN** | Here, above the sea cliffs in North Kohala, sustainability meets luxury without sacrificing comfort: the resort generates its own solar and wind-turbine power, harnesses its own water, and grows much of its own food. **Pros:** stunning location; emphasis on organic food; affordable yurts are one lodging option. **Cons:** somewhat isolated and not within walking distance of restaurants; yurts don't have in-unit showers; four-night minimum. ⓢ *Rooms from: $425* ✉ *250 Maluhia Rd., Kapaau* ✛ *Off Hwy. 270 in Hawi* ☎ *808/889–6336* ⊕ *www.hawaii-islandretreat.com* ⮐ *20 rooms* ⦿l *Free Breakfast.*

★ Puakea Ranch

$$$ | **HOUSE** | **FAMILY** | Four beautifully restored ranch houses and bungalows occupy this historic country estate in Hawi, where guests enjoy their own private swimming pools, horseback riding, round-the-clock concierge availability, and plenty of fresh fruit from the orchards. **Pros:** charmingly decorated; washer and dryer in each house; private swimming pools. **Cons:** 15 minutes to the beach; spotty cell-phone coverage; sometimes windy. ⓢ *Rooms from: $359* ✉ *56-2864 Akoni Pule Hwy., Hawi* ☎ *808/315–0805* ⊕ *www.puakearanch.com* ⮐ *4 houses* ⦿l *No Meals.*

⬤ Shopping

ARTS AND CRAFTS

Bamboo Gallery

CRAFTS | The real draw of the Bamboo Restaurant is its attached art gallery, which tempts browsers with elegant koa-wood furniture and an array of gift items, such as hand-sewn crafts, boxes, jewelry, and even upscale aloha shirts. There's something for everyone here, and the prices are affordable. ✉ *55-3415 Akoni Pule Hwy., Hawi* ☎ *808/889–1441* ⊕ *www.bamboorestauranthawaii.com.*

Elements Jewelry and Fine Crafts

CRAFTS | The tiny shop carries lots of original jewelry handmade by local artists, as well as carefully chosen gifts including unusual ceramics, paintings, prints, glass items, baskets, fabrics, bags, and toys. Look for their 100% cotton *pareau* (sarongs) designed in Hawaii. ✉ *55-3413 Akoni Pule Hwy., Hawi* ⊹ *Next to Bamboo Restaurant* ☎ *808/889–0760* ⊕ *www. elementsjewelryandcrafts.com* ⊗ *Closed Mon.*

CLOTHING

★ As Hawi Turns

CLOTHING | Housed in the 1932 Toyama Building, this landmark North Kohala shop stocks sophisticated women's resort wear made of hand-painted silk or high-quality cotton in tropical designs by local artists. There are also plentiful vintage treasures, jewelry, gifts, hats, bags, and toys, plus handmade ukuleles by local luthier David Gomes. ✉ *55-3412 Akoni Pule Hwy., Hawi* ☎ *808/889–5023.*

GALLERIES

Ackerman Galleries

ART GALLERY | This small, family-owned gallery features fine art, glass, jewelry, aloha wear, and island souvenirs. ✉ *3897 Akoni Pule Hwy., Kapaau* ☎ *808/889– 5138* ⊕ *www.ackermangalleries.com* ⊗ *Closed Sun.*

Rankin Gallery

ART GALLERY | Watercolorist and oil painter Patrick Louis Rankin showcases his own work at his shop in a restored plantation store next to the bright-green Chinese community and social hall. The building sits right at a curve in the road on the way to Pololu Valley, at the first gulch past Kapaau. ✉ *53-4380 Akoni Pule Hwy., Kapaau* ☎ *808/889–6849* ⊕ *www.patricklouisrankin.net.*

LOCAL SPECIALTIES

Hawaii Cigar and Ukulele

MUSIC | It may seem like an odd combination to offer, but this funky little shop knows how to do both right. Handcrafted instruments start at just $100 and are made by local master luthiers David Gomes and Mark Evans. One lesson is included with your purchase, and they also have a great selection of other stringed instruments and accessories. Cigar lovers can sit in the lounge and enjoy a custom, hand-rolled Nicaraguan cigar for just $10. Or you can partake of the CBD option if cigars aren't your thing, then browse the cool selection of Hawaiiana in the gift shop before you leave. ✉ *55-3419 Akoni Pule Hwy., Hawi* ☎ *808/889–1282* ⊕ *hawicenter.com* ☞ *By appointment only.*

Kohala Grown Market

FOOD | This popular natural market carries handmade soaps and lotions, clothing, honey, organic groceries, and fresh vegetables. The deli counter offers a wide variety of smoothies and an excellent roast beef sandwich served with chips. Hot foods are available from 1 to 3 pm; eat outside on one of their small tables. There's even Ola Brew beer on tap and Big Island Booch kombuchas available. It's a great alternative if you don't want sit-down dining at the town's only restaurant. ✉ *55-3419 Akoni Pule Hwy., Hawi* ☎ *808/937–4930* ⊕ *kohalagrownmarket. com.*

 Activities

SPAS

Hawaii Island Retreat Maluhia Spa

SPA | Remote and elegant, this sanctuary in North Kohala offers three artfully appointed indoor treatment rooms and two outdoor massage platforms that overlook the valley. The spa is first-rate, with handcrafted wooden lockers, rain-style showerheads, and a signature line of lotions and scrubs made locally. The owners also create their own scrubs and wraps from ingredients grown on the property. Massage options include Hawaiian lomilomi, Thai, and deep tissue. ⊠ *250 Maluhia Rd., Kapaau* ☎ *808/889–6336* ⊕ *www.hawaiiislandretreat.com* ⊠ *Massages from $130, facials from $70.*

Waimea

10 miles east of the Kohala Coast, 23 miles southeast of Kapaau, 40 miles northeast of Kailua-Kona.

Thirty minutes over the mountain from Kohala, Waimea (sometimes called "Kamuela" to distinguish it from the similarly named places on Kauai and Oahu) offers a completely different experience from the rest of the island. Rolling green hills, large open pastures, light rain, cool evening breezes, and morning mists, along with abundant cattle, horses, and regular rodeos, are just a few of the surprises you'll stumble upon here in *paniolo* (cowboy) country. Parker Ranch, one of the largest privately held cattle ranches in the United States, surrounds this attractive little town.

Waimea is also where some of the island's top Hawaii Regional Cuisine chefs practice their art using local ingredients, which makes it an ideal place to find yourself at dinnertime. In keeping with the restaurant trend toward featuring local farm-to-table ingredients, a handful of Waimea farms and ranches supply most of the restaurants on the island, and many sell to the public as well. With its galleries, coffee shops, brewpubs, restaurants, beautiful countryside, and *paniolo* culture, Waimea is well worth a stop if you're heading to Hilo or Maunakea. ■ TIP→ **The short highway, or mountain road, that connects Waimea to North Kohala (Highway 250) affords some of our favorite Big Island views.**

GETTING HERE AND AROUND

From the Kohala Coast, it's a reasonable drive to Waimea. From the Mauna Kea and Hapuna resorts, it's about 12 miles; from the Waikoloa resorts, it's about 19 miles via Waikoloa Road. You can see most of what Waimea has to offer in one day, but if you're heading up to Maunakea for stargazing—which you should—it could easily be stretched to two. If you stay in Waimea overnight (there are many B&B options), spend the afternoon browsing through town or touring some of the area's ranches and historic sites, and then indulging in a delicious meal.

Sights

★ Anna Ranch Heritage Center

HISTORIC SIGHT | On the National and State Registers of Historic Places, this stunning heritage property belonged to the "first lady" of Hawaii ranching, Anna Lindsey Perry-Fiske, and now provides a rare opportunity to see a fully restored cattle ranch compound and learn about the life of this fascinating woman. She rounded up and butchered cattle by day and threw lavish parties by night. Wander the picturesque grounds and gardens on a self-guided walk, watch a master saddlemaker and an ironsmith in action, and take a guided tour (by appointment only) of the historic house, where Anna's furniture, gowns, and elaborate *pau* (parade riding) costumes are on display. The knowledgeable staff shares anecdotes about Anna's life. (Some staff and visitors have even reported strange goings-on in the main house, suggesting that Anna may still be "hanging around.") ⊠ *65-1480 Kawaihae Rd., Waimea (Hawaii County)* ☎ *808/885–4426* ⊕ *www.annaranch.org* ⊠ *Grounds and Discovery Trail free, historic home tours $10* ⊗ *Closed Sat.–Mon.*

Imiola Congregational Church

CHURCH | Highlights of this stunning church, which was established in 1832 and rebuilt in 1857, include a gleaming, restored koa interior and unusual wooden

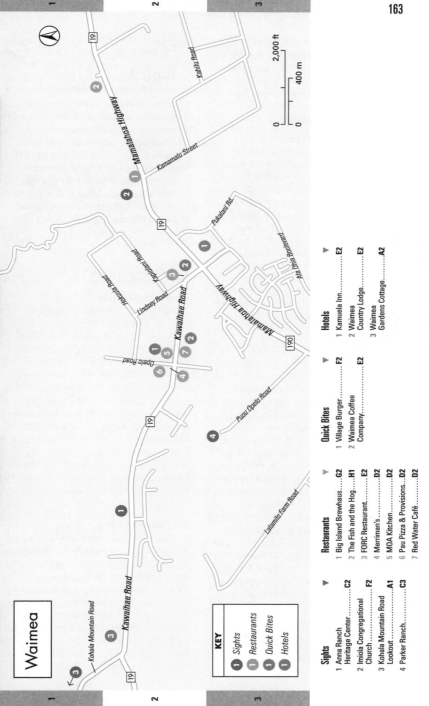

Waimea

KEY
- ① Sights
- ① Restaurants
- ① Quick Bites
- ① Hotels

Sights ▶
1. Anna Ranch Heritage Center..........**C2**
2. Imiola Congregational Church..........**F2**
3. Kohala Mountain Road Lookout..........**A1**
4. Parker Ranch..........**C3**

Restaurants ▶
1. Big Island Brewhaus.....**G2**
2. The Fish and the Hog....**H1**
3. FORC Restaurant..........**E2**
4. Merriman's..........**D2**
5. MOA Kitchen..........**D2**
6. Pau Pizza & Provisions...**D2**
7. Red Water Café..........**D2**

Quick Bites ▶
1. Village Burger..........**F2**
2. Waimea Coffee Company..........**E2**

Hotels ▶
1. Kamuela Inn..........**E2**
2. Waimea Country Lodge..........**E2**
3. Waimea Gardens Cottage..........**A2**

0 ____ 2,000 ft
0 ____ 400 m

calabashes hanging from the ceiling. Be careful not to walk in while a service is in progress, as the front entry is behind the pulpit. ✉ *65-1084 Mamalahoa Hwy., on "Church Row," Waimea (Hawaii County)* ☎ *808/885–4987* ⊕ *www.imiola.org* ✉ *Free; donations welcome.*

Kohala Mountain Road Lookout

VIEWPOINT | The road between North Kohala and Waimea is one of the most scenic drives in Hawaii, passing Parker Ranch, open pastures, rolling hills, quaint homesteads, and tree-lined mountains. There are a few places to pull over and take in the view; the lookout at mile marker 8 provides a splendid vista of the Kohala Coast and Kawaihae Harbor far below. On clear days, you can see well beyond the resorts to Maui, while at other times an eerie mist drifts over the view. ✉ *Kohala Mountain Rd. (Hwy. 250), Waimea (Hawaii County).*

★ Parker Ranch

FARM/RANCH | Exceeding 130,000 acres and regularly running tens of thousands of head of cattle, Parker Ranch is an impressive and compelling backdrop for the scenic town of Waimea. It was established in 1847 by a sailor from Massachusetts, John Palmer Parker, who was permitted by the Hawaiian ruler King Kamehameha I to cull vast herds of out-of-control cattle; thus, the ranch was born. It later grew into the empire it is today, and the foundation started by Parker's descendants supports community health care, the arts, and education, as well as a commitment to sustainability. In addition to taking self-guided tours of two of the ranch's historic homes—Hale Mana and Puuopelu—you can also visit Parker Ranch Center, the town's largest shopping and restaurant complex. The Round Up Club, founded by Parker Ranch employees, holds rodeos year round. ✉ *66-1304 Mamalahoa Hwy., Waimea (Hawaii County)* ☎ *808/885–7311* ⊕ *parkerranch.com* ✉ *$20* ⊗ *Closed Sat. and Sun.*

Waimea or Kamuela?

Both, actually. Everyone knows the town as Waimea, but the sign on the post office says Kamuela, which is Hawaiian for "Samuel," referring to Samuel Parker, the son of the founder of Parker Ranch. That designation is used to avoid confusion with communities named Waimea on the islands of Kauai and Oahu. But the official name of the town is Waimea.

🍴 Restaurants

Big Island Brewhaus

$ | **AMERICAN** | A hands-down island favorite, this casual brewpub from owner and veteran brewmaster Tom Kerns churns out premium ales, lagers, and specialty beers from his on-site brewery in Waimea. With a focus on fresh ingredients, the brewpub's menu includes falafels, burgers, poke, fish tacos, burritos, and quesadillas fresh to order. **Known for:** coconut-infused White Mountain porter; affordable sampler with six beer choices; amazing grass-fed burgers. ⑤ *Average main: $12* ✉ *64-1066A Mamalahoa Hwy., Waimea (Hawaii County)* ☎ *808/887–1717* ⊕ *www.bigislandbrewhaus.com.*

The Fish and the Hog

$ | **ECLECTIC** | This casual little restaurant along the highway serves up generous sandwiches, salads, and melt-in-your-mouth barbecue items. Because the owners are fisherpeople, the poke and nightly specials showcase fish caught from their boat. **Known for:** enormous, puffy onion rings; kiawe-smoked pulled pork, ribs, pork ribs, and brisket; yummy banana cream pie. ⑤ *Average main: $15* ✉ *64-957 Mamalahoa Hwy. (Hwy. 11),*

Waimea (Hawaii County) ☎ *808/885–6268* ⊕ *fishandthehog.com.*

FORC Restaurant

$$$$ | **HAWAIIAN** | Their name stands for "Farmer, Ocean, Rancher, Cook" but this little gem is a great example of the magic that happens when a famous resort chef creates his own vibe and brand. Chef Allen Hess blends the unique nuances of Hawaii Regional Cuisine with flavors from the ocean and land and throws in a dash of comfort food. **Known for:** ube lemon drop martini; goat tacos; chef's table. ⑤ *Average main: $45* ⊠ *65-1214 Lindsey Rd., Waimea (Hawaii County)* ☎ *808/731–4656* ⊕ *forchawaii.com* ⊙ *Closed Tues. and Wed. No lunch.*

Merriman's

$$$$ | **MODERN HAWAIIAN** | The signature restaurant of Peter Merriman, one of the pioneers of Hawaii Regional Cuisine, is the home of the original wok-charred ahi: it's seared on the outside, leaving sashimi on the inside. Although lunch prices are reasonable, dinner is "resort pricey," so prepare to splurge; there's also a reasonable prix fixe option. **Known for:** grilled-to-order New York steak; locally raised Kahua Ranch braised lamb; reservations essential. ⑤ *Average main: $45* ⊠ *Opelo Plaza, 65-1227 Opelo Rd., Waimea (Hawaii County)* ☎ *808/885–6822* ⊕ *www.merrimanshawaii.com.*

MOA Kitchen

$ | **JAPANESE** | Just like an authentic Japanese *izakaya* (bar/restaurant), this hip little place serves *yakatori* (skewered chicken) grilled on a *binchotan* (grill) that the restaurant owners imported from Japan. Ramen is served with a variety of broths—regular shoyu, spicy, and vegetarian. **Known for:** uni nigiri; Hawaiian spicy ramen; island-grown ingredients. ⑤ *Average main: $12* ⊠ *65-1298 Kawaihae Rd., Waimea (Hawaii County)* ☎ *808/339–7887* ⊙ *Closed Mon. No lunch Sun.*

Pau Pizza & Provisions

$ | **ITALIAN** | **FAMILY** | Its name is Hawaiian for "done," perhaps an allusion to how eagerly the pizzas are gobbled up at this eatery with cool artwork and a relaxed vibe. On offer is a wide selection of appetizers, salads, sandwiches, pastas, and pizzas loaded with lots of local ingredients. **Known for:** popular build-your-own-pizza option; superfood salad with quinoa and brown rice; triple slice lunch special. ⑤ *Average main: $12* ⊠ *65-1227 Opelo Rd., Waimea (Hawaii County)* ⊹ *Near Merriman's* ☎ *808/885–6325* ⊕ *www.paupizza.com.*

Red Water Café

$$$ | **ECLECTIC** | **FAMILY** | Chef David Abrahams serves upscale café fare with a twist and a side of aloha. Although it opens fairly early (at 2 pm Tuesday–Friday, noon on Saturday), there's only a single, all-day menu, and this place is busy, so reserve ahead. **Known for:** worthy saketini (sake martini); Kansas City rib-eye steak, Berkshire pork chops, and short ribs; sushi menu. ⑤ *Average main: $36* ⊠ *65-1299 Kawaihae Rd., Waimea (Hawaii County)* ☎ *808/885–9299* ⊕ *www.redwatercafe.com* ⊙ *Closed Sun. and Mon. No lunch weekdays.*

☕ Coffee and Quick Bites

Village Burger

$ | **AMERICAN** | **FAMILY** | At this little eatery that brings a whole new meaning to gourmet hamburgers, locally raised, grass-fed, hormone-free beef is ground fresh, hand-shaped daily on-site, and grilled to perfection right before your eyes. Top your burger (be it ahi, veal, Kahua Ranch Wagyu beef, Hamakua mushroom, or Waipio taro) with everything from local avocados, baby greens, and chipotle goat cheese to tomato marmalade. **Known for:** brioche buns baked fresh in nearby Hawi; order online for quicker service; ice cream for milkshakes made fresh in Waimea. ⑤ *Average main: $12* ⊠ *Parker Ranch*

Big Island Farm Tours

As local ingredients continue to play a more prominent role on Big Island menus, chefs and farmers are working together to support a burgeoning agritourism industry in Hawaii. Several local farms make specialty items that cater to the island's gourmet restaurants. The **Hawaii Island Goat Dairy** (⊕ *hawaiiislandgoatdairy.com*) on the Hamakua Coast produces specialty cheese; **Big Island Bees** (⊕ *bigislandbees.com*) boasts its own beekeeping museum and tasting room at Kealakekua Bay; and **Hamakua Mushrooms**

(⊕ *hamakuamushrooms.com*) has turned harvested koa forests into a safe haven for gourmet mushrooms.

Many farms—like **Greenwell Farms** (⊕ *greenwellfarms.com*), which produces 100% organic Kona coffee, and **Hawaiian Vanilla Company** (⊕ *hawaiianvanilla.com*), which is cultivating vanilla from orchids on the Hamakua Coast—are open to the public and offer free tours. And don't forget the chocolate: take a tour of the farm and cacao orchards at **Honokaa Chocolate Company** (⊕ *honokaachocolateco.com*).

Center, 67-1185 Mamalahoa Hwy. (Hwy. 11), Waimea (Hawaii County) ☎ 808/885–7319 ⊕ www.villageburgerwaimea.com.

Waimea Coffee Company

$ | **CAFÉ** | Right next to the Waimea General Store, this is a good stop for a steaming latte and a warm pastry, a cup of hot soup, or a freshly made salad. The small lanai offers enjoyable views of Waimea's compact, rolling hills dappled with rain, fog, sunlight, and, often, rainbows. **Known for:** specialty coffee drinks; convenient to Waimea shopping; limited seating. ⑤ *Average main: $4* ⊠ *Parker Square, 65-1279 Kawaihae Rd., Waimea (Hawaii County)* ☎ *808/885–8915* ⊕ *www.waimeacoffeecompany.com* ⊗ *No dinner.*

 Hotels

Though it seems a world away, Waimea is only about a 15- to 20-minute drive from the Kohala Coast resorts, which places it considerably closer to the island's best beaches than Kailua-Kona. Yet few visitors think to book lodging in this pleasant upcountry ranching community, where you can enjoy cool mornings

and evenings after a day spent basking in the sun.

There are some very good restaurants, and sightseeing is easy from Waimea: Maunakea is a short drive away, Hilo is 90 minutes away, and Kailua-Kona is about an hour's drive. There aren't as many condos and hotels, but Waimea has some surprisingly good B&B and cottage options—as well as some great deals, especially considering their vantage point. Many have spectacular views of Maunakea, the ocean, and the beautiful green hills of Waimea.

Kamuela Inn

$$$ | **HOTEL** | With a prime location in the center of Waimea, this newly renovated boutique inn offers beautiful accommodations that feature Hawaiian-style bed linens and *paniolo* (cowboy) art, along with polished, upgraded decor such as barn doors, high-definition TVs, granite countertops, and rainfall showerheads. **Pros:** kitchenettes in some rooms; beautiful decor; good value for the price. **Cons:** sometimes noisy; no elevator; rooms on the smaller side. ⑤ *Rooms from: $329* ⊠ *65-1300 Kawaihae Rd., Waimea*

(Hawaii County) ☎ 808/885–4243 ⊕ thek-amuelainn.com ➷ 17 suites ⦿ Free Breakfast.

Waimea Country Lodge

$ | **HOTEL** | In the heart of cowboy country, this quaint ranch house–style lodge offers views of the green, rolling slopes of Waimea and a distant view of Mau-nakea. **Pros:** large rooms; kitchenettes in some rooms; free coffee in morning. **Cons:** not near the beach; no pool; no on-site restaurant. ⑤ *Rooms from: $159* ✉ *65-1210 Lindsey Rd., Waimea (Hawaii County)* ☎ 808/885–4100, 800/367–5004 ⊕ www.waimeacountrylodge.com ➷ 22 rooms ⦿ No Meals.

Waimea Gardens Cottage

$$ | **HOUSE** | Surprisingly luxe yet cozy and quaint, the three charming country cottages and one suite at this historical Hawaiian homestead are surrounded by flowering private gardens and a backyard stream. **Pros:** charming, self-contained units; lush, bird-filled grounds; kitchens include food for breakfast. **Cons:** 50% deposit within two weeks of booking and payment in full six weeks before arrival; only personal or bank checks accepted; three-night minimum stay. ⑤ *Rooms from: $205* ✉ *Waimea (Hawaii County)* ⊹ *Located off Kawaihae Rd., 2 miles from Waimea Town* ☎ 808/885–8550 ⊕ www.waimeagardens.com ▤ No credit cards ➷ 4 units ⦿ Free Breakfast.

 Performing Arts

THEATER

★ Kahilu Theatre

PERFORMANCE VENUES | The intimate theater regularly hosts internationally acclaimed performers such as Mikhail Baryshnikov and renowned Hawaiian artists such as Jake Shimabukuro, Kealii Reichel, and the Brothers Cazimero. They share the calendar with regional and national modern-dance troupes, community theater and dance groups, ukulele festivals, and classical music

performances. The theater also supports the community by welcoming local artists to exhibit in its lobby, which doubles as a gallery. ✉ *Parker Ranch Center, 67-1185 Mamalahoa Hwy., Waimea (Hawaii County)* ☎ 808/885–6868 ⊕ kahilutheatre.org.

Shopping

FOOD AND WINE

Crackseed, Etc.

FOOD | As local as it gets, this little shop is a classic Big Island tradition, selling preserved Hawaiian-style seeds, *li hing mui* (sweet and sour plums), Japanese snacks such as *arare* (small crackers), and handmade candies, in addition to authentic Hawaiian souvenirs. ✉ *65-1290 Kawaihae Rd, Waimea (Hawaii County)* ☎ 808/885–6966.

Kamuela Liquor Store

WINE/SPIRITS | From its plain name and exterior, this store doesn't look like much, but it sells the best selection of premium spirits, wines, and gourmet items on the island. Alvin, the owner, is a collector of fine wines, as evidenced by his multiple cellars. Wine tastings take place Friday afternoon from 3 to 6 and Saturday at noon. ✉ *64-1010 Mamalahoa Hwy., Waimea (Hawaii County)* ☎ 808/885–4674.

★ Waimea General Store

GENERAL STORE | Since 1970, this Waimea landmark at Parker Square has been a favorite of locals and visitors alike. Although specialty kitchenware takes center stage, the shop brims with local gourmet items, books, kimonos, and Hawaiian gifts and souvenirs. ✉ *Parker Square, 65-1279 Kawaihae Rd., Suite 112, Waimea (Hawaii County)* ☎ 808/885–4479 ⊕ www.waimeageneralstore.com.

GALLERIES

Firehouse Gallery

ART GALLERY | Supporting the Waimea Arts Council, this gallery presents annual juried shows of local art as well as solo and group exhibitions by its many award-winning multimedia artists and artisans. It's in Waimea's original firehouse building at the intersection of Lindsey Road and Mamalahoa Highway. ■ TIP➜ **Always call to check before visiting, as the gallery is staffed by volunteers and hours aren't always regular.** ⊠ *67-1201 Mamalahoa Hwy., Waimea (Hawaii County)* ⊹ *Across from Waimea Chevron* ☎ *808/887–1052* ⊕ *www.waimeaartscouncil.org.*

★ Gallery of Great Things

ART GALLERY | You might lose yourself exploring the trove of fine art and collectibles in every price range at this gallery, which represents hundreds of local artists and has a low-key, unhurried atmosphere. The "things" include hand-stitched quilts, ceramic sculptures, vintage kimonos, original paintings, koa-wood bowls and furniture, etched glassware, Niihau shell lei, and feather art by local artist Beth McCormick. Paintings by such beloved artists as impressionist William Wingert are among the offerings. ⊠ *Parker Square, 65-1279 Kawaihae Rd., Waimea (Hawaii County)* ☎ *808/885–7706* ⊕ *www.galleryofgreatthingshawaii.com.*

SHOPPING CENTERS

Parker Ranch Center

SHOPPING CENTER | With a welcoming, ranch-style motif, this shopping hub includes a large supermarket, some fun food court eateries, gift shops, and clothing boutiques. During the holidays, they install a very large Christmas tree and garlands by their classic stone fireplace, great for photos. ⊠ *67-1185 Mamalahoa Hwy. (Hwy. 11), Waimea (Hawaii County)* ⊕ *parkerranchcenter.com.*

Parker Square

SHOPPING CENTER | Although the Gallery of Great Things, known for art and collectibles, is this shopping center's star attraction, it's also worth looking into the Waimea General Store; Sweet Wind, for books, chimes, and beads; Bentley's, which sells locally crafted and imported home decor and gifts; and Hula Moon, for upscale women's fashions. Waimea Coffee Company satisfies with salads, sandwiches, and Kona coffee. ⊠ *65-1279 Kawaihae Rd., Waimea (Hawaii County).*

Chapter 6

THE HAMAKUA COAST

Updated by
Kristina Anderson

◉ Sights	🍴 Restaurants	🛏 Hotels	🛍 Shopping	🍸 Nightlife
★★★★★	★★★☆☆	★★☆☆☆	★☆☆☆☆	★☆☆☆☆

WELCOME TO THE HAMAKUA COAST

TOP REASONS TO GO

★ **Waipio Valley:** This stunning "amphitheater" valley, surrounded by sheer cliffs and plunging waterfalls, and edged with an expansive black-sand beach, is one of Hawaii's most dramatic gems.

★ **Akaka Falls State Park:** An easy, ½-mile loop trail takes you to gorgeous falls that plunge 420 feet into cascading pools.

★ **Honokaa:** Remnants of its sugar-plantation past dot this little town, with its historic buildings, small shops, and cafés.

★ **Kalopa State Recreation Area:** The park's 2,000-foot elevation gives visitors a break from the heat to enjoy native forests and birds.

★ **Honomu:** Quaint and tiny, the town is a fun place to poke through or grab a bite after you've visited Akaka Falls.

★ **Maunakea:** Located in the middle of the island, this 13,796-foot volcanic peak rises above 40% of the Earth's atmosphere, making it the best place in the world for astronomy.

From Hilo, Highway 19 passes through the beautiful Hamakua Coast on the island's northeast. If you're driving from Kailua-Kona, cut across on the Mamalahoa Highway (Highway 190) to Waimea and then catch Highway 19 to the Hamakua Coast. Once you've stopped to explore the quiet little villages with vintage buildings, wooden boardwalks, and dogs dozing in backyards, or if you've spent time in Waipio Valley, night will undoubtedly be falling. Don't worry: you can stop in Honokaa if you are heading south toward Hilo, about an hour away. If you are heading west back toward the Kailua-Kona side (about 25 to 45 minutes), you can stop in Waimea for dinner at one of the nice restaurants or brewpubs.

Although you can explore the Hamakua Coast in a day, a few romantic bed-and-breakfasts are available if you want to spend more time and soak in the peaceful country vibe.

1 Waipio Valley. The "Valley of the Kings," an emerald-green valley surrounded by steep cliff faces, is a must-see whether you view it from a spectacular lookout or explore further.

2 Honokaa. A sleepy little town with a spark of the past, Honokaa offers little boutiques and a handful of restaurants.

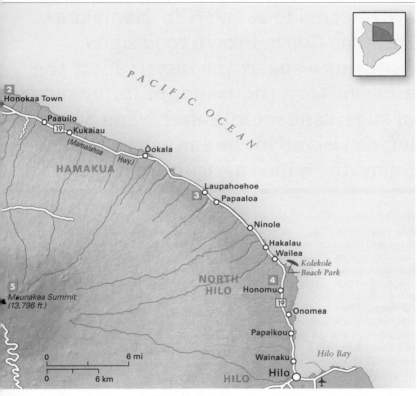

3 Laupahoehoe. Laupahoehoe Point marks the spot where 24 people died during a tsunami in 1946. This area has a beach park (no swimming allowed) and a history museum.

4 Honomu. Sweet and small, this town borders the Akaka Falls area and has some cafés, ice cream shops, and antiques stores. Upper Akaka Falls is spectacular, dropping more than 442 feet.

5 Maunakea. The nearly 14,000-foot Maunakea volcano, home to 11 active observatories, is the world's best place to view the heavens. There's an excellent visitor center at 9,200 feet. It's best to go with an outfitter if you're heading for the summit.

The spectacular waterfalls, jungles, emerald slopes, and ocean vistas along Highway 19 northwest of Hilo are referred to as the Hilo–Hamakua Heritage Coast. Brown road signs featuring a sugarcane tassel reflect the area's history: thousands of former acres of sugarcane sat idle after "King Sugar" left the island in the early 1990s, but today diversified agriculture is growing.

This is a great place to wander off the main road and see "real" Hawaii—untouched valleys, overgrown banyan trees, tiny coastal villages, and little plantation towns such as Honomu, Laupahoehoe, and Honokaa. Some small communities are still hanging on quite nicely after the demise of the big sugar plantations that first engendered them. The towns have homey cafés, gift shops, galleries, and a way of life from a time gone by. Plenty of farmers here use premium agricultural lands serviced by former cane roads and the restored and repaired Hamakua Ditch, growing crops such as Hamakua mushrooms, sweet potatoes, tomatoes, vanilla, coffee, and lettuce.

The dramatic Akaka Falls is only one of the area's hundreds of waterfalls, many of which tumble into a series of cascading pools. The falls may expand or retract depending on inclement weather. The pristine Waipio Valley was once a favorite getaway spot for Hawaiian royalty. Residents of the isolated valley floor have maintained the ways of old Hawaii, with taro patches, wild horses, and a handful of homes. The view from the lookout is breathtaking.

Before you head out to the coast, consider taking a side trip to Maunakea, the tallest peak in the Hawaiian Islands and home to 11 powerful telescopes that are co-managed by a consortium of nations, universities, and researchers. You can go with a licensed guide to the summit· (recommended) or just drive up to the visitor center at 9,200 feet to peruse exhibits and check out the stars above for yourself.

MAJOR REGIONS

Hamakua Coast. Offering a look at a Hawaii far different from the state's big resorts, the Hamakua Coast has waterfalls, dramatic cliffs, ocean views, ancient hidden valleys, rain forests, sleepy small towns like Honokaa, Laupaehoe, and Honomu, and the stunning Waipio Valley.

Maunakea. From the coast, you can head inland and up to Maunakea for what's considered the world's best stargazing; multiple observatories are perched on top of the mountain. The safest, easiest way to get to the top is to book a tour with a licensed guide.

Planning

Planning Your Time

Two days is sufficient time to explore the Hamakua Coast as well as Maunakea. Take one day to view the magnificent Waipio Valley and then stroll around the small, quaint towns of Honokaa and Honomu. The coast's fading sugar plantation past lives on in these sleepy towns, where modest workers' bunga- lows have been turned into charming cafés or antiques stores. About 5 miles from Honomu is spectacular Akaka Falls, a state park located just off the highway.

Maunakea, one of the tallest mountains on Earth as measured from the ocean floor, sits in a fairly central location on the island, so give yourself at least a full day to get there and experience it. You can drive to the Onizuka visitor center at 9,200 feet yourself with a regular vehicle, but you'll be prohibited from driving past Hale Pohaku unless you have true 4WD. For this and other reasons, it's better to go to the top with a licensed, permitted outfitter that leads summit tours. These tours depart from Kona and Hilo.

Getting Here and Around

AIR

Most visitors to the Hamakua Coast fly into Ellison Onizuka Kona International Airport on the west side, which is about 1¼ hours away.

CAR

A car is by far the best and most efficient way to see the Hamakua Coast. You will want the freedom to leisurely stop off at various lookouts to take in the scenery or pause in a little town to grab a snack or lunch.

Beaches

Beaches along the Hamakua Coast are extremely limited. This is the windward side of the island, where the coast tends to be rocky and rugged and the surf violent. And that's on a calm day. Although at time of writing, visitors can't access Waipio Beach due to the road closure, you can wade, swim, or body board here if conditions are good. If you go, never venture out too, far and keep in mind there are no lifeguards, as this is a remote area. Be careful crossing the river mouth, as waters can rise quickly and leave you stranded. For the novice, Waip- io is probably best as a toe-dipping place rather than a swimming one. The beach parks beneath the Hakalau Bridge are currently closed due to lead contamina- tion. Laupahoehoe is best for surf-watch- ing; not even locals venture in.

Hotels

The stretch of coastline between Waimea and Hilo is an ideal spot for those seeking peace, tranquility, and beautiful views, which makes it a favorite with honeymooners avoiding the big resorts. Several über-romantic B&Bs dot the coast, each with its own personality and views. The beaches are an hour's drive away or more, so most visitors spend a few nights here and a few closer to the beaches on the west side. Vacation homes or home shares provide an extra level of comfort for couples, groups, or families. Honokaa is a charming spot with restaurants, shops, banks, a small market, convenience stores, and even a theater.

⇨ *Hotel prices in the reviews are the lowest cost of a standard double room in high season. Restaurant prices in the reviews are the average cost of a main course at dinner, or if dinner is not served, at lunch. Hotel and restaurant reviews have been shortened. For full information, see Fodors.com.*

What It Costs in U.S. Dollars			
$	**$$**	**$$$**	**$$$$**
HOTELS			
under $200	$200– $280	$281– $380	over $380
RESTAURANTS			
under $20	$20–$30	$31–$40	over $40

Restaurants

Although there aren't a lot of dining choices along the Hamakua Coast, the few options available are surprisingly good. One of the standout stops is Tex Drive-In, with a full menu of local favorites, burgers, vegetarian burritos, pizza, and their famous *malasadas* (the Portuguese doughnuts that are popular in Hawaii). At Cafe il Mondo, the specialty is homemade Italian, and at the Honokaa Public House you can get a great pizza or pastrami on rye with an artisan beer. If you plan on dinner, just know the area generally closes down at 8 pm.

Tours

A guided tour from a locally owned and operated company is one of the best (and easiest) ways to see Waipio Valley. Many are given by lifelong residents of the area. You can walk down and up the steep, narrow road yourself, but you need to be in good shape and you may not see as much. And as locals say, it's 15 minutes to walk down but about 45 minutes to walk back up, which can be rather grueling. There's something for everyone here, and a guided tour is also great fun for the kids. The cost of tours depends on both the company and the mode of transportation.

■ TIP→ **At the time of writing, the Waipio Valley Road was closed for all but essential uses by residents and businesses due to the need for repairs. Check with operators for the availability of tours.**

Waipio Naalapa Stables

GUIDED TOURS | Friendly horses and friendly guides take guests on tours of the valley floor, where they are treated to unforgettable sights of taro fields, waterfalls, lush trails, and freshwater streams. The 2½-hour tours run Monday through Saturday (the valley rests on Sunday), with check-in times of 9 and 12:30. Riders meet at Waipio Valley Artworks, near the lookout, where they are transported to the valley floor in a four-wheel-drive van. ⊠ *Waipio Valley Artworks Bldg., 48-5416 Kukuihaele Rd., Kukuihaele* ☎ *808/775–0419* ⊕ *www.naalapastables. com* ⊠ *From $115.*

Waipio on Horseback

GUIDED TOURS | On guided, 2½-hour horseback-riding tours on the Waipio Valley floor, riders experience lush tropical foliage, curving rivers, flowering trees, a scenic beach, tranquil streams, and 2,000-foot-tall cliff walls. Local *paniolo* (cowboy) guides share the history, culture, and mythology of this magical valley and give you a peek into a traditional family farm where the owners tend Hawaiian staples such as taro. You'll also get to see the stunning Naalapa Falls. ⊠ *Hwy. 240 at mile marker 7.5, Honokaa* ✛ *Northwest of Honokaa* ☎ *808/775–7291* ⊕ *www. waipioonhorseback.com* ⊠ *From $150.*

Waipio Valley Shuttle

GUIDED TOURS | Not up for hiking in and out of the valley on foot? Informative and affordable, these 1½- to 2-hour, four-wheel-drive tours do the driving for you, exploring the valley with lots of stops Monday through Saturday. The windows on the van are removed, allowing you to snap unobstructed photos. You have the option to stay at the beach for two to four hours and come back up with the next tour. ⊠ *48-5416 Kukuihaele Rd.,*

Kukuihaele ☎ *808/775–7121* ⊕ *www. waipiovalleyshuttle.com* ✉ *From $65.*

Waipio Valley

24 miles east and then north of Waimea.

Bounded by 2,000-foot cliffs, the "Valley of the Kings" was once a favorite retreat of Hawaiian royalty, and it remains one of the most picturesque spots in all of Hawaii. Waterfalls drop thousands of feet from the North Kohala watershed to the Waipio Valley floor. The lush valley is breathtaking in every way and from every vantage, with tropical foliage, abundant flowers, wild horses, misty pastures, curving rivers, stands of ironwood trees, and a wide, gray, boulder-strewn shore. Though almost completely off the grid today, Waipio (the word means "curved water") was once a center of Hawaiian life. Somewhere between 4,000 and 20,000 people made it their home between the 13th and 17th centuries. In addition, this highly historic and culturally significant area housed *heiau* (temples) and *puuhonua* (places of refuge) in addition to royal residences. King Kamehameha the Great launched a great naval battle from here, which marked the start of his unification of (some would say conquest) and reign over the Hawaiian Islands. To preserve this pristine part of the island, commercial transportation permits are limited—only a few outfitters offer organized valley floor trips.

A treacherous paved road leads down from the Waipio Valley Lookout, but no car rental companies on the island allow their cars to be driven down. Please don't try, even if you rented a four-wheel drive. You can walk it, and you should if you can. The distance is actually less than a mile from the lookout point—just keep in mind that the climb back gains 1,000 feet in elevation and is highly strenuous, so bring water and a walking stick. Area landowners do not look kindly on public trespassing to access Hiilawe Falls at the back of the valley, so stick to the front by the beach. Hike all the way to the end of the beach for a glorious vantage point. Swimming (for experienced swimmers only), surfing, and picnics are all popular here, conditions permitting; exercise caution. You can also take the King's Trail from the end of the beach to access another waterfall not far down the trail. Keep in mind that waterfalls can come and go depending on the level of recent rains. If you do visit here, kindly respect this area, as it is considered highly sacred to Hawaiians and is still home to several hundred full-time residents who cultivate taro on family farms.

■ TIP➔ **At the time of writing, the Waipio Valley Road was closed to visitors for repairs; only essential uses by residents and businesses or farms were being allowed. Check ahead and with any outfitters before visiting. The Waipio Valley Lookout remains open.**

GETTING HERE AND AROUND
After driving through the tiny hamlet of Kukuihaele on Highway 240, continue west for just under a mile to the Waipio Valley Lookout. There's plenty of free parking at the lookout.

 Sights

★ **Waipio Valley Lookout**
VIEWPOINT | An easily accessible access point to see the beauty of the Waipio Valley, this lookout offers a stunning view of the valley and the high cliffs that surround it. Not surprisingly, it's a popular spot, but there's plenty of parking to handle the cars on most days; Hawaii County maintains the park at the top. A treacherous paved road leads down (Big Island car rental companies don't allow their cars to be driven down because it's so steep, but you can walk down if you wish, though it's 1,000 feet back up). Your best bet for seeing the wonders of the valley floor is with a guided four-wheel-drive tour such as the Waipio

Valley Shuttle. ■ TIP→ **Due to repair work, Waipio Valley Road going down to the valley was closed at the time of writing for all but essential uses. Check ahead and confirm with outfitters.** ⊠ *Hwy. 240, 8 miles west of Honokaa, Kukuihaele* ⊠ *Free.*

🛍 Shopping

GALLERIES

Waipio Valley Artworks

ART GALLERY | In a vintage home, this quaint gallery showcases finely crafted wooden bowls, koa furniture, paintings, and jewelry—all made by local artists. There's also a great little café where you can pick up a sandwich or house-made ice cream before descending into Waipio Valley. ⊠ *48-5416 Kukuihaele Rd., Kukuihaele* ☏ *808/775–0958.*

Honokaa

8 miles east of Waipio Valley Lookout, 15 miles northeast of Waimea.

Cool antiques shops, a few interesting galleries, funky gift shops, and cozy cafés abound in this quaint, cliff-top village fronting the ocean. It was built in the 1920s and 1930s by Japanese and Chinese workers who quit the nearby plantations to start businesses that supported the sugar economy. The intact historical character of the buildings with a Western vibe, bucolic setting, and friendliness of the merchants provide a nice reason to stop and stroll. There's even a vintage theater that often showcases first-rate entertainment. Most restaurants close by 8 pm.

GETTING HERE AND AROUND

If you're traveling to Honokaa from Waimea, you will not need to make any turns; just follow Highway 19 as it veers right. Keep driving until you reach the town of Honokaa on the *makai* (ocean side) of the highway. Coming from Hilo, turn right into the town after mile marker 53.

👁 Sights

★ Kalopa State Recreation Area

STATE/PROVINCIAL PARK | FAMILY | Northwest of the old plantation town of Paauilo, at a cool elevation of 2,000 feet, lies this sweet 100-acre state park with a lush forested area with picnic tables and restrooms. There's an easy .7-mile loop trail with additional paths in the adjacent forest reserve. Small signs identify some of the plants, including the Gothic-looking native ohia and the rare loulu palm. It's chilly and damp here, making it a good escape from the heat at sea level. Three campground areas with full-service kitchens, as well as four cabins, can be reserved online. ⊠ *44-3375 Kalopa Mauka Rd., Honokaa* ✛ *12 miles north of Laupahoehoe and 3 miles inland off Hwy. 19* ☏ *808/775–8852* ⊕ *dlnr.hawaii. gov* ⊠ *Free.*

🍴 Restaurants

★ Cafe il Mondo

$ | ITALIAN | Unquestionably the fanciest spot in Honokaa, this cozy Italian bistro known for its pizza and other options feels like you've taken a step into Florence. Wood details, a full bar, travertine finishes, warm woods, antique furnishings, pendant lighting, and a fantastic stone pizza oven combine to create a thoroughly welcoming atmosphere. **Known for:** variety of house-made calzones; pasta primavera; Paauilo penne. $ *Average main: $15* ⊠ *3580 Mamane St., Honokaa* ☏ *808/775–7711* ⊕ *www.facebook.com/p/ Cafe-il-Mondo-100030921806845.*

Honokaa Public House

$ | AMERICAN | The signature plate here is the pastrami on rye, and it's no ordinary sandwich. This one, possibly rivaling those in New York City, boasts locally raised, grass-fed sirloin that is brined for 13 days, then slow smoked, sliced razor thin, and served with handcrafted dressing and Swiss cheese.

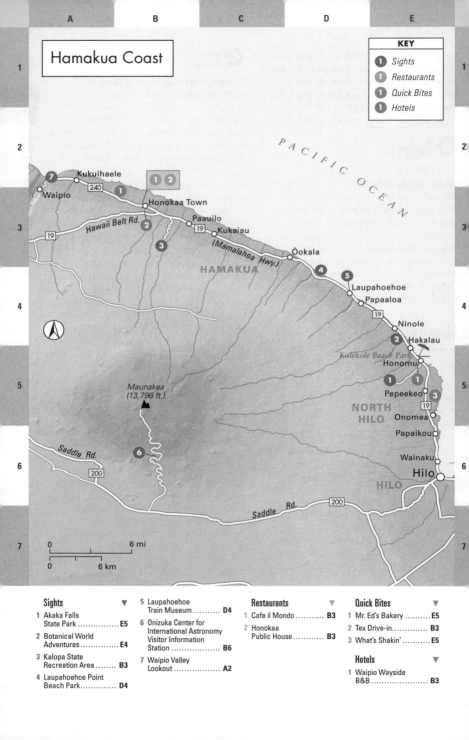

Hamakua Coast

PACIFIC OCEAN

HAMAKUA

Kukuihaele

Waipio

240

Honokaa Town

Hawaii Belt Rd.

19

Paauilo

19 Kukaiau

(Mamalahoa Hwy.)

Ōokala

Laupahoehoe

Papaaloa

19

Ninole

Hakalau

Kolekole Beach Park

Honomu

Pepeekeo

19

NORTH HILO

Onomea

Papaikou

Maunakea
(13,796 ft.)

Saddle Rd.

200

Wainaku

Hilo

HILO

Saddle Rd.

200

0   6 mi

0   6 km

Known for: specialty cocktails; variety of comfort foods; pastrami on rye. $ *Average main: $14* ✉ *45-3490 Mamane St., Honokaa* ☎ *808/775–1666* ⊕ *honokaapub.com* ✪ *Closed Mon. and Tues.*

Coffee and Quick Bites

★ Tex Drive-In
$ | **DINER** | A local institution and icon, this casual place is famous for its *malasadas,* the puffy, doughy, deep-fried Portuguese doughnuts without a hole, best eaten hot; there are also vanilla, chocolate, and coconut cream-filled versions. For more than a snack, go for the Hawaiian burger, with a fat, juicy slice of sweet pineapple on top; the overstuffed burrito; or some decent house-made pizza. **Known for:** the island's best malasadas; food cooked to order; long waits. $ *Average main: $6* ✉ *45-690 Pakalana St., at Hwy. 19, Honokaa* ☎ *808/775–0598* ⊕ *www.texdriveinhawaii.com.*

🛏 Hotels

Waipio Wayside B&B
$ | **B&B/INN** | Nestled amid the avocado, mango, coffee, and kukui trees of a historical plantation estate (circa 1932), this serene home provides a retreat close to the Waipio Valley. **Pros:** ocean views from many of the rooms; gracious owner; full breakfast served in the dining room. **Cons:** remote location; close quarters; no lunch or dinner on property. $ *Rooms from: $165* ✉ *42-4226 Waipio Rd. (Hwy. 240), Honokaa* ☎ *808/775–0275* ⊕ *www.waipiowayside.com* ⇌ *5 rooms* ⦿ *Free Breakfast.*

🎭 Performing Arts

FILM

Honokaa People's Theatre
FILM | Screening art films during the week and more mainstream releases on weekends, the largest cinema on the Big Island features a 50-foot screen as well

as a huge stage and dance floor. Hula competitions, big-name concert performers, community theater performances, and other special events are also held at this gorgeous, beloved vintage theater built in 1930. ∎**TIP→ Park properly, as police officers eagerly write tickets while theatergoers are watching the show.** ✉ *45-3574 Mamane St., Honokaa* ☎ *808/775–0000* ⊕ *honokaapeople.com.*

Laupahoehoe

19 miles southeast of Honokaa.

After the devastating events of 1946, in which a tsunami raged ashore and 24 people were swept away, the once-thriving railway town of Laupahoehoe was relocated to higher ground. Now all that's there is a small museum, convenience store, and beach park. It's a quick turn off the highway and well worth it to see the memorial to the schoolteachers and children who died here.

Sights

Laupahoehoe Point Beach Park
STATE/PROVINCIAL PARK | Here the surf pounds the jagged black rocks at the base of a stunning point, lending a savage beauty to the place. But be advised: this is not a safe place for swimming, so bring only cameras and picnics, not swimsuits. Still vivid in the minds of longtime area residents is the 1946 tragedy in which 21 schoolchildren and three teachers were swept out to sea by a tsunami, back in the days when there was no early warning system. ✉ *Hwy. 19, Laupahoehoe* ⊹ *Makai (ocean) side, north of Laupahoehoe* ☎ *808/961–8311* 🎫 *Free.*

Laupahoehoe Train Museum
HISTORY MUSEUM | **FAMILY** | Behind a stone loading platform of the once-famous Hawaii Consolidated Railway, constructed about 1900, the former manager's

house is now a museum and a reminder of the era when sugar was the local cash crop. It displays artifacts from the sugar plantation era, the 1946 tsunami, local railway history, and the rich culture of the Hamakua Coast. The museum's Wye railyard has a vintage switch engine, large standard-gauge caboose, and narrow-gauge explosives boxcar. The trains even run a few yards along the restored tracks on special occasions. Call before coming: hours may vary according to docent availability. ✉ 36-2377 Mamalahoa Hwy., Laupahoehoe ☎ 808/962–6300 ⊕ www.thetrainmuseum.com ⊠ $10 ⊘ Closed Sat. and Sun. (except by appointment).

Honomu

12 miles southeast of Laupahoehoe.

Bordering Akaka Falls State Park, this tiny town did not die when sugar did, and its sugar-plantation past is reflected in its wooden boardwalks and metal-roofed buildings. You can check out homemade baked goods, have an espresso, or browse the local art at one of the fine galleries. It's also fun to wander through some old, dusty shops filled with little treasures such as antique bottles.

GETTING HERE AND AROUND
On your way to Akaka Falls from Highway 19, you will pass through the quaint town of Honomu, which is about 5 miles from the park.

Sights

★ Akaka Falls State Park
WATERFALL | A paved, 10-minute loop trail (approximately ½ mile) takes you to the best spots to see the spectacular cascades of Akaka, including the majestic upper Akaka Falls, which drops more than 442 feet. It tumbles far below into a pool drained by Kolekole Stream amid a profusion of fragrant white, yellow,

and red torch ginger and other tropical foliage. Another 400-foot falls is on the lower end of the trail. Restroom facilities are available but no drinking water. The park is 4 miles inland, and vehicle parking closes at 6. Visitors are encouraged to reserve parking online in advance at this popular spot. ■ TIP→ **A series of steps along parts of the trail may prove challenging for some visitors, and they are not wheelchair accessible.** ✉ 875 Akaka Falls Rd., Honomu ✛ At the end of Akaka Falls Rd. (Hwy. 220) ☎ 808/974–6200 ⊕ dlnr. hawaii.gov ⊠ $5 per vehicle; parking $10.

Botanical World Adventures
GARDEN | FAMILY | Just off the highway, this garden park on more than 300 acres of former sugarcane land has wide views of the countryside and the ocean; it's also the place to see the beautiful Kamaee waterfalls. During a visit you can follow a walking trail with old-growth tropical gardens including orchids, palm trees, ginger, hibiscus, and heliconia; visit the 10-acre arboretum, which includes a maze made of orange shrubs; explore the river walk; ride the relatively small zip line; and take the only off-road Segway adventure on the island. You can tour the garden only for a nominal fee, which is waived if you take the zip line or Segway. If you skip the zip line, you can see it all in a few hours. This place is 3 miles north of Honomu. ✉ 31-240 Old Mamalahoa Hwy., Hakalau ✛ Just past mile marker 16 from Hilo, on mountain side ☎ 808/963–5427 ⊕ www.botanical-world.com ⊠ $10 garden, $187 zip line, Segway from $137.

☕ Coffee and Quick Bites

Mr. Ed's Bakery
$ | BAKERY | There's been a bakery in this building since 1912, when the previous owner served cookies and treats to the kids of plantation workers. Dean and June Edmoundson took over the spot in 1990 and have been treating visitors and residents to delectable goodies, including

guava bear claws, *paniolo* (cowboy) cookies, homemade preserves, ice cream, and shave ice. **Known for:** fresh-baked pastries and desserts every morning; to-go food such as hot dogs and manapua (pork in a steamed bun); proximity to Akaka Falls State Park. $ *Average main: $4* ⊠ *28-1672 Old Mamalahoa Hwy., Honomu* ☎ *808/960–5000* ⊕ *mredsbakeryhawaii.com* ⊗ *Closed Sun. No dinner.*

What's Shakin'

$ | **AMERICAN** | **FAMILY** | A cute vintage shack, painted a cheery yellow, is home to the best smoothies and shakes on the Hamakua Coast. Order at the counter and take away, or sit awhile under the canopy while you indulge in a Mango Tango, Lava Java, Bananarama, or any of about 15 selections of creative smoothies; you can pair it with tasty turkey, fish, or chicken roll-ups and other wraps. **Known for:** healthy vegetarian and vegan wraps; smoothies made from fruit grown on location; one of the few places to stop on the way to Honokaa. $ *Average main: $10* ⊠ *27-999 Old Mamalahoa Hwy., Pepeekeo* ☎ *808/964–3080* ⊕ *whatsshakinbigisland.com* ⊗ *No dinner.*

 ## Shopping

ANTIQUES AND COLLECTIBLES

Glass from the Past

ANTIQUES & COLLECTIBLES | A fun place to shop for a quirky gift or just to browse before or after a visit to Akaka Falls, the store is chock-full of old Hawaii bottles, antiques, vintage clothing, Japanese collectibles, and interesting ephemera. A super-friendly owner loves to engage with customers. There's often even a "free" table out front to add to the discovery. ⊠ *28-1672 Old Mamalahoa Hwy., Honomu* ☎ *808/963–6449.*

Maunakea

Maunakea's summit is 18 miles southeast of Waimea and 34 miles northwest of Hilo.

Maunakea ("white mountain"), a major attraction for stargazers, offers the antithesis of the typical tropical island experience: freezing temperatures and arctic conditions are common at the summit, and snow can fall year-round. You can even snowboard or ski up here, though you should be in very good shape and a close-to-expert boarder or skier to get down the slopes near the summit and then up again in the thin air—with no lifts.

Winter sports, however, are the least of the reasons that most people visit this starkly beautiful mountain, a dormant volcano. From its base below the ocean's surface to its summit, Maunakea is the tallest island mountain on the planet. It's also home to little Lake Waiau, one of the highest natural lakes in the world.

Maunakea's summit—at 13,796 feet—is the world's best place for viewing the night sky. For this reason, the summit is home to the largest and most productive astronomical observatories in the world—and $1 billion worth of equipment. Research teams from 11 different countries operate 11 telescopes. There are actually 13, but several are being decommissioned now. Decommissioning takes time, so while they aren't doing science, the telescopes are still there. On Maunakea, several telescopes are record holders: the world's largest optical-infrared telescopes (the dual Keck telescopes), the world's largest dedicated infrared telescope (UKIRT), and the largest submillimeter telescope (the JCMT). The still-larger Thirty Meter Telescope (TMT) had been cleared for construction and was slated to open its record-breaking eye to the heavens until it was delayed by protests in 2019. The project's future is unknown, as the

The world's largest optical and infrared telescopes are located at the Keck Observatory on Maunakea's summit.

mountain transitions to the management of the Maunakea Stewardship Oversight Authority, which includes Native Hawaiians in the dialogue.

Maunakea is tall, but there are higher mountains in the world, so what makes this spot so superb for astronomy? It has more to do with atmosphere than with elevation. A tropical-inversion cloud layer below the summit keeps moisture from the ocean and other atmospheric pollutants down at the lower elevations. As a result, the air around the Maunakea summit is extremely dry, which helps in the measurement of infrared and submillimeter radiation from stars, planets, and other astronomical points of interest. There are also rarely clouds up here; the annual number of clear nights here blows every other place out of the water. In addition, because the mountain is far away from any interfering artificial lights (not a total coincidence—in addition to the fact that the nearest town is nearly 30 miles away, there's an official ordinance limiting certain kinds of streetlights on the island), skies are dark for the astronomers' research. To quote the staff at the observatory, astronomers here are able to "observe the faintest galaxies that lie at the very edge of the observable universe."

Teams from various nations and universities around the world must submit proposals years in advance to get the chance to use the telescopes on Maunakea. They have made major astronomical discoveries, including several about the nature of black holes, super planets, new satellites around Jupiter and Saturn, new Trojans (asteroids that orbit, similar to moons) around Neptune, new moons and rings around Uranus, and new moons around Pluto. Their studies of galaxies are changing the way scientists think about time and the evolution of the universe.

What does all this mean for you? A visit to Maunakea is a chance to see more stars than you've likely ever seen before and an opportunity to learn more about mind-boggling scientific discoveries in the very spot where these discoveries are being made. Only the astronomers, though, are allowed to use the telescopes and other equipment, but the scenery is available to all. (You must leave the summit before dark for your safety.) We recommend going with a licensed summit tour company that takes care of the details.

If you're in Hilo, be sure to visit the Imiloa Astronomy Center. It offers presentations and planetarium films about the mountain and the science being conducted there, as well as exhibits describing the deep knowledge of the heavens possessed by the ancient Hawaiians.

GETTING HERE AND AROUND

The summit of Maunakea isn't terribly far, but the drive takes about 90 minutes from Hilo and an hour from Waimea thanks to the steep road. Between the ride there, sunset on the summit, and stargazing, allot at least five hours for a Maunakea visit.

To reach the summit, you must take Saddle Road (Highway 200, the Daniel K. Inouye Highway), which is a beautiful shortcut across the middle of the island. At mile marker 28, John A. Burns Way, the access road to the visitor center (9,200 feet), is fine, but the road from there to the summit is a lot more precarious because it's unpaved washboard and steep. As of 2022, new rules have restricted the road to true four-wheel-drive vehicles. These must have a 4-low or a 4-high on the transfer case; all-wheel-drive and two-wheel-drive vehicles are no longer allowed. Every vehicle will be inspected, and those deemed unsuitable will be turned away by rangers and prohibited past Hale Pohaku.

If you haven't rented a four-wheel-drive vehicle from Harper or Big Island Jeep Rentals—the only rental companies that allow their vehicles on the summit—the best thing to do is book a commercial tour. Operators provide transportation

to and from the summit led by expert guides; they also provide parkas, gloves, telescopes, dinner, hot beverages, and snacks. All give their own star talks a few thousand feet below the summit, which is actually a better spot to view stars for amateur stargazers than the actual summit. Companies that offer summit tours are headquartered in Hilo and Kona.

Although you can park at the visitor center and hike to the summit if you are in good shape, the trip takes approximately seven hours one way, and no camping is allowed. That means you must leave in the predawn hours in order to be back before dark; a permit is also required for this hike.

The last potential obstacle to visiting the summit: it's cold—as in freezing—usually with significant wind chill, ice, and snow. Winds have been clocked exceeding 135 miles per hour. This is a wilderness area, and there are no services or rangers, except in an absolute emergency.

SAFETY

Maunakea's extreme altitude can cause altitude sickness, leading to disorientation, headaches, and light-headedness. Keeping hydrated is crucial. Scuba divers must wait at least 24 hours before traveling to the summit. Children under 16, pregnant women, and those with heart, respiratory, or weight problems should not go higher than the visitor center.

TOURS

Arnott's Lodge and Hiking Adventures
SPECIAL-INTEREST TOURS | This outfitter takes small tours (maximum nine guests) to the summit of Maunakea for sunset and then stops on the way down the mountain, where guides give visual lectures (dependent on clear skies) using handheld lasers. They focus on major celestial objects and Polynesian navigational stars. The excursion departs from Hilo, offers pickup from Hilo hotels, and includes hot beverages. The company also offers a traveler's lodge

Mauna Loa

Mauna Loa is the world's largest active volcano, making up more than 50% of the Big Island of Hawaii. This shield volcano is so massive and heavy that it creates a depression in the sea floor (part of the Pacific tectonic plate) of 8 kilometers (5 miles). In fact, if measured from its base on the ocean floor, Mauna Loa would dwarf Everest. It's been erupting for nearly 700,000 years and shows no signs of stopping. And indeed, it erupted for two weeks in November 2022 after a rest period of 38 years, sending lava flows toward the northeast, fortunately well away from populated areas.

The volcano remains enigmatic to visitors and locals and is not often visited. On the rare days when the summit is visible from the southeast highway, the view of its gentle shield formation does not appear very commanding. You might drive by and simply think it's just a rather large hill.

Looks can be deceiving. Mauna Loa is one of 16 "Decade Volcanoes," so designated by the International Association of Volcanology and Chemistry of Earth's Interior. These volcanoes are particularly dangerous to populated areas. Needless to say, the volcano looms large in the history and the daily life of Hawaii residents.

Visiting Mauna Loa

Despite its size, Mauna Loa is often forgotten in the typical visitor's itinerary. One reason for this is the long drive; a single-lane, paved, 17½-mile road, accessed from mile marker 28 on the Daniel K. Inouye Highway (Highway 200, also called the Saddle Road), takes you to the Mauna Loa Observatory at 11,500 feet, where the road ends. It's then a steep, rugged 6.4-mile hike (which can take all day) to the summit, a trek recommended only for the fit, the well-prepared, and the adventurous. There is a cabin at the summit caldera, called Mokuaweoaweo Caldera (13,250 feet), where you may sleep if you obtain a permit (available from the Kilauea Visitor Center at Hawaii Volcanoes National Park). The other way to access the summit is even more difficult and takes a minimum of three to four days. It's a 19½-mile journey, during which you ascend in altitude by some 6,600 feet to reach the crater. Most hikers stop to acclimatize properly and camp in one of two basic cabins. You need a backcountry wilderness permit for this hike. But there are no services whatsoever in this subfreezing wilderness environment. It was from this vantage that several campers were awakened with the shock of their lives in 1984, when the summit erupted and sent lava flows within 6 miles of Hilo.

and a number of volcano park and Puna eruption site adventure hikes. Private tours are available, as are alternate trips to the mountain for sunrise, when the summit is far less crowded. ⊠ *98 Apapane Rd., Hilo* ☎ *808/339–0921* ⊕ *www. arnottslodge.com* ⌨ *From $228.*

★ **Hawaii Forest & Trail**

SPECIAL-INTEREST TOURS | The ultracomfortable, highly educational Summit & Stars tour packs a lot of fun into a few hours. Guides are knowledgeable about astronomy and Hawaii's geologic and cultural history, and the small group size (maximum of 12) encourages camaraderie while attending to safety. Included in the tour are dinner at an old ranching station, sunset on the summit, and a private star show midmountain. The company's powerful 11-inch Celestron Schmidt-Cassegrain telescope reveals many celestial objects and constellations, and you are given a chance to look. Everything from water bottles, parkas, and gloves to hot chocolate and brownies is included.

The company's Maunakea Sunrise tour begins in the wee hours before the sun comes up and includes a hike among the endangered silverswords as well as breakfast at the visitor center. Of course the main event is a spectacular sunrise on the summit. The company also offers a daytime version of the summit tour. ⊠ *73-5593 Olowalu St., Kailua-Kona* ☎ *808/331–8505, 800/464–1993* ⊕ *www.hawaii-forest.com* ⌧ *From $275.*

Mauna Kea Summit Adventures
SPECIAL-INTEREST TOURS | The first company to specialize in tours to the mountain is a small outfit that focuses on stars. Cushy vans with panoramic windows journey first to the visitor center, where participants eat dinner on the lanai and acclimatize for 45 minutes before donning hooded arctic-style parkas and ski gloves for the sunset trip to the 14,000-foot summit. With the help of knowledgeable guides, stargazing through a powerful Celestron telescope happens midmountain, where the elevation is more comfortable and skies are just as clear. The tour includes dinner, hot cocoa and biscotti, and west-side pickup; it runs 364 days a year, weather permitting. ■TIP→ **Book at least one month in advance, as these tours sell out fast.** ⊠ *Kailua-Kona* ☎ *808/322–2366, 888/322–2366* ⊕ *www.maunakea.com* ⌧ *From $282.*

Sights

★ **Onizuka Center for International Astronomy Visitor Information Station**
VISITOR CENTER | At 9,200 feet, this excellent amateur observation site is a great way to get a sense of the mountain and the observatory work without going all the way to the summit. It's open daily from 9 am to 9 pm and offers free monthly stargazing events (which require preregistration and are weather dependent). The center is also a good place to stop to acclimatize yourself to the altitude if you're heading for the summit. Peruse the gift shop and exhibits about ancient Hawaiian celestial navigation, the mountain's significance as a quarry for the best basalt in the Hawaiian Islands, and Maunakea as a revered spiritual destination. You'll also learn about modern astronomy and ongoing projects at the summit. Nights are clear 90% of the year, so the chances are good for seeing some amazing sights in the sky. Surprisingly, stargazing here is actually better than at the summit itself because of reduced oxygen there. The parking lot can get crowded. ⊠ *Maunakea Access Rd.* ☎ *808/934–4550 visitor center, 808/935–6268 current road conditions* ⊕ *hilo.hawaii.edu/maunakea* ⌧ *Free, donations welcome.*

Chapter 7

HILO

Updated by
Karen Anderson

7

◉ Sights	🍴 Restaurants	🛏 Hotels	💼 Shopping	🍸 Nightlife
★★★★☆	★★★★☆	★★★☆☆	★★★☆☆	★☆☆☆☆

WELCOME TO HILO

TOP REASONS TO GO

★ **Rainbow Falls and Boiling Pots:** The iconic Rainbow Falls puts on quite a show just above downtown Hilo, especially after heavy rains. Located 1 mile above Rainbow Falls, Boiling Pots are natural cauldrons fed by the Wailuku River.

★ **Liliuokalani Gardens:** Ornamental Japanese gardens feature arched bridges and meandering pathways in historic downtown Hilo by the bay.

★ **Downtown shopping and dining:** Interesting shops and restaurants, as well as museums, occupy historic buildings along the Hilo bayfront.

★ **Hilo Farmers Market:** This open-air market downtown features up to 200 vendors and is best visited on Saturday and Wednesday; a smaller market takes place on other days.

★ **Imiloa Astronomy Center:** Located above the campus of the University of Hawaii at Hilo, this planetarium and museum features daily presentations about the skies above Hawaii.

The Hilo District encompasses more than 58 square miles including Hilo Bay, so you'll need a car to explore the area. Highway 19 is the main artery in and out of Hilo. Also known as the Hawaii Belt Road, Highway 19 parallels Kamehameha Avenue, which leads straight to downtown. The airport is on the town's eastern edge, just a few minutes' drive from downtown and about 40 minutes from Volcano.

1 Downtown. Cooled by sea breezes from scenic Hilo Bay, the walkable downtown area brims with shops, parks, and historic buildings. Side streets lead to museums, a theater, and eateries.

2 Liliuokalani Gardens and Reeds Bay. Hilo's hotel district wraps around tree-lined Banyan Drive and is within walking distance of serene Liliuokalani Gardens and Reeds Bay.

3 Greater Hilo. Popular visitor destinations extend beyond downtown. You can learn about Hawaiian coffee in the area, visit botanical gardens, or stop by the Imiloa Astronomy Center to learn about Hawaii's starry skies. There's even a county zoo.

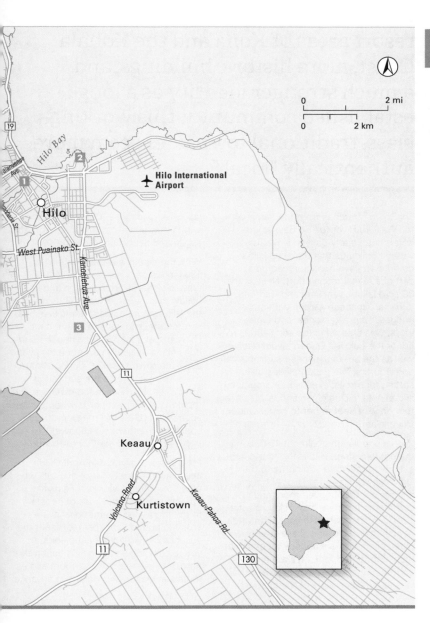

In comparison to Kailua-Kona, Hilo is often deemed "the old Hawaii." With significantly fewer visitors than the resort areas of Kona and the Kohala Coast, more historic buildings, and a much stronger identity as a long-established community, this working-class, traditional town does seem more authentically "local."

The town stretches from the banks of the Wailuku River to Hilo Bay, where hotels line stately Banyan Drive. The vintage buildings that make up Hilo's downtown have been spruced up as part of a revitalization effort. Nearby, the 30-acre Liliuokalani Park and Gardens, a formal Japanese garden with arched bridges, stepping-stones, and waterways, was created in the early 1900s to honor the beloved Queen Liliuokalani as well as the area's Japanese sugar-plantation laborers. The park provides a serene setting for strolls, exercise, photography, and events, including an annual hula performance in September to honor Queen Liliuokalani's birthday.

With a population of almost 45,000 in the entire district, Hilo is the fourth-largest city in the state and home to the University of Hawaii at Hilo. Although it is the center of government and commerce for the island, Hilo is clearly a residential town. Mansions with yards of lush tropical foliage share streets with older, plantation-era houses topped with rusty corrugated roofs. It's a friendly community, populated by Native Hawaiians and descendants of the contract laborers—Japanese, Chinese, Filipino, and Portuguese—brought in to work the sugarcane fields during the 1800s.

With the district's average rainfall of 130 inches per year, it's easy to see why Hilo's yards are so green and its buildings so weatherworn. Outside town, the Hilo District boasts scenic beaches, rain forests, and waterfalls. Although Hilo can get a lot of rain, when the sun does shine—usually part of nearly every day—the town sparkles; during winter, the snow glistens on the summit of Maunakea, 25 miles in the distance. The most magical time of all is when the sun appears while it's still misty, producing spectacular *anuenue* (rainbows) that earn Hilo its nickname: the City of Rainbows.

For a week every year in April, Hilo becomes the epicenter of the hula world when the Merrie Monarch Festival attracts tens of thousands of people to the renowned international event steeped in traditions that represent the essence of Hilo's pioneering spirit. If you're planning a stay in Hilo during this time, be sure to book your room and car rentals at least eight months in advance.

Planning

Planning Your Time

Hilo is a great base for exploring the eastern and southern parts of the island, including Hawaii Volcanoes National Park; just be sure to bring an umbrella and rainwear for the sporadic—and sometimes torrential—showers. If you're passing through town or making a day trip from either side of the island, you can focus your itinerary on the downtown area's museums, shops, and historical buildings. Street parking is relatively easy to find, and downtown is best experienced on foot. To experience all of what Hilo and the surrounding areas have to offer, book a two- or three-night stay. This will give you time to explore the sights in "Hawaii time," from seeing gardens and nature-oriented destinations to meeting mochi makers and chocolate purveyors. Early mornings in Hilo give you the best chance to enjoy sunny skies before the afternoon clouds. If you're in the mood for a dip in the water or a quiet spot for picnicking, Reeds Bay Beach Park offers calm waters and easy access.

There are plenty of gas stations and restaurants in the area. Hilo is a good spot to load up on food and supplies— just south of downtown there are several large budget retailers. If you're here on Wednesday or Saturday, be sure to stop by the expansive Hilo Farmers Market to peruse the myriad stalls of produce, flowers, baked goods, coffee, honey, and more.

Getting Here and Around

AIR

Hilo International Airport is one of the island's two international airports, although flights to and from Kailua-Kona are more frequent. Still, this is the best airport to fly into if your main goal is to visit Hilo and Hawaii Volcanoes National Park.

AIRPORT Hilo International Airport (ITO).
✉ *2450 Kekuanaoa St., Hilo* ☎ *808/961–9300* ⊕ *www.airports.hawaii.gov/ito.*

AIRPORT TRANSFERS

The Hilo airport is a five-minute drive from the hotels. There are no hotel shuttles to and from the airport. Take a taxi, Uber, or Lyft. You can also catch a Hele-On bus from the airport once every hour.

BUS

The Hele-On (⊕ *www.heleonbus.org*) public bus offers intra-Hilo transit service throughout town, but buses don't operate at night. For ultrabudget travelers, the Hele-On bus is a cost-effective way to visit Hawaii Volcanoes National Park or Pahoa Town without having to rent a car. Thanks to some federal funding, the Hele-On Bus system began offering free service for everyone in June 2022, but it could revert back to $2 per ride if the fare-free initiative is discontinued in 2025.

CAR

The bottom line is you must have a car to get around Hilo. The rental car companies at the Hilo airport include Enterprise, Alamo, Budget, Dollar, Hertz, and National. Off-site rental car companies in Hilo include Aiona Car Rentals, Affordable Rentals, and Island Discount Car Rentals. Daily rates average $125 a day, not including taxes and fees. Reserve early, as fleets in Hilo are not as large as on the Kona side. If you're coming during the Merrie Monarch Festival, rental cars will be in short supply.

TAXI

A couple of taxi companies in Hilo provide relatively affordable rates. There are 17 taxi companies that service Hilo airport. Approximate cost to Hilo from the airport is $15–$17, and to Banyan Drive hotels $13–$15. A taxi from Hilo to

Volcano would cost around $100. There are rideshare (Uber and Lyft) services in Hilo, but wait times can be long.

CONTACTS AA Marshall's Taxi. ✉ *391 Kukuau St., Hilo* ☎ *808/936–2654* ⊕ *www.taxihilo.com.* **Da Best Taxi Service.** ✉ *Hilo* ☎ *808/557–7059.*

Beaches

Hilo isn't exactly known for tropical white-sand beaches, but a few nice ones in the area offer good swimming and snorkeling opportunities, and you can watch surfers riding the waves at spots like Honolii Beach Park.

Hotels

Hilo has several decent hotels and one higher-end resort hotel. Bed-and-breakfasts occupy lovely historical homes and offer breakfasts that sometimes include ingredients from backyard gardens. Hawaii Volcanoes National Park is only a 40-minute drive away, as are the sights of the Lower Puna region. The incredible Hamakua Coast is north of Hilo.

⇨ *Hotel prices in the reviews are the lowest cost of a standard double room in high season. Restaurant prices in the reviews are the average cost of a main course at dinner, or if dinner is not served, at lunch. Hotel and restaurant reviews have been shortened. For full information, see Fodors.com.*

What It Costs in U.S. Dollars			
$	$$	$$$	$$$$
HOTELS			
under $200	$200– $280	$281– $380	over $380
RESTAURANTS			
under $20	$20–$30	$31–$40	over $40

Restaurants

The restaurant scene in Hilo is both eclectic and off the beaten path. As the saying goes, you can't judge a book by its cover: in this case some of the great culinary discoveries in Hilo are at seemingly hole-in-the-wall places. Some of the best eateries serve local specialties such as *laulau* (pulled pork, beef, salted butterfish, or chicken steamed with taro luau leaves and wrapped in ti leaf), *loco moco* (meat, rice, and eggs smothered in gravy), or mochi-covered strawberries. Most Hilo restaurants have immediate access to fresh-off-the-boat seafood from fishers.

Downtown

Local flavor abounds in downtown Hilo, where vintage homes are the norm and businesses occupy older buildings, many historic. The Hilo Farmers Market, in full swing on Wednesday and Saturday, is a must-see. Also downtown are the Pacific Tsunami Museum, the historic Palace Theater, and the Mokupapapa Discovery Center. Visitors to downtown Hilo might wonder why the bayfront shops, galleries, and businesses are located such a distance from the actual bayfront. That's because the devastating tsunamis of 1946 and 1960 decimated the populated shoreline areas of Hilo's former downtown center.

GETTING HERE AND AROUND
Driving around downtown Hilo can be confusing, even for longtime residents. The many one-way streets crisscross one another and meander in directions that can take you astray. The best thing to do is turn on your GPS app and hope that it can pronounce Hawaiian street names well enough to be deciphered. Free street parking is plentiful in the downtown area.

A Walking Tour of Hilo

Put on some comfortable shoes, because all the best downtown destinations are within easy walking distance of each other. Start your excursion in front of the public library (✉ *300 Waianuenue Ave.*), four blocks from Kamehameha Avenue. Here you'll find the massive Naha and Pinao stones, one of which legend says King Kamehameha I was able to move as a teenager, thus foretelling that someday he would be a powerful king. Cross the road to walk southeast along Kapiolani Street, and turn right on Haili Street to visit the historic Lyman Museum and Mission House. Back on Haili Street, follow this busy road toward the ocean; on your right you'll pass Haili Congregational Church.

Soon you'll reach Keawe Street with its vintage, early-1900s shop fronts.

Turn left, you'll be on Kalakaua Street; for a quick respite, make another left and rest on the benches in Kalakaua Park. Continue *makai* (toward the ocean) on Kalakaua Street to visit the Pacific Tsunami Museum on the corner of Kalakaua and Kamehameha Avenues. Nearby, on the corner of Kamehameha and Waianuenue Avenues, is the free Mokupapapa Discovery Center, showcasing the Marine National Monument north of the Island chain. After heading three blocks east along the picturesque bayfront, you'll come across the S. Hata Building, with its interesting shops and restaurants. You can't miss the Hilo Farmers Market, bustling with vendors and customers. Allow at least an hour to take in all the major sights, more if you want to linger.

7

Hilo
DOWNTOWN

◉ Sights

Haili Congregational Church
CHURCH | Constructed in 1859 by New England missionaries, this church is known for its services in Hawaiian and for the choir, which sings hymns in Hawaiian. In 1902, Hawaiian musical legends Harry K. Naope Sr. and Albert Nahalea Sr. began the choral traditions still practiced by their descendants. The church, with its iconic yellow spire, has an interesting history that dates to 1824 when it was a thatched structure. ✉ *211 Haili St., Hilo* ☏ *808/935–4847* ⊕ *www.hailichurch.org* 🖼 *Free, donations welcome.*

★ Hilo Farmers Market
MARKET | The 200 vendors here—stretching a couple of blocks at the bayfront—sell a profusion of tropical flowers, locally grown produce, aromatic honey, tangy goat cheese, hot breakfast and lunch items, and fresh baked specialties at extraordinary prices. This colorful, open-air market—the largest and most popular on the island—opens for business Wednesday and Saturday from 7 am to 3 pm. A smaller version on the other days features more than 30 vendors. Free parking is available. ✉ *Kamehameha Ave. and Mamo St., Hilo* ☏ *808/933–1000* ⊕ *www.hilofarmersmarket.com* 🖼 *Free.*

Kalakaua Park
CITY PARK | A bronze statue in this park, the central town square for more than a century, depicts King David Kalakaua (1836–1891), who revived the hula and is the inspiration for Hilo's Merrie Monarch Festival. Erected in 1988, the statue depicts the king with a taro leaf in his left hand to signify the Hawaiian people's bond with the land. The park is surrounded by civic buildings and a war memorial. There is a huge, spreading banyan tree and small fishponds but no

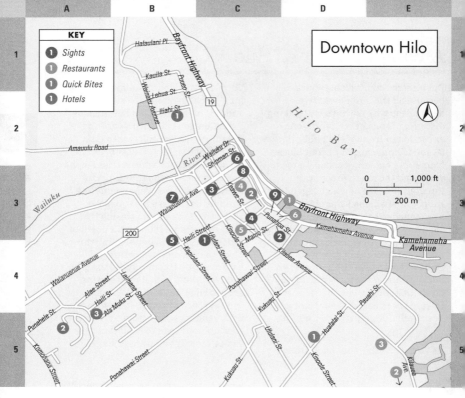

Downtown Hilo

KEY

- ① Sights
- ① Restaurants
- ① Quick Bites
- ① Hotels

Hilo Bay

| 0 | 1,000 ft |
| 0 | 200 m |

Sights ▼

1 Haili Congregational Church **C4**
2 Hilo Farmers Market **C3**
3 Kalakaua Park............ **C3**
4 Keawe Street............. **C3**
5 Lyman Museum and Mission House **B4**
6 Mokupapapa Discovery Center for Hawaii's Remote Coral Reefs **C2**
7 Naha and Pinao Stones.................... **B3**
8 Pacific Tsunami Museum **C3**
9 S. Hata Building.......... **C3**

Restaurants ▼

1 Café Pesto................ **C3**
2 Hawaiian Style Cafe..... **E5**
3 Hilo Burger Joint......... **E5**
4 Moon and Turtle **C3**
5 Pineapple's Island Fresh Cuisine............. **C3**
6 Reuben's Mexican Restaurant..... **C3**

Quick Bites ▼

1 K's Drive-In **D5**
2 Puka Puka Kitchen **C3**

Hotels ▼

1 Dolphin Bay Hotel **B2**
2 Hilltop Legacy Vacation Rental **A5**
3 Hilo Honu Inn............ **A5**

picnic or recreation facilities. According to local tradition, families of military personnel often leave leftover floral displays and funeral wreaths along the fishpond walkway as a way of honoring their loved ones. ⊠ *Kalakaua and Kinoole Sts., Hilo.*

Keawe Street
STREET | Buildings here have been restored to their original 1920s and '30s vintage plantation styles. Although most shopping is along Kamehameha Avenue two blocks below, the ambience on Keawe Street offers a nostalgic sampling of Hilo as it might have been decades ago. ⊠ *Hilo.*

★ Lyman Museum and Mission House
HISTORY MUSEUM | Built in 1839 by missionary couple Sarah and David Lyman from New England, the beautifully restored Lyman Mission House is the Island's oldest wood-frame building. On display are household utensils, artifacts, tools, and furniture used by the family, giving visitors a peek into the day-to-day lives of Hawaii's first missionaries. The Lymans hosted such literary dignitaries as Isabella Bird and Mark Twain here. The home is on the State and National Registers of Historic Places, and docent-guided tours are offered. An adjacent museum has wonderful exhibits on volcanoes, island formation, island habitats and wildlife, marine shells, and minerals and gemstones; it also showcases Native Hawaiian culture and the culture of immigrant ethnic groups. On permanent exhibit is a full-size replica of a traditional 1930s Korean home. The gift shop sells superb Hawaiian-made items. ⊠ *276 Haili St., Hilo* ☎ *808/935–5021* ⊕ *www. lymanmuseum.org* 🎟 *$7* 🕑 *Closed Sat. and Sun.*

Mokupapapa Discovery Center for Hawaii's Remote Coral Reefs
SCIENCE MUSEUM | **FAMILY** | This is a great place to learn about the stunning Papahanaumokuakea Marine National Monument, which encompasses nearly 140,000 square miles in the northwestern Hawaiian Islands and is the only mixed UNESCO World Heritage site (meaning one that has both natural and cultural significance) in the United States. Giant murals, 3D maps, and hands-on interactive kiosks depict the monument's extensive wildlife, including millions of birds and more than 7,000 marine species, many of which are found only in the Hawaiian archipelago. Knowledgeable staff and volunteers are on hand to answer questions. A 3,500-gallon aquarium and short films give insight into the unique features of the monument, as well as threats to its survival. Located in the refurbished F. Koehnen Building, the center is worth a stop just to get an up-close look at its huge stuffed albatross with wings outstretched or the monk seal exhibit. ⊠ *F. Koehnen Bldg., 76 Kamehameha Ave., Hilo* ☎ *808/933–8180* ⊕ *www.marinesanctuary.org/mokupapapa-discovery-center* 🎟 *Free* 🕑 *Closed Sun. and Mon.*

Naha and Pinao Stones
INDIGENOUS SIGHT | These two huge, oblong stones in front of the Hilo Public Library are legendary: the Pinao stone is purportedly an entrance pillar of an ancient temple built near the Wailuku River. King Kamehameha I is said to have moved the 5,000-pound Naha stone when he was still in his teens. Legend decreed that he who did so would become king of all the islands. ⊠ *300 Waianuenue Ave., Hilo.*

Pacific Tsunami Museum
SCIENCE MUSEUM | **FAMILY** | A small but informative museum in a vintage First Hawaiian Bank building designed by noted Hawaii-raised architect C. W. Dickey provides tsunami education and scientific information. It may seem odd that downtown Hilo businesses tend to be far from the scenic bayfront, but the 1946 tsunami alone killed 158 people in Hilo. Visitors can peruse the history

of these devastating disasters, with accounts taken from tsunami survivors from Hawaii and worldwide. Exhibits include a wave machine and interactive tsunami warning center simulation as well as films and pictographs detailing tsunamis in Japan, Alaska, and Indonesia. A safety-wall exhibit demonstrates how to be prepared and what steps to take during an evacuation. ⊠ *130 Kamehameha Ave., Hilo* ☎ *808/935–0926* ⊕ *www.tsunami.org* 🎫 *$15.*

S. Hata Building

NOTABLE BUILDING | Built as a general store in 1912 by Japanese immigrant and businessman Sadanouke Hata and his family, this two-story building now houses galleries, a restaurant, and small shops, with offices upstairs. When first built, it was one of the only buildings in Hawaii constructed out of concrete. During World War II, when Hata family members were interned because of their heritage, the building was confiscated by the U.S. government. When the war ended, a daughter repurchased it for $100,000. A beautiful example of Renaissance Revival architecture, the building won a state award for the authenticity of its restoration. ⊠ *308 Kamehameha Ave., at Mamo St., Hilo.*

 **Restaurants**

Café Pesto

$$ | **ITALIAN** | Located in a beautiful high-ceiling venue in the historic S. Hata Building, Café Pesto offers artisan pizzas with ingredients such as fresh Hamakua mushrooms, artichokes, and rosemary Gorgonzola sauce. **Known for:** exhibition kitchen detailed in brass; wood-fired pizza; featured on the Food Network. ⑤ *Average main: $20* ⊠ *308 Kamehameha Ave., Hilo* ☎ *808/969–6640* ⊕ *www.cafepesto.com.*

Hawaiian Style Cafe

$ | **HAWAIIAN** | **FAMILY** | Come hungry: there's a reason the line is usually out the door at this popular hole-in-the-wall eatery in a shopping center downtown. Not only does the Hawaiian comfort food hit the spot, it's affordable and served in sizable portions. **Known for:** breakfast available all day; massive pancakes; signature homemade Portuguese sausage. ⑤ *Average main: $11* ⊠ *681 Manono St., Suite 101, Hilo* ☎ *808/969–9265* ⊕ *www.hawaiianstylecafe.us* ⊘ *No dinner Sun. and Mon.*

★ Hilo Burger Joint

$ | **AMERICAN** | **FAMILY** | What this casual former Irish pub lacks in space and parking is more than made up for in burger choices: more than 22 varieties of gourmet burgers, from a bacon ranch burger to a southern BBQ burger. Many of the ingredients come straight from the Big Island, and non-beef selections such as fish burgers are available as well, so it's definitely worth checking out. **Known for:** Wagyu burger; live entertainment; more than 21 beers on tap. ⑤ *Average main: $16* ⊠ *776 Kilauea Ave., Hilo* ☎ *808/935–8880* ⊕ *www.hiloburgerjoint.com.*

Moon and Turtle

$$$ | **INTERNATIONAL** | This sophisticated, intimate restaurant in a bayfront building offers a classy selection of international fare with the focus on locally sourced meats, produce, and seafood. The menu changes daily (see their Facebook page), but mushroom pappardelle is a highlight, along with seafood chowder, spicy *kajiki* (marlin) tartare, and crispy whole-fried *moi* (Pacific threadfin). **Known for:** "Smokey" ahi sashimi; lychee martinis infused with Hawaiian influences; changing daily menu. ⑤ *Average main: $30* ⊠ *51 Kalakaua St., Hilo* ☎ *808/961–0599* ⊕ *facebook.com/moonandturtle* ⊘ *Closed Sun. and Mon.*

Pineapple's Island Fresh Cuisine

$ | **AMERICAN** | **FAMILY** | If you expect that a restaurant named Pineapple's would serve tropical beverages in hollowed-out pineapples, you'd be exactly correct. Always packed, this open-air bistro looks like a tourist trap, but there is a fine-dining component to the menu, which includes fresh catch, *kalbi* ribs (grilled, Korean-style), teriyaki flank steak, burgers, wraps, and sandwiches. **Known for:** surprisingly inventive island cuisine; vegan-friendly; live entertainment Thursday–Sunday. $ *Average main: $15* ⊠ *332 Keawe St., Hilo* ☎ *808/238–5324* ⊕ *www.pinappleshilo.net* ⊗ *Closed Mon.*

Reuben's Mexican Restaurant

$ | **MEXICAN** | **FAMILY** | It's not the best Mexican food you've ever had, but if you're jonesing for some carne asada or chicken flautas, Reuben's has you covered. You can make a meal out of the warm chips and salsa alone. **Known for:** local landmark open since 1979; generous portions; homemade margarita mix with flavors such as lilikoi (passion fruit), guava, and mango. $ *Average main: $10* ⊠ *336 Kamehameha Ave., Hilo* ☎ *808/961–2552* ⊗ *Closed Sun.*

☕ Coffee and Quick Bites

K's Drive-In

$ | **HAWAIIAN** | **FAMILY** | Unassuming from the outside, this small, local-style plate-lunch eatery serves top-quality, genuine Hawaiian specialties in Hilo. All the staples are here, from *kalua* pork (slow-cooked and pulled) to *shoyu* chicken (cooked in a sauce including fermented soy sauce), *loco moco* (meat, rice, and eggs smothered in gravy), and pork adobo. **Known for:** daily specials like oxtail soup; home of the Twist Cone; favorite among locals since 1964. $ *Average main: $14* ⊠ *194 Hualalai St., Hilo* ☎ *808/935–5573* ⊕ *www.ksdrivein.com.*

Puka Puka Kitchen

$ | **HAWAIIAN** | *Puka* means a small space in Hawaiian, and this little takeout eatery certainly fits the bill. This is where you can experience authentic local fare such as lunch plates, a chicken katsu plate, or *onolicious* (delicious) fish-and-chips. **Known for:** bento boxes; ample portions; true local vibe. $ *Average main: $14* ⊠ *270 Kamehameha Ave., Hilo* ☎ *808/933–2121* ⊗ *Closed Sun. No dinner.*

Hotels

Dolphin Bay Hotel

$ | **HOTEL** | **FAMILY** | Units in this circa-1950s motor lodge are modest but charming, as well as clean and inexpensive; a glowing lava-flow sign marks the office and testifies to owner John Alexander's passion for the volcano. **Pros:** great value; full kitchens in all units; within walking distance to shops and restaurants. **Cons:** no pool; no phones in the rooms; dated decor. $ *Rooms from: $139* ⊠ *333 Iliahi St., Hilo* ☎ *808/935–1466* ⊕ *www.dolphinbayhotel.com* ⇥ *18 rooms* ⊚ *No Meals.*

Hilltop Legacy Vacation Rental

$ | **HOUSE** | Built in the 1930s by a Japanese doctor, this vintage home offers stunning views of downtown Hilo and the bay. **Pros:** garden to relax in; billiard table; close to downtown. **Cons:** two of the four rooms don't have views; kitchen is shared; parking issues. $ *Rooms from: $122* ⊠ *57 Hina St., Hilo* ☎ *808/896–2074* ⊕ *www.hilltoplegacy.com* ⇥ *4 rooms* ⊚ *No Meals.*

Hilo Honu Inn

$ | **B&B/INN** | A charming old Craftsman home lovingly restored by a friendly and hospitable couple from North Carolina, the inn offers variety in guest room size and decor, though every room has a fridge. **Pros:** spectacular Hilo Bay views;

historical setting; within walking distance of Hilo bayfront. **Cons:** no toddlers in the upstairs suite; not on the beach; air-conditioning in only two of the three rooms. ⑤ *Rooms from: $175* ⊠ *465 Haili St., Hilo* ☎ *808/935–4325* ⊕ *www.hilohonu.com* ⊷ *3 rooms* ⑩ *Free Breakfast.*

Nightlife

BARS

Cronies Bar & Grill

BARS | A sports bar by night and a good hamburger joint by day, Cronies is a local favorite. When the lights go down, the bar gets packed. ⊠ *11 Waianuenue Ave., Hilo* ☎ *808/935–5158* ⊕ *www.cronieshawaii.com.*

 Performing Arts

FESTIVALS

KWXX Hoolaulea

MUSIC FESTIVALS | Since 1993, a local radio station has sponsored the island's largest free concert, a famous *hoolaulea* (festival) that takes place mid-September in downtown Hilo and attracts a bounty of Big Island musical talent. Music styles featured included Hawaiian, reggae, and island music. Some big names play here on four different stages, and there's dancing in the streets along the bayfront, rain or shine. ⊠ *257 Kamehameha Ave., Hilo* ☎ *808/935–5461* ⊕ *www.kwxx.com* ⌦ *Free.*

★ Merrie Monarch Festival

CULTURAL FESTIVALS | The mother of all Hawaii festivals, the world-class Merrie Monarch Festival in Hilo celebrates all things hula for one fantastic week every April with competitions, activities, a parade, and more. The esteemed event honors the legacy of King David Kalakaua (1836–1891), the man responsible for reviving fading Hawaiian cultural traditions including hula. The three-day hula competition is staged at the Edith Kanakaole Multi-Purpose Stadium during

the first week following Easter Sunday. Hula *halau* (studios) worldwide come to perform both *kahiko* (ancient) and *auana* (modern) dance styles, solo and in groups. Tickets are not expensive, but they are hard to get. ■ TIP→ **You should reserve accommodations and rental cars up to a year in advance. Ticket requests must be mailed and postmarked after December 1 of the preceding year.** ⊠ *Edith Kanakaole Multi-Purpose Stadium, 350 Kalanikoa St., Hilo* ☎ *808/935–9168* ⊕ *www.merriemonarch.com.*

THEATER

★ Palace Theater

THEATER | Beautifully restored through community support, this historic theater dating from the silent-movie era (1925) survived Hilo's many tsunamis and now showcases everything from film festivals and old movies to musical productions and holiday concerts. There are even performances by big-name artists. The lovely vintage details inside the theater make you feel as if you stepped back in time. ⊠ *38 Haili St., Hilo* ☎ *808/934–7010* ⊕ *www.hilopalace.com.*

⬤ Shopping

There's a nice vibe of both past and present as you stroll streets lined with local shops in vintage buildings.

CLOTHING AND SHOES

Sig Zane Designs

CLOTHING | This acclaimed boutique for women and men sells island wearables with bold colors and motifs designed by the legendary Sig Zane, known for his artwork honoring Hawaii's native flora and fauna. All apparel is handcrafted in Hawaii and is often worn by local celebrities and businesspeople. ⊠ *122 Kamehameha Ave., Hilo* ☎ *808/935–7077* ⊕ *www.sigzanedesigns.com* ⊘ *Closed Sun.*

FOOD

⭐ Sugar Coast Candy

CANDY | FAMILY | Located on the bayfront in downtown Hilo, this beautifully decorated candy boutique is a blast from the past, featuring an amazing array of nostalgic candies, artisan chocolates, and wooden barrels overflowing with saltwater taffy and other delights. ✉ *274 Kamehameha Ave., Hilo* ☎ *808/935–6960.*

⭐ Two Ladies Kitchen

CANDY | FAMILY | This hole-in-the-wall confections shop has made a name for itself thanks to its pillowy mochi. The proprietors are best known for their huge, ripe strawberries wrapped in a white mochi covering, which won't last as long as a box of chocolates—most mochi items are good for only two or three days. To guarantee you get your fill, call and place your order ahead of time. ✉ *274 Kilauea Ave., Hilo* ☎ *808/961–4766* ☾ *Closed Sun. and Mon.*

GIFTS AND SOUVENIRS

Most Irresistible Shop in Hilo

SOUVENIRS | FAMILY | Living up to its name, this store stocks unique gifts from around the Pacific, like pure Hawaiian ohia lehua honey, Kau coffee, aloha wear, and tinkling wind chimes. ✉ *256 Kamehameha Ave., Hilo* ☎ *808/935–9644* ⊕ *www.mostirresistibleshop.com.*

HOME DECOR

Dragon Mama

HOUSEWARES | Step into this hip downtown Hilo spot to find authentic Japanese fabrics, futons, and gifts along with elegant clothing, sleepwear, and tea-service accoutrements. Handmade comforters, pillows, and futon pads are sewn of natural fibers on-site. ✉ *266 Kamehameha Ave., Hilo* ☎ *808/934–9081* ⊕ *www.dragonmama.com* ☾ *Closed Sun. and Mon.*

Liliuokalani Gardens and Reeds Bay

The hotel district near Banyan Drive is within walking distance of nearby scenic Liliuokalani Gardens. To the east, Reeds Bay is small and idyllic, surrounded by a tiny sand beach and some parks with picnic tables. There's a lot of local activity here, including biking, jogging, kayaking, fishing, swimming, and stand-up paddleboarding. Several bayside restaurants are within walking distance of the hotels, some with spectacular bayfront views.

GETTING HERE AND AROUND

Located along Banyan Drive and Lihiwai Street, beautiful Liliuokalani Gardens is within easy walking distance of the Banyan Drive hotels. If driving, you can park on Lihiwai Street to the west, or on Banyan Drive by Alii Ice Company.

 ## Sights

Banyan Drive

STREET | More than 50 enormous banyan trees with aerial roots dangling from their limbs were planted along the road, mostly during the 1930s but also after World War II, by visiting celebrities. Names such as Amelia Earhart, Babe Ruth, and Franklin Delano Roosevelt appear on plaques affixed to the trees. A scenic loop beginning at the Grand Naniloa Hotel Hilo (✉ *93 Banyan Dr.*) makes a nice walk, especially in the evening when thousands of mynah birds roost in the trees. ✉ *Hilo.*

Liliuokalani Gardens

GARDEN | Designed to honor Hawaii's first Japanese immigrants and named after Hawaii's last reigning monarch, Liliuokalani Gardens' 30 acres of fish-filled ponds, stone lanterns, half-moon bridges, elegant pagodas, and a ceremonial teahouse make it a favorite Sunday destination, or any day of the week for

Liliuokalani Gardens, a 30-acre ornamental Japanese garden, was built in 1917 to honor the island's first Japanese immigrants.

that matter. You'll see weddings, picnics, and family gatherings as you stroll. The surrounding area, once a busy residential neighborhood on Waiakea Peninsula, was destroyed by a devastating 1960 tsunami that killed 61 people. ⊠ *Banyan Dr., at Lihiwai St., Hilo* ⊠ *Free.*

Moku Ola (*Coconut Island*)

ISLAND | **FAMILY** | Also known as Coconut Island, this small island sits just offshore from Liliuokalani Gardens and is a nicely manicured spot where children play in the tide pools and anglers try their luck. Accessible via a footbridge, it was considered a place of healing and refuge in ancient times. There's a grassy picnic area, swimming spots, and a restroom, plus incredible views. ⊠ *Off Banyan Dr., Hilo.*

Wailoa Center

ARTS CENTER | At the Wailoa River State Recreation Area, a beautiful park setting near downtown Hilo, this circular exhibition center hosts monthly exhibits in two galleries featuring impressive work from local artists. Pieces range from photography, pottery, contemporary painting, quilts, glassworks, multimedia, and woodworking to musical instruments and artwork depicting Hawaii's native species. There's also an educational space for workshops and community events. ⊠ *200 Piopio St., off Kamehameha Ave., Hilo* ☎ *808/933–0416* ⊕ *www. wailoacenter.com* ⊠ *Free* ⊘ *Closed Sun.*

Beaches

Reeds Bay Beach Park

BEACH | Safe swimming, proximity to downtown Hilo, and the Ice Pond—a freshwater-fed swimming hole that flows into the backwaters of Hilo Bay—are the enticements of this cove. No, there really isn't ice in the swimming hole; it just feels that way on a hot, sultry day. The large pond, between SCP Hilo Hotel and the Ponds Hilo Restaurant, is a favorite of local kids, who enjoy jumping into and frolicking in the fresh- and saltwater mix. The water is usually calm. **Amenities:** parking (no fee); showers. **Best for:** swimming. ⊠ *277 Kalanianaole Ave., Hilo.*

🍴 Restaurants

⭐ Hilo Bay Cafe

$$ | **JAPANESE FUSION** | Overlooking Hilo Bay from its towering perch on the waterfront, this popular, upscale restaurant with great water views has a sophisticated second-floor dining room that looks like it's straight out of Manhattan. A sushi bar complements the excellent selection of fresh fish, pork, beef, and vegan options. **Known for:** creative use of fresh local produce; artisan sushi; Hilo's most upscale restaurant. $ *Average main: $26 ⊠ 123 Lihiwai St., Hilo ☎ 808/935–4939 ⊕ www.hilobaycafe. com ⊘ Closed Sun. and Mon.*

⭐ Ken's House of Pancakes

$ | **DINER** | **FAMILY** | For years, this legendary diner near Banyan Drive between the airport and the hotels has been a gathering place for Hilo residents and visitors. Breakfast is the main attraction: Ken's serves 11 types of pancakes, plus all kinds of fruit waffles (banana, peach) and popular omelets, like Da Bradda, teeming with meats. **Known for:** local landmark with old-fashioned diner vibe; variety of homemade syrups; breakfast served all day. $ *Average main: $16 ⊠ 1730 Kamehameha Ave., Hilo ☎ 808/935–8711 ⊕ www.kenshouseofpancakes.com.*

Ponds Hilo

$$ | **AMERICAN** | **FAMILY** | Perched on the waterfront overlooking a scenic pond at Reeds Bay Beach Park, this restaurant has the look and vibe of an old-fashioned, harborside steak house and bar. The menu features a good range of burgers and salads, steak, and seafood. **Known for:** live music; excellent fish-and-chips; popular Sunday brunch. $ *Average main: $20 ⊠ 135 Kalanianaole Ave., Hilo ☎ 808/934–7663 ⊕ www.pondshilo.com ⊘ Closed Tues. and Wed.*

⭐ Sombat's Fresh Thai Cuisine

$$ | **THAI** | There's a reason why locals flock to this hideaway for the best Thai cuisine in Hilo. Proprietor Sombat Saenguthai's menu highlights fresh local ingredients (many of the herbs come from her own garden) in authentic and tasty Thai treats like coconut curries, fresh basil rolls, eggplant stir-fry, and green papaya salad. **Known for:** famous pad Thai sauce available for purchase; friendly service; single owner and chef. $ *Average main: $20 ⊠ Waiakea Kai Plaza, 88 Kanoelehue Ave., Hilo ☎ 808/969–9336 ⊕ www. sombats.com ⊘ Closed Sat. and Sun. No lunch.*

☕ Coffee and Quick Bites

Cafe 100

$ | **HAWAIIAN** | **FAMILY** | Established in 1948, this casual spot is famous for its tasty *loco moco,* prepared in more than three dozen ways (with different meats, chicken, vegetables, and fish), and its low-priced breakfast and lunch specials. The word "restaurant," or even "café," is used loosely—you order at a window and eat on one of the outdoor benches provided—but you come here for the food, prices, and authentic, old-Hilo experience. **Known for:** family-owned eatery; the Super Loco Moco; generous portions. $ *Average main: $6 ⊠ 969 Kilauea Ave., Hilo ☎ 808/935–8683 ⊕ www.cafe100. com ⊘ Closed Sat. and Sun.*

Verna's Drive-In

$ | **HAWAIIAN** | Verna's is tried-and-true among locals, who come for the juicy house-made burgers and filling plate lunches; and the price is right with a burger combo that includes fries and a drink. If you're hungry for more, try the traditional Hawaiian plate with either *laulau,* beef stew, chicken long rice, or *lomi lomi* salmon (salted salmon "salsa" made with tomatoes and onions). **Known for:** local grindz (food) with outdoor seating; open 24 hours; superlow prices. $ *Average main: $6 ⊠ 1765 Kamehameha Ave., Hilo ☎ 808/935–2776 ⊘ Closed Sun.*

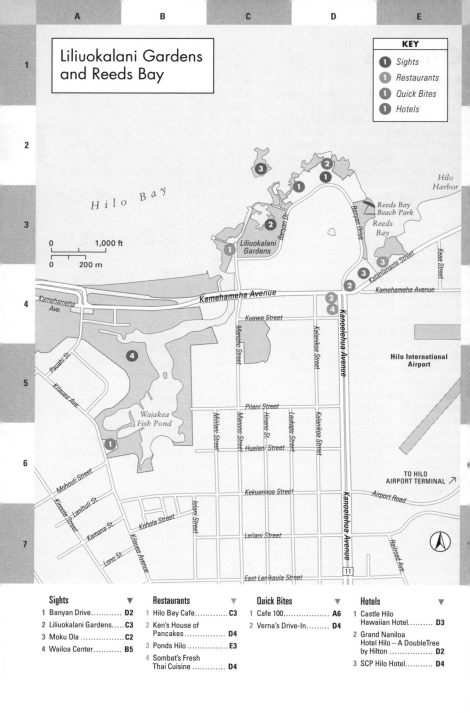

Liliuokalani Gardens and Reeds Bay

KEY
- ❶ Sights
- ❶ Restaurants
- ❶ Quick Bites
- ❶ Hotels

Hilo Bay

Hilo Harbor

Reeds Bay Beach Park

Reeds Bay

Liliuokalani Gardens

Kalanianaole Street

Kamehameha Avenue

Kamehameha Ave.

Kamehameha Avenue

Kuawa Street

Waiakea Fish Pond

Manono Street

Mililani Street

Manono Street

Hinano St.

Laukapu Street

Kalanikoa Street

Kanoelehua Avenue

Hilo International Airport

Pilani Street

Hualani Street

Kekuanaoa Street

Airport Road

TO HILO AIRPORT TERMINAL ↗

Mohouli Street

Kinoole Street

Lanihuli St.

Kamana St.

Kohola Street

Iolani Street

Leilani Street

Kilauea Avenue

Lono St.

Pauahi St.

Kilauea Ave.

Kalanikoa Street

Keaa Street

Railroad Ave.

East Lanikaula Street

11

0 ⸻ 1,000 ft
0 ⸻ 200 m

Hotels

Castle Hilo Hawaiian Hotel

$ | **HOTEL** | **FAMILY** | This landmark hotel has large bayfront rooms offering spectacular views of Maunakea and Coconut Island on Hilo Bay; street-side rooms overlook the golf course, and the hotel is within walking distance of Liliuokalani Gardens. **Pros:** private lanai in most rooms; 24-hour front desk; free parking. **Cons:** dated decor; some rooms don't have bayfront views; no beach. ⑤ *Rooms from: $159* ✉ *71 Banyan Dr., Hilo* ☎ *808/935–9361 direct, 800/367–5004 from mainland* ⊕ *www.castleresorts.com* ➷ *286 rooms* ❶ *No Meals.*

Grand Naniloa Hotel Hilo – A DoubleTree by Hilton

$$ | **HOTEL** | **FAMILY** | Hilo isn't known for its fancy resort hotels, but the Grand Naniloa, built in 1939, attempts to remedy that situation in grand fashion, paying homage to hula, Hawaiian culture, and Big Island adventures. **Pros:** walking distance to Japanese gardens and Coconut Island; rental kayaks, paddleboards, and bikes; free golf at adjacent 9-hole course and driving range. **Cons:** some rooms don't have ocean views; limited parking; small swimming pool. ⑤ *Rooms from: $214* ✉ *93 Banyan Dr., Hilo* ☎ *808/969–3333* ⊕ *www.grandnaniloahilo.com* ➷ *388 rooms* ❶ *No Meals.*

SCP Hilo Hotel

$$ | **HOTEL** | This mindfully designed boutique hotel features a minimalist Zen style combined with Hawaiiana accents. **Pros:** fantastic location across from Reeds Bay; wellness amenities and sustainable practices; walking distance to several restaurants. **Cons:** parking lot can be tight; no TVs in rooms; no hot tub. ⑤ *Rooms from: $233* ✉ *126 Banyan Way, Hilo* ☎ *808/935–0821* ⊕ *scphotel.com/hilo* ➷ *128 rooms* ❶ *No Meals.*

Shopping

BOOKSTORES

★ **Basically Books**

BOOKS | This legendary shop stocks one of Hawaii's largest selections of maps, including topographical and relief maps, and Hilo's largest selection of Hawaiian music (feel free to ask for advice about your selection). It also has a wealth of books about Hawaii, with great choices for children. If you need an umbrella on a rainy Hilo day, this bookstore has plenty of them. ✉ *334 Kilauea Ave., Hilo* ☎ *808/961–0144* ⊕ *www.basicallybooks.com* ❍ *Closed Sun.*

Greater Hilo

Sights beyond the downtown area spread out in every direction and are often interspersed among residential neighborhoods and industrial parks. Be sure to check out Panaewa Rainforest Zoo and Gardens with more than 200 animals and hundreds of species of tropical plants. Above the University of Hawaii at Hilo campus, the Imiloa Astronomy Center has a planetarium, restaurant, and gift shop. For a delicious side trek, Big Island Candies is a must-visit destination for world-class confections.

GETTTING HERE AND AROUND

You need a car to explore the spread-out sights of the area, but drive carefully. Some roads around Hilo are treacherous, riddled with potholes, unexpected turns, fast traffic, one-way streets, and confusing intersections. Take extra precautions at night, and always make sure you know where you're going before you start your car. Don't get discouraged if you get temporarily lost. Getting disoriented when driving in Hilo happens to the best of Big Island residents.

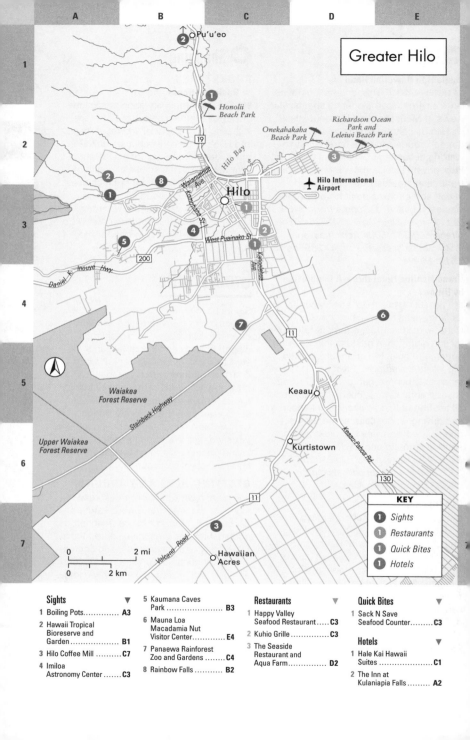

Greater Hilo

Pu'u'eo

Honolii
Beach Park

Onekahakaha
Beach Park

Richardson Ocean
Park and
Leleiwi Beach Park

Hilo Bay

Waianuenue Ave.

Hilo

Kamehameha St.

Hilo International
Airport

West Puainako St.

Kanoelehua Ave.

Daniel K. Inouye Hwy.

Waiakea
Forest Reserve

Stainback Highway

Upper Waiakea
Forest Reserve

Keaau

Kurtistown

Keaau-Pahoa Rd.

Hawaiian
Acres

Volcano Road

0   2 mi

0   2 km

KEY

1 *Sights*

1 *Restaurants*

1 *Quick Bites*

1 *Hotels*

Sights ▼

1 Boiling Pots............. **A3**

2 Hawaii Tropical
Bioreserve and
Garden.................. **B1**

3 Hilo Coffee Mill **C7**

4 Imiloa
Astronomy Center **C3**

5 Kaumana Caves
Park **B3**

6 Mauna Loa
Macadamia Nut
Visitor Center............ **E4**

7 Panaewa Rainforest
Zoo and Gardens **C4**

8 Rainbow Falls **B2**

Restaurants ▼

1 Happy Valley
Seafood Restaurant..... **C3**

2 Kuhio Grille **C3**

3 The Seaside
Restaurant and
Aqua Farm............... **D2**

Quick Bites ▼

1 Sack N Save
Seafood Counter......... **C3**

Hotels ▼

1 Hale Kai Hawaii
Suites **C1**

2 The Inn at
Kulaniapia Falls **A2**

👁 Sights

Boiling Pots

WATERFALL | Four separate streams fall into a series of circular pools here, fed by Peepee Falls just above, and the resulting turbulent action—best seen after a good rain—has earned this scenic stretch of the Wailuku River the nickname Boiling Pots. Swimming is not allowed at Boiling Pots or anywhere in the Wailuku River, due to extremely dangerous currents and undertows. The falls are 3 miles northwest of downtown Hilo off Waianuenue Avenue; keep to the right when the road splits and look for the sign. The gate opens at 7 am and closes at 6 pm. You may want to combine a drive to this site with a visit to Rainbow Falls, a bit closer to downtown. ⚠ **You may be tempted, as you watch others ignore the signs and climb over guardrails, to jump in, but resist. Swimming is prohibited and unsafe, and people have died here.** ✉ *Wailuku River State Park, off Waianuenue Ave., Hilo* ✛ *At the end of Peepee Falls Dr.* ⊕ *dlnr.hawaii.gov/dsp/parks/hawaii* ✉ *Free.*

★ Hawaii Tropical Bioreserve and Garden

GARDEN | Stunning coastline views appear around each curve of the 4-mile scenic jungle drive that accesses this privately owned nature preserve next to Onomea Bay. Paved pathways in the 17-acre botanical garden lead past ponds, waterfalls, and more than 2,000 species of plants and flowers, including palms, bromeliads, torch ginger, heliconia, orchids, and ornamentals. With its stunning boardwalk entry, the garden is well worth a stop, and your entry fee helps the nonprofit preserve plants, seeds, and rain forests. ■TIP→ **Trails can get slippery when it's raining.** ✉ *27-717 Old Mamalahoa Hwy., Papaikou* ✛ *8 miles north of downtown Hilo* ☎ *808/964–5233* ⊕ *www.htbg.com* ✉ *$30.*

Hilo Coffee Mill

FARM/RANCH | With all the buzz about Kona coffee, it's easy to forget that estate-grown coffee is produced throughout the rest of the island; the Hilo Coffee Mill, on 24 acres in lush Mountain View, is a pleasant reminder of that. In addition to farming its own coffee on-site, the mill has partnered with several small coffee farmers in East Hawaii in an effort to put the region on the world's coffee map. You can sample the company's efforts, tour the mill, and watch the roasters in action. They host a farmers' market every Saturday from 9 to 2. ✉ *17-995 Volcano Rd. (Hwy. 11), between mile markers 12 and 13, Mountain View* ☎ *808/968–1333* ⊕ *www.hilocoffeemill.com* ✉ *Free* ⊘ *Closed Sun., Mon., and Fri.*

★ Imiloa Astronomy Center

SCIENCE MUSEUM | Part Hawaiian cultural center, part astronomy museum, part planetarium, this center provides community outreach for the astronomy program at the University of Hawaii at Hilo. With its interactive exhibits, full-dome planetarium shows, and regularly scheduled talks and events, the center is a must-see for anyone interested in the stars and planets, Hawaiian cultural history, and early Polynesian navigation. Admission includes one planetarium show and an all-day pass to the exhibit hall, which features more than 100 interactive displays. The lunch buffet at the adjoining Sky Garden Restaurant is popular and affordable. A five-minute drive from downtown Hilo, the center is located above the main campus at the university's Science and Technology Park. ✉ *University of Hawaii at Hilo Science and Technology Park, 600 Imiloa Pl., off Nowelo and Komohana Sts., Hilo* ☎ *808/969–9700* ⊕ *www.imiloahawaii.org* ✉ *$19* ⊘ *Closed Mon. and Tues.*

Kaumana Caves Park

CAVE | Thanks to Hilo's abundant rainfall, this lava tube is lush with plant life. Concrete stairs lead down to the 2½-mile-long tube, which has no lighted areas. The ground is uneven and damp, so wear sturdy shoes, bring a flashlight, and explore as far as you dare to go. There are restrooms and a covered picnic table at the cave, and parking across the street. ■TIP→ **Heed all warning signs when entering the caves.** ✉ *1492 Kaumana Dr., Hilo* 🖾 *Free.*

Mauna Loa Macadamia Nut Visitor Center

FACTORY | FAMILY | Acres of macadamia nut trees lead to a giant roasting facility and processing plant with viewing windows and self-guided tours. You can even watch demonstrations showing how they coat nuts and shortbread cookies with milk chocolate to create their famous products. There are free samples and plenty of gift boxes with mac nuts in every conceivable form of presentation for sale in the visitor center. Children can burn off extra energy on a nature trail here after enjoying dairy-free ice cream for sale. ✉ *16-701 Macadamia Rd., off Hwy. 11, Hilo* ✛ *5 miles south of Hilo in Keaau* 🕾 *808/966–8614* ⊕ *www.maunaloa.com* 🖾 *Free* ⊗ *No factory processing Sat. and Sun.*

★ Panaewa Rainforest Zoo and Gardens

ZOO | FAMILY | Billed as "the only natural tropical rain forest zoo in the United States," this 12-acre county zoo features native Hawaiian species such as the nene goose and the *io* (hawk), as well as many other rare birds such as the highly endangered Hawaiian crow, or *alala*. Two Bengal tigers are also part of the collection. The white-faced whistling tree ducks are a highlight, along with monkeys, sloths, and lemurs. There's also a petting zoo on Saturdays from 1:30 to 2:30. Myriad species of lush, unusual tropical plants fill the grounds. To get here, turn left on Mamaki off Highway 11; it's just past the "Kulani 19, Stainback Hwy." sign. ✉ *800 Stainback Hwy., Hilo* 🕾 *808/959–7224* ⊕ *www.hilozoo.org* 🖾 *Free, donations encouraged.*

Rainbow Falls

WATERFALL | After a hard rain, these impressive falls thunder into the Wailuku River gorge, often creating magical rainbows in the mist. Rainbow Falls, sometimes known as the Hilo Town Falls, are located just above downtown Hilo at Wailuku River State Park. Take Waianuenue Avenue west for a mile; when the road forks, stay right and look for the Hawaiian warrior marker sign. The falls remain open during daylight. If you're visiting the falls, drive up to Boiling Pots, also inside the park but a bit farther up the road. At Boiling Pots, four streams fall into turbulent pools that resemble cauldrons. ✉ *Wailuku River State Park, Rainbow Dr., Hilo* ⊕ *dlnr.hawaii.gov/dsp/parks/hawaii* 🖾 *Free.*

 Beaches

Honolii Beach Park

BEACH | One of the most consistent places on the east side to catch a wave, Honolii is popular with the local surf crowd. The beach is a mix of black sand, coral, and sea glass, with plenty of rocks. A shady grassy area is great for picnics while you watch the surfers. Note that the presence of surfers is not an indication that an area is safe for swimmers; winter surf is very rough. A pond just to the north is good for swimming, but it's deep and there is a drop-off. There's limited parking on the narrow roadside. Walk down the stairs and veer left over the rocks. **Amenities:** lifeguards; toilets. **Best for:** surfing. ✉ *Hwy. 19, Hilo* ✛ *1½ miles north of Hilo* 🕾 *808/961–8311.*

Onekahakaha Beach Park

BEACH | FAMILY | Shallow, rock-wall-enclosed tide pools and an adjacent grassy picnic area make this park a favorite among Hilo families with small children. The protected pools are great places to look for Hawaiian marine life like crabs and *opihi* (limpets). There isn't much white sand, but access to the water is easy. The water is usually rough beyond the line of large boulders protecting the inner tide pools, so be careful if the surf is high. This beach gets crowded on weekends. **Amenities:** lifeguards (weekends, holidays, and summer only); parking (no fee); restrooms; showers. **Best for:** swimming. ✉ *Onekahakaha Rd. and Kalanianaole Ave., Hilo* ⊕ *3 miles east of Hilo* 🕾 *808/961–8311.*

Richardson Ocean Park and Leleiwi Beach Park

BEACH | FAMILY | Just east of Hilo, almost at the end of the road, is one of the best snorkeling sites on this side of the island, as rocky outcrops provide shelter for schools of reef fish and sea turtles. Richardson Ocean Park is also the only beach in Hilo with black and green sand. Don't get close to turtles or disturb them; they are protected from harassment by federal and state law. The shaded grassy areas are great for picnics. The surrounding area unfolds into bays, protected inlets, fishponds, and lagoons, as well as the adjacent Leleiwi Beach Park. Local kids use the small black-sand beach for body boarding. The annual Richardson Rough Water Swim event takes place in October. **Amenities:** lifeguards (weekends, holidays, and summer only); parking (no fee); showers; toilets. **Best for:** snorkeling; walking. ✉ *2349 Kalanianaole Ave., Hilo* ⊕ *4 miles east of Hilo* 🕾 *808/961–8311.*

🍽 Restaurants

Happy Valley Seafood Restaurant

$ | CHINESE | Hilo's best Chinese restaurant specializes in seafood but also offers many other Cantonese treats, including salt-and-pepper pork, Mongolian lamb, and vegetarian specialties like garlic eggplant and crispy green beans. The food is good, portions are large, and the price is right, but don't come here expecting any ambience—this is a funky, no-frills Chinese restaurant, with random pieces of artwork tacked up here and there. **Known for:** authentic Cantonese Chinese food; salt-and-pepper prawns; good soups. 💲 *Average main: $12* ✉ *1263 Kilauea Ave., Suite 320, Hilo* 🕾 *808/933–1083* ☞ *Lunch hours vary.*

Kuhio Grille

$ | HAWAIIAN | There's no atmosphere to speak of at this diner, and water is served in unbreakable plastic tumblers, but if you're searching for local fare—that undefinable fusion of ethnic cuisines—this is the place. Choose from "grindz" that include *loco moco* (meat, rice, and eggs smothered in gravy), oxtail soup, plate lunches, pork chops, steaks, saimin, stir-fry, and daily specials. **Known for:** authentic Hawaiian experience; good plate lunches; award-winning one-pound laulau. 💲 *Average main: $12* ✉ *80 Pauahi St., Hilo* 🕾 *808/959–2336* ⊕ *www.kuhiogrille.com* 🕙 *Closed Tues.*

★ The Seaside Restaurant and Aqua Farm

$$ | SEAFOOD | FAMILY | Owned and operated by the Nakagawi family since the early 1920s, this landmark restaurant features three separate dining rooms that overlook a 30-acre natural brackish fishpond, making this one of the most interesting places to eat in Hilo. Some highlights are *paniolo* (cowboy) prime rib, New York steak, and shrimp scampi. **Known for:** authentic local experience; ocean and pond views at sunset; fried aholehole (young Hawaiian flagtail). 💲 *Average main: $30* ✉ *1790 Kalanianaole Ave., Hilo* 🕾 *808/935–8825* ⊕ *seasidehilo.square. site* 🕙 *Closed Mon. and Tues. No lunch.*

☕ Coffee and Quick Bites

Sack N Save Seafood Counter

$ | HAWAIIAN | FAMILY | It may sound strange, but the takeout seafood counter tucked in the back of this grocery store serves some of the finest poke in Hilo. For $13 a bowl, you get enough seafood on a steaming pile of rice to feed two people. **Known for:** variety of fresh, Hawaiian-style seafood; house-made sauces; good-value grab-and-go lunch spot. 💲 *Average main: $13* ✉ *Puainako Center, 2100 Kanoelehua Ave., Suite 101, Hilo* 🕾 *808/935-3113* ⊕ *www.foodland.com/ stores/sack-n-save-hilo.*

7

Hilo GREATER HILO

Hotels

Hale Kai Hawaii Suites

$ | **B&B/INN** | On a bluff above Honolii surfing beach, this modern, 5,400-square-foot home is 2 miles from downtown Hilo and features four rooms—each with patio, deluxe bedding, and grand ocean views within earshot of the surf. **Pros:** daily fresh breakfast items in room; intimate, romantic vibe; free on-site parking. **Cons:** no kids under 13; just outside walking distance to downtown Hilo; no air-conditioning. $ *Rooms from: $199* ✉ *111 Honolii Pl., Hilo* ☎ *808/935–6330* ⊕ *www.halekaihawaii.com* 🛏 *4 rooms* ◉l *Free Breakfast.*

The Inn at Kulaniapia Falls

$$ | **B&B/INN** | Overlooking downtown Hilo and the ocean beyond, this inn sits next to a 120-foot waterfall that tumbles into a 300-foot-wide natural pond—enticing for swimming, conditions permitting. **Pros:** guest rooms in different buildings; delicious full breakfast (not included with cabins); eco-friendly option. **Cons:** isolated location; paved road is dark at night (drive slow); no air-conditioning. $ *Rooms from: $231* ✉ *100 Kulaniapia Dr., Hilo* ☎ *808/935–6789* ⊕ *www.waterfall.net* 🛏 *14 rooms* ◉l *Free Breakfast.*

🎭 Performing Arts

ARTS CENTERS

University of Hawaii at Hilo Performing Arts Center

PERFORMANCE VENUES | The 600-seat venue hosts a full season of dance, drama, music, lectures, and other events, with about 150 performances held from September to May. The quality of the performers rivals that of any mainland university, and tickets are affordable, too. ✉ *University of Hawaii at Hilo, 200 W. Kawili St., Hilo* ☎ *808/932–7490* ⊕ *artscenter.uhh.hawaii.edu.*

Shopping

FOOD

★ Big Island Candies

CHOCOLATE | A local legend in the cookie- and chocolate-making business, Big Island Candies is a must-see for connoisseurs of fine chocolates. The packaging is first-rate, which makes these world-class confections the ideal gift or souvenir. Enjoy a free cookie sample and a cup of Kona coffee as you watch through a window as sweets are being made. The store has many interesting products, but it is best known for its chocolate-dipped shortbread cookies. ✉ *585 Hinano St., Hilo* ☎ *808/935–8890* ⊕ *www.bigislandcandies.com.*

SHOPPING CENTERS

Hilo Shopping Center

SHOPPING CENTER | **FAMILY** | Among this shopping plaza's 40 shops are a guitar store, a pharmacy, a brewpub, a trendy boutique, and the popular Island Naturals Market & Deli. Other dining destinations include Happy Valley Seafood Restaurant, Sunlight Cafe, and Restaurant Miwa, a Japanese restaurant. There's plenty of free parking. Across the street, the Kilauea Market has a wide variety of hard-to-find Asian cooking ingredients. ✉ *1261 Kilauea Ave., Hilo* ☎ *808/935–6874* ⊕ *www.thehiloshoppingcenter.com.*

Prince Kuhio Plaza

MALL | **FAMILY** | The Big Island's most comprehensive mall has indoor shopping, entertainment (a multiplex), and dining, including KFC, Hot Dog on a Stick, Cinnabon, Genki Sushi, IHOP, and Maui Tacos. The kids might like the arcade (near the food court), while you enjoy the stores, anchored by Macy's and Old Navy. ✉ *111 E. Puainako St., Hilo* ☎ *808/959–3555* ⊕ *www.princekuhioplaza.com.*

Chapter 8

HAWAII VOLCANOES NATIONAL PARK, PUNA, AND KAU

8

Updated by
Karen Anderson

👁 **Sights**
★★★★★

🍴 **Restaurants**
★★★☆☆

🛏 **Hotels**
★★★★☆

🛍 **Shopping**
★★☆☆☆

🍸 **Nightlife**
★☆☆☆☆

WELCOME TO HAWAII VOLCANOES NATIONAL PARK, PUNA, AND KAU

TOP REASONS TO GO

★ **Thurston Lava Tube:** This 600-foot-long underground cavern is traversed by foot.

★ **Halemaumau Crater:** Home to Hawaii's fire goddess, Pele, the magnificent summit crater is the park's star attraction.

★ **Chain of Craters Road:** The scenic 18.8-mile road winds through historic eruption sites all the way down to the coast. It also provides access to a number of trailheads.

★ **Kilauea Iki Trail:** A switchback trail descends into breathtaking Kilauea Iki Crater, which last erupted in 1959.

★ **Punaluu Black Sand Beach:** If you're driving from Ka Lae (South Point) to Volcano, this is a must for swimming, picnicking, and turtle viewing.

★ **Pahoa:** This small town in Lower Puna features shops, cafés, and a lava museum that documents life in a lava zone.

Hawaii Volcanoes National Park in the island's southeast is a prime draw for tourists to the Big Island of Hawaii. From charming Volcano Village and the park itself to the wider Puna region, there are extraordinary sights around every corner. Most travelers who visit may do so only for a day. Those who have the time and interest should base themselves on the east side of the island for two to three days, allowing enough time to explore some of the less-visited sights beyond the national park.

1 **Volcano Village.** The artsy small town that surrounds the park has galleries, restaurants, shops, vacation accommodations, a golf course, and a winery.

2 **Summit Area.** Volcano House hotel, the Kilauea Visitor Center, Volcano Art Center Gallery, Halemaumau crater, and intriguing steam vents and sulfur banks are all located at the park's summit.

3 **Greater Park Area.** The park's dynamic geology extends all the way to the ocean, encompassing enormous pit craters, historic eruption sites, cinder cones, and more, as well as hiking trails and a coastal sea arch.

Holualoa
Kealakekua
Captain Cook
Keei
Honaunau
Kealia
Hookena
Kipahoehoe National Area Reserve
Hoopuloa
Manuka State Wayside
Ocean View
Mamalahoa Hwy
KAUNA POINT
Kahuku
SOUTH POINT (KA LAE)
Papakolea Be (Green Sand Bec
Hawaii Belt Rd.

Hawaii Volcanoes National Park, Puna, and Kau

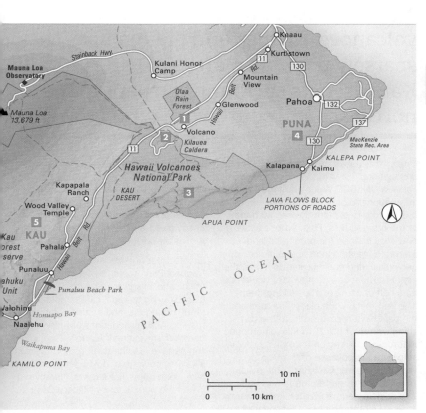

4 Puna. Whether you're headed to Hawaii Volcanoes National Park from the island's east side or the west, Highway 11/Hawaii Belt Road is the road you'll take. If you're going to Lower Puna, the Keaau–Pahoa Road intersection will lead to Highway 130 and the town of Pahoa, 11 miles farther down the road. For extra adventure, take Highway 130 all the way to Kalapana.

5 Kau. Any destination in the Kau District is accessed from Highway 11, also known as Hawaii Belt Road. The 12-mile road to South Point is easily accessed from the highway.

Dynamic, dramatic, and diverse, Hawaii Volcanoes National Park encompasses 333,308 acres across two active shield volcanoes: Kilauea and Mauna Loa. The sparsely populated areas of the Puna and Kau districts surround the park to the northeast and southwest, respectively.

One of the state's most popular visitor destinations, Hawaii Volcanoes National Park—a UNESCO World Heritage site and International Biosphere Reserve—beckons visitors to explore the sacred home of the fire goddess, Pele, whose active presence shapes the primordial landscape. Presenting incomparable scenic, geological, and ecological attractions, the park is a must-see destination, whether for a half-day trek or a weeklong deep dive into this unique place. The area and the park have recovered from the damaging events of the 2018 Kilauea eruption that rocked the region for months, beginning with the collapse of the Puu Oo Vent in the lower East Rift Zone in April 2018. Soon thereafter, the famed lava lake at Halemaumau Crater, known for its ethereal nighttime glow, disappeared for several years, only to return once more in December 2020. It has been putting on a show intermittently ever since. The seismic events of 2018 at the summit did cause permanent damage, however, to the Jaggar Museum and the Hawaii Volcano Observatory facility that overlooked the crater; both are closed.

While the dramatic changes to the Summit Caldera are evident to anyone who visited the park before the 2018 eruption, most of the park's favorite attractions survived intact including Thurston Lava Tube, Devastation Trail, and Kilauea Iki Trail. Although it's hard to keep up with the on-again, off-again nature of Kilauea's eruptions within Halemaumau Crater, there are always plenty of activities such as hiking, biking, and picnicking to enjoy at any given time if there's a pause with the visible lava.

Located just outside Hawaii Volcanoes National Park, the artsy, forested enclave of Volcano Village features galleries, glassblowing studios, cafés, restaurants, boutiques, and a Sunday farmers' market. Accommodations are plentiful here. When visiting Volcano Village, you can partake in wine tastings and tours at a local winery, go bird-watching, or ride a bike along quiet, flat streets. Nearby but inside the park, Kilauea Military Camp has an arcade, a bowling alley, a general store, and the Lava Lounge cocktail bar, all open to the public. And of course, you can always take in the nighttime celestial sights or the ever-changing daytime skies unveiling random rain showers, rainbows, rolling clouds, or crystal clear, sunny weather.

The districts of Kau and Puna lie adjacent to each other and are big and sparse, requiring lots of drive time to get to the places of most interest. The Kau area is known for its wide-open spaces, vast desert regions, rugged coastline, dense macadamia groves, and windswept ranchlands. The Puna district encompasses Lower and Upper Puna.

With an active volcano looming directly upslope on the flank of Kilauea, Pahoa Town in Lower Puna has been threatened by lava through the years, including in 2014 and 2018, but has survived. Despite the natural disasters that have inundated some of the area, there is still much to experience in Lower Puna, including cafés, restaurants, boutique shops, artisan markets, festivals, a Lava Zone museum, and yoga retreats. Add Lava Tree State Monument and Kalapana to your itinerary.

MAJOR REGIONS

Volcano Village. Located outside the Hawaii Volcanoes National Park, this quiet residential enclave offers gas, food, lodging, shops, and recreational opportunities. The close-knit town has attracted artists of all kinds, and their works are on display in local galleries.

Summit Area. The Summit Area of Kilauea Volcano encompasses the park visitor center, Volcano House hotel, Volcano Art Center Gallery, Kilauea Military Camp, and a host of geological sights highlighted by the massive Kilauea Caldera.

Greater Park Area. The area beyond the summit spans vast open spaces, miles of lava flows, lush rain forests, and coastal regions. A drive along Chain of Craters Road takes you past trailheads and geological wonders to the coast and memorable, wide-open ocean views.

Puna. The large Puna District is divided into a lower and an upper region. Most of Upper Puna comprises portions of Hawaii Volcanoes National Park and the neighboring town of Volcano Village. Closer to sea level, Lower Puna includes the towns of Keaau, Mountain View, Kurtistown, and Pahoa, as well as the coastal community of Kalapana.

Kau. Stretching from Ocean View on the southwest side of the Big Island, the Kau District spans all the way to South Point, Naalehu, and Pahala to Hawaii Volcanoes National Park.

Planning

Planning Your Time

When you're headed to Hawaii Volcanoes National Park for the day, allow a minimum of three hours to see the summit area's main attractions. Also make time to visit Volcano Village, with its art galleries and cafés. If there is visible lava activity within Halemaumau Crater during your visit, you might time your trip so that you are still in the park at dusk or into the evening to see the orange glow, or at predawn, which is less crowded. For short day hikes, there are easy trails within the summit area, as well as off Chain of Craters Road, that can be enjoyed within an hour. A full day trip could include wine tasting, bike riding, shopping, bowling, and even live music at Lava Lounge after dark. A two- or three-day stay in Volcano will yield many compelling discoveries in the park off the beaten track. If you want to fully explore the sights in Lower Puna or Kau, add another day or two to your visit.

Getting Here and Around

The 27-mile drive on Highway 19 from Hilo to Volcano takes about 40 minutes. From downtown Kailua-Kona, the drive requires traversing Saddle Road to Hilo and then heading up to Volcano; one-way takes approximately 2½ hours. If you're heading south to Volcano from South Kona, you'll drive past Ocean View, South Point and Pahala along Highway 11 to the park, which takes about two hours. The park itself is easy to drive around, as there are only two main roads: Chain of Craters Road and Crater Rim Drive.

8

Hawaii Volcanoes National Park, Puna, and Kau PLANNING

AIR

If your primary goal for visiting the Big Island is to spend most of your time at Hawaii Volcanoes National Park and vicinity, then fly into Hilo if you can. It's a long drive from Kona International Airport (about 2½ hours) to Volcano, versus about 40 minutes from Hilo.

BUS

Six public Hele-On buses (⊕ *www.hele-onbus.org*) travel from Volcano to downtown Hilo and back on weekdays and Saturday. Stops include Volcano Village and the Kilauea Visitor Center inside the park. The last bus leaves the park's visitor center around 6 pm. (Always check the latest bus schedules to confirm.) Once you're in the park, though, you'll be limited to sights within walking distance of the Kilauea Visitor Center. You can bring a bike with you on the bus; biking is a great way to see the park when it's not raining. Transportation to points farther in the Kau district is even more limited. Only one bus departs each morning from Ocean View, traveling all the way to Hilo and returning to Ocean View in the evening.

CAR

You'll need a car to explore this vast region, but there's no need to rent a four-wheel drive. There are two main roads inside the park: Crater Rim Drive, which is at the summit, and Chain of Craters Road, which leads all the way down to the coast. It's easy to plan a driving itinerary within the park's boundaries. Speed limits in the park are enforced for a reason. The area is highly visited, and the park strives to maintain visitor safety for all, as well as provide protection for the endangered Hawaiian nene geese that roam the area.

The 31-mile drive from Volcano to Pahoa takes 45 minutes one way along Hawaii Belt Road. The road connecting Pahoa to Kalapana is 13 miles long, about a half-hour drive depending on the stops you make along the way. There are

restaurants, stores, and gas stations in Pahoa, and services are also available in Keeau closer to Hilo. Long stretches of the road may be completely isolated at any given point; it's a little dark at night but tranquil during the day.

The drive from Kailua-Kona to South Point is a long one (roughly two hours). You can fill up on gas and groceries on the way in Ocean View and also dine, fuel up, and get picnic fixings in Naalehu. From Hilo, you can get to Pahoa in 24 minutes, barring traffic, via Highway 130 (Keeau-Pahoa Rd). The drive from Hilo to Volcano takes about 40 minutes on Highway 11.

Beaches

The Puna and Kau districts are known for black-sand beaches, including the famous black-sand beach of Punaluu in Kau and Pohoiki Black Sand Beach near Pahoa. Currently, there are no beaches within Hawaii Volcanoes National Park. There once was a black-sand beach within the park at the end of Chain of Craters Road, but lava covered it in the early '90s.

Hotels

If you visit Hawaii Volcanoes National Park—and you should—spend at least one night in Volcano Village. This allows you time to explore additional hiking trails and park attractions, as well as to see the village with its art galleries, winery, cafés, and gift stores. There are plenty of places to stay, and many are both charming and reasonably priced. There is one hotel in the park, the landmark Volcano House. (Kilauea Military Camp inside the park offers lodging in 90 vintage cottages only for military members/veterans and their families.) Volcano Village has just enough visitor destinations to satisfy you for a day or two.

Puna is a world apart—thick rain forests, rugged shorelines, and homes that are decidedly off the beaten track. There is, however, a handful of well-priced vacation homes and funky bed-and-breakfasts. It's not your typical vacation spot; there are a few black-sand beaches (some of them clothing optional), scant dining or entertainment options, and quite a few, er, interesting locals. That said, for those who want to have a unique experience and get away from everything, and who don't mind the sound of the chirping coqui frogs at night, this is the place to do it. The Kilauea eruption of 2018, however, destroyed some of Lower Puna's most beautiful bays, coastal neighborhoods, and beach parks.

Far from the major South Kohala resorts, the Kau district is a good place for those looking to get away from it all. You won't find a lot in terms of amenities, but there are several nice options including vacation rental cottages, a B&B, and a condo resort complex with a golf course. The main visitor attraction is the beautiful Punaluu Black Sand Beach, home of the endangered hawksbill turtle.

⇨ *Hotel prices in the reviews are the lowest cost of a standard double room in high season. Restaurant prices in the reviews are the average cost of a main course at dinner, or if dinner is not served, at lunch. Hotel and restaurant reviews have been shortened. For full information, see Fodors.com.*

What It Costs in U. S. Dollars			
$	$$	$$$	$$$$
HOTELS			
under $200	$200–$280	$281–$380	over $380
RESTAURANTS			
under $20	$20–$30	$31–$40	over $40

Restaurants

At the park, a restaurant (The Rim) and lounge inside Volcano House serves breakfast, lunch, and dinner overlooking the summit from the rim of Kilauea Caldera. There are also casual public eateries at Kilauea Military Camp within the park. You'll find a handful of dining options, and a general store, in Volcano Village. If you can't find what you're looking for, Hilo is about a 40-minute drive away, and in Keaau, there's a grocery store, natural foods store, eateries, and fast-food joints just 30 minutes away.

The best restaurants in the Puna District are in Volcano Village and Pahoa. Dining in Kau is limited, with a handful of diners scattered throughout the district.

Safety

When visiting Hawaii Volcanoes National Park, don't venture off marked trails or into closed areas, and avoid walking near open steam vents, ground cracks, or steep cliffsides. Many hikes in the park are on rugged, open lava fields where winds, rain, and searing sun can happen at a moment's notice. Wear plenty of sunscreen, a hat or a hooded light jacket, and close-toed shoes; always carry plenty of water with you. Volcanic fumes can be hazardous. Heed any air-quality warnings that are posted at the Kilauea Visitor Center and throughout the park. Down along the coast, strong winds and high surf are possible.

There is a bit of a "locals-only" vibe in parts of Lower Puna, and some areas suffer crime, car theft, and drug problems. Don't wander around alone at night or risk getting lost on backcountry roads.

Tours

Volcano Art Center Forest Tour

WALKING TOURS | Volcano Art Center offers a free Monday morning forest tour where visitors can learn about old-growth koa and ohia rain forests. These hour-long walks take place on easily traversed gravel trails, rain or shine. No reservations are required, but a group of five or more is recommended. The center offers additional customized rain forest tours, as well as forest restoration activities. ✉ *Volcano Art Center, 99-150 Crater Rim Dr., Hawaii Volcanoes National Park ☎ 866/967–8222 for administration, 808/967–7565 for gallery ⊕ www. volcanoartcenter.org ☜ Free.*

Visitor Information

Hawaii Volcanoes National Park is open 24/7. When you arrive at the park entrance during normal visiting hours, you'll receive a complimentary detailed map and brochure about the park. The park entrance fee (good for seven days) is $30 per vehicle, $15 per pedestrian, and $25 per motorcycle. (The park no longer accepts cash for entrance fees and passes; debit or credit cards only.)

Inside Kilauea Visitor Center, trail guide booklets written by park geologists are available for less than $3 each. Operated by Hawaii Pacific Parks, the park store features educational materials, apparel, gifts, books, and art. A small theater plays educational films about the history of the park, and park rangers are available to answer questions. There is always an itinerary of ranger-led activities.
■ TIP→ **Purchase the Hawaii Tri-Park Annual Pass for $55, which allows full access to Hawaii Volcanoes National Park and Puuhonua O Honaunau National Historical Park on the Big Island, and Haleakala National Park on Maui.**

Volcano Village

Located right outside the park boundary and surrounded by rain forest, Volcano Village is a residential neighborhood that offers vacation rental accommodations, B&Bs, a gas station, a post office, an art school, galleries, shops, a general store, and a fun Sunday farmers' market. The immediate area also has a country club and golf course, as well as the popular Volcano Winery. Next door to the winery, the Keauhou Bird Conservation Center is not open to the public, but if you listen closely, you may be able to hear the call of the highly endangered *alala* (Hawaiian crow), a species being bred in captivity at the center.

Sights

Volcano Farmers' Market

MARKET | Local produce, flowers, crafts, and food products, including fresh-baked breads, pastries, coffee, pancakes, fresh coconuts with straws, and homemade Thai specialties, are available every Sunday morning from 6 to 10 at this decidedly down-home farmers' market in Volcano Village. It's best to get there early, before 7, as vendors tend to sell out of the best stuff quickly. There's also a small bookstore (paperbacks 50¢, hardcovers $1, and magazines 10¢) and a thrift store with clothes and knickknacks. The market is held in the covered Cooper Center, so it's safe from the rain. ✉ *Cooper Center, 19-4030 Wright Rd., Volcano ☎ 808/936–9705 ⊕ www.thecoopercenter.org ⊗ Closed Mon.–Sat.*

Volcano Garden Arts

ART GALLERY | Located on beautifully landscaped grounds dotted with intriguing sculptures, this delightful gallery and garden lend credence to Volcano Village's reputation as an artists' haven. The complex includes an eclectic gallery representing more than 100 artists, a gourmet organic café in redwood buildings built in

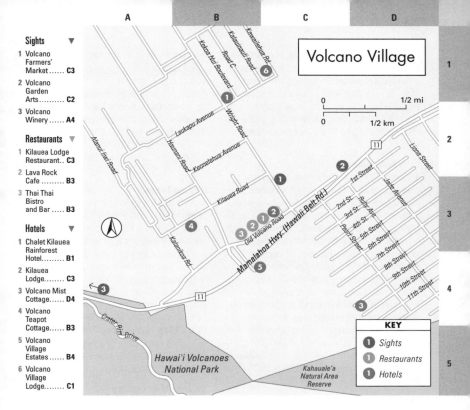

Volcano Village

KEY

1 Sights
1 Restaurants
1 Hotels

1908, and a cute, one-bedroom vacation cottage, available for rent. If you're lucky, you'll get to meet the award-winning owner/caretaker of this enclave, the multitalented Ira Ono, known for his mixed-media art, recycled trash creations, and friendly personality. ⊠ 19-3834 Old Volcano Rd., Volcano ☎ 808/985–8979 ⊕ www.volcanogardenarts.com ⊠ Free ⊗ Café closed Mon.–Wed.

★ **Volcano Winery**

WINERY | Not all volcanic soils are ideal for the cultivation of grapes, but this winery grows its own grapes and produces some interesting vintages. The Macadamia Nut Honey Wine is a nutty, very sweet after-dinner drink. The Infusion Tea Wine pairs estate-grown black tea with South Kona's fermented macadamia nut honey for a smooth concoction perfect for brunch through early evening. Though

this isn't Napa Valley, the vintners take their wine seriously, and the staff is friendly and knowledgeable. Wine tasting and flights are available; you can also enjoy wine and cheese inside or in a shaded picnic area. A gift store carries a selection of local crafts. ⊠ 35 Pii Mauna Dr., Volcano ✦ Past entrance to Hawaii Volcanoes National Park, by golf course ☎ 808/967–7772 ⊕ www.volcanowinery. com ⊠ Free; tastings from $15 for a flight of 6 wines.

🍽 Restaurants

Kilauea Lodge Restaurant

$$ | **MODERN AMERICAN** | At this historic lodge in the heart of Volcano Village, the fare ranges from gourmet grass-fed Big Island beef burgers and locally sourced lamb burgers to Cajun shrimp and sausage pasta, catch of the day, and farm-fresh salads. The restaurant serves breakfast, lunch, and dinner seven days a week. **Known for:** Fireplace of Friendship; fine dining with prices to match; popular Sunday brunch. ⑤ *Average main: $30* ⊠ *19-3948 Old Volcano Rd., Volcano* ☎ *808/967–7366* ⊕ *www.kilauealodge.com.*

Lava Rock Cafe

$ | **DINER** | **FAMILY** | This is an affordable place to grab a sandwich or a coffee and check your email (Wi-Fi is free with purchase of a meal) before heading to Hawaii Volcanoes National Park. The homey, sit-down diner caters to families, serving up heaping plates of comfort food like pancakes and French toast for breakfast; on the lunch menu, burger options include bacon and cheese, turkey, and *paniolo* (cowboy) burgers made with Hawaii grass-fed beef. **Known for:** roadhouse atmosphere; volcano-themed floors; full bar. ⑤ *Average main: $18* ⊠ *19-3972 Old Volcano Hwy., Volcano* ⊹ *Next to Kilauea General Store* ☎ *808/967–8526* ⊘ *No dinner Sun. Closed Mon.*

Thai Thai Bistro and Bar

$$ | **THAI** | **FAMILY** | The food is authentic and the prices are reasonable at this little Volcano Village find with Thai art and silk wall hangings in the pleasant dining room. A steaming-hot plate of curry is the perfect antidote to a chilly day at the volcano, and the chicken satay is excellent—the peanut dipping sauce a good blend of sweet and spicy. **Known for:** reliable Thai cuisine with plenty of spice; full bar; vegan and gluten-free options. ⑤ *Average main: $30* ⊠ *19-4084 Old Volcano Rd., Volcano* ☎ *808/967–7969* ⊕ *www.lavalodge.com* ⊘ *Closed Wed. and Thurs.*

 Hotels

Chalet Kilauea Rainforest Hotel

$ | **B&B/INN** | **FAMILY** | Quirky yet upscale, this accommodation features four artistically distinctive rooms that unveil beautiful views of the rain forest from a great location five minutes from Hawaii Volcanoes National Park. **Pros:** unique decor; friendly front desk; hot tub on property. **Cons:** space heaters; stairs to upper floor; can get cold at night. ⑤ *Rooms from: $75* ⊠ *19-4178 Wright Rd., Volcano* ☎ *808/967–7786, 800/937–7786* ⊕ *www.volcano-hawaii.com* ⇋ *4 rooms* ⦿ *No Meals.*

Kilauea Lodge

$$$ | **HOTEL** | A mile from the entrance to Hawaii Volcanoes National Park, this lodge built as a YMCA camp in the 1930s is now a pleasant inn, tastefully furnished with European antiques, photographs, and authentic Hawaiian quilts. **Pros:** great restaurant; close to volcano; historic ambience. **Cons:** no TV or phone in lodge rooms; 45 minutes to downtown Hilo; books up quickly. ⑤ *Rooms from: $300* ⊠ *19-3948 Old Volcano Rd., Volcano* ⊹ *1 mile northeast of national park* ☎ *808/967–7366* ⊕ *www.kilauealodge.com* ⇋ *12 rooms* ⦿ *No Meals.*

Volcano Mist Cottage

$$$$ | **HOUSE** | Both rustic and Zen, this magical cottage in the rain forest features cathedral ceilings, spruce walls, cork flooring, and amenities not usually found at Volcano vacation rentals, like bathrobes, a Bose home theater system, and Trek mountain bikes. **Pros:** isolated and private cottage; outdoor Jacuzzi tub; upscale amenities. **Cons:** not large enough for families; 45 minutes from downtown Hilo; pricey for the area. ⑤ *Rooms from: $465* ⊠ *11-3932 9th St., Volcano* ☎ *808/895–8359* ⊕ *www.volcanomistcottage.com* ⇋ *1 cottage* ⦿ *Free Breakfast* ⊘ *2-night minimum stay.*

Volcano Teapot Cottage

$$ | **HOUSE** | A near-perfect spot for couples seeking a romantic getaway in Volcano Village, this historical 1912 two-bedroom cottage evokes a vintage country feeling in keeping with the summer homes of the era. **Pros:** near town restaurants; fireplace and hot tub; laundry

facilities. **Cons:** accommodates three people max; can get cold at night; books up fast. $ *Rooms from: $215* ✉ *19-4041 Kilauea Rd., Volcano* ☎ *808/937–4976* ⊕ *www.volcanoteapot.com* ⛵ *1 cottage* ❑ *Free Breakfast.*

Volcano Village Estates

$$ | **B&B/INN** | **FAMILY** | A stately and comfortable Queen Anne–style mansion, the Dillingham House is the centerpiece of the property and was built in the 1930s as a summer home for a wealthy Scotsman (the property is listed on the State Historic Register). **Pros:** unique architecture; within walking distance of HVNP; private location. **Cons:** no TVs; simple breakfast offerings; can get cold at night. $ *Rooms from: $275* ✉ *11-3968 Hale Ohia Rd., Volcano* ☎ *808/967–7986, 800/455–3803* ⊕ *volcanovillageestates. com* ⛵ *18 units* ❑ *Free Breakfast.*

★ Volcano Village Lodge

$$$ | **B&B/INN** | Hospitality abounds at this luxurious B&B in a secluded rain forest, where the separate suites (connected by paths) offer amenities including fine furnishings, dining niches, jetted bathtubs, heated blankets, and private forest entrances. **Pros:** secluded and quiet; hospitable staff; outdoor hot tub. **Cons:** no covered parking; far from Hilo town; no restaurants within walking distance. $ *Rooms from: $310* ✉ *19-4183 Kawailehua Rd., Volcano* ☎ *808/985–9500* ⊕ *www.volcanovillagelodge.com* ⛵ *5 suites* ❑ *Free Breakfast.*

🛍 Shopping

ARTS AND CRAFTS

★ Kilauea Kreations

FABRICS | Beautiful hand-stitched Hawaiian quilts grace the walls here, quilting kits and books are plentiful, and the vast inventory of tropical fabrics is amazing. The friendly proprietors also offer fine art, photography, cards, and cool souvenirs you won't find anywhere else. ✉ *19-3972 Volcano Rd., Volcano* ✛ *Next to Lava*

Rock Cafe ☎ *808/967–8090* ⊕ *www. kilaueakreations.com* ⊘ *Closed Mon.*

2400 Fahrenheit

ART GALLERY | At the end of Old Volcano Road near Volcano Village, this small gallery and studio has handblown glass inspired by the eruption of Kilauea and the colors of the tropics. You can see the artists in action Thursday through Sunday from 10 to 4, and other days by appointment. ✉ *Old Volcano Rd., off Hwy. 11 between mile markers 23 and 24, Volcano* ☎ *808/985–8667* ⊕ *www.2400f.com* ⊘ *Closed Mon.–Wed.*

🏃 Activities

SPAS

Hale Hoola Volcano's Spa

SPA | For those staying in Volcano, this spa is a sweet alternative to the big resorts, with a menu featuring a bounty of local ingredients and traditional Hawaiian treatments. These include *lomi hula,* which is lomilomi massage choreographed to hula music, and *laau hamo,* which blends lomilomi with traditional Hawaiian and Asian healing herbs and plant extracts. Body scrubs use traditional ginger, coconut, and macadamia nuts but also some surprises, including taro, vanilla, and volcanic clay. Rejuvenation packages include a full-body scrub, massage, and hot steam. Couples are welcome. Treatments are by appointment only. ✉ *Mauna Loa Estates, 11-3913 7th St., Volcano* ☎ *808/756–2421* ⊕ *www. halehoola.net* ✉ *Massages from $115.*

Summit Area

In the heart of Hawaii Volcanoes National Park, a primeval landscape unfolds at the summit of Kilauea volcano, where steam rises continuously from cracks in the earth and volcanic gases create malodorous sulfur banks. Here, Halemaumau

Continued on page 226

HAWAII VOLCANOES NATIONAL PARK

Exploring the surface of the world's most active volcano—from the moonscape craters at the summit to the red-hot lava flows on the coast to the kipuka, pockets of vegetation miraculously left untouched—is the ultimate ecotour and one of Hawaii's must-dos.

The park sprawls over 520 square miles and encompasses Kilauea and Mauna Loa, two of the five volcanoes that formed the Big Island nearly half a million years ago. Kilauea, youngest and most rambunctious of the Hawaiian volcanoes, erupted at its summit from the 19th century through 1982. Since then, the top of the volcano had been more or less quiet, frequently shrouded in mist; an eruption in the Hale-maumau Crater in 2008 ended this period of relative inactivity. A major eruption in 2018, and several smaller eruptions since, have caused further changes in the park.

Kilauea's eastern side sprang to life on January 3, 1983, shooting molten lava four stories high. This eruption has been ongoing, and lava flows are generally steady and slow, appearing and disappearing from view. Over 500 acres have been added to Hawaii's eastern coast since the activity began, and scientists say this eruptive phase is not likely to end anytime soon. However, the famed lava lake at Halemaumau Crater, which drained in 2018, began to refill by 2020.

The damaging events of 2018 have now subsided, and you can see the effects of creation elemental—where molten lava meets the ocean, cools, and solidifies into brand-new stretches of coastline. Although some popular park sights have had to close, you can hike 150 miles of trails and camp amid wide expanses of *aa* (rough) and *pahoehoe* (smooth) lava. There's nothing quite like it.

- ✉ 1 Crater Rim Dr., Hawaii Volcanoes National Park, HI 96718
- ☎ 808/985–6000
- 🌐 www.nps.gov/havo
- 💲 $30 per vehicle; $15 for pedestrians and bicyclists. Ask about passes. Admission is good for seven consecutive days.
- 🕐 The park is open daily, 24 hours. Kilauea Visitor Center: 9 am–5 pm. Volcano Art Center Gallery: 9–5.

(Top) Kilauea Iki Trail (Left) Halemaumau Crater

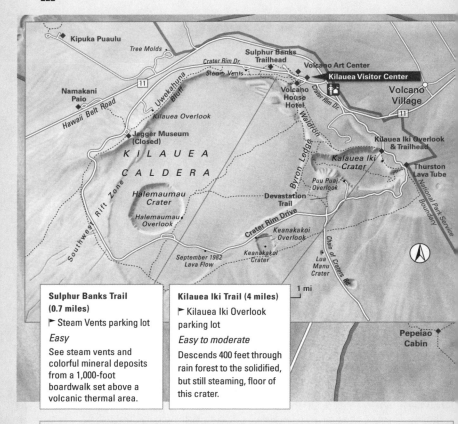

Sulphur Banks Trail (0.7 miles)

⚲ Steam Vents parking lot

Easy

See steam vents and colorful mineral deposits from a 1,000-foot boardwalk set above a volcanic thermal area.

Kilauea Iki Trail (4 miles)

⚲ Kilauea Iki Overlook parking lot

Easy to moderate

Descends 400 feet through rain forest to the solidified, but still steaming, floor of this crater.

SEEING THE SUMMIT

The best way to explore the summit of Kilauea is to cruise along Crater Rim Drive to Kilauea Overlook. From Kilauea Overlook you can see all of Kilauea Caldera and Halemaumau Crater, an awesome depression in Kilauea Caldera measuring 3,000 feet across and nearly 300 feet deep. It's a huge and breathtaking view with pluming steam vents. Halemaumau Crater's most recent on-and-off eruption has been taking place since December 2020, creating a lake that has risen within view of several observation points accessible to the public.

Regrettably, the events of 2018 damaged the Thomas A. Jaggar Museum beyond repair, and it is now permanently closed. You can visit the nearby Kilauea Military Camp, with its recreational activities and general store, and the park's star attractions, the Thurston Lava Tube, which you can walk through.

Other highlights along Crater Rim Drive include sulfur and steam vents, fractures, and gullies along Kilauea's flanks. Kilauea Iki Crater, on the way down to Chain of Craters Road, is smaller, but just as fascinating when seen from Puu Pai Overlook.

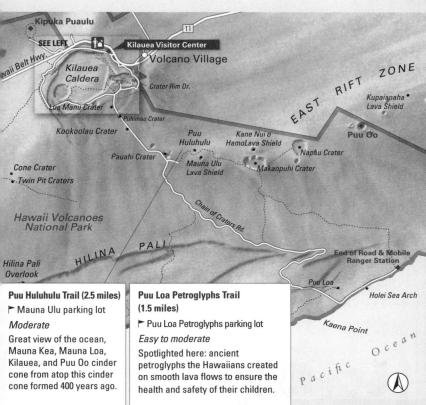

Kipuka Puaulu

SEE LEFT

Kilauea Visitor Center

Volcano Village

11

awaii Belt Hwy.

Kilauea Caldera

Crater Rim Dr.

EAST RIFT ZONE

Loa Manu Crater

Kupaianaha Lava Shield

Puhimau Crater

Kookoolau Crater

Puu Huluhulu

Kane Nui o HamoLava Shield

Puu Oo

Pauahi Crater

Napau Crater

Cone Crater

Mauna Ulu Lava Shield

Makaopuhi Crater

Twin Pit Craters

Hawaii Volcanoes National Park

Chain of Craters Rd.

HILINA PALI

End of Road & Mobile Ranger Station

Hilina Pali Overlook

Puu Loa

Holei Sea Arch

Kaena Point

Pacific Ocean

Puu Huluhulu Trail (2.5 miles)

▶ Mauna Ulu parking lot

Moderate

Great view of the ocean, Mauna Kea, Mauna Loa, Kilauea, and Puu Oo cinder cone from atop this cinder cone formed 400 years ago.

Puu Loa Petroglyphs Trail (1.5 miles)

▶ Puu Loa Petroglyphs parking lot

Easy to moderate

Spotlighted here: ancient petroglyphs the Hawaiians created on smooth lava flows to ensure the health and safety of their children.

SEEING LAVA

There are three guarantees about lava flows in HVNP. First: They constantly change. Second: Because of that, you can't predict when and where you'll be able to see them. Third: New land formed where lava meets the sea is highly unstable and can collapse at any time. Never go into areas that have been closed.

■ TIP→ **Even without flowing lava, Chain of Craters Road is a magnificent drive, and the park's best hiking trails have now reopened fully.**

PLANNING YOUR TRIP TO HVNP

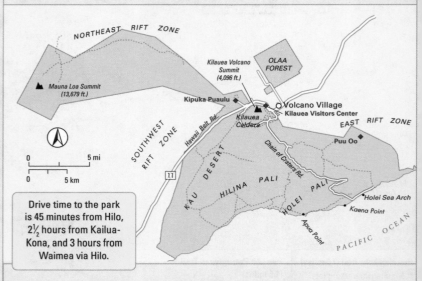

NORTHEAST RIFT ZONE

Kilauea Volcano
Summit
(4,096 ft.)

OLAA
FOREST

▲ Mauna Loa Summit
(13,679 ft.)

Kipuka Puaulu ◆

○ Volcano Village
Kilauea Visitors Center

Kilauea
Caldera

SOUTHWEST RIFT ZONE

Hawaii Belt Rd.

EAST RIFT ZONE

Puu Oo ◆

Chain of Craters Rd.

KAU DESERT

HILINA PALI

HOLEI PALI

11

Holei Sea Arch •

Kaena Point •

Apua Point •

PACIFIC OCEAN

0 ___ 5 mi
0 ___ 5 km

Drive time to the park
is 45 minutes from Hilo,
2½ hours from Kailua-
Kona, and 3 hours from
Waimea via Hilo.

Lava entering the ocean

WHERE TO START

Begin your visit at the Visitor Center, where you'll find maps and books; information on trails, ranger-led walks, and special events; and current weather, road, and lava-viewing conditions. Free volcano-related film showings, lectures, and other presentations are regularly scheduled.

WEATHER

Weather conditions fluctuate daily, sometimes hourly. It can be rainy and chilly even during the summer; the temperature usually is 14° cooler at the 4,000-foot-high summit of Kilauea than at sea level.

Expect hot, dry, and windy coastal conditions at the end of Chain of Craters Road. Bring rain gear, and wear layered clothing, sturdy shoes, sunglasses, a hat, and sunscreen.

Visitors hike to Halemaumau

FOOD

It's a good idea to bring your own favorite snacks and beverages; stock up on provisions in Volcano Village, 1½ miles away. Kilauea Military Camp, near the summit, has a general store as well as casual dining options, and all are open to the public.

PARK PROGRAMS

Rangers lead daily walks at 10:30 and 1:30 into different areas; check with the Visitor Center for details as times and destinations depend on weather conditions and eruptions.

Over 60 companies hold permits to lead hikes at HVNP. Good choices are Hawaii Forest & Trail (⊕ *www.hawaii-forest.com*) and KapohoKine Adventures (⊕ *www.kapohokine.com*).

CAUTION

"Vog" (volcanic smog) can cause headaches; breathing difficulties; lethargy; irritations of the skin, eyes, nose, and throat; and other health problems. Pregnant women, young children, and people with asthma and heart conditions are most susceptible, and should avoid areas such as Halemaumau Crater where fumes are thick.

Wear long pants and boots or closed-toe shoes with good tread for hikes on lava. Stay on marked trails and step carefully. Lava is composed of 50% silica (glass) and can cause serious injury if you fall.

Carry at least 2 quarts of water on hikes. Temperatures near lava flows can rise above 100°F, and dehydration, heat exhaustion, and sunstroke are common consequences of extended exposure to intense sunlight and high temperatures.

Remember that these are active volcanoes, and eruptions can cause parts of the park to close at any time. Check the park's website or call ahead for last-minute updates before your visit.

Pay for and download a digital park entrance pass from ⊕ *recreation.gov* to save time at the entry gate. The pass can be downloaded to your smart phone or printed.

Crater's on-and-off eruption has been taking place throughout the decades, creating a lake that most recently has been putting on a fiery extravaganza within view of several observation points accessible to the public. In addition to the many geological sights, the summit area of the park includes Kilauea Visitor Center, Volcano Art Center Gallery, and Volcano House—a landmark hotel perched above the rim of Kilauea Caldera. The visitor center is a good place to begin your park adventure.

Sights

Devastation Trail

TRAIL | A paved pathway takes visitors across a barren lavascape strewn with chunky cinders that descended from towering lava fountains during the 1959 eruption of nearby Kilauea Iki Crater. The easy 1-mile (round-trip) hike ends at the edge of the Kilauea Iki Crater. This must-see view of the crater could yield such memorable sights as white-tailed tropic birds gliding in the breeze or a rainbow stretching above the crater's rim after a sunlit rain shower. *Easy.* ⊠ *Hawaii Volcanoes National Park* ⊹ *Trailhead: 4 miles from visitor center at intersection of Crater Rim Dr. and Chain of Craters Rd.* ☎ *808/985–6101* ⊕ *www.nps.gov/havo.*

★ Halemaumau Crater

VOLCANO | For Native Hawaiians, Halemaumau Crater is the sacred home of Pele, the fire goddess; for scientists at the Hawaiian Volcano Observatory, this mighty pit crater within the massive Kilauea Caldera is an ever-changing force to be reckoned with. Prior to Kilauea's 2018 eruption, Halemaumau's visible lava lake awed visitors for 10 consecutive years. Then Puu Oo Vent, which had been erupting farther away in the East Rift Zone for 35 years, collapsed in April 2018. As lava from the vent drained, so did the lava lake at Halemaumau Crater. A relentless series of seismic events at the summit followed, doubling the

diameter of Halemaumau Crater and deepening it by 1,300 feet, after which a lake of water began forming, eventually growing to 160 feet deep. On December 20, 2020, an eruption within the crater instantly vaporized the water lake, sending molten lava cascading into the crater from vents within the walls and commencing the return of an active lava lake to Halemaumau, which has erupted intermittently in the years that followed through 2023 and likely beyond. There are many places in the park to view the magnificent crater, including at the Steaming Bluff Overlook and at Volcano House hotel. To get a glimpse of the lava lake during an eruption phase, there is a lookout area between the Steam Vents and the former Jaggar Museum area; another lookout point is on the crater's other side near the Devastation Trail parking lot. ■ **TIP**→ **For the best lava-viewing experience of Halemaumau Crater during an eruption phase, visit the park after 10 pm when crowds are smaller.** ⊠ *Crater Rim Dr., Hawaii Volcanoes National Park* ☎ *808/985–6101* ⊕ *www.nps.gov/havo.*

★ Kilauea Iki Trail

TRAIL | The stunning 4-mile loop hike descends 400 feet into a massive crater via a forested nature trail. When you hike across the crater floor, you're actually walking on a solidified lava lake. Still steaming in places, the crater is dotted with baby ohia trees emerging from the cracks. Venture across the crater floor to the Puu Puai cinder cone that was formed by spatter from a towering lava fountain during the 1959 Kilauea Iki eruption. There are three different trailheads for Kilauea Iki; the main one, which takes two or three hours, begins at the Kilauea Iki Overlook parking lot off Crater Rim Drive. You can also access the crater from Devastation Trail or Puu Puai on the other side. *Easy.* ■ **TIP**→ **Bring water, snacks, a hat, sunscreen, and hooded rain gear, as weather can change at a moment's notice.** ⊠ *Crater Rim Dr., Hawaii Volcanoes National Park* ⊹ *Trailhead: 3* miles from visitor center ☎ 808/985–6011 ⊕ www.nps.gov/havo.

Kilauea Military Camp

NATIONAL PARK | FAMILY | Located inside the park, Kilauea Military Camp, established in 1916, offers visitor accommodations to members of the military and their families but also has places open to the public, including an arcade, bowling alley, diner, buffet, general store, and gas station. The Lava Lounge cocktail bar is open nightly and features live music on weekends. ⊠ 99-252 Crater Rim Dr., Hawaii Volcanoes National Park ☎ 808/967–8333 ⊕ www.kilaueamilitarycamp.com.

Kilauea Visitor Center

VISITOR CENTER | FAMILY | Rangers and volunteers greet people and answer all questions at this visitor center, located just beyond the park entrance. There are lots of educational murals and displays, maps, and guidebooks. Also check out the daily itinerary of ranger-led activities. The gift shop operated by the Hawaii Pacific Park Association stocks excellent art, books, apparel, and more. A small theater plays documentaries about the park. ⊠ 1 Crater Rim Dr., Hawaii Volcanoes National Park ☎ 808/985–6011 ⊕ www.nps.gov/havo.

Steam Vents and Sulphur Banks

VOLCANO | A short walk from the Kilauea Visitor Center leads to the pungent yet fascinating Sulphur Banks, where gases composed of hydrogen sulfide produce a smell akin to rotten eggs. Most of the rocks surrounding the vents are chemically stained with a yellow hue due to constant gas exposure. Throughout the surrounding landscape, dozens of active steam vents emit white, billowing vapors that originate from groundwater heated by volcanic rocks. Located on the caldera's edge, Steaming Bluff is a short walk from a nearby parking area. ■ TIP→ **The best steam vents are across the road from the main steam vent parking area; they vary in size and are scattered alongside the dirt trails.** ⊠ Crater Rim Dr., Hawaii Volcanoes

National Park ✛ Within walking distance of Kilauea Visitor Center ☎ 808/985–6101 ⊕ www.nps.gov/havo.

Thurston Lava Tube (Nahuku)

NATURE SIGHT | FAMILY | One of the park's star attractions, Thurston Lava Tube (named "Nahuku" in Hawaiian) spans 600 feet underground. The massive cavelike tube, discovered in 1913, was formed by hot molten lava traveling through the channel. To reach the entrance of the tube, visitors descend a series of stairs surrounded by Hawaiian rain forest and the sounds of native birds. The Kilauea eruption of 2018 resulted in an almost two-year closure of the tube. During the closure, the drainage system was improved to reduce standing water on the cave's floor, and electrical lines and lighting were replaced. Visitors should not touch the walls or delicate tree root systems that grow down through the ceiling. ■ TIP→ **Parking is limited near the tube. If the lot is full, you can park at the Kilauea Iki Overlook parking lot, ½ mile away.** ⊠ Crater Rim Dr., Hawaii Volcanoes National Park ✛ 1½ miles from the park entrance ☎ 808/985–6101 ⊕ www.nps. gov/havo.

Volcano Art Center Gallery

ART GALLERY | Occupying a portion of the original Volcano House hotel built in 1877, this mesmerizing art gallery, within walking distance of the hotel, has showcased works by local artists since 1974. From stained and handblown glass to wood crafts, paintings, sculptures, block prints, jewelry, photographs, and more, the gallery features fine art (for sale) that depicts indigenous and cultural themes of Hawaii Island. In addition, live hula shows in the ancient style are often featured on the lawn that fronts the gallery. ⊠ Crater Rim Dr., Hawaii Volcanoes National Park ✛ Within walking distance of Kilauea Visitor Center ☎ 808/967–8222 ⊕ www.volcanoartcenter.org.

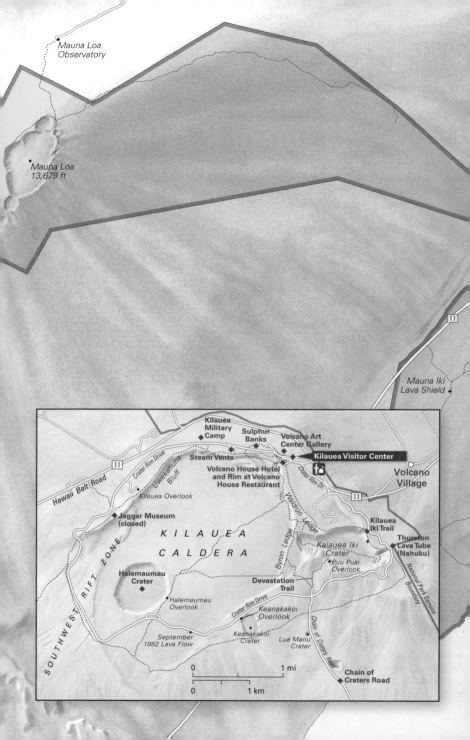

Mauna Loa
Observatory

Mauna Loa
13,679 ft

11

Mauna Iki
Lava Shield

Kilauea
Military
Camp

Sulphur
Banks

Volcano Art
Center Gallery

Kilauea Visitor Center

Crater Rim Drive

Uwekahuna
Bluff

Steam Vents

Volcano House Hotel
and Rim at Volcano
House Restaurant

Volcano
Village

Hawaii Belt Road

Kilauea Overlook

Waldron Ledge

11

Jaggar Museum
(closed)

K I L A U E A

C A L D E R A

Byron Ledge

Kilauea
Iki Trail

Thurston
Lava Tube
(Nahuku)

Kalauea Iki
Crater

Puu Puai
Overlook

National Park Service

Halemaumau
Crater

Devastation
Trail

Halemaumau
Overlook

Crater Rim Drive

Keanakakoi
Overlook

SOUTHWEST RIFT ZONE

September
1982 Lava Flow

Keanakakoi
Crater

Lua Manu
Crater

Chain of Craters Road

National Park Service Boundary

0   1 mi

0   1 km

Chain of
Craters Road

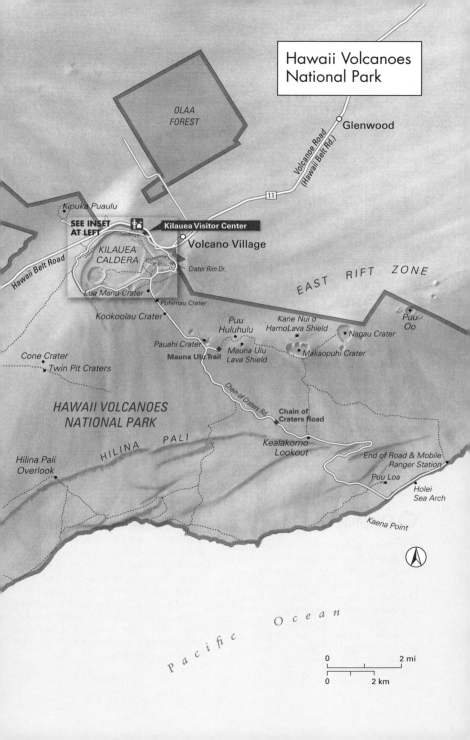

Restaurants

The Rim at Volcano House

$$ | **HAWAIIAN** | **FAMILY** | This fine-dining restaurant overlooks the rim of Kilauea Caldera and the expansive Halemaumau Crater. Featuring two bars (one of which is adjacent to a lounge) and live entertainment nightly, the restaurant highlights island-inspired cuisine and locally sourced ingredients. **Known for:** views of Halemaumau Crater; Hawaii Ranchers 14-oz rib eye; Taste of Hawaii lunch menu. $ *Average main: $25* ✉ *Volcano House, 1 Crater Rim Dr., Hawaii Volcanoes National Park* ☎ *808/756–9625* ⊕ *www.hawaiivolcanohouse.com.*

🛏 Hotels

★ Volcano House

$$$ | **HOTEL** | Hawaii's oldest hotel—and the only one in Hawaii Volcanoes National Park—is committed to sustainable practices and promoting Hawaiian culture and history through its locally sourced restaurants, artisan-crafted decor, and eco-focused guest programs. **Pros:** unbeatable location; views of crater; sense of place and history. **Cons:** basic amenities; books up quickly; some rooms have parking lot views. $ *Rooms from: $285* ✉ *1 Crater Rim Dr., Hawaii Volcanoes National Park* ☎ *808/756–9625* ⊕ *www.hawaiivolcanohouse.com* ⬏ *33 rooms* ⎮❍⎮ *No Meals.*

🛍 Shopping

In addition to recreational activities, Kilauea Military Camp has a general store and a gas station, making it the best place in the park to stop if you need supplies. The park visitor center has a gift store, and Volcano Art Center Gallery sells lovely crafts and fine art. Volcano-themed souvenirs, apparel, and art can be found at Volcano House's two gift shops.

Greater Park Area

Spanning landscapes from sea level to the summits of two of the most active volcanoes in the world, Hawaii Volcanoes National Park boasts a diverse landscape with rain forests, rugged coastlines, surreal lava fields, and sacred cultural sites. There's also a sense of peace and tranquility here, despite the upheavals of nature. A drive down Chain of Craters Road toward the ocean allows you to access the greater area of the park, affording opportunities for exploration beyond the summit destinations. Along the way are birding trails, backcountry hikes, two campgrounds, pit craters, and a dramatic sea arch at the coast.

Sights

★ Chain of Craters Road

SCENIC DRIVE | The coastal region of Hawaii Volcanoes National Park is accessed via the spectacularly scenic Chain of Craters Road, which descends 18.8 miles to sea level. You could drive it without stopping, but it's well worth spending a few hours or a day exploring the stops and trails. Winding past ancient craters and modern eruption sites, this scenic road was realigned in 1979 after parts of it were buried by the Mauna Ulu eruption. Marked stops along the way include Lua Manu Crater, Hilina Pali Road, Pauahi Crater, the Mauna Ulu eruption site, Kealakomo Lookout, and Puu Loa Petroglyphs. As you approach the coast, panoramic ocean vistas prevail. The last marked stop features views of the stunning natural Holei Sea Arch from an overlook. In recent decades, many former sights along the coast have been covered in lava, including a black-sand beach and the old campground. ✉ *Hawaii Volcanoes National Park* ☎ *808/985–6101* ⊕ *www.nps.gov/havo.*

★ Mauna Ulu Trail

TRAIL | The Mauna Ulu lava flow presents an incredible variety of geological attractions within a moderate, 2½-mile round-trip hike. The diverse lava landscape was created during the 1969–74 Mauna Ulu flow, which produced enormous "lava falls" the size of Niagara Falls. Visitors can see everything from lava tree molds and fissure vents to cinder cones and portions of the old highway still exposed under the flow. Hawaiian nene geese roam the area, feeding on ripe ohelo berries. Hike to the top of a small hill that survived the flow for incredible views of the distant geological landmarks. On clear days, you can see Mauna Loa, Maunakea, and the Pacific Ocean from atop this hill, known as Puu Huluhulu. *Moderate.* ■ TIP→ **Purchase the Mauna Ulu trail booklet at the Kilauea Visitor Center for under $3. This excellent resource includes trailside attractions, trail maps, history, and photographs.** ⊠ *Chain of Craters Rd., Hawaii Volcanoes National Park* ✛ *Trailhead: 7 miles from Kilauea Visitor Center* ☎ *808/985–6101* ⊕ *www.nps.gov/havo.*

Puna

The Puna District begins 6 miles from the town of Hilo; Pahoa is 19 miles south of downtown Hilo.

The Puna District is wild in every sense of the word, with a jagged black coastline that is changing all the time. The albizzia trees grow out of control, forming canopies over roads; the residential areas are remote; and the people—well, there's something about living in an area that could be destroyed by lava at any moment (as Kalapana was in 1990, or Kapoho in 1960, or Kapoho Vacationland and half of Leilani Estates in 2018) that makes the norms of modern society seem silly. Vets, surfers, hippies, yoga teachers, and other free spirits abound. And there are also a few ruffians. So it is that Puna has its well-deserved

reputation as an "outlaw" region of the Big Island. That said, it's well worth a detour, especially if you're near this part of the island. Some mighty fine people-watching opportunities exist in Pahoa, a funky little town that the "Punatics" call home.

This is also farm country for an array of agricultural products. Local farmers grow everything from orchids and anthuriums to papayas, bananas, and macadamia nuts. Several of the island's larger, rural, residential subdivisions are nestled between Keaau and Pahoa, including Hawaiian Paradise Park, Orchidland Estates, Hawaiian Acres, and Hawaiian Beaches. When dusk falls here, the air fills with the high-pitched symphony of thousands of coqui frogs. Though they look cute and seem harmless, the invasive frogs are considered pests by local residents weary of their shrieking, all-night calls.

GETTING HERE AND AROUND

The sprawling Puna District stretches from the mountain to the sea. If you're staying in Hilo for the night, driving around Lower Puna to Pahoa and beyond is a great way to spend a morning.

◉ Sights

★ Kilauea Caverns of Fire

CAVE | This way-out adventure explores the underbelly of the world's most active volcano via the Kazamura Lava Tube system. The world's longest lava tube system—more than 40 miles long, with sections up to 80 feet wide and 80 feet tall—is 500 to 700 years old and filled with bizarre lava formations and mind-blowing colors. Tours, customized to groups' interests and skill levels, focus on conservation and education and take visitors through beautiful lava caves unlike any others in the world. The tours are by reservation only and are well worth the extra detour (about 40 minutes off the main highway) and planning. Equipment is included. ■TIP→ **When you make your reservation, you will be given detailed directions to the location.** ✉ *Hawaiian Acres, off Hwy. 11, between Kurtistown and Mountain View* ☎ *808/217–2363* ⊕ *www.kilaueacavern-soffire.com* 💲 *$39 for 1-hour walking tour; $99 for 3-hour adventure tour; $269 day in the cave.*

Lava Tree State Monument

STATE/PROVINCIAL PARK | Tree molds that rise like blackened smokestacks formed here in 1790, when a lava flow swept through the ohia forest. Some reach as high as 12 feet. A meandering trail provides close-up looks at some of Hawaii's tropical plants and trees, and there are restrooms and a couple of picnic pavilions and tables. ■TIP→ **Mosquitoes live here in abundance, so be prepared.** ✉ *Hwy. 132, Pahoa* ☎ *808/974–6200* ⊕ *dlnr. hawaii.gov/dsp* 💲 *Free.*

MacKenzie State Recreation Area

STATE/PROVINCIAL PARK | This park was one of the few coastal parks in the Lower Puna region spared in the 2018 Kilauea eruption. A breezy ironwood grove overlooks rocky shoreline cliffs and offers a pavilion, picnic tables, and restrooms—but no drinking water. The park is significant for the restored section of the old King's Trail system, which circled the coast in the pre-contact era. In those days, regional chiefs used the trails to connect coastal villages and for the transportation of food and materials. Views take in the rugged coast, rocky beach, and coastal dry forest. There's good shore fishing here, so you might see some locals with a line or two in the water. ✉ *Hwy. 137, Pahoa* ⊕ *dlnr.hawaii. gov/dsp/parks* 💲 *Free.*

Pahoa Town

TOWN | Founded to serve the sugar plantation community, this little town is reminiscent of the Wild West, with its wooden boardwalks and vintage buildings. Secondhand stores, tie-dye/hemp clothing boutiques, smoke shops, and art and antiques galleries add to the "trippy" experience. In 2014, lava flows from Kilauea almost intruded into the town, destroying a couple of farmers' sheds as residents braced for the worst when plumes billowed in the near distance and flows glowed after dark. Then it all stopped within 500 yards of Pahoa Village Road, again ensuring the town's status as a survivor—until 2018, when Pahoa became command central for disaster assistance, Hawaii County Civil Defense, and reporters covering the nearby destructive eruption of Kilauea. Today Pahoa's funky main street—with buildings dating from 1910—boasts a handful of excellent, local-style eateries. To get here, turn southeast onto Highway 130 at Keaau, drive 11 miles and follow signs to the Village. (Traffic on Highway 130 can back up during rush hour.) ✉ *Pahoa.*

Star of the Sea Painted Church

HISTORIC SIGHT | Dating from the 1930s, this historic church, now a community center, is known for its colorfully painted folk-art interior. It was moved to its present location in 1990 just ahead of the advancing lava flow that destroyed the Kalapana area. The church was built by a Belgian Catholic missionary priest, Father Evarist Gielen, who also painted the detailed scenes on the church's interior. Though similar in style, the Star of the Sea and St. Benedict's (in South Kona) were painted by two different Belgian priests. Star of the Sea also holds several stained-glass windows and is on the National Register of Historic Places. ✉ *12-4815 Pahoa–Kalapana Rd., Kalapana* ✛ *1 mile north of Kalapana* 💲 *Free, donations welcome.*

⊕ Beaches

Puna's few beaches have some unusual attributes—swaths of new black sand, volcano-heated springs, and a coastline that is beyond dramatic, with sheer walls of lava rock.

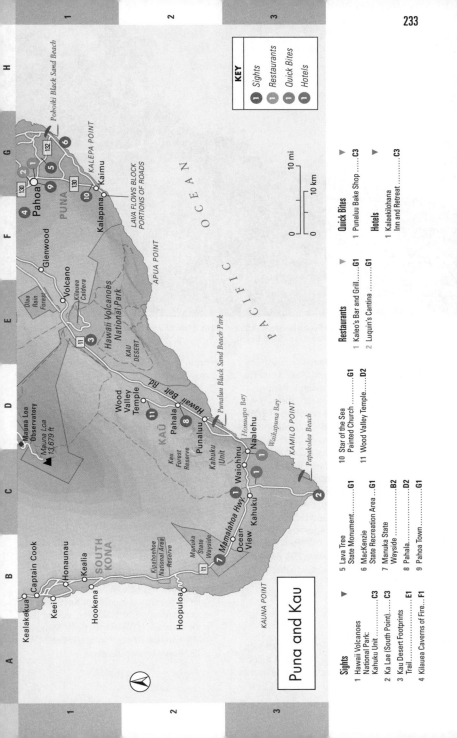

Puna and Kau

Sights ▶

1 Hawaii Volcanoes
National Park:
Kahuku Unit **C3**

2 Ka Lae (South Point) **C3**

3 Kau Desert Footprints
Trail **E1**

4 Kilauea Caverns of Fire ... **F1**

5 Lava Tree
State Monument **G1**

6 MacKenzie
State Recreation Area ... **G1**

7 Manuka State
Wayside **B2**

8 Pahala **D2**

9 Pahoa Town **G1**

10 Star of the Sea
Painted Church **G1**

11 Wood Valley Temple **D2**

Restaurants ▶

1 Kaleo's Bar and Grill **G1**

2 Luquin's Cantina **G1**

Quick Bites ▶

1 Punaluu Bake Shop **C3**

Hotels ▶

1 Kalaekilohana
Inn and Retreat **C3**

KEY

① Sights

① Restaurants

① Quick Bites

① Hotels

Lava from the 2018 Lower Puna eruption was pulverized as it flowed into the sea, creating the very rough black sand of the new Pohoiki Black Sand Beach.

Pohoiki Black Sand Beach

BEACH | Located next to Isaac Hale Beach is Madame Pele's newest creation, Pohoiki Black Sand Beach, formed when molten lava from the eruption of 2018 became pulverized as it flowed into the ocean. This added newly created—albeit rough—sand that washed up on the shore and cut off access to the boat ramp. The beach is open daily from 7 am to 6 pm. There is a portable restroom but no running water in the area. This is not a good swimming beach since the water can be rough and dangerous. To get there, take Highway 137 from Kalapana and turn left on Highway 137. **Amenities:** toilets. **Best for:** walking. ✉ *Kalapana Kapoho Beach Rd., Pahoa.*

 Restaurants

Kaleo's Bar and Grill

$ | **HAWAIIAN** | Pahoa Town isn't known for gourmet dining choices, but Kaleo's is pretty sophisticated for a small-town restaurant and remains a local favorite. Hawaiian-inspired fare blends the gamut of the island's international influences with tempura ahi rolls, grilled burgers, and catch of the day. **Known for:** good people-watching from the porch; nightly entertainment; jumbo calamari. ⑤ *Average main: $17* ✉ *15-2969 Pahoa Village Rd., Pahoa* ☎ *808/965–5600* ⊕ *www. kaleoshawaii.com.*

Luquin's Cantina

$ | **MEXICAN** | **FAMILY** | Long an island favorite for tasty, albeit greasy, Mexican grub, this landmark has made a comeback in funky Pahoa in a different space after a fire destroyed the original restaurant in 2017. Tacos are great (go for crispy), especially when stuffed with grilled, seasoned local fish. **Known for:** good service; affordable fare; delicious pork carnitas. ⑤ *Average main: $9* ✉ *15-1448 Kahakai Blvd., Pahoa* ☎ *808/333–3390* ⊕ *www.luquins.com.*

Puna and the 2018 Kilauea Eruption

The infamous Kilauea eruption in 2018 sent molten lava throughout the Lower Puna region near the town of Pahoa, decimating more than 700 homes as well as farmlands and agricultural operations.

Unrelenting flows from the prolific Fissure 8 vent destroyed some of Puna's most treasured destinations including Green Lake, Kapoho Tidepools, Kapoho Bay, and the warm ponds of Ahalanui. The beloved seaside residential communities of Kapoho Vacationland and Hawaiian Beach Lots were wiped off the face of

the map by lava flows that completely transformed the coastline. A popular surf spot and fishing area, Pohoiki now features a new black-sand beach that surrounds the old boat ramp. Closer to Pahoa Town, the enormous subdivision of Leilani Estates became ground zero for dozens of fissure eruptions that took out hundreds of homes and changed residents' lives forever.

Pahoa Town survived, though, and today there is still plenty to do and see in the area.

Kau

South Point in the District of Kau is 50 miles south of Kailua-Kona.

Perhaps the most desolate region of the island, the Kau District is nevertheless home to some spectacular sights. Mark Twain wrote some of his finest prose here, where macadamia nut farms, remote green-sand beaches, and tiny communities offer rugged, largely undiscovered beauty. The drive from Kailua-Kona to windswept South Point winds away from the ocean through a surreal moonscape of lava fields and swaths of ohia forest. At the end of the 12-mile, two-lane road to South Point, you can park and hike about an hour to Papakolea (Green Sand Beach). Back on the highway, you'll descend into Waiohinu and the village of Naalehu, then pass by vast ranchlands that unfold into lush vistas, sheer ocean cliffs, and verdant pastures. The little town of Pahala is just past the black-sand beach of Punaluu, a nesting place of the Hawaiian hawksbill turtle.

GETTING HERE AND AROUND
Sightseeing in Kau is usually combined with a quick trip to Hawaii Volcanoes National Park. If you're driving all the way from Kona, this is probably cramming too much into one day, however. Visiting the volcano fills up at least a day (two is better), and the sights of this southern end of the island are worth more time. Instead, make Green Sand Beach or Punaluu a full beach day, and see some nearby sights on the way there or back. Bring sturdy shoes, water, and a sun hat if Green Sand Beach is your choice (reaching the beach requires a hike). It's much calmer. and you can sometimes snorkel at Punaluu, but use caution at all Hawaii beaches.

Sights

Hawaii Volcanoes National Park: Kahuku Unit
NATIONAL PARK | Located off Highway 11 at mile marker 70.5, the Kahuku section of the park takes visitors over many trails through ancient lava flows and native forests. Ecological wonders abound in this beautiful but isolated region that

encompasses more than 116,000 acres. Guided hikes with knowledgeable rangers are a regularly scheduled highlight. ✉ Hwy. 11, at mile marker 70.5, Kahuku ☎ 808/985–6101 ⊕ www.nps.gov/havo ✆ $30 per car, $15 for pedestrians ☉ Closed Mon. and Tues.

Ka Lae (South Point)

NATURE SIGHT | According to ancient Hawaiian lore, the first Polynesians came ashore at South Point, known in Hawaiian as "Ka Lae." The southernmost point of land in the United States, the South Point Complex is a National Historic Landmark known for the oldest Hawaiian settlement in the Islands, uncovered by archaeologists in 1956. Old canoe-mooring holes, still visible, were carved through the rocks, possibly by settlers from Tahiti as early as AD 750. Today, visitors come here for the views and access to Green Sand Beach. To get to the beach, drive 12 miles down the turnoff road, past rows of giant electricity-producing windmills powered by the nearly constant winds sweeping across this coastal plain. Bear left when the road forks, and park in the lot at the end. Walk past the boat hoists toward the little lighthouse. South Point is just past the lighthouse at the southernmost cliff. You may see brave locals jumping off the cliffs and then climbing up rusty old ladders, but swimming here is not recommended. Don't leave anything of value in your car. The area is isolated and without services. Green Sand Beach is a 40-minute hike down the coast. ✉ South Point Rd. off Mamalahoa Hwy., near mile marker 70, Naalehu ✆ Free.

Kau Desert Footprints Trail

TRAIL | People take this short hike, 1.6 miles round-trip, to see faded human footprints, fossilized in hardened volcanic ash. Easy. ✉ Naalehu ✛ Take Hwy. 11 approximately 15 minutes west of the park entrance, between mile markers 38 and 39 ✆ Free.

Manuka State Wayside

STATE/PROVINCIAL PARK | FAMILY | Located near the subdivision of Ocean View, this lowland forest reserve spreads across several relatively recent lava flows, offering a semi-rugged trail that follows a 2-mile loop past a pit crater and winding around interesting trees such as hau and kukui (candlenut). You can wander through the well-maintained arboretum, snap photos of the eerie forest, and let the kids scramble around trees so large they can't get their arms around them. The pathways can get muddy and rough, so bring appropriate shoes if you plan to hike. Large populations of the Hawaiian hoary bat inhabit the area, which, in totality, encompasses 25,000 acres of forest reserve. Restrooms and picnic areas are available. ✉ Hwy. 11, north of mile marker 81, Naalehu ☎ 808/974–6200 ⊕ dlnr.hawaii.gov/dsp ✆ Free.

Pahala

TOWN | About 16 miles east of Naalehu, beyond Punaluu Beach Park, Highway 11 passes directly by this sleepy little town, once a thriving sugar-plantation town and still inhabited by retired cane workers and their descendants. You'll miss it if you blink. There is a Longs Pharmacy, a gas station, a small supermarket, a hospital, a bank, and a post office, but not much else in terms of sightseeing. ✉ Pahala.

Wood Valley Temple (Nechung Temple)

TEMPLE | Behind the remote town of Pahala, this serene and beautiful Tibetan Buddhist temple, established in 1973, has hosted more than 50 well-known lamas, including the Dalai Lama on two occasions. Known as Nechung Dorje Drayang Ling (Immutable Island of Melodious Sound), this peaceful place welcomes all creeds. You can visit and meditate, leave an offering, walk the lush gardens shared by strutting peacocks, browse the gift shop, or stay in the temple's guesthouse. ✉ 96-2285 Wood Valley Rd., Pahala ☎ 808/928–8539 ⊕ www. nechung.org ✆ $5.

Did You Know?

You can see turtles at the Big Island's Punaluu Black Sand Beach Park, a popular resting and feeding spot for endangered Hawaiian hawksbill sea turtles. There's absolutely no touching the animals—it's a hefty fine.

Beaches

The rocky coasts of Kau don't have sparkling white-sand beaches, but the black-and green-sand beaches here are well worth the visit. There's also the chance to see endangered hawksbill or Hawaiian green sea turtles.

Papakolea Beach (*Green Sand Beach*)
BEACH | Those tired of the same old white- or black-sand beaches can lace up good hiking shoes or sneakers to get to this olive-green crescent, one of the most unusual beaches on the island. It lies at the base of Puu O Mahana, at Mahana Bay, where a cinder cone formed during an early eruption of Mauna Loa. The greenish tint is caused by an accumulation of olivine crystals that form in volcanic eruptions. The dry, barren landscape is totally surreal but stunning, as aquamarine waters lap on green sand against reddish cliffs. Drive down to South Point; at the end of the 12-mile paved road, take the road to the left and park at the end. To reach the beach, follow the 2¼-mile coastal trail, which ends in a steep and dangerous descent down the cliffside on an unimproved trail. The hike takes about two hours each way and can get hot and windy, so bring lots of drinking water. Four-wheel-drive vehicles are no longer permitted on the trail. The surf is often rough and swimming can be hazardous due to strong currents, so caution is advised. **Amenities:** none. **Best for:** solitude; walking. ⊠ *Hwy. 11, Naalehu* ⊕ *2½ miles northeast of South Point.*

★ **Punaluu Black Sand Beach Park**
BEACH | A must-do on a south-southeast-bound trip to the volcano, this easily accessible black-sand beach is backed by low dunes, brackish ponds, and tall coco palms. The shoreline is jagged, reefed, and rocky. Most days, large groups of sea turtles nap on the sand—a stunning sight. Resist the urge to get too close or disturb them; they're protected by federal and state law, and fines for harassment

can be hefty. Removing black sand is also prohibited. ■TIP→ **Extremely strong rip currents prevail, so only experienced ocean swimmers should consider getting in the water here.** A popular stop for locals and tour buses alike, this beach park can get busy; the north parking lot is usually quieter. Shade from palm trees provides an escape from the sun, and at the northern end of the beach lie the ruins of Kaneeleele Heiau, an old Hawaiian temple. **Amenities:** parking (no fee); showers; toilets. **Best for:** walking. ⊠ *Hwy. 11, between mile markers 55 and 56, Naalehu* ⊕ *27 miles south of Hawaii Volcanoes National Park* ☎ *808/961–8311* ☜ *Free.*

Coffee and Quick Bites

Punaluu Bake Shop
$ | **CAFÉ** | **FAMILY** | Billed as the southernmost bakery in the United States, this is a good spot to grab a snack or lunch. Hawaiian sweetbread is the specialty here. **Known for:** sweet bread; all goods baked on-site; malasada (Portuguese doughnuts) glazed with lilikoi (passion fruit). Ⓢ *Average main: $8* ⊠ *5642 Mamalahoa Hwy., Naalehu* ☎ *808/929–7343* ⊕ *www.bakeshophawaii.com* ☾ *No dinner.*

Hotels

Kalaekilohana Inn and Retreat
$$$ | **B&B/INN** | You wouldn't expect to find a top-notch B&B in Kau, but this grand residence offers large private suites with locally harvested hardwood floors and private lanai with ocean and mountain views. **Pros:** big, comfy beds with down comforters; beautiful decor reminiscent of old Hawaii; delicious breakfast. **Cons:** not for children under 12; no pool; very limited nearby shopping. Ⓢ *Rooms from: $379* ⊠ *94-2152 South Point Rd., Naalehu* ☎ *808/939–8052* ⊕ *www.kau-hawaii.com* ☛ *4 suites* ⦶ *Free Breakfast.*

ACTIVITIES AND TOURS

Updated by
Kristina Anderson

With the Big Island's predictably mild year-round climate, it's no wonder you'll find an emphasis on outdoor activities. After all, this is the home of the annual Ironman World Championship triathlon and numerous other world-class athletic events. Whether you're an avid hiker or a beginning bicyclist, a casual golfer or a serious scuba diver, there are plenty of adventures to lure you away from your resort or condo.

You can explore by bike, helicopter, ATV, zip line, or horse, or you can put on your hiking boots and use your own horsepower. No matter how you get around, you'll be treated to breathtaking backdrops along the Big Island's 266-mile coastline and within its 4,028 square miles (and still growing!). Aerial tours take in any eruption activity and lava flows, as well as the island's gorgeous tropical valleys, gulches, and coastal plains. Trips into the backcountry wilderness explore the rain forest, private ranchlands, and coffee farms, while sleepy sugar plantation villages offer a glimpse of Hawaii's bygone days. Golfers will find acclaimed championship golf courses at the Kohala Coast resorts—Mauna Kea Beach Hotel, Autograph Collection; the Westin Hapuna Beach Resort; Mauna Lani, Auberge Resorts Collection; and the Waikoloa area resorts, among others.

The ancient Hawaiians, who took much of their daily sustenance from the ocean, also enjoyed playing in the water, so it follows that visitors want to get out onto the water as well. In fact, surfing was the sport of kings, born in the Hawaiian Islands. Though it's easy to be lulled into whiling away the day baking in the sun on a white-, gold-, black-, or green-sand beach, getting into or onto the water is a highlight of most trips.

All the Hawaiian Islands are surrounded by the Pacific Ocean and blessed with a temperate latitude, making them some of the world's greatest natural playgrounds. Still, certain experiences are even better on the Big Island of Hawaii: nighttime diving trips to see manta rays; deep-sea fishing in Kona's fabled waters, where dozens of Pacific blue marlin of 1,000 pounds or more have been caught; and kayaking in pristine bays, to name a few.

From almost any point on the Big Island, the ocean is not far. From body boarding and snorkeling to kayaking and surfing, there is a water sport for everyone. For most activities, you can rent gear from a local vendor and go it alone. Or book a group excursion with experienced guides who offer convenience and security, as well as special insights into Hawaii's marine life, ecology, history, and culture. Want to try surfing? Contrary to what you may have heard, there *are* waves on the Big Island. You can take lessons from pros who take you to special spots and promise to have you standing the first day out.

The Kona and Kohala Coasts of West Hawaii have the largest number of ocean sports outfitters and tour operators. They operate from the small-boat harbors and piers in Kailua-Kona, Keauhou, and Kawaihae, and out of the Kohala Coast resorts. There are also several outfitters in East Hawaii.

As a general rule, the waves are gentler here than on the other Islands, especially in summer, but there are a few things to be aware of. First, never turn your back on the ocean. It's unlikely, but if conditions are right, a wave could come along and push you face-first into the sand or drag you out to sea. Second, when the Big Island does experience high surf, dangerous conditions prevail nearly everywhere and can change rapidly. Watch the ocean for a few minutes before going out to scan for waves, which arrive in sets, and wait for three to go by. If it looks too rough, don't chance it. Third, realize that ultimately you must keep yourself safe. We strongly encourage you to obey lifeguards and high surf advisories, and heed the advice of outfitters from whom you rent equipment, and even advice from locals on shore. If you are not a strong swimmer, find a baby beach and use a life vest. It could save your trip—or even your life.

Aerial Tours

There's nothing quite like the aerial view of a waterfall crashing down a couple thousand feet along a steep valley wall into cascading pools below. You can get this and other bird's-eye views from a helicopter or a fixed-wing small plane. All operators pay strict attention to safety and will take off only if conditions are safe. ■TIP→ **Before you choose a company, be a savvy traveler, read up on the experience offered, and ask the right questions. What kind of aircraft do they fly? What is their safety record?**

Blue Hawaiian Helicopters

FLIGHTSEEING | Hawaii Island's premier aerial tour is on Blue Hawaiian's roomy Eco-Star helicopters—so smooth and quiet you hardly realize you're taking off. There are no worries about what seat you get because each has great views. Pilots are State of Hawaii–certified tour guides, too, so they are knowledgeable and experienced but not overly chatty. In the breathtaking Waimanu Valley, the helicopter hovers close to 2,600-foot cliffs and cascading waterfalls. Departing from Waikoloa, the two-hour Big Island Spectacular also takes in the incredible landscapes of Hawaii Volcanoes National Park (over the permissible areas), as well as stunning windward valleys. Leaving from Hilo, the more affordable, 50-minute Circle of Fire tour showcases Kilauea Volcano and other major island sites. Should you wish to splurge, private charters are also offered. ✉ *Waikoloa Heliport, Hwy. 19, Waikoloa* ☎ *808/961–5600* ⊕ *www. bluehawaiian.com* ✈ *From $369.*

★ Paradise Helicopters

FLIGHTSEEING | Even in areas where the volcano is not actively flowing, there's plenty to see from the air, with great options from this locally owned and operated company. Departing from Kona, the Circle Island Experience and Experience Hawaii tours both fly over the Hawaii

Did You Know?

A helicopter tour is a great way to see the Big Island's most inaccessible areas. It's hard to beat aerial views, whether of the coast and its rocky cliff faces or a waterfall plunging into the valley below.

Volcanoes National Park area including the once-active Puu Oo vent. Departing from Hilo, the Doors-Off Lava and Rainforest Adventure offers an unforgettable excursion in a Hughes 500 helicopter for unobstructed views of Kilauea Volcano. Even when it's erupting, volcanic flows are difficult to see in the daytime. That's why our favorite flights are ones that tour the isolated valleys of the windward side, hovering for a breathtaking few minutes while you take 3,000-foot valleys. There are also options in which you land, take a hike through rugged rain forests or explore the beautiful Kohala region, as well as a number of charter options. ■TIP→ **Check online for monthly coupons and specials.** ⊠ *Kailua-Kona* ☎ *808/969–7392, 866/876–7422* ⊕ *www.paradise-copters.com* ⤳ *From $360.*

Safari Helicopters

FLIGHTSEEING | Departing from the Hilo airport, Safari is the most affordable operator on the island. They offer a 55-minute tour that includes Hawaii Volcanoes National Park and the Hilo-area waterfalls. Book online for substantial discounts. ⊠ *Hilo International Airport, 2350 Kekuanaoa St., Hilo* ☎ *808/969–1259* ⊕ *www. safarihelicopters.com* ⤳ *From $299.*

ATV Tours

A super fun way to experience the Big Island's rugged coastline and wild ranchlands is through an off-road adventure—a real backcountry experience. At higher elevations, the weather gets nippy and rainy, but views can be awesome. Protective gear is provided, and everyone gets a mini driving lesson. Generally, you must be 16 or older to drive your own ATV; some outfitters allow children seven and older as passengers while others do the driving for you.

AATV Adventures

FOUR-WHEELING | Their name stands for "all about the view," and they aren't

joking. These 2½-hour ATV tours offer panoramic views of the glorious Hamakua coast along trails meandering through private ranchlands. You'll journey across a traditional Hawaiian land division called an *ahupuaa*, which showcases native and introduced plants and trees and lots of animals. The tour also takes you along the historic engineering marvel, the Hamakua Ditch, built in 1906 to transport water from the wet Kohala Mountains down to drier elevations to irrigate sugarcane lands. Tandem two-seats or quad four-seaters accommodate passengers age seven and up. Drivers must be licensed and at least 18. ⊠ *Honokaa* ✛ *Mile marker 7.5, highway 240* ☎ *808/775–7291* ⊕ *aatvadventure.com* ⤳ *from $150.*

Aloha Adventure Farms ATV Tours

FOUR-WHEELING | The outfitter's unique approach takes you through the "islands" of Polynesia (Hawaii, Fiji, Tonga, and Samoa) on an ATV or UTV (off-road, utility task vehicle) while educating and informing about the history, culture, and people of these places. As you traverse untouched dryland forests near Kailua-Kona, you'll stop periodically to try different local foods and activities. If you add an optional carving class, a fourth-generation master carver from Tonga helps you create your own souvenir tiki piece. Snacks and gifts are available at the gift shop. ⊠ *77-6261 Mamalahoa Hwy., Holualoa* ☎ *808/796–0110* ⊕ *alohaadventurefarms. com* ⤳ *From $199.*

Kohala UTV Adventure

FOUR-WHEELING | After closing their Hamakua Ditch kayak ride due to structural damage to the ditch, this local company opened a UTV ride that explores the same area by riding the rim along seven stunning North Kohala valleys. Guides share history of the area while taking guests through pastures on a private cattle ranch and then to the mists and cool forests and meandering streams of the top of the valleys. Drivers must be 21 or older, and prepared to get wet and muddy. ✉ *55-517 Hawi Rd., Hawi* ☎ *808/933–4294* ⊕ *kohalautv.com* ☞ *From $330.*

Biking

The Big Island's biking trails and road routes range from easy to moderate coastal rides to rugged backcountry wilderness treks that challenge the most serious cyclists. You can soak up the island's storied scenic vistas and varied geography—from tropical rain forest to rolling ranch country, from high-country mountain meadows to dry lava deserts. It's dry, windy, and hot on Kona's and Kohala's coastal trails, mountainous through South Kona, and cool, wet, and muddy in the upcountry Waimea and Volcano areas, as well as in lower Puna. There are long distances between towns, few bike lanes, narrow single-lane highways, and scanty services in the Kau, Puna, South Kona, and Kohala Coast areas, so plan accordingly for your weather, water, food, and lodging needs before setting out. ■ TIP➔ **Your best bet is to book with an outfitter who has all the details covered.**

Hawaii Cycling Club

BIKING | This nonprofit club based in Kailua-Kona has tons of information on every type of bicycling on the Big Island. The club also sponsors scheduled rides, time trials, and social events such as picnics. They welcome visitors to join (with a small fee) and participate in their activities. ✉ *Kailua-Kona* ⊕ *www.hawaiicyclingclub.com* ☞ *$20 membership fee.*

BEST SPOTS
Alii Drive

BIKING | If all you have is a beach cruiser or low-gear hybrid bike, it's fun to take a simple ride down super-scenic oceanfront Alii Drive in downtown Kailua-Kona. From the south end of the road at Keauhou, hop on your bike and head north. It's pretty much flat riding the whole way,

and there are some bike lanes. (That said, you must be cautious around traffic and wear a helmet.) We recommend riding to Magic Sands Beach Park, taking a dip in the ocean, and then having a bite at the snack bar next door. The full ride from Keauhou to the Kailua pier is about 7½ miles. By paying a small subscription fee, you can check out a bike at one of the Hawaii Island Bikeshare kiosks located here and there on Alii Drive; return it to the kiosk of your choice. ✉ *Alii Dr., Kailua-Kona.*

★ Ke Ala o Kulanihakoi (*Kulani Trails*)

BIKING | It has been called the state's best mountain bike ride—if you want to get gnarly. The technically demanding ride, which passes majestic eucalyptus trees, is for advanced cyclists; muddy conditions prevail. To reach the trailhead from the intersection of Highway 11 and Highway 19 in Hilo, take Highway 19 south about 4 miles, turn right on Stainback Highway, and continue 2½ miles. Turn right at the Waiakea Arboretum and park near the gate. Once known as Kulani Trails, the newly renamed mountain bike system is now officially part of the state of Hawaii Na Ala Hele trail system, and a permit is no longer required. Download a copy of the trail map online. ✉ *Stainback Hwy., Hilo* ⊕ *dlnr.hawaii.gov.*

Kohala Mountain Road

BIKING | On one of the state's most scenic rides, the climb (3% to 11% grade) is steep and challenging, but the views from the summit at 3,500 feet (called the Summit Pickup) make it well worth the effort. The starting point can be reached on Highway 250 across from the Island Short Stop on Akoni Pule Highway in Kapaau, in North Kohala. Although the ride uphill is more than 13½ miles one-way, the downhill ride back is superfast. Although the road is not usually that busy, there are no shoulders; it does have some blind curves, so use caution. Come prepared for wind and rain, as conditions can get foggy and wet. ✉ *Kapaau.*

Old Puna Trail

BIKING | A 10½-mile ride through the subtropical jungle in Puna, this trail leads into one of the island's most isolated areas. It starts on a cinder road, which becomes a four-wheel-drive trail. If it's rained recently, you'll have to deal with puddles—the first few of which you'll gingerly avoid until you give in and go barreling through the rest for the sheer fun of it. This is a great ride for all abilities and takes about 90 minutes. The ride ends at Haena Beach. To get to the trailhead from Highway 130, take Kaloli Drive to Beach Road. ■TIP→ **Ride at your own risk; this is not a maintained trail.** ⊠ *Kaloli Dr. at Hwy. 130, Pahoa.*

EQUIPMENT AND TOURS

Bike shops around the island offer daily or weekly rentals, and many resorts rent beach cruisers that can be used around the properties. Most outfitters can provide a bicycle rack for your car, and all have reduced rates for rentals longer than one day. All retailers offer excellent advice about where to go; they know the areas well. **Hawaii Island Bikeshare** (⊕ *hawaiiislandbikeshare.org*) offers access to bikes across the island at their well-placed stations, using a subscription key. One of the best and easiest ways to see the island is to take a bike tour.

Bike Works Kona

BIKING | This company caters to cyclists of all skill levels with race services; suggested rides for moderate to advanced riders; and rentals of deluxe road bikes, full-suspension mountain bikes, e-bikes, and high-end triathlon bikes. Their impressive shop feels like a superstore, full to the brim with top-notch brands. ⊠ *75-5660 Kopiko St., Kailua-Kona* ☎ *808/326–2453* ⊕ *www.bikeworkskona.com* 🚲 *From $25/day.*

Hilo Bike Hub

BIKING | An enthusiast shop specializing in servicing bikes to fit the ruggedness of Hawaii's east-side terrain, this is a good resource for those wishing to mountain bike in these off-the-beaten-path areas. A sponsor of rides and local events, Hilo Bike Hub was instrumental in helping to establish Kulani Trails, part of the Waiakea Forest reserve, as an official mountain biking area. The shop also carries gear and accessories but does not rent bikes. ⊠ *318 E. Kawili St., Hilo* ☎ *808/961–4452* ⊕ *www.hilobikehub.com.*

Kona Fat Bikes

BIKING | This small store rents e-bikes (with helmets) by the hour. Save more with a multiday rental. The shop also rents towels, snorkels, and other accessories, and sells sunscreen, water, and snacks for your excursion. ⊠ *75-5719 Alii Dr., #1A, Kailua-Kona* ☎ *808/830–9680* ⊕ *konafatbikes.com* 🚲 *From $22.50/hr.*

Mid Pacific Wheels

BIKING | The oldest bike shop on the Big Island, this community-oriented shop near the university carries a full line of bikes and accessories and rents mountain bikes for exploring the Hilo area. The friendly staff provides expert advice on where to go and what to see and do on a self-guided tour. They also carry a large selection of cycling accessories, bikes, and repair parts. ⊠ *1133C Manono St., Hilo* ☎ *808/935–6211* ⊕ *www.midpacificwheelsllc.com* 🚲 *From $35/day.*

Volcano Bike Tours

BIKING | This friendly outfitter rents e-bikes that you can use on self-guided excursions in Hawaii Volcanoes National Park. You'll take in fantastic sights from rain forests to craters to lava tubes. With an e-bike you can opt to use the pedal assist or not, depending on whether you want more of a workout. Use the self-guided map to follow the routes they recommend. ⊠ *19-3972 Old Volcano Rd., Volcano* ☎ *808/934–9199* ⊕ *www.bikevolcano.com* 🚲 *Rentals from $119/day.*

Body Boarding and Bodysurfing

Although they share the same ocean, and sometimes the same surfing spots, there's always been a little friction between the three types of board users—paddle, surf, and body. Fortunately, there's usually enough room for all, even along the Big Island's somewhat limited surf spots.

However, the different users generally do keep to their own separate areas. Often the body boarders, who lie on their bellies on shorter boards, stay closer to shore and leave the outside breaks to the board surfers. Or the board surfers may stick to one side of the beach and the body boarders to the other. The truth is, body boarding (often called "boogie boarding," in homage to the first commercial manufacturer of this slick, little, flexible-foam board whose inventor debuted his creation at Honl's Beach, right here in Kona) is a blast. Most surfers also sometimes carve waves on a body board, no matter how much of a purist they claim to be.

You'll need a pair of short fins to get out to the bigger waves offshore, though novice body boarders should catch shorebreak waves only. Ask lifeguards or locals for the best spots, and of course heed high surf warnings. As for bodysurfing, you don't need a board—just catch a wave and make like Superman going faster than a speeding bullet.

Paddleboarding is easy to learn and more stable than it looks. It's best to try paddleboarding in a calm location such as Kamakahonu Beach; there are rental vendors offering lessons nearby.

BEST SPOTS

Hapuna Beach State Recreation Area. Often considered one of the top 10 beaches in the world, Hapuna Beach offers fine white sand, turquoise water, and easy rolling surf on most days, making it great for bodysurfing and body boarding at all levels. Ask the lifeguards—who cover only areas south of the rocky cliff that juts out near the middle of the beach—about conditions before heading into the water, especially in winter. Sometimes northwest swells create a dangerous undertow, so use caution here. ⊠ *Hwy. 19, near mile marker 69, just south of Mauna Kea Beach Hotel, Kohala Coast* ⊕ *dlnr.hawaii.gov/dsp.*

Honolii Cove. North of Hilo, this is the best body boarding spot on the east side of the island. ⊠ *Off Hwy. 19, near mile marker 4, Hilo.*

Kohanaiki Beach Park ("Pine Trees"). A popular local surfing spot, this newish county park is one of the best places to find waves and is recommended for experienced surfers. Be sure to watch your belongings here and lock your car. ⊠ *Hwy. 19, 7 miles north of Kailua-Kona.*

Magic Sands Beach Park (White Sands Beach). This white-sand, shorebreak cove is great for beginning to intermediate bodysurfing and body boarding. Sometimes, randomly, much of the sand here washes out to sea and forms a sandbar just offshore, creating fun wave conditions, only to "reappear" a few days later. Also known as White Sands, the beach is popular and can get crowded with locals, especially when school is out. Watch for large, overwhelming surf and nasty rip currents at high tide. Listen to lifeguards when they tell you to get out of the water. ■TIP→ **If you're not using fins, wear reef shoes for protection against sharp rocks.** ⊠ *Alii Dr., just north of mile marker 4, Kailua-Kona.*

EQUIPMENT

Equipment rental shacks are located at many beaches and boat harbors, along the highway, and at most resorts. Bodyboard rental rates are around $12–$15 per day and around $60 per week. You can also buy snorkeling equipment at one of the big-box retailers if you plan to be out every day, want to ensure sanitation, or need a perfect fit. Most also carry body boards. Ensure that the vendor has attached a leash to your board. Some lifeguards won't let you in the water without one.

Honolua Surf Company

WATER SPORTS | Surfboards, surf apparel, logowear, gear, sunglasses, and hats are available at these moderately priced surf shops. There are several locations state-wide. ⊠ Kona Shopping Village, 75-5744 Alii Dr., Kailua-Kona ☎ 808/329–1001 ⊕ www.honoluasurf.com.

Caving

The Kanohina Lava Tube system is about a thousand years old and was used by the ancient Hawaiians for water collection and for shelter. More than 56 miles of braided lava tubes have been mapped so far in the Kau District of the Big Island, near Ka Lae (South Point). About 45 miles south of Kailua-Kona, these lava tubes are a great experience for cavers of all age levels and abilities. The Kazamura lava-tube system is the longest lava-tube system in the world and is located on the east side of the island not far from Hawaii Volcanoes National Park. Each set of caves is a unique experience to visit and explore.

⭐ **Kula Kai Caverns**

SPELUNKING | Expert cave guides lead groups into the fantastic underworld of these caverns near South Point in Kau. The braided lava-tube system attracts scientists from around the world, who come to study and map them (more than 56 miles so far). Tours range from the Lighted Trail (in the lighted show cave, which is easy walking) to the Two Hour, a deep-down-under spelunking adventure that often takes closer to three hours and allows you to see archaeological evidence of the ancient Hawaiians.

Longer, customized tours are available; all gear is provided. Tours start at an Indiana Jones–style expedition tent and divulge fascinating details about the caves' geological and cultural history. Reservations are required. ⊠ Kula Kai Estates, Lauhala Dr., at Kona Kai Blvd., Ocean View ☎ 808/929–9725 ⊕ www.kulakaicaverns. com ☎ From $28.

Deep-Sea Fishing

The Kona Coast boasts some of the world's most exciting "blue-water" fishing. The island's steep, sloping underwater geography means that just 3 miles out to sea, the ocean plunges to depths of more than 6,000 feet, making it a sportfisher's dream. Although July, August, and September are peak months, with the best fishing and a number of tournaments, charter fishing goes on year-round. Some 60 charter boats, averaging 26 to 58 feet in length, are available for hire, all of them out of **Honokohau Harbor,** north of Kailua-Kona.

The Kona Coast is world-famous for the presence of large marlin, particularly the Pacific blue. In fact, it's also known as "Grander Alley" for the fish caught here that weigh more than 1,000 pounds. The largest blue marlin on record was caught in 1984 and weighed 1,649 pounds. In total, more than 60 granders have been reeled in here by top sportfishing teams.

For an exclusive charter, prices generally range from $700 to $950 for a half-day trip (about four hours) and $800 to $1,700 for a full day at sea (about eight hours). For share charters, rates are about $100 to $140 per person for a half day and $200 for a full day. If fuel prices increase, expect charter costs to rise. Most boats are licensed to take up to six passengers, in addition to the crew. Tackle, bait, and ice are furnished, but you usually have to bring your own lunch. You won't be able to keep your catch, although if you ask, many captains will send you home with a few fillets.

Honokohau Harbor's Fuel Dock

FISHING | Show up around 11 am and watch the weigh-in of the day's catch from the morning charters, or around 3:30 for the afternoon charters, especially during the summer tournament season. Weigh-ins are fun when the big ones come in, but these days, with most of the marlin being released, it's not a sure thing. ■TIP→ **In the foyer of the Kona Inn in Kailua-Kona, look for some of the "granders" on display.** ✉ *Honokohau Harbor, Kealakehe Pkwy. at Hwy. 11, Kailua-Kona.*

BOATS AND CHARTERS

Before you sign up with anyone, think about the kind of trip you want. Looking for a romantic cruise? A rockin' good time with your buddies? Serious fishing in one of the "secret spots"? A family-friendly excursion? A private charter customized to your needs? Be sure to describe your expectations so a booking agent can match you with a captain and a boat that suit your style.

Bite Me Sportfishing Fleet

FISHING | **FAMILY** | This multifaceted sportfishing company offers a full fleet with shared, half-day, or three-quarter-day charters as well as invitational championships; they know how, when, and where to catch fish along the Kona Coast. They specialize in a family-friendly experience and can accommodate private parties of six or more. The boats have the newest gear and accessories, shady top and bottom decks, restrooms, showers, and comfy seating. Lots of charters for different excursions are also available, and the company follows catch-and-release practices to help sustain local fisheries. Dolphin-watching cruises and seasonal whale-watching excursions are other options. A cool retail store sells everything from logo T-shirts to hats. ■TIP→ **Bonus: they will share the catch with you so you can enjoy some while on**

the island, or they'll recommend a restaurant that can cook it for you. ✉ *Honokahau Harbor, 74-425 Kealakehe Pkwy., Suite 17, Kailua-Kona* ☎ *808/936–3442* ⊕ *www. bitemesportfishing.com* 💲 *From $159.*

Bwana Sportfishing

FISHING | Half-, three-quarter-, and full-day charters, as well as overnight charters, are available on the 46-foot *Bwana*, a boat with the latest electronics, top-of-the-line equipment, and air-conditioned cabins. You get outstanding, quality tackle and lots of experience here. Captain Teddy comes from a fishing family; father Pete was a legend on Kona waters for decades. ✉ *Honokohau Harbor, Slip H-17, 74-381 Kealakehe Pkwy., Kailua-Kona* ⊹ *Just south of Kona airport* ☎ *808/936–5168* ⊕ *facebook.com/bwanasportfishing* 💲 *From $1,250.*

Charter Locker

FISHING | Half- and full-day charter fishing trips on 36- to 53-foot vessels are offered by this experienced company. Featured boats include *Kona Blue, JR's Hooker, Strong Persuader,* and *Kila Kila*. Rates depend on the boat. ✉ *Honokohau Harbor, 74-381 Kealakehe Pkwy., #16, Kailua-Kona* ⊹ *Just south of Kona airport* ☎ *808/326–2553* ⊕ *www.charterlocker. com* 💲 *From $699.*

Humdinger Sportfishing

FISHING | The father-son team here brings more than five decades of fishing experience in Kona waters, and the expert crew are marlin specialists. Their 37-foot Rybovich, the *Humdinger*, features the latest in electronics and top-line rods and reels. Book online for discounts and specials; they sell out quickly, so plan ahead. ■TIP→ **They will let you keep your catch (except for billfish) and will even fillet it for you.** ✉ *Honokohau Harbor, 74-381 Kealakehe Pkwy., Slip B-4, Kailua-Kona* ☎ *808/425–9225, 800/926–2374, 808/425–9228 boat phone* ⊕ *www.humdingersportfishing.com* 💲 *From $699.*

Kona Charter Desk at Honokohau Harbor

FISHING | The longtime booking agent works with all the big-name boats and will book just the right charter for you (even manta dives and whale-watching cruises). They will greet you on return and give you a tag-and-release certificate if you caught and released a billfish. For those who boat a fish, they will hoist it, weigh it, and issue a weigh tag to take home. The company also provides photos and runs a gift shop. All boats call in their catches to this desk before returning, so they know which boats are the most active and have the best daily catches. ■TIP→ **You can make arrangements through hotel activity desks, but it's better to come here and look things over for yourself.** ⊠ *Honokohau Harbor Fuel Dock, 74-381 Kealakehe Pkwy., Kailua-Kona* ☎ *808/264–2495* ⊕ *konacharterdesk.com* ⊠ *From $859.*

Golf

For golfers, the Big Island is a big deal, starting with the Mauna Kea Golf Course, which opened in 1964 and remains one of the state's top courses. Black lava and deep blue sea are the predominant themes on the island. In the roughly 40 miles from the Kona Country Club to the Mauna Kea resort, nine courses are carved into sunny seaside lava plains, with four more in the hills above. Indeed, most of the Big Island's best courses are concentrated along the Kohala Coast, statistically the sunniest spot in Hawaii. Vertically speaking, the majority of courses are seaside or at least near sea level, and three are located above 2,000 feet. This is significant because in Hawaii temperatures drop 3°F for every 1,000 feet of elevation gained.

Greens fee: Greens fees listed here are the highest course rates per round on weekdays for U.S. residents. (Some courses charge non–U.S. residents

higher prices.) Courses with varying weekend rates are noted in the individual listings. ■TIP→ **Discounts are often available for resort guests and for those who book tee times online, as well as for those willing to play in the afternoon. Twilight rates are also usually offered.**

Hamakua Country Club

GOLF | FAMILY | While the typical, modern 18-hole golf course requires at least 250 acres, this public course fits into just 19. Compact is the word, and with several holes crisscrossing, this place may require you to BYO hard hat. Holes run up and down a fairly steep slope overlooking the ocean—the views are spectacular. Cheerfully billed as an old-world golf experience, the course works on the honor system ("if no one is there, put your money in the slot"), and the ninth green is square, but for 20 bucks (kids under 17 play free), whaddaya expect? Most golfers prefer to walk, but there are carts available. ⊠ *Hwy. 19 at mile marker 41, Honokaa* ✛ *43 miles north of Hilo* ☎ *808/775–7244* ⊕ *hamakuagolf.com* ⊠ *$20; cart $13* ⛳ *Two sets of 9 holes, 4,800 yards, par 66 (men), 74 (women).*

Hapuna Golf Course

GOLF | Hapuna's challenging play and environmental sensitivity make it one of the island's most unusual courses. Designed by Arnold Palmer and Ed Seay, it nestles into the natural contours of the land from the shoreline to about 700 feet above sea level. There are spectacular views of mountains and sea; Maui is often visible in the distance. Holes wind through kiawe scrub, beds of jagged lava, and tall fountain grasses. Hole 12 is favored for its beautiful views and challenging play. The course is within walking distance of the Westin Hapuna Beach Resort. ⊠ *Westin Hapuna Beach Resort, 62-100 Kanunaoa Dr., Mauna Kea* ☎ *808/880–3000* ⊕ *marriott.com* ⊠ *$200, cart required* ⛳ *18 holes, 6,875 yards, par 72.*

Tips for the Green

Golf is golf, and Hawaii is part of the United States, but island golf nevertheless has its own quirks. Here are a few tips to make your golf experience in the Islands more pleasant.

■ Wear sunscreen, even in December. We recommend zinc-based, with a minimum SPF of 30; you should reapply on the 10th tee.

■ Stay hydrated. Spending four-plus hours in the tropical sun and heat means you'll perspire away considerable fluids and energy.

■ Private courses may allow you to play at their discretion.

■ All resort courses and many daily-fee courses provide rental clubs. In many cases, they're the latest lines from Titleist, Ping, Callaway, and the like. This is true for both men and women, as well as left-handers, which means you don't have to schlep clubs across the Pacific.

■ Pro shops at most courses are stocked with balls, tees, and other accoutrements, so even if you bring a bag, it needn't weigh a ton.

■ Come spikeless—very few Hawaii courses permit metal spikes.

■ Resort courses, in particular, offer more than the usual three sets of tees, sometimes four or five. So bite off as much or little challenge as you like. Tee it up from the tips and you'll end up playing a few 600-yard par 5s and see a few 250-yard forced carries.

■ In theory, you can play golf in Hawaii 365 days a year. But there's a reason the Hawaiian Islands are so green. Better to bring an umbrella and light jacket and not use them than not to bring them and get soaked.

■ Unless you play a muni or certain daily-fee courses, plan on taking a cart. Carts are mandatory at most courses and are included in the greens fee.

Hilo Municipal Golf Course

GOLF | Hilo Muni is proof that you don't need sand bunkers to create a challenging course. Trees and several meandering creeks are the danger here. The course, which offers views of Hilo Bay from most holes, has produced many of the island's top players over the years. Taking a divot reminds you that you're playing on a volcano—the soil is dark-black crushed lava. Due to heavy demand as the only public course on the Big Island, tee-time reservations (required) are by phone only. ⊠ 340 Haihai St., Hilo ☎ 808/959–7711 ⌨ $40 weekdays, $47 weekends; $24 cart ⅄. 18 holes, 6,325 yards, par 71.

★ Kona Country Club

GOLF | Renovated in 2016, this William F. Bell–designed golf course is perched high above historic Keauhou Bay, with spectacular views of the sea from almost every hole. Stands of mature coco trees, several remarkable lava features, wide fairways, and challenging Bermuda greens make this course a classic Hawaii golf experience that's open to the public. The most prominent feature is the "blowhole" (puka in Hawaiian), fronting the par-4 13th tee, where seawater propelled through a lava-tube formation erupts forcefully like a geyser—try timing your drive to penetrate the shooting water! In the winter months, golfers may also be treated to the sight of migrating

Most of the Big Island's top golf courses are located on the sunny Kohala Coast.

humpback whales splashing and breaching within a tee shot of the shoreline. The View, the on-site restaurant, is a favorite of locals, whether they golf or not, and has some of the best sunset views on the Kona Coast. ✉ 78-7000 Alii Dr., Kailua-Kona ☎ 808/322–2595 ⊕ www.konacountryclub.com ✆ $189, $105 9-hole; includes cart 🏌 18 holes, 6,613 yards, par 72.

Makalei Golf Club

GOLF | Set on the slopes of Hualalai Volcano at an elevation of 2,900 feet, Makalei is one of the rare Hawaii courses with bent-grass putting greens, which means they're quick and without the grain associated with Bermuda greens. Former PGA Tour official Dick Nugent designed holes that play through thick forest and open to wide ocean views. Elevation change is a factor on many holes, especially the par-3 eighth, whose tee is 80 feet above the green. In addition to fixed natural obstacles, wild peacocks and turkeys can make for an entertaining game. ■TIP→ **Check tourist and car rental guides for coupons and discounts.** ✉ 72-3890 Hawaii Belt Rd., Kailua-Kona ☎ 808/325–6625 ⊕ www.makalei.com ✆ $109, $89 after noon 🏌 18 holes, 7,091 yards, par 72.

Makani Golf Club

GOLF | At 2,000 feet above sea level on the slopes of Hualalai, this course is out of the way but well worth the drive. In 1997, Pete and Perry Dye created a gem that plays through upland woodlands—more than 2,500 trees line the fairways. On the par-5 16th, a giant tree in the middle of the fairway must be avoided with the second shot. Five lakes and a meandering natural mountain stream bring water into play on nine holes. The most dramatic is the par-3 17th, where Dye created a knockoff of his infamous 17th at the TPC at Sawgrass. ✉ 71-1420 Hawaii Belt Rd., Kailua-Kona ☎ 808/325–5044 ⊕ makanigolfclub.com ✆ $135 with cart, bottled water; $99 after noon 🏌 18 holes, 7,075 yards, par 72.

★ Mauna Kea Golf Course

GOLF | Originally opened in 1964, this golf course is one of the state's most revered. In 2008, it underwent a tee-to-green renovation by Rees Jones, son of the original architect, Robert Trent Jones Sr. Hybrid grasses were planted, the number of bunkers increased, and the overall yardage expanded. The par-3 third is one of the world's most famous holes—and one of the most photographed. You play from a cliffside tee across a bay to a cliffside green. Getting across the ocean is half the battle because the green is surrounded by seven bunkers, each one large and undulated. The course is a shot-maker's paradise and follows Jones's "easy bogey, tough par" philosophy. The course may be undergoing some upcoming minor renovations, so call first to check the status. ⊠ 62-100 Kaunaoe Dr., Mauna Kea ☎ 808/882–5400 ⊕ maunakeabeach-hotel.com ⊡ $295, $245 after 11 am, $195 after 1:30 pm ⛳ 18 holes, 7,250 yards, par 72.

★ Mauna Lani Golf Courses

GOLF | Black lava flows, lush green turf, white sand, and the Pacific's many blue hues define the 36 holes at Mauna Lani. The **South Course** includes the par-3 15th across a turquoise bay, one of Hawaii's most photographed holes. It shares "signature hole" honors with the seventh, a long par 3, which plays downhill over convoluted patches of black lava, with the Pacific immediately to the left and a dune to the right. The **North Course** plays a couple of shots tougher. Its most distinctive hole is the 17th, a par 3 with the green set in a lava pit 50 feet deep. The shot from an elevated tee must carry a pillar of lava that rises from the pit and partially blocks a view of the green. ⊠ 68-1310 Mauna Lani Dr., Waimea (Hawaii County) ☎ 808/885–6655 ⊕ aubergeresorts.com/maunalani ⊡ From $295, with dynamic pricing ⛳ South Course: 18 holes, 6,025 yards, par 72. North Course: 18 holes, 6,057 yards, par 72.

The Village Course at Waikoloa

GOLF | Robert Trent Jones Jr., who created some of the most expensive courses on the Kohala Coast, also designed this little gem 20 minutes from the coast. At a 450-foot elevation, it offers ideal playing conditions year-round; ask about summer rates. Holes run across rolling hills with sweeping mountain and ocean views. ■TIP→ **The 9-hole sunset special starts at 3 pm.** ⊠ 68-1792 Melia St., Waikoloa ☎ 808/883–9621 ⊕ thevillagecourse.com ⊡ $130, $60 sunset ⛳ 18 holes, 6,230 yards, par 72.

Volcano Golf Course

GOLF | Just outside Hawaii Volcanoes National Park—and barely a stone's throw from Halemaumau Crater—this is by far Hawaii's highest course. At 4,200 feet elevation, shots tend to fly a bit farther than at sea level, even in the often cool, misty air. Because of the elevation and climate, this Hawaii course features Bermuda and seashore paspalum grass putting greens. The course is mostly flat, and holes play through stands of ohia lehua (flowering native trees) and multitrunk hau trees. The uphill par-4 15th doglegs through a tangle of hau. ⚠ **Hawaii's highly endangered native goose, the nene, love golf courses and are especially prevalent here. Please do not approach or feed.** ⊠ 99-1621 Pii Mauna Dr., off Hwy. 11, Volcano ☎ 808/319–4745 ⊕ www.volcanogc.com ⊡ From $56; $15 cart ⛳ 18 holes, 6,106 yards, par 72.

★ Waikoloa Beach Resort

GOLF | Robert Trent Jones Jr. built the Beach Course at Waikoloa (1981) on an old flow of crinkly aa lava, which he used to create holes that are as artful as they are challenging. The par-5 12th hole is one of Hawaii's most picturesque and plays through a chute of black lava to a seaside green. At the Kings' Course (1990), Tom Weiskopf and Jay Morrish built a links-esque track. It turns out lava's natural humps and declivities replicate the contours of seaside Scotland. There

Hawaii Volcanoes National Park's 155 miles of trails offer easy to moderately difficult day hikes.

are a few island twists—such as seven lakes. This is "option golf," as Weiskopf and Morrish provide different risk-reward tactics on each hole. Resort guests receive a lower rate. ⊠ *600 Waikoloa Beach Dr., Waikoloa* ☎ *808/886–7888* ⊕ *www.waikoloabeachgolf.com* ✉ *From $194* ⅃. *Beach Course: 18 holes, 6,566 yards, par 70. Kings' Course: 18 holes, 7,074 yards, par 72.*

Hiking

Ecologically diverse, Hawaii Island has four of the five major climate zones and eight of 13 subclimate zones—a lot of variation for one island—and you can experience almost all of them on foot. The ancient Hawaiians cut trails across the lava plains, through the rain forests, and up along the mountain heights. Many of these paths are still in use today. Part of the King's Trail at Anaehoomalu winds through a field of lava rock covered with ancient petroglyphs. Many other trails—historic and modern—crisscross the huge

Hawaii Volcanoes National Park and other parts of the island. The three national parks here are replete with fantastic hiking opportunities for all abilities. If you like coastal hiking, the serenity of certain remote beaches is accessible only to hikers. Check the statewide trail system website (⊕ *hawaiitrails.ehawaii.gov*) for up-to-date information on hiking trails.

Department of Land and Natural Resources, State Parks Division
HIKING & WALKING | The division provides information on all the Big Island's state parks and jurisdictions. Check online for the latest additions, information, and advisories. ⊠ *75 Aupuni St., Hilo* ☎ *808/961–9544* ⊕ *dlnr.hawaii.gov/dsp.*

BEST SPOTS
Hawaii Volcanoes National Park. Perhaps the Big Island's premier area for hikers, the park has more than 155 miles of trails providing close-up, often jaw-dropping views of fern and rain-forest environments, cinder cones, craters, steam vents, lava fields, rugged coastline, and current eruption activity. Day hikes

Hiking Big Island Trails

■ Trails on the eastern, or windward, side of the island and at higher elevation are often wet and muddy, making them slippery and unstable. Wear good hiking shoes or boots.

■ Bring plenty of water, rain protection, a hat, sunblock, and a cell phone (but be aware that service can be spotty).

■ Always hike with a buddy or let someone know your plans. Obtain a permit where required.

■ Don't eat any unknown fruits or plants, or drink unfiltered water from streams.

■ Darkness comes suddenly here, so carry a flashlight or headlamp if you'll be out after sunset.

■ Always obey posted warning signs.

range from easy to moderately difficult, and from one or two hours to a full day. For a bigger challenge, consider an overnight or multiday backcountry hike with a stay in a park cabin (available en route to the remote coast, in a lush forest, or atop frigid Mauna Loa). To do so, you must first obtain a permit ($10) at the Backcountry Office, off Chain of Craters Road. Daily guided hikes are led by knowledgeable, friendly park rangers. The bulletin boards outside Kilauea Visitor Center have the day's schedule of guided hikes. ⊠ *Hwy. 11, 30 miles south of Hilo, Hawaii Volcanoes National Park* ☎ *808/985–6000* ⊕ *www.nps.gov/havo.*

Kekaha Kai State Park. A 1.8-mile unimproved road leads to Mahaiula Bay, a gorgeous little piece of paradise, while on the opposite side is lovely Kua Bay. Connecting the two is the 4½-mile Ala Kahakai historic coastal trail. Midway between the two white-sand beaches, you can hike to the summit of Puu Kuili, a 342-foot-high cinder cone with an excellent view of the coastline. Mahaiula has picnic tables and vault toilets but no other amenities. It's dry and hot, with no drinking water, so pack sunblock, hats, and extra water. Park gates close at 7 pm sharp. ⊠ *Trailhead on Hwy. 19, about 2 miles north of Kona airport, Kailua-Kona* ⊕ *dlnr.hawaii.gov/dsp.*

Muliwai Trail. On the western side of mystical Waipio Valley on the Hamakua Coast, this trail leads to the back of the valley, then switchbacks up through a series of gulches and finally emerges at Waimanu Valley. Only very experienced hikers should attempt the entirety of this remote 18-mile trail, the hike of a lifetime. It can take two to three days of backpacking and camping, which requires camping permits from the Division of Forestry and Wildlife in Hilo. At the time of this writing, the road to Waipio is closed due to repairs. ⊠ *Trailhead at end of Hwy. 240, Honokaa* ☎ *808/974–4221* ⊕ *hawaiitrails.ehawaii.gov.*

Onomea Bay Trail. This short but beautiful trail is packed with stunning views of the cliffs, bays, and gulches of the Hamakua Coast, on the east side of the island. The trail is just under a mile and fairly easy, with access down to the shore if you want to dip your feet in; we don't recommend swimming in the rough waters. Unless you pay the entry fee to the nearby Hawaii Tropical Bioreserve & Garden, entering its gates (even by accident) will send one of the guards running after you to point you back to the trail. ⊠ *Trailhead on Old Hawaiian Belt Rd., just before botanical garden* ⊕ *hawaiitrails.ehawaii. gov.*

GOING WITH A GUIDE

To get to some of the best trails and hiking spots (some of which are on private property), it's worth going with a skilled, professional guide, many of whom are certified national park guides. Costs range from about $150 to more than $285, and some hikes include transportation, full meals, refreshments, and gear such as binoculars, ponchos, parkas, and walking sticks. The outfitters mentioned here also offer customized adventure tours.

★ Hawaii Forest and Trail

WALKING TOURS | Since 1993, this locally owned and operated outfit has built a reputation for outstanding nature tours and eco-adventures. Sustainability, cultural sensitivity, and forging island connections are company missions. They have access to thousands of acres of restricted or private lands and employ expert, certified guides who are entertaining and informative. Choose one of the bird-watching tours, a journey that takes you deep into the Hakalau Forest National Wildlife Refuge with local bird experts at the helm. Other tours include treks to Kilauea Volcano in Hawaii Volcanoes National Park, a Kohala waterfall trip, or the uncrowded, awe-inspiring Hidden Craters Tour, which takes you over private land to explore the slopes of Hualalai Volcano. They can also design custom private tours. ⊠ 73-5593A Olowalu St., Kailua-Kona ☎ 808/331–8505, 800/464–1993 ⊕ www.hawaii-forest.com ☞ From $175.

Kailani Tours

WALKING TOURS | This ambitious local outfitter embarks on "luxe" tours of the Kilauea Volcano, including hikes of Kilauea Iki, Puuhuluhulu Cinder Cone, and the Devastation Trail. They also take guests to visit the national park's Holei Sea Arch and the wonders along Chain of Craters Road, finishing with Hilo's extraordinary Kaumana Caves and Rainbow Falls. Tours include a gourmet picnic lunch, snacks, and beverages during a full day of walking and adventures. The Big Island Highlights Day Tour promises volcanoes, coffee, turtles, wine, and waterfalls. ⊠ 74-555 Honokohau St., Suite B8, Kailua-Kona ☎ 808/938–4057 ⊕ kailanitourshawaii. com ☞ From $239.

★ KapohoKine Adventures

WALKING TOURS | **FAMILY** | One of the best-loved outfitters on the island, locally owned KapohoKine Adventures offers a number of excellent hiking tours that depart from both Hilo and Kona. The epic full-day Elite Volcano Hike (departing from both Kona and Hilo) hits all the great spots, including now-quiet areas in Puna impacted by the 2018 eruption. Hikers will encounter a 40-foot wall of lava and follow it to the sea and an enormous black-sand beach. Also included are Kalapana, the Kaumana Caves, the Steaming Bluffs, and a tour of Hawaii Volcanoes National Park. All tours are led by a national park–certified guide. Enjoy a final stop at Volcano House for views from the enormous picture windows overlooking the crater. A hearty dinner is included, as well as lunch and snacks. ⊠ Grand Naniloa Hotel Hilo, 93 Banyan Dr., Hilo ☎ 808/964–1000 ⊕ www.kapohokine. com ☞ From $295.

Horseback Riding

With its *paniolo* (cowboy) heritage and the ranches it spawned, the Big Island is a great place for equestrians. Riders can gallop through upcountry green pastures or saunter through lush valleys for a taste of old Hawaii.

TOURS

4D Quarter Horses

HORSEBACK RIDING | Owned by a Native Hawaiian family, this working ranch at 3,000 feet offers 90-minute, open-range rides on quarter horses along rolling hills, meaning this is not nose-to-tail trail riding. Depending on the day, you may even get the chance to drive cattle. The horses are accustomed to riders of all abilities and are gentle. You won't generally be running on this ride, as you mainly traverse 4½ miles over hilly terrain. Bring appropriate foul-weather gear; it can get cold and rainy. The ranch is located midway between Waimea and Honokaa. ⊠ 68-1936 Waikoloa Rd ☎ 808/987–4872 ⊕ 4dquarterhorses.com 💲 $110.

Paniolo Adventures

HORSEBACK RIDING | The company offers an open-range horseback ride on a working Kohala Mountain cattle ranch, spectacular views of three volcanoes and the coastline, and an authentic *paniolo* (cowboy) experience from 3,000 feet up. You don't ride nose-to-tail and can spread out and trot or canter if you wish: this is an 11,000-acre ranch, so there's room to roam. The company caters to beginning and experienced riders and offers special private rides as well. ⊠ Kohala Mountain Rd. (Hwy. 250) at mile marker 13.2 ☎ 808/889–5354 ⊕ www.panioloadventures.com 💲 From $139.

Waipio on Horseback

HORSEBACK RIDING | Riders are treated to rides through coconut, guava and banana groves, fishponds, flower patches, and outstanding views on this 500-acre, private working ranch above Waipio Valley. There's 2½ hours in the saddle, and you'll ride along some sections of the famous Hamakua Ditch, which was built in the early 1900s to ship water down to irrigate sugarcane lands. ⊠ 48-5158 Honokaa-Waipio Rd. ☎ 808/775–7291 ⊕ waipioonhorseback.com 💲 From $150.

Kayaking

The leeward (west coast) areas of the Big Island are protected for the most part from the northeast trade winds, making for ideal near-shore kayaking conditions. Miles and miles of uncrowded Kona and Kohala coastline present close-up views of stark, raw, lava-rock shores and cliffs; lava-tube sea caves; pristine, secluded coves; and deserted beaches.

Ocean kayakers can get close to shore—places the commercial snorkel and dive cruise boats can't reach. This opens up all sorts of possibilities for adventure, such as near-shore snorkeling among the expansive coral reefs and lava-rock formations that teem with colorful tropical fish and Hawaiian green sea turtles. You can pull ashore at a quiet cove for a picnic and a plunge into turquoise waters. With a good coastal map and some advice from the kayak vendor, you might paddle past ancient battlegrounds, burial sites, bathing ponds for Hawaiian royalty, or old villages.

Kayaking can be enjoyed via a guided tour or on a self-guided paddling excursion. Either way, the kayak outfitter can brief you on recommended routes, safety, and how to help preserve and protect Hawaii's ocean resources and coral reef system.

Whether you're a beginning or experienced kayaker, choose appropriate location, distance, and conditions for your excursion.

■ Ask the outfitter about local conditions and hazards, such as tides, currents, and advisories, but also judge conditions for yourself and *never* launch in rough weather.

■ Beginners should practice getting into and out of the kayak and capsizing (called a *huli*, the Hawaiian word for "flip over") in shallow water.

■ Before departing, secure the kayak's hatches to prevent water intake.

■ Use a line to attach the paddle to the kayak to avoid losing it.

■ Always use a life vest or jacket, and wear a rash guard and hat; apply plenty of reef-safe sunblock.

- Carry appropriate amounts of water and food.

- Don't kayak alone. Create a float plan; tell someone where you're going and when you will return.

BEST SPOTS

Hilo Bay. This is a favorite kayak spot. The best place to put in is at Reeds Bay Beach Park. Parking is plentiful and free at the bayfront. Most afternoons you'll share the bay with local paddling clubs. Stay inside the breakwater unless the ocean is calm (or you're feeling unusually adventurous). Conditions range from extremely calm to quite choppy. ⊠ *Banyan Way and Banyan Dr., 1 mile from downtown Hilo.*

Hookena Beach Park. Located in South Kona, this lovely little bay is perfect for kayaking. A concessionaire offers both double and single kayaks for rent by the hour. ⊠ *86-4322 Mamalahoa Hwy, Captain Cook.*

Kailua Bay and Kamakahonu Beach. The small sandy beach that fronts the Courtyard King Kamehameha's Kona Beach Hotel is a nice place to rent or launch kayaks. You can unload in the cul-de-sac and park in nearby paid lots. The water here is especially calm, and the surroundings are historical and scenic. ⊠ *Alii Dr., next to Kailua Pier, Kailua-Kona.*

Kealakekua Bay State Historical Park. The excellent snorkeling and likelihood of seeing dolphins (morning is best) make Kealakekua Bay one of the most popular kayaking spots on the Big Island. An underwater Marine Life Conservation District, the bay is usually calm and tranquil. (⚠ **Use caution and common sense during surf advisories.**) Tall coral pinnacles and clear visibility surrounding the Captain James Cook Monument also make for stupendous snorkeling. Regulations permit only a few operators to lead kayak tours in the park. ⊠ *Napoopoo Rd. and Manini Beach Rd., Captain Cook* ⊕ *dlnr. hawaii.gov/dsp.*

Oneo Bay. Right in downtown Kailua, this is usually a placid place to kayak. It's fairly easy to access. If you can't find parking along the road, there's a free lot across the street from the library and farmers' market. ⊠ *Alii Dr., Kailua-Kona.*

EQUIPMENT, LESSONS, AND TOURS

There are several rental outfitters on Highway 11 between Kainaliu and Captain Cook, but only a few are permitted to lead kayak trips in Kealakekua Bay.

Aloha Kayak Co.

KAYAKING | The outfitter is one of the few permitted to guide kayaking tours to the stunningly beautiful Kealakekua Bay, leaving from Napoopoo, including about 1½ hours at the Captain Cook Monument. The 3½-hour morning and afternoon tours include snacks and drinks, while the five-hour tour includes lunch. Local guides discuss the area's cultural, historical, and natural significance. You may see spinner dolphins, but you will observe them from a distance only, as this is a protected marine reserve and dolphins are protected by federal law. Keauhou Bay tours are also available, including a two-hour evening manta ray tour. Advance reservations are highly recommended. ⊠ *82-5674 Kahau Pl., Captain Cook* ☎ *808/322–2868* ⊕ *www. alohakayak.com* 🖼 *Tours from $105 (price includes mandatory wharf fee).*

KapohoKine Adventures Kayak Tour

KAYAKING | Exploring Hilo Bay like no other trip, this two-hour, fully guided kayak or paddleboard (your choice) tour departs Hilo Bay and includes a fascinating tour of the area by a lifeguard-certified guide. Points of interest include Moku Ola (Coconut Island), waterfalls, breakwaters, beaches, and even a hydroelectric plant. You'll learn about what happened when a catastrophic tsunami swept over this area in 1946. Snacks and water are provided. ⊠ *Grand Naniloa Hotel Hilo, 93 Banyan Dr., Lobby, Hilo* ☎ *808/964–1000* ⊕ *kapohokine.com* 🖼 *$152.*

★ Kona Boys

KAYAKING | On the highway above Kealakekua Bay, this full-service, environmentally conscious outfitter handles kayaks, body boards, surfboards, stand-up paddleboards, and snorkeling gear. Single-seat and double kayaks are offered. Surfing and stand-up paddleboarding lessons are available for private or group instruction. One of the few companies permitted to lead tours in Kealakekua Bay, Kona Boys offers their Morning Magic and Midday Meander tours, two half-day guided kayaking and snorkeling trips with gear, lunch, snacks, and beverages. They also run a beach shack fronting the Courtyard King Kamehameha's Kona Beach Hotel, with everything for the beachgoer such as rentals of beach mats, chairs, and other gear. ■TIP→ **The Kailua-Kona location offers Hawaiian outrigger canoe rides and SUP lessons.** ⊠ 79-7539 Mamalahoa Hwy., Kealakekua ☎ 808/328–1234 Kealakekua location, 808/329–2345 Kailua-Kona location ⊕ www.konaboys.com ⊠ Tours from $199.

Ocean Safari's Kayak Adventures

KAYAKING | On the guided, 3½-hour morning sea-cave tour that begins in Keauhou Bay, you can visit lava-tube sea caves along the coast, then swim ashore for a snack. The kayaks are already on the water, so you won't have the hassle of transporting them. The company also offers stand-up paddleboard rentals and lessons. Book online for best availability. ⊠ 78-7128 Kaleiopapa St., Kailua-Kona ☎ 808/326–4699 ⊕ www.oceansafariskayaks.com ⊠ From $89.

Running

Ironman World Championship

RUNNING | Staged annually since 1978, the Ironman World Championship is the granddaddy of all triathlons. For about two weeks in mid-October, Kailua-Kona takes on the vibe of an Olympic Village, as up to 2,000 top athletes from across the globe and their supporters roam the town, carb-loading, training, and prepping in advance of the world's premier swim-bike-run endurance event. The competition starts at Kailua Pier with a 2.4-mile open-water swim, followed by a 112-mile bicycle ride and a 26.2-mile marathon. In 2022, a new two-day format debuts, allowing men and women to race on different days. The week prior is filled with fun community events such as the Underpants Run, in which locals and visitors—including well-known celebrities—run through town in only their knickers. ■TIP→ **Only qualified athletes may participate, but if you are visiting during Ironman and want to volunteer, contact** ✉ **kona@ironmanvolunteers.com.** ⊠ Kailua-Kona ⊕ www.ironman.com.

★ Peaman Biathlon Series

RUNNING | Beloved by the community, Sean "Peaman" Pagett has been a Kona icon for decades, putting on no-cost biathlon events that are suitable for the whole family. Run and swim lengths vary according to the day's event, but Peaman emphasizes there are no "rules" here. He even says contestants are free to make up their own, as the only goal is to promote fun, fitness, and community. There are snacks and water at the finish, and Peaman has awesome prizes for kids. Normally held the last Sunday of every month at 8:08 am at the Kona pier, the event welcomes visitors. ⊠ Kailua Pier, 75-5660 Palani Rd., Kailua-Kona ☎ 808/938–2296 ⊠ Free.

Sailing

For old salts and novice sailors alike, there's nothing like a cruise on the Kona or Kohala Coast. Calm waters, serene shores, and the superb scenery of Maunakea, Mauna Loa, and Hualalai, the Big Island's primary volcanic peaks, make for a great sailing adventure. You can drop a line over the side and try your luck at catching dinner, or grab some snorkel gear and explore when the boat stops in one of the quiet coves and bays. A cruise may well be the most relaxing and adventurous part of a Big Island visit.

Kona Sail Charters

SAILING | The fully equipped, 32-foot cutter-rigged sloop *Honu* (Hawaiian for sea turtle) carries up to six passengers on full-day, half-day, and sunset sailing excursions along the scenic Kona Coast, including time to snorkel in clear waters over coral reefs during the day tours and heavy *pupus* (appetizers) for the sunset excursion. This friendly outfitter allows passengers to get some hands-on sailing experience or to kick back and relax, and there are plenty of cushions and lots of shade. Private charters are an option. ⊠ *Honokohau Harbor, Kailua-Kona* ☎ *808/896–4668* ⊕ *www.sailkona.com* ✉ *Tours from $250/hr.*

Paradise Sailing Hawaii

SAILING | Married Captains Eric and Yumi Wakely spent 20 years running charters in West Hawaii and decided to open their own charter company. *Kolea*, a comfortable, sleek, 36-foot Kurt Hughes catamaran, provides plenty of shade, ample seating, tables, restrooms, and a shower. Take a private morning, afternoon, or sunset sail along the Kona Coast. ⊠ *Honokohau Marina, 74-380 Kealakehe Pkwy., #J24, Kailua-Kona* ☎ *808/883–0399* ⊕ *paradisesailinghawaii.com* ✉ *From $995 for maximum of 8 people.*

Scuba Diving

The Big Island's underwater world is the setting for a dramatic diving experience. With generally warm and calm waters, vibrant coral reefs and rock formations, and plunging underwater drop-offs, the Kona and Kohala Coasts offer premier scuba diving. There are some good dive locations in East Hawaii, not far from the Hilo area, but the best spots are all on the west coast. Divers find much to occupy their time, including marine reserves teeming with tropical reef fish, Hawaiian green sea turtles, an occasional and critically endangered Hawaiian monk seal, and some playful spinner dolphins. On special night dives to see manta rays, divers descend with underwater lights that attract plankton, which in turn attract these otherworldly creatures.

BEST SPOTS

Garden Eel Cove. Accessible only by boat, this is a great place to see manta rays somersaulting overhead as they feast on a plankton supper. It's also home to hundreds of tiny garden eels darting out from their sandy homes. There's a steep drop-off and lots of marine life. ⊠ *Rte. 19, near the Kona Airport, Kailua-Kona.*

Manta Village. Booking with a night-dive operator is required for the short boat ride to this area, one of Kona's best night-dive spots. If you're a diving or snorkeling fanatic, it's well worth it to experience manta rays drawn by the lights of the hotel. ■**TIP**→ **If night swimming isn't your cup of tea, you can catch a glimpse of the majestic creatures from the Outrigger's viewing areas. No water access is allowed from the hotel's property.** ⊠ *78-128 Ehukai St., off Outrigger Kona Resort and Spa at Keauhou Bay, Kailua-Kona.*

Pawai Bay Marine Preserve. Clear waters, abundant reef life, and interesting coral formations make this protected preserve ideal for diving. Explore sea caves, arches, and lava-rock formations and dive into lava tubes. An easy boat-only dive spot is a half mile north of Old Airport Park. (No shoreline access to protected Pawai Bay is available due to its cultural and environmental significance.) ⊠ *Kuakini Hwy., north of Old Kona Airport Park, Kailua-Kona.*

Puako. Just south of Hapuna Beach State Recreation Area, beautiful Puako (a small oceanfront neighborhood) offers easy entry to some fine reef diving. Deep

Hawaii's Manta Rays

Manta rays, one of Hawaii's most fascinating marine-life species, can be seen on some nighttime diving excursions along the Kona and Kohala Coasts. They are generally completely harmless to divers, though of course no wild animal is totally predictable. If you don't want to get wet, head to the beach fronting the Mauna Kea Beach Hotel, on the Kohala Coast, or to the Outrigger Kona Resort and Spa at Keauhou Bay, where each evening, visitors gather by the hotel's lights to watch manta rays feed in the shallows.

■ The manta ray (*Manta birostris*), called the devil fish by some, is known as *hahalua* by Hawaiians.

■ Its winglike fins, reaching up to 20 feet wide, allow the ray to skim through the water like a bird gliding through air.

■ The manta ray uses the two large, flaplike lobes extending from its eyes to funnel food to its mouth. It eats microscopic plankton, small fish, and tiny crustaceans.

■ Closely related to the shark, the manta can weigh more than 3,000 pounds.

■ The manta's skeleton is made of cartilage, not bone.

■ A female ray gives birth to one or two young at a time; pups can be 45 inches long and weigh 20 pounds at birth.

chasms, sea caves, and rock arches abound with marine life. Trade winds pick up in the afternoons. ⊠ *Puako Rd., off Hwy. 19, Kailua-Kona.*

EQUIPMENT, LESSONS, AND TOURS

There are quite a few good dive shops along the Kona Coast. Most are happy to take on all customers, but a few focus on specific types of trips. Trip prices vary, depending on whether you're already certified and whether you're diving from a boat or from shore. Instruction with PADI, SDI, or TDI certification in three to five days costs $600 to $850. Most instructors rent dive equipment and snorkel gear, as well as underwater cameras. Most also organize otherworldly manta ray dives at night and whale-watching cruises in season.

Aquatic Life Divers

SCUBA DIVING | Dedicated to local coral reef conservation, this dive company not only provides two-tank dives, black-water

dives, manta dives, snorkeling, and whale-watching excursions but also educates guests on coral reef ecology and other issues. ⊠ *74-381 Kealakehe Pkwy, Kailua-Kona* ☎ *808/345–4411* ⊕ *aquaticlifedivers.com* ☎ *From $219.*

Big Island Divers

SCUBA DIVING | This company offers several levels of certification as well as numerous excursions, including night dives, two-tank charters, and in-season whale-watching. ⊠ *74-5467 Kaiwi St., Kailua-Kona* ☎ *808/329–6068* ⊕ *bigislanddivers.com* ☎ *From $199.*

Jack's Diving Locker

SCUBA DIVING | Good for novice and intermediate divers, Jack's has trained and certified tens of thousands of divers since 1981, with classrooms and a dive pool for instruction. Four boats that accommodate up to 18 divers and six snorkelers visit more than 80 established dive sites along the Kona Coast, yielding sightings of turtles, manta rays, garden

The Kona Coast's relatively calm waters and colorful coral reefs offer excellent scuba diving.

eels, and schools of barracuda. They even take you lava-tube diving. Snorkelers can accompany their friends on the dive boats or take guided morning trips and manta night trips, and dolphin-watch and reef snorkels. Combined sunset/night manta ray dives are offered as well. ■TIP→ **Kona's best deal for scuba newbies is Jack's pool-and-shore dive combo.** ✉ *75-5813 Alii Dr., Kailua-Kona* ☎ *808/329–7585, 800/345–4807* ⊕ *www.jacksdivinglocker.com* ✉ *Tours from $199 certified divers, $300 intro divers and privates.*

★ Kohala Divers

SCUBA DIVING | The Kohala Coast's gorgeous underwater topography of lava tubes, caves, vibrant coral reefs, and interesting sea life makes it a great diving destination. This full-service PADI dive shop has been certifying divers since 1984. A one-day intro dive course has you in the ocean the same day. A four-day, full-certification course is offered, too. The company rents any equipment needed for boat or shore excursions and takes divers to the best diving spots on their fully outfitted, comfortable 46-foot Newton dive boat. The retail shop is packed with everything needed for diving, snorkeling, and beach-going. ✉ *Kawaihae Harbor Shopping Center, Hwy. 270, Kawaihae* ☎ *808/882–7774* ⊕ *www.kohaladivers.com* ✉ *Two-tank dive $179; open-water certification from $699.*

Torpedo Tours

SCUBA DIVING | Owner-operators Mike and Nikki Milligan, both dive instructors, love to take divers out on their 40-foot custom dive boat, the *Na Pali Kai II*. They specialize in small groups, which means you'll get personalized attention and spend more time diving and less time waiting to dive. Morning excursions feature two-tank dives. Certified divers should try the spectacular Blackwater Night Dive. They also offer full PADI certification and private charters. ✉ *Honokohau Harbor, 74-425 Kealakehe Pkwy., Kailua-Kona* ☎ *808/938–0405* ⊕ *www.torpedotours.com* ✉ *Dives from $169.*

Sightseeing

Polynesian Adventures

BUS TOURS | In business since 1977, this company offers motorcoach tours at a great price. Take their eco-friendly, ultra-comfortable tour on a relaxing excursion halfway around the island, hitting all the highlights. On the Coffee, Culture and Craters tour, you'll stop at a coffee plantation, Puuhonua of Honaunau National Historical Park, Punaluu Black Sand Beach, Naalehu Town, and finally, Hawaii Volcanoes National Park. Park fees, snacks, and lunch are included in this very affordable tour, which departs from both Kona and Waikoloa. ☎ 877/930–1740 ⊕ polyad.com ✉ $202.

Snorkeling

A favorite pastime on the Big Island, snorkeling is perhaps one of the easiest and most enjoyable water activities for visitors. By floating on the surface, peering through your mask, and breathing through your snorkel, you can see lava-rock formations, sea arches, sea caves, and coral reefs teeming with colorful tropical fish. While the Kona and Kohala Coasts boast more beaches, bays, and quiet coves to snorkel, the east side around Hilo is also a great place to get in the water.

If you don't bring your own equipment, you can easily rent all the gear needed from a beach activities vendor, who will happily provide directions to the best sites for snorkeling in the area. For access to deeper water and assistance from an experienced crew (to say nothing of typically great food and drink), you can opt for a snorkel cruise. Excursions generally range from two to five hours; be sure to ask what equipment and food is included. ■TIP→ **Use a few drops of baby shampoo on your mask for a cheap and easy-on-the-eyes defogger.**

BEST SPOTS

Carlsmith Beach Park. This calm group of lagoons near Hilo is a great place to bring kids. Freshwater springs might cloud your mask and keep the water cool, but you'll see lots of turtles and tropical fish here. There are showers, a lifeguard, and picnic tables. ⊠ 1815 Kalanianaole Ave., 10 min. east of Hilo on Hwy. 137.

Honaunau Bay. This lovely spot presents expansive coral gardens and relatively easy access. You'll see lots of yellow tangs here. Please be respectful at this beloved local spot, and don't stand on coral, chase dolphins, or use reef-toxic sunscreens. There's very limited parking. ⊠ Next to Puuhonua o Honaunau NHP, South Kona.

Kahaluu Beach Park. Since ancient times, the waters around Kahaluu Beach have provided traditional throw net–fishing grounds. With super-easy access, the bay offers good swimming and outstanding snorkeling, revealing turtles, angelfish, parrotfish, needlefish, puffer fish, and many types of tangs. ■TIP→ **Stay inside the breakwater and don't stray too far, as dangerous and unpredictable currents swirl outside the bay.** ⊠ Alii Dr., Kailua-Kona.

Kealakekua Bay State Historical Park. This protected Marine Life Conservation District is hands down one of the best snorkeling spots on the island, thanks to clear visibility, fabulous coral reefs, and generally calm waters. Pods of dolphins can be abundant, but they're protected under federal law and may not be disturbed or approached. Access to the area is restricted, but a few companies are permitted to escort tours to the bay. ■TIP→ **Overland access is difficult, so opt for one of the guided snorkel cruises permitted to moor here.** ⊠ Napoopoo, at end of Beach Rd. and Hwy. 160, Captain Cook.

Continued on page 268

SNORKELING IN HAWAII

Molokini Crater

The waters surrounding the Hawaiian Islands are filled with life—from giant manta rays cruising off the Big Island's Kona Coast to humpback whales giving birth in the waters around Maui. Dip your head beneath the surface to experience a spectacularly colorful world: pairs of milletseed butterflyfish dart back and forth, redlipped parrotfish snack on coral algae, and spotted eagle rays flap past like silent spaceships. Sea turtles bask at the surface while tiny wrasses give them the equivalent of a shave and a haircut. The water quality is typically outstanding; many sites afford 30-foot-plus visibility. On snorkel cruises, you can often stare from the boat rail right down to the bottom.

Certainly few destinations are as accommodating to every level of snorkeler as Hawaii. Beginners can tromp in from sandy beaches while more advanced divers descend to shipwrecks, reefs, craters, and sea arches just offshore. Because of Hawaii's extreme isolation, the island chain has fewer fish species than Fiji or the Caribbean—but many of the fish that live here exist nowhere else. The Hawaiian waters are home to the highest percentage of endemic fish in the world.

The key to enjoying the underwater world is slowing down. Look carefully. Listen. You might hear the strange crackling sound of shrimp tunneling through coral, or you may hear whales singing to one another during winter. A shy octopus may drift along the ocean's floor beneath you. If you're hooked, pick up a waterproof fish-key from Long's Drugs. You can brag later that you've looked the Hawaiian turkeyfish in the eye.

Picasso triggerfish

Milletseed butterflyfish*

Yellow tang

Moorish idol

Hawaiian whitespotted toby*

Saddleback wrasse*

Redlip parrotfish

Hawaiian turkeyfish*

Zebra moray eel

Stocky hawkfish

Green sea turtle (honu)

Spotted eagle ray

*Endemic to Hawaii

POLYNESIA'S FIRST CELESTIAL NAVIGATORS: HONU

Honu is the Hawaiian name for two native sea turtles, the hawksbill and the green sea turtle. Little is known about these dinosaur-age marine reptiles, though snorkelers regularly see them foraging for *limu* (seaweed) and the occasional jellyfish in Hawaiian waters. Most female honu nest in the uninhabited Northwestern Hawaiian Islands, but a few sociable ladies nest on Maui and Big Island beaches. Scientists suspect that they navigate the seas via magnetism—sensing the earth's poles. Amazingly, they will journey up to 800 miles to nest—it's believed that they return to their own birth sites. After about 60 days of incubation, nestlings emerge from the sand at night and find their way back to the sea by the light of the stars.

SNORKELING

Many of Hawaii's reefs are accessible from the shore.

The basics: Sure, you can take a deep breath, hold your nose, squint your eyes, and stick your face in the water in an attempt to view submerged habitats . . . but why not protect your eyes, retain your ability to breathe, and keep your hands free to paddle about when exploring underwater? That's what snorkeling is all about.

Equipment needed: A mask, snorkel (the tube attached to the mask), and fins. In deeper waters (any depth over your head), life jackets are advised.

Steps to success: If you've never snorkeled before, it's natural to feel a bit awkward at first, so don't sweat it. Breathing through a mask and tube, and wearing a pair of fins take getting used to. Like any activity, you build confidence and comfort through practice.

If you're new to snorkeling, begin by submerging your face in shallow water or a swimming pool and breathing calmly through the snorkel while gazing through the mask.

Next you need to learn how to clear water out of your mask and snorkel, an essential skill since splashes can send water into tube openings and masks can leak. Some snorkels have built-in drainage valves, but if a tube clogs, you can force water up and out by exhaling through your mouth. Clearing a mask is similar: lift your head from water while pulling forward on mask to drain. Some masks have built-in purge valves, but those without can be cleared underwater by pressing the top to the forehead and blowing out your nose (charming, isn't it?), allowing air to bubble into the mask, pushing water out the bottom. If it sounds hard, it really isn't. Just try it a few times and you'll soon feel like a pro.

Never touch or stand on coral.

Now your goal is to get friendly with fins—you want them to be snug but not too tight—and learn how to propel yourself with them. Fins won't help you float, but they will give you a leg up, so to speak, on smoothly moving through the water or treading water (even when upright) with less effort.

Flutter kicking is the most efficient underwater kick, and the farther your foot bends forward the more leg power you'll be able to transfer to the water and the farther you'll travel with each stroke. Flutter kicking movements involve alternately separating the legs and then drawing them back together. When your legs separate, the leg surface encounters drag from the water, slowing you down. When your legs are drawn back together, they produce a force pushing you forward. If your kick creates more forward force than it causes drag, you'll move ahead.

Submerge your fins to avoid fatigue rather than having them flailing above the water when you kick, and keep your arms at your side to reduce drag. You are in the water—stretched out, face down, and snorkeling happily away—but that doesn't mean you can't hold your breath and go deeper in the water for a closer look at some fish or whatever catches your attention. Just remember that when you do this, your snorkel will be submerged, too, so you won't be breathing (you'll be holding your breath). You can dive head-first, but going feet-first is easier and less scary for most folks, taking less momentum. Before full immersion, take several long, deep breaths to clear carbon dioxide from your lungs.

If your legs tire, flip onto your back and tread water with inverted fin motions while resting. If your mask fogs, wash condensation from the lens and clear water from your mask.

TIPS FOR SAFE SNORKELING

■ Snorkel with a buddy and stay together.

■ Plan your entry and exit points prior to getting in the water.

■ Swim into the current on entering and then ride the current back to your exit point.

■ Carry your flippers into the water and then put them on, as it's difficult to walk in them, and rocks may be slippery.

■ Make sure your mask fits properly and is not too loose.

■ Pop your head above the water periodically to ensure you aren't drifting too far out, or too close to rocks.

■ Think of the water as someone else's home—don't take anything that doesn't belong to you, or leave any trash behind.

■ Don't touch any sea creatures; they may reveal hidden stingers.

■ Wear a rash guard; it will help you from being fried by the sun..

■ When in doubt, don't go without a snorkeling professional; try a guided tour.

■ Don't go in if the ocean seems rough.

Green sea turtle (honu)

Magic Sands Beach Park. Also known as White Sands or Disappearing Sands Beach Park, this is a great place for beginning and intermediate snorkelers. In winter, it's also a prime spot to watch for whales. ⊠ *Alii Dr., Kailua-Kona.*

Puako Tide Pools. The large shelf of extensive reef and tide pools at this sleepy beach town along the Kohala Coast makes for fantastic snorkeling, as long as conditions are calm. ⊠ *South end of Puako Beach Rd., Puako, off Hwy. 11.*

EQUIPMENT, LESSONS, AND TOURS

Body Glove Cruises
SNORKELING | FAMILY | A good choice for families, this operator has a waterslide and a high-dive platform that kids love. On the daily Snorkel and BBQ Adventure, the 65-foot catamaran sets off from Kailua-Kona pier for stunning Red Hill in uncrowded South Kona. The morning snorkel cruise includes breakfast and a barbecue burger lunch, with vegetarian options. A three-hour historical dinner cruise to Kealakekua Bay is a great way to relax, watch the sunset, and learn about Kona's history. It includes an excellent Hawaiian-style meal, complimentary cocktail, and live music. Seasonal whale-watch cruises and all dolphin snorkel cruises guarantee you will see the featured mammals or you can go again for free. The company follows a NOAA-approved Dolphin SMART policy, encouraging responsible viewing, on all their cruises. Children under five are always free. ⊠ *75-5629 Kuakini Hwy., Kailua-Kona* ☎ *808/326–7122, 800/551–8911* ⊕ *www.bodyglovehawaii.com* ☙ *From $158.*

★ Fair Wind Cruises
SNORKELING | FAMILY | In business since 1971, Fair Wind offers morning and afternoon snorkel trips into breathtaking Kealakekua Bay. Great for families with small kids, the custom-built, 60-foot catamaran *Fair Wind* has two 15-foot waterslides, freshwater showers, and a staircase descending directly into the water for easy access. Snorkel gear is included, along with flotation equipment and prescription masks. The 4½-hour cruise is known for its delicious meals; 3½-hour snack cruises are offered, too. For ages seven and older, the company also operates the *Hula Kai* snorkel cruise, on a 55-foot luxury hydrofoil catamaran that takes guests to several remote South Kona locations. Their five-hour morning snorkel cruise includes gourmet breakfast and barbecue lunch. ■ TIP→ **The morning cruise is a bit more expensive, but you will have a better chance of clear, sunny conditions than aboard the afternoon boat.** ⊠ *Keauhou Bay, 78-7130 Kaleiopapa St., Kailua-Kona* ☎ *808/322–2788, 800/677–9461* ⊕ *www.fair-wind.com* ☙ *From $159.*

Sea Quest
SNORKELING | Careful stewardship of the Kona Coast and its sea life is a major priority for this company, which offers catamaran charters and other snorkeling excursions. They support the Hawaii Eco-Tourism Association's commitments to sustainable underwater tourism management. Trips leave from Keauhou Bay and head to Captain Cook Monument and other points south. When night falls, they are one of the best manta ray outfitters on the west side. ⊠ *78-7138 Kaleiopapa St., Kailua-Kona* ☎ *808/329–7238* ⊕ *www.seaquesthawaii.com* ☙ *From $105.*

Snorkel Bob's
SNORKELING | You're likely to see Snorkel Bob's wacky ads in your airline in-flight magazine or rack cards. The company offers a wide selection of rental gear packages and options; they often run specials, so be sure to ask. They also rent beach chairs and flotation devices. The two Big Island locations are in Kona and at Mauna Lani, but if you book online they will give you a small discount.

■TIP→ **If you happen to be traveling inter-island, you can rent your gear on one island and return it to another.** ✉ *75-5831 Kahakai St., Kailua-Kona* ☎ *808/329–0770, 800/262–7725* ⊕ *www.snorkelbob.com* ✆ *From $68/week.*

Stand-Up Paddleboarding

Stand-up paddleboarding (or stand-up paddling; SUP for short), a sport with roots in the Hawaiian Islands, has grown popular worldwide in recent years. It's available for all skill levels and ages, and even novice stand-up paddleboarders can get up, stay up, and have a great time paddling around a protected bay or exploring the gorgeous coastline. All you need to get started is a large body of calm water, a board, and a paddle. The workout tests your core strength as well as your balance and offers an unusual vantage point from which to enjoy the beauty of island and ocean.

BEST SPOTS

Anaehoomalu Bay Beach. In this well-protected bay, it's usually fairly calm even when surf is rough on the rest of the island, though trade winds pick up heartily in the afternoon. Boards are available for rent at the north end, and the safe area for stand-up paddling is marked by buoys. ✉ *Off Waikoloa Beach Dr., south of Waikoloa Beach Marriott, Kohala Coast.*

Hilo Bay. The bay is calm most days, as well as shallow, so it's a great place for novices to try stand-up paddling. The beach is about 3,000 feet long, one of the longest in Hawaii, so there's lots of room on the beach and in the water. Free parking is abundant fronting the bay off Bayfront Highway, so you won't usually have to schlep your board and paddle too far from your car. ✉ *Bayfront Hwy., downtown Hilo.*

Kailua Bay and Kamakahonu Beach. The small sandy beach that fronts the Courtyard King Kamehameha's Kona Beach Hotel is great for kids; the water here is especially calm and gentle. If you're more daring, you can easily paddle out of the bay and along the coast for some great exploring. ✉ *Alii Dr., next to Kailua Pier, Kailua-Kona.*

EQUIPMENT AND LESSONS
Alii Adventure Shack

STAND UP PADDLEBOARDING | This small company specializes in paddleboard rentals and can give you some great tips about where to go in Kailua-Kona for the best experience. They also rent coolers and Go-Pro cameras so you can record your outing. ✉ *75-5663 Palani Rd., Kailua-Kona* ☎ *808/657-4606* ⊕ *aliiadventureshack.com* ✆ *From $20/hr.*

★ Hypr Nalu Hawaii

STAND UP PADDLEBOARDING | **FAMILY** | Veteran waterman and fitness enthusiast Ian Foo, his wife, Lauren, and their adult kids, run this top-of-the-line board shop at the beach fronting the Waikoloa Beach Marriott Resort. From stand-up paddleboards and surfboards, to lessons, accessories, clothing, and gear, they do it all with passion and expertise. More impressively, they make the elegant stand-up boards themselves—arguably the most beautiful paddleboards in the world—and will ship worldwide. So if you take a lesson, fall in love with the sport, and want one sent home, this is the place to go. ✉ *69-275 Waikoloa Beach Dr., Waikoloa* ☎ *808/960–4667* ⊕ *www.hyprnalu.com* ✆ *Lessons from $125.*

Submarine Tours

Atlantis Submarines

BOATING | **FAMILY** | Want to stay dry while exploring the tropical undersea world? Climb aboard the 48-passenger *Atlantis X* submarine, anchored off Kailua Pier, across from Courtyard

Passengers aboard the *Atlantis X* submarine visit the aquatic world without getting wet. They may even see a scuba diver in action.

King Kamehameha's Kona Beach Hotel. A large glass dome in the bow and 13 viewing ports on each side allow clear views of the aquatic world more than 100 feet down. They take you to a pristine, 25-acre coral garden brimming with sea creatures of all kinds. This is a great trip for kids and nonswimmers. ■TIP➔ **Book online for discounts and specials.** ⊠ *75-5669 Alii Dr., Kailua-Kona* ☎ *808/326–7939, 800/381–0237* ⊕ *www. atlantisadventures.com* ⊠ *$148.*

Surfing

The Big Island does not have the variety of great surfing spots found on Oahu or Maui, but it does have decent waves and a thriving surf culture. Local kids and avid surfers frequent a number of places up and down the Kona and Kohala Coasts of West Hawaii; some have become famous surf champions. Expect high surf in winter and much calmer conditions

during summer. The surf scene is much more active on the Kona side.

BEST SPOTS

Honolii Cove. North of Hilo, this is the best surfing spot on the eastern side of the island. It hosts many exciting surf contests. ⊠ *Off Hwy. 19, near mile marker 4, Hilo.*

Kahaluu Beach Park. Slightly north of this beach park and just past the calm lagoon filled with snorkelers, beginning and intermediate surfers can have a go at some nice waves. Heed lifeguard warnings. ⊠ *Alii Dr., Kailua-Kona.*

Kohanaiki Beach Park. Also known as Pine Trees, this community beach park is among the best places to catch waves. Keep in mind that it's a very popular local surf spot on an island where there aren't all that many surf spots, and be respectful. ⊠ *Off Hwy. 11, Kohanaiki entrance gate, about 2 miles south of Kona airport, Kailua-Kona.*

Old Kona Airport Park. The park is a good place for catching wave action. A couple of the island's outfitters conduct surf lessons here, as the break is far from potentially dangerous rocks and reefs. ⊠ *Kuakini Rd., Kailua-Kona.*

EQUIPMENT, LESSONS, AND TOURS

★ Hawaii Lifeguard Surf Instructors

SURFING | This family-owned, lifeguard-certified school helps novices become wave riders at Kahaluu Beach Park in Kailua-Kona and offers lessons for more experienced riders at Kona's top surf spots. A two-hour introductory lesson has one instructor per two to four students and is gentle and reassuring. Private instruction is available as well. If the waves are on the smaller side, the school converts to stand-up paddleboard lessons for the same prices as surfing. ⊠ *75-5909 Alii Dr., Kailua-Kona* ☎ *808/324–0442, 808/936–7873* ⊕ *www.surflessonshawaii.com* ⊠ *From $139.*

Kahaluu Bay Surf & Sea

SURFING | Specializing in being family-friendly, this outfit offers individual and group lessons given by certified lifeguards who are also certified in CPR and First Aid and are right by your side. If you'd rather learn to stand-up paddle, no problem; they also have SUP lessons for all abilities available. If you already know how to surf or paddle, this is a great place for rentals. They have showers, safe storage, and parking on-site. ⊠ *78-6685 Alii Dr., Kailua-Kona* ☎ *808/322–4338* ⊕ *learntosurfkona.com* ⊠ *From $99.*

Ocean Eco Tours Surf School

SURFING | Family owned and operated, Kona's oldest surf school emphasizes the basics and specializes in beginners. It's one of a handful of operators permitted to conduct business in Kaloko-Honokohau National Historical Park, which gets waves even when other spots on the west side are flat. All lessons are taught by certified instructors, and the school guarantees that you will surf. There's an authentic soul surfer's vibe to this operation, and they are equally die-hard about teaching you about the ocean and having you standing up riding waves on your first day. Group, private, and semiiprivate lessons are available. ⊠ *Gentry Marina, 74-425 Kealakehe Pwy., Suite 16, Kailua-Kona* ☎ *808/324–7873* ⊕ *www. oceanecotours.com* ⊠ *From $95.*

★ Orchidland Surfboards and Surf Shop

WATER SPORTS | This venerable shop in historic downtown Hilo—in business since 1972—carries a wide variety of surf and other water sports equipment for sale or rent. It stocks professional custom surfboards and surf apparel. Owner Stan Lawrence, famous for his "Drainpipe" legacy, was one of the last people to surf that famous break before lava flows claimed the entire Kalapana area. Old photos and surfing posters on the walls celebrate the sport and add to the nostalgia. Through the shop, Stan hosts surfing contests and does the daily surf report for local radio stations. Orchidland, the longest continually operating surf shop on the Big Island, is as authentic as it gets. ⊠ *262 Kamehameha Ave., Hilo* ☎ *808/935–1533* ⊕ *www.orchidlandsurfshop.com* ⊠ *$30, 8-ft. soft surfboard/day.*

★ Pacific Vibrations

SURFING | Family-owned, this surf shop—in business since 1978—stocks tons of equipment, surf wear and gear, sunglasses, and GoPro cameras. It's worth a stop just to soak in the cool Hawaii surf vibe and to talk story with the friendly owners. The owners are activists in protecting local surf spots from development, and their grassroots efforts have been very successful. ⊠ *74-5614 Palani Rd., Kailua-Kona* ☎ *808/329–4140.*

Tennis and Pickleball

Many of the island's resorts rent rackets, balls, and shoes, and allow nonguests to play for a fee. On the Kohala Coast, try the Fairmont Orchid Hawaii, the Hilton Waikoloa Village, and Waikoloa Beach Marriott. In Keauhou, there's Holua Tennis and Pickleball Center; in Kailua-Kona, you can play at the Courtyard King Kamehameha's Kona Beach Hotel and the Royal Kona Resort. There are also several free public courts on both sides of the island. Call the County of Hawaii Department of Parks and Recreation (☎ 808/961–8311) for information about public courts.

Edith Kanakaole Multi-Purpose Stadium

TENNIS | The stadium is used for large events, but there are public courts in the same complex. ⊠ Hoolulu County Park, Piilani and Kalanikoa Sts. ☎ 808/961–8720 ⛶ Free.

Higashihara Park

TENNIS | You can play for free at this nearly always uncrowded park near Honalo, south of Kailua-Kona. ⊠ Off Hwy. 11 before Honalo ⛶ Free.

★ Holua Racquet and Paddle Center

TENNIS | By far the nicest tennis center in Kona town, and the largest in the state, this center has five beautiful, tournament-quality courts and 20 new pickleball courts. Drop-in play, lessons, and a pro shop (with shoe and racket rental) are available. There's ice-cold water on every court, a very nice shower and changing room, and a breezy lounge with vending machines. The center also hosts major tournaments and actively supports the local tennis and racquet-sports community. Beloved local coach Richard Kahalioumi manages the center and teaches tennis to all ages. You can purchase a one-month membership for a reasonable fee, or opt for an affordable punch card. ⊠ 78-7190 Kaleiopapa St.

☎ 808/322–6090 ⊕ holuaracquetandpaddle.com ⛶ 7 sessions, $60.

Kona Old Airport Park

TENNIS | A community tennis organization nicely maintains the courts here. It can get very hot midday, so bring water and plan on using hats, sunscreen, and long-sleeve rash guards to play comfortably. ⊠ North end of Kuakini Hwy. ☎ 808/961–8561 ⛶ Free.

Royal Kona Resort Tennis Club

TENNIS | Open to the general public, the club features four lighted Latexite hard courts. They offer lessons along with stringing and pro shop services. You can purchase a one-month, single membership or even day passes for a reasonable fee. ⊠ Royal Kona Resort, 75-5852 Alii Dr. ☎ 808/349-3455 ⊕ playtennis.usta.com/royalkona ⛶ $10/daily.

Whale- and Dolphin-Watching

One of the most highly anticipated Hawaii experiences for visitors and residents alike from December through May is the annual migration of the North Pacific humpback whales. They travel about 3,200 miles from Alaska's icy waters to the Hawaiian Islands in as few as 40 days, swimming 24 hours a day. As early as October, mother whales with nursing calves arrive first, followed by mothers with yearlings. These cetacean moms have taught the migration routine to their offspring and then begin to wean them. Adult males arrive next, followed by adult females, and finally by pregnant mothers who maximize their feeding in Alaska before making the journey and giving birth. Once here, they do not feed. The population of migrating humpbacks in Hawaiian waters is now estimated at about 12,000 individuals.

Humpback whales are visible off the coast of the Big Island between December and April.

Behaviors that you might witness include pectoral slapping, spy-hops, tail slapping, and the most spectacular of all—leaping barrel rolls. Toward the end of the season, you may see mothers nurturing newborn calves. Humpbacks tend to stick close to shore, so you will often witness them from many accessible locations, especially along the Kohala Coast.

Eighteen species of dolphins live here year-round, including spotted, spinner, rough-toothed, and bottlenose. Be sure to choose excursions that respect the natural boundaries of dolphins and that don't disturb or impact their resting states, as they are all protected by federal law. ■TIP→ **If you take a morning cruise, you're more likely to see dolphins.**

⇨ *In addition to the outfitters listed below, see the Snorkeling section for more outfitters that offer whale- and dolphin-watching cruises.*

TOURS

Captain Dan McSweeney's Whale Watch Learning Adventures

WILDLIFE-WATCHING | Captain Dan McSweeney, self-described whale researcher and conservationist, offers three-hour trips on his double-decker, 40-foot cruise boat. In addition to humpbacks (in winter), he'll try to show you dolphins and some of the six other whale species that live off the Kona Coast throughout the year. McSweeney guarantees you'll see whales or he'll take you out again for free. ⌧ *Honokohau Harbor, 74-381 Kealakehe Pkwy., Kailua-Kona* ☎ *808/322–0028, 888/942–5376* ⊕ *www.ilovewhales.com* ⌧ *$135.*

Hawaiian Adventures Kona

WILDLIFE-WATCHING | See humpbacks in the wild with this outfitter, who employs professional naturalists to educate and inform so that you come away with greater respect and knowledge of these magnificent creatures of the deep. Tours

Be Dolphin SMART

Dolphin Smart

The idea of swimming with Hawaii's wild spinner dolphins may seem like an amazing experience, but in actuality it's neither ecologically advisable nor safe for the animals. Oh, and did we mention that it's illegal to feed, chase, harass, or swim too closely to wild dolphins? Instead, visitors should follow the Dolphin SMART guidelines (⊕ *sanctuaries.noaa.gov/dolphinsmart*) developed by NOAA, Whale and Dolphin Conservation, and the Dolphin Ecology Project. These guidelines break down the cans and cannots when it comes to wildlife, and the rules are proudly followed by most tour operators and businesses; if you're looking into a company that does not follow these practices, we suggest you look elsewhere.

S is for Stay Away. People must stay at least 50 yards from dolphins at all times.

M is for Move Cautiously Away. Move away cautiously from dolphins who are showing signs of disturbance.

A is for Always Put Your Engine in Neutral. Always put your boat engine in neutral when dolphins are near. The same can be said for humans—put yourself in neutral and stop to think about the negative impact you may have by getting too close.

R is for Refrain. This means refrain from swimming with, feeding, or touching dolphins.

T is for Teach. Share your knowledge with others.

Keep these guidelines in mind for Hawaii's other protected species such as sea turtles, humpback whales (and other whales and dolphins), and Hawaiian monk seals.

---

are led aboard the comfortable *Those Guys,* a 20-passenger, 38-foot Delta vessel. The owners have been leading tours in Kona waters since 1997. They keep a safe and legal distance from these protected mammals, so you can still enjoy seeing creatures in the wild without disturbing their habitat and activities. ■ TIP→ **Book online for substantial discounts.** ✉ *247 Kealakehe Pkwy., Kailua-Kona* ☏ *808/339–3604* ⊕ *hawaiianadventureskona.com* 🍽 *From $119.*

Hawaii Nautical

WILDLIFE-WATCHING | A NOAA-designated Dolphin SMART operator, this company practices strict guidelines for viewing protected marine animals, including dolphins and whales. You can be assured that you'll enjoy a wonderful ocean tour,

see plenty of animals, and not be a part of harming or impacting the animals' activities or habitats. Excursions include affordable powerboat cruises, catamaran snorkel sails, and even a pampering yacht adventure that takes a maximum of six guests to Pawai Bay or Makalawena. Private charters are also available. ✉ *74-425 Kealakehe Pkwy., Slip I-10, Kailua-Kona* ☏ *808/234–7245* ⊕ *www.hawaiinautical.com* 🍽 *From $54.*

Zip Line Tours

One of the few ways to really see the untouched beauty of the Big Island is to fly over its lush forests, dense tree canopies, and glorious rushing waterfalls on a zip line. You strap into a harness, get clipped to a cable, step off a platform, and then zip, zip, zip your way through paradise. Most companies start you out easy on a slower, shorter line and graduate you to faster, longer zips. It's an exhilarating adventure for all ages and, between the zipping, rappelling, and suspension bridges, has been known to help some put aside their fear of heights (at least for a few minutes). If you have a fear of flying, most companies have tandem zips so you can fly with a friend.

Kohala Zipline

ZIP–LINING | Located in the canopy of the Halawa Gulch in North Kohala, this tour features nine zips and five suspension bridges for a thrilling, within-the-canopy adventure in the forest. You'll bounce up to the site in a six-wheel-drive, military-style vehicle. Two certified guides accompany each small group. Designed for all ability levels, the Kohala Zipline focuses on fun and safety, offering a dual line for efficient, confident braking. You'll soar more than 100 feet above the ground and feel like a pro by the last platform. A quickie lesson in rappelling is included. Zip and Dip tours (combining zip line, nature walk, lunch, snacks, and waterfall swim) are also available. ⊠ 54-3676 Akoni Pule Hwy. ☎ 808/331–8505 ⊕ www.kohalazipline.com ⊠ From $215.

Umauma Zipline Experience

ZIP–LINING | This is the quickest, most adventurous way to see 14 waterfalls, including the dramatic Umauma Falls, as you soar overhead via nine zip lines (four are dual, so you can ride next to a friend). Suspension bridges take you over rain forests, gorges, grottoes, and lava tubes in the beautiful Hakalau Bay region on the Hamakua Coast. You can also opt for the Waterfall Rappel and River Experience and rappel down a waterfall and over caves to the river. ⊠ 31-313 Old Mamalahoa Hwy. ☎ 808/930–9477 ⊕ umaumaexperience.com ⊠ From $219.

Index

Photo Credits

Front cover: Douglas Peebles/eStock Photo [Descr.: Hawaii, Island of Hawaii, Waimanu Valley, Helicopter.]. **Back cover, from left to right:** Fominayaphoto/Shutterstock. Marek Poplawski/Shutterstock. Maridav/Shutterstock. **Spine:** Aquatic creature/Shutterstock. **Interior, from left to right:** Shane Myers Photography/Shutterstock (1). Fremme/Shutterstock (2-3). Shane Myers Photography/Shutterstock (5). **Chapter 1: Experience Big Island:** Ademyan/Dreamstime (6-7). Robert Randall/Dreamstime (8-9). Swaengpic/Dreamstime (9). Michael DeFreitas North America/Alamy Stock Photo (9). Galina Barskaya/Dreamstime (10). Kailua Village Business Improvement District (10). Melissa Burovac (10). Kilauea Military Camp (10). George Burba/Shutterstock (11). FotoMonkey/Shutterstock (12). Anita Gould/Flickr (12). Michael Hanano/Shutterstock (12). Sam Antonio/Dreamstime (13). Robin Runck/Dreamstime (13). Ujjwalstha/Dreamstime (14). Phillip B. Espinasse/Shutterstock (14). Jason Kolenda/Dreamstime (14). John Elk III/Alamy Stock Photo (15). Kirk Lee Aeder/Big Island Visitors Bureau (20). Cameron Brooks/Hawaii Tourism Authority (20). Tor Johnson/Hawaii Tourism Authority (20). Christopher Mazmanian/Shutterstock (21). Anna Pacheco/Hawaii Tourism Authority (21). Tyler Schmitt/Island of Hawaii Visitors Bureau (22). Kirk Lee Aeder/Island of Hawaii Visitors Bureau (22). Emperorcosar/Shutterstock (22). Tor Johnson/Hawaii Tourism Authority (23). Png-Studio/iStockphoto (23). Brent Hofacker/Shutterstock (24). Hawaii Tourism (24). Dana Edmunds (24). Magdanatka/Shutterstock (25). Kirk Lee Aeder/Big Island Visitors Bureau (25). Marilyn Gould/Dreamstime (26). Douglas Peebles Photography/Alamy Stock Photo (26). Ancha Chiangmai/Shutterstock (26). Pr2is/Dreamstime (26). Vfbjohn/Dreamstime (26). Eddygaleotti/Dreamstime (27). Koondon/Shutterstock (27). Caner CIFTCI/Dreamstime (27). Elmar Langle/iStockphoto (27). Kirk Lee Aeder/Big Island Visitors Bureau (27). Lost Mountain Studio/Shutterstock (28). Alla Machutt/iStockphoto (28). Brooke Dombroski/Hawaii Tourism Authority (28). Temanu/Shutterstock (28). Mongkolchon Akesin/Shutterstock (28). Heather Goodman/Hawaii Tourism Authority (29). Olgakr/iStockphoto (29) Dana Edmunds/Hawaii Tourism Authority (29). Hawaii Tourism Authority (29). Heather Goodman/Hawaii Tourism Authority (29). Cathy Locklear/Dreamstime (33). HVCB (34). Thinkstock LLC (35). Linda Ching/HVCB (37). Sri Maiava Rusden/HVCB (37). Kelly Alexander Photography (38). Leis of Hawaii/leisofhawaii.com (38). Leis of Hawaii/leisofhawaii.com (38). Leis of Hawaii/leisofhawaii.com (38). Kelly Alexander Photography (38). Tim Wilson/Flickr (39). Douglas Peebles Photography/Alamy Stock Photo (40). Douglas Peebles Photography/Alamy Stock Photo (40). Dana Edmunds/Polynesian Cultural Center's Alii Luau (40). Douglas Peebles Photography/Alamy Stock Photo (40). Purcell Team/Alamy Stock Photo (40). Hawaii Visitors and Convention Bureau (41). Hawaii Visitors and Convention Bureau (41). Hawaii Visitors and Convention Bureau (41). Oahu Visitors Bureau (41). **Chapter 3: Kailua-Kona:** Atommy/Shutterstock (79). Mariusz S. Jurgielewicz/Shutterstock (90). Mhgstan/Shutterstock (109). **Chapter 4: South Kona:** Uheheu/Shutterstock (111). Cphoto/Dreamstime (119). Kauai Visitors Bureau (120). Jack Jeffrey (121). Heather Goodman/Hawaii Tourism Authority (122). Marek Poplawski/Shutterstock (125). Martywakat/Dreamstime (126). **Chapter 5: The Kohala Coast and Waimea:** George Burba/Dreamstime (131). Alexander Demyanenko/Shutterstock (149). Maria Luisa Lopez Estivill/Dreamstime (150). Instacruising/Shutterstock (153). Georgeburba/Dreamstime (159). **Chapter 6: The Hamakua Coast:** Ujjwalstha/Dreamstime (169). Estivillml/iStockphoto (176). Russ Bishop/Alamy Stock Photo (181). JMP Traveler/iStockphoto (183). **Chapter 7: Hilo:** Emperorcosar/Shutterstock (187). Risaacman/Dreamstime (200). **Chapter 8: Hawaii Volcanoes National Park, Puna, and Kau:** Maridav/Shutterstock (209). Douglas Peebles Photography/Alamy Stock Photo (220). Dmitri Kotchetov/iStockphoto (221). Janice Wei/iStockphoto (223). Theartist312/iStockphoto (224). Sergi Reboredo/Alamy Stock Photo (225). Billy McDonald/Shutterstock (234). MNStudio/Dreamstime (237). **Chapter 9: Activities and Tours:** Maridav/Shutterstock (239). Cameron Nelson (242). Russ Bishop/Alamy Stock Photo (251). MNStudio/Dreamstime (253). Andre Seale/Alamy Stock Photo (261). Ron Dahlquist/HVCB (263). Shane Myers Photography/Shutterstock (264). Gert Vrey/Dreamstime (266) Orxy/Shutterstock (266). Shane Myers Photography/Shutterstock (267). David Fleetham/Alamy Stock Photo (270). Yaroslav Williams/Shutterstock (273). **About Our Writers:** All photos are courtesy of the writers.

*Every effort has been made to trace the copyright holders, and we apologize in advance for any accidental errors. We would be happy to apply the corrections in the following edition of this publication.

Notes

Notes

Notes

Fodor's BIG ISLAND OF HAWAII

Publisher: Stephen Horowitz, *General Manager*

Editorial: Douglas Stallings, *Editorial Director;* Jill Fergus, Amanda Sadlowski, *Senior Editors;* Brian Eschrich, Alexis Kelly, *Editors;* Angelique Kennedy-Chavannes, Yoojin Shin, *Associate Editors*

Design: Tina Malaney, *Director of Design and Production;* Jessica Gonzalez, *Senior Designer;* Jaimee Shaye, *Graphic Design Associate*

Production: Jennifer DePrima, *Editorial Production Manager;* Elyse Rozelle, *Senior Production Editor;* Monica White, *Production Editor*

Maps: Rebecca Baer, *Map Director;* Mark Stroud (Moon Street Cartography) and David Lindroth, *Cartographers*

Photography: Viviane Teles, *Director of Photography;* Namrata Aggarwal, Neha Gupta, Payal Gupta, Ashok Kumar, *Photo Editors;* Jade Rodgers, Shanelle Jacobs, *Photo Production Intern*

Business and Operations: Chuck Hoover, *Chief Marketing Officer;* Robert Ames, *Group General Manager*

Public Relations and Marketing: Joe Ewaskiw, *Senior Director of Communications and Public Relations*

Fodors.com: Jeremy Tarr, *Editorial Director;* Rachael Levitt, *Managing Editor*

Technology: Jon Atkinson, *Executive Director of Technology;* Rudresh Teotia, *Associate Director of Technology;* Alison Lieu, *Project Manager*

Writers: Karen Anderson, Kristina Anderson

Editor: Brian Eschrich

Production Editor: Monica White

9th Edition

ISBN 978-1-64097-691-7

ISSN 1934-5542

All details in this book are based on information supplied to us at press time. Always confirm information when it matters, especially if you're making a detour to visit a specific place. Fodor's expressly disclaims any liability, loss, or risk, personal or otherwise, that is incurred as a consequence of the use of any of the contents of this book.

SPECIAL SALES
This book is available at special discounts for bulk purchases for sales promotions or premiums. For more information, e-mail SpecialMarkets@fodors.com.

PRINTED IN CANADA

10 9 8 7 6 5 4 3 2 1

About Our Writers

Karen Anderson resides in Kona, Hawaii, and works as a freelance journalist, managing editor, and professional photographer. For 13 consecutive years, she has been the managing editor of *At Home, Living with Style in West Hawaii.* She also writes for a variety of publications including *West Hawaii Today; Hawaii Island Midweek; Hawaii Luxury Magazine; Ke Ola Magazine; Hawaii Drive Magazine; Edible Hawaiian Islands Magazine;* and *USA Today Travel Tips.* Karen is the author of *The Hawaii Home Book: Practical Tips for Tropical Living,* which reached #1 on the *Honolulu Advertiser*'s nonfiction bestseller list and received the Award of Excellence from the Hawaii Book Publishers Association. Her monthly humor column is known throughout the Big Island. She also writes the weekly "Onolicious Dining Guide" for *West Hawaii Today,* as well as feature articles for local real estate publications. She is the longtime advertising/marketing chairperson for the annual King Kamehameha Day Celebration Parade in Kailua-Kona. For this edition, Karen updated Travel Smart; Hilo; and Hawaii Volcanoes National Park, Puna, and Kau.

Kristina Anderson has been writing professionally for more than 30 years. After working as an advertising director in Southern California for more than a decade, she moved to Hawaii in 1992 and began working as a senior copywriter and broadcast producer for Hawaii agencies and client direct. Since 2006, she has also written for national and regional publications, most notably for *At Home in West Hawaii* magazine, which profiled a variety of homes—from coffee shacks to resort mansions—and for *Hawaii Island Midweek* magazine. When there's time, she runs, paddles outrigger canoes competitively, and plays tennis very noncompetitively. Her brightest accomplishment of all, however, is raising twin sons as a single mom. For this book, Kristina updated Experience Big Island; Kailua-Kona and the Kona Coast; The Kohala Coast and Waimea; The Hamakua Coast; and Activities and Tours.